UNPLUGGED
PLAY

No Batteries. No Plugs. Pure Fun.

Bobbi Conner

Illustrations by Amy Patacchiola

Workman Publishing • New York

Library of Congress Cataloging-in-Publication Data is available.

ISBN-13: 978-0-7611-4114-3 (hc)
ISBN-13: 978-0-7611-4390-1 (pbk)

This book references websites that may be of interest to the reader. Every effort has been made to ensure that the information about these websites is correct and up-to-date as of press time.

Cover designed by Paul Gamarello
Interior designed by Paul Gamarello and Orlando Adiao
Photo Credits: *Front cover*—Girl with kitchen pot: Sean Justice/Corbis; Boy playing sack race: Photodisc/Punchstock; Girl with plane: David Katzenstein/Corbis; Hose: Photodisc/Getty Images; *Back Cover*—Girl: Rubber Ball/Veer; *Spine*—Girl with plane: David Katzenstein/Corbis.

Workman books are available at special discounts when purchased in bulk for premiums and sales promotions as well as for fund-raising or educational use. Special editions or book excerpts can also be created to specification. For details, contact the Special Sales Director at the address below.

Workman Publishing Company, Inc.
225 Varick Street
New York, NY 10014-4381
www.workman.com

NOTE: The games and activities in this book were developed for specific age groups and abilities; however, not all toddlers, preschoolers, or grade-school children have the same capabilities. Please supervise your child carefully and select only games and activities that are appropriate and safe for your individual child.

Printed in the United States of America
First printing May 2007

10 9 8 7 6 5 4 3 2 1

Dedication

To Billy, Cassidy, Olivia, and Peter for the joy you bring to my life each day.

And to my mother, Charlotte, for giving me a childhood filled with fun and imaginative play.

Acknowledgments

This book is built upon the play experiences of real children who have engaged in all sorts of creative, active play. Let me begin by thanking my own children, Cassidy, Olivia, and Peter, for being such enthusiastic unplugged players during every stage of their childhood. Their exuberant, clever play ideas are woven into each section of this book.

I am deeply indebted to the fabulous game brainstormer and play reviewer (and extraordinary mom) Kiki Walker. Her marvelous can-do attitude made the research phase of this book a delightful experience.

Thank you also to the following children and parents who provided play ideas and tested games:

Lakeshia Alexander; Carol Brown; Tom Daldin; John, Molli, Samantha, and Patricia Dowd; Jonnie, Bud, Andrew, Christian, Joanna, and Mary Grace Furmanchik, Anne, Ed, Claire, and Sam Gutshall; Ann Jenkins; Virginia McCann; Fulton and Ren Mills; Rob, Susan, Teddy, Julia, and Daniel Monyak; Christina, Chris, Jack, Kate, and Lucy Oxford; Liz and Bob Sauntry; Duncan, Lisa, Will, and Catherine Sherer; Els Sincebaugh; Breonna Tiller; Jacob Ufkes; Doug, Jack, George, Harry, and Lucy Walker; and Debbie Willis.

Olivia Conner's creative thinking skills and artistic talents helped shape many of the arts and crafts projects in the book.

In my professional life, I have had the great pleasure of interviewing hundreds of wise and compassionate child development specialists about play, friendships, growing, and learning in my twenty-one years as host of *The Parent's Journal* public radio show. I offer a special thanks to these childhood experts, who have generously shared their insight, words of wisdom, and interview quotes in this book. (Julia Vanderelst stayed busy, typing hundreds of hours of program transcripts from *The Parent's Journal* to capture these quotes.) Also, I could not have written this book without the dedication of my radio coworkers: Ellen Pruitt, Bruce Roberts, and Madeleine Thomas.

My first-rate agent (and terrific human being), Jim Levine, found just the right publisher for my book. Nina Graybill wears two hats marvelously well—both talented writer and outstanding attorney—and her advice and suggestions are much appreciated.

The exceptional team at Workman has made the publishing of this book a wonderful, collaborative experience. In the beginning, Peter Workman gave his enthusiastic "yes" to the importance of *Unplugged Play*. Megan Nicolay has been an outstanding editor and a delight to work with, providing creative ideas, careful editing, and great attention to detail. Suzie Bolotin nurtured this book from start to finish, offering a brilliant combination of encouragement, review, and fine editing along the way. The splendid art, illustrations, typesetting, and design provided by Paul Gamarello, Orlando Adiao, Dove Pedlosky, Barbara Peragine, Catherine Leonardo, and Amy Patacchiola capture the essence of children at play and provide an easy-to-navigate format. Others at Workman I especially wish to thank are Melanie Bennitt, Amy Corley, Amanda Pritzker, Doug Wolff, Haley Pelton, and Savannah Ashour. It has been a great pleasure to work with each and every one of you.

And finally, a word of thanks to my husband, Billy, whose playful spirit enhances my life each day, and who offered just the right mix of encouragement and humor to lighten my routine during long stretches of writing.

Contents

Preface:

Play Matters

Why—and How—I Wrote This Book

Children like to play. And why wouldn't they? It's fun! So it makes sense that the more they play, the more they want to play again. It's a lovely, self-perpetuating cycle that most parents intuitively understand. But what is harder to grasp is the power of play to shape a child's world, particularly a world that is high-tech, fast paced, and plugged in.

And that's why I wrote this book. During my twenty years as host of the nationally syndicated *The Parent's Journal* public radio show, I've chatted with many of the leaders in the world of child development. Whether it was David Elkind or Penelope Leach, Fred Rogers or Benjamin Spock, they all—every one of them—spoke of the significance of play. And now I want to help parents help their children enjoy the wholesome, old-fashioned experience of playing creatively and freely . . . *without batteries.* I started by collecting and inventing hundreds of games, and then I tested them one by one on different groups of children, ages twelve months to ten years. When the kids rejected a game or an activity, I rejected it too. When a game inspired them to come up with a variation of their own, I appropriated their invention. The result is the nearly seven hundred "unplugged" games that you have here.

But why "unplugged," you may ask. Since most of us embrace technology to some extent every day—can you imagine a world without e-mail?—it may seem far-fetched to suggest that parents minimize the amount of time their child spends connected to anything with a screen, a plug, or a battery. Besides, it's so easy to plunk a kid in front of a TV! But children need to interact with living, breathing human playmates, and not be held captive by the lights, sounds, and images on a screen. They need to run, chase, ride, skip, and jump, and not *sit still* for prolonged blocks of time. We need only look at the huge rise in childhood obesity to understand how children suffer physically when they remain inactive.

But the toll on kids who rely primarily on electronics for their entertainment goes way beyond some extra pounds. When a child sits in front of a screen, he has no opportunity to connect with the natural world outside—mud, water, sand, stones, leaves, seeds, animals, insects, sunshine, and rain. It might not seem like such a huge loss at the moment when your child is contentedly clicking buttons on the keypad, but there is something essential about a child getting his hands messy. In addition, because electronic games are preprogrammed with finite possible responses, they limit the imagination. A child who draws, paints, builds, and invents experiences a creativity that has no boundaries. By learning that he has the ability to shape his world—either alone or in the company of others—he gains the self-confidence he needs to grow into a problem-solving, creative adult.

And who could ask for more?

—*Bobbi Conner*

Introduction:
The Power of Play

You may feel as though life has changed in an essential way, and that there is no time for the kind of old-fashioned, wholesome, playful childhood that you had envisioned for your child. But there are the same twenty-four hours in each day and the same seven days in each week. What's changed is the pace of life.

To a large extent you, as the parent, are the keeper of the time in your family. You arrange the family schedule; you set dinnertime, bath time, and bedtime; and you get your child to appointments, child care, playgroups, and school *on time.* As the keeper of the time, you have the power and authority to slow time down. And if you make that choice, you'll probably find that your child has more time for all sorts of unplugged play.

Let me give you an example from my own life as a mom. When my son was in kindergarten and my daughter was three, I worked full-time. I was a single parent earning a living for our family of three by day and doing all the typical parenting tasks by night. I always felt rushed. I picked my children up from their Montessori school each day at 5:00 P.M. and headed home. The moment I walked in the door I jumped right into making dinner. (And in the back of my mind I was thinking about the time needed for baths, bedtime stories, and laundry too.) So I scurried around the kitchen making dinner while the children played on their own. Or at least that's what they were supposed to do. Often, after just a minute or two, a sibling squabble would set off a group meltdown.

This went on for several days in a row that first week of school, and I realized something needed to change. The next day I put a happier plan in place. I walked in the house and said to my children, "Let's get a snack and read a story together!" (I meant now, not later tonight.) We grabbed three apples from the fruit bowl and a small plate of sliced cheese. We went into the living room, snuggled up on the couch, and ate our snack while I began to read *Caps for Sale.* It was a nourishing, calming time, and after fifteen minutes my son said, "I want to play with my LEGOs now." My daughter said, "Me too." Off they went. I started dinner knowing everyone was happy and reconnected. We all had the time and attention we needed to make a graceful transition into our evening together as a family. Our new after-work and after-school routine made an immediate, positive difference in our lives over the years. I often recalled how I had *slowed down time* and applied this same smart thinking whenever our routine and mood felt off-kilter.

> **"** *Play is not trivial. When children play, they're doing important work.* **"**
>
> **—Fred Rogers**
> Emmy Award–winning creator and host of *Mister Rogers' Neighborhood*

I mention this lesson from my own life for three reasons. One, to assure you that simple solutions are often best for fixing family routines that are out of synch. Two, to encourage you to stop, take a breath, and make whatever changes are necessary to diminish that anxious feeling that comes when time closes in on you. And finally, to remind you that *children need time to play.* It was true when *you* were a child and it is just as true for infants, toddlers, preschoolers, and older children today.

Dare to Unplug

Play is fun, which is the primary reason children want to do it. And the more fun children have while they play, the more they want to play again next time. This basic cause-and-effect law keeps children in perpetual motion, in search of more and more fun and more and more play. But the full story about play doesn't end here. Play is also a powerful way for children to experience the world.

Children learn through their everyday play experiences. In fact, play is perhaps the best way for toddlers, preschoolers, and children six to ten to learn about themselves (and their own capabilities), to learn about one another, and to learn how all things work in the world. What's absolutely brilliant about this evolutionary mechanism is that children don't know and don't particularly care about the learning component to their play. For example, when two little toddlers play side by side, each loading miniature blocks into his own dump truck, they don't see small hints of cooperation, sharing, or a budding friendship unfolding. They are just doing what toddlers love to do. The four-year-old who pinches and sorts pasta shapes into a muffin tin at the kitchen table while you cook isn't concerned with fine motor development or early math concepts. When two eight-year-olds use plastic flyswatters to bat a balloon back and forth across the lawn, they don't take notice of the agility, muscles, and hand–eye coordination they are developing. The child who plays Dog Diaries (page 247) and writes ad-lib adventures about the dogs in her neighborhood is not striving to get accepted into an award-winning school for creative writers. She is just having a good time. And so it goes, with physical, intellectual, social, and emotional growth happening as children go about the everyday business of play.

We parents can't be satisfied, however, with knowing that our children are out there playing, either alone or with others. We need to do everything in our power to encourage *unplugged* play—those marvelous, nonelectronic, time-tested games and activities that build strong bodies (climbing, hopping, running, jumping, tossing, catching), expand the mind (guessing, figuring, remembering, numbering, interpreting), spark creativity (inventing, building, wordplay, jokes, stories, drawing, painting, songs), and forge friendships. Children stretch their attention spans and learn to manage their emotions. They become the masters of their own destiny and directors of their own experience. This is true in the first year of life and every week, month, and year thereafter. Children also learn that they are capable of entertaining and amusing themselves, without machines and without Mom or Dad!

Within this broad category of unplugged play, there are many types of games for your child to experience, at every age. First up are the loads of clever and creative games a child can play alone—on-the-spot activities that parents can offer whenever they need a few minutes to make dinner, work, or chat on the phone. But teaching kids how

> **" **If you've been around kids, particularly young kids, for any length of time, [you know] it's absolutely true that all the most important things in life are learned through play. **"**
>
> **—Penelope Leach, Ph.D.**
> psychologist and author of *Your Baby and Child*

to amuse themselves is not some selfish act; rather, showing them that they don't have to reach for a video console whenever a parent or friend is not around is a lifelong gift.

And then, of course, there are hundreds upon hundreds of games to play with one or two friends, or with large groups (such as at birthday parties or playgroups)—the absolute best way for a child to develop social skills, again, whatever the child's age. This holds true for the shy child, the child who gravitates toward one particular playmate, or the child who thrives in a large group. Play is a magnificent way to learn to get along with others, to take turns, to negotiate; it also teaches children about fairness, making amends, and what it feels like to have a friend.

Finally, there are games that parents and children can enjoy together, in the park or at the kitchen table. Bringing an entire family together creates another wonderful tradition of play (see *Family Game Night,* page 359.) I've tried to include games that do not require Mom or Dad to wear a donkey hat or sing "Yankee Doodle Dandy" while standing on one foot. But far be it from me to tell you to put dignity in the way of a good time!

The Simple Pleasures

Here are just a few of the sensations and experiences that come alive through unplugged play. When you read this list, the essential question to ask yourself is this: *Can a screen or machine bring the same joyful experience into my child's life?*

Play for Joy
- Feel the sunshine on your face as you kick a ball.
- Run after a friend and catch her!
- Put on a costume and pretend to be a grown-up.
- Squish your toes and fingers in mud.
- Jump, skip, and roll down the hill.
- Pick up a caterpillar and look at its fur.
- Pour sand into containers; make a castle.
- Make yourself go higher on the swing and feel the thrill in your stomach.
- Catch a frog and feel his slimy skin.
- Pedal a bike without falling off.
- Learn how to turn a cartwheel.
- Pull a wagon full of dolls as fast as you can.
- Run through the sprinkler in the backyard.
- Dig up worms in the dirt with a stick.
- Throw a water balloon and watch it splash.
- Learn to dribble a ball.
- Make a paper-plate hat, put it on your head, look in the mirror, and have a laugh.
- Jump rope with two friends.

Play for Intelligence
- Line up wooden blocks on the floor and count them for the first time.
- Watch how your older sister builds a tower and make one just like hers.
- Learn to add and subtract by counting buttons from the button box.
- Use cups to scoop water out of a bucket to determine how many cups are in a gallon.
- Build a fort and add heavy books to keep the sheets from slipping off the table.
- Turn over cards on the table that have matching pictures underneath.
- Learn which pans make the loudest noises when you hit them with a spoon.
- Invent a story from your own imagination and tell it to a friend.
- Experiment at a sink full of water to see which things sink and which ones float.
- Find the treasure box in the backyard by guessing the correct answers to all the clues.
- Learn to write your name in cursive.

Play for Connection
- Listen to a story and know when it's time to turn the page.
- See that a friend is sad and offer her a teddy bear.
- Say "I'm sorry" after grabbing a shovel from your friend.
- Learn to take turns on the slide.
- Do the Hokey-Pokey with four other friends.
- Learn not to tell the answer to the riddle until everyone has had a chance to guess.
- Make a big playhouse out of a box and let your friend color the door red when you wanted to paint it blue.
- Imitate exactly what your friend does and take your own turn being the leader.
- Make a giant get-well card for Grandma and take it to the hospital.
- Give a puppet show where all the bunnies act happy, then sad.
- Play house with your friends, and you get to be the dad.

What's Wrong with Electronic Play?

Okay, I can hear you muttering in the background—*what world does she live in?*—so it's time to get real. I am not suggesting that electronic games and high-tech play have no place in a child's world, but I feel very strongly that they should occupy only a minor amount of a child's playtime.

> **"** *Most of the television viewing that goes on in under twos is not useful, partly because a television program moves at quite the wrong pace for a baby of eighteen months. He turns his head to call your attention to something on the screen. By the time he turns back, it's gone, it's over.* **"**
>
> **—Penelope Leach, Ph.D.**
> psychologist and author of *Your Baby and Child*

Do you want to know why? I've covered some of these points earlier, but they're worth remembering. To begin with, many children play these games in isolation. So rather than interacting with human playmates, they're being captivated by lights, sounds, and moving images. The ramifications on developing social skills (and friendships) are huge. Furthermore, it's a good bet that your child will not be running around while playing video games. (Is it any wonder that we are witnessing a huge rise in childhood obesity?) And it's not just the physical benefits that he'll be missing. When your child draws, paints, builds, and invents, or writes music, songs, poems, and stories, there are no artificial boundaries or predetermined limits to his creativity. And when he's playing outside, there's even more—in the form of mud, water, sand, stones, leaves, seeds, animals, insects, sunshine, rain.

Fighting the Fight: Not Giving in to High-Tech Pressure

Given all this, you may be wondering how in the world these games have become so popular—there's so much pressure to buy them, and nearly everyone seems to be paying and playing. The short answer has to do with successful advertising. The longer answer includes peer pressure, the mistaken belief among parents and educators that children must learn to be proficient on the computer at age four or five or ten or they will be left in the dust academically, and the fact that popping in a videotape to amuse a child is just easier to do when you need a quiet moment for yourself.

But that's only part of the story. Put a toddler in front of a large video screen with bright, quick-moving images, and chances are his eyes will light up, and that he will follow the movement on the screen with intensity. Now add interesting sounds, and your child's auditory attention will be fixed on that screen as well. So your child appears to be having fun. That's one thing. The other is that high-tech gadgets are so much a part of our adult lives—and we value them so highly—that we imagine they must be of use to children too. They can be. Children with physical limitations or special needs can really benefit from gadgets and games that allow them to connect to friends. And all children, once they get into school, will need to learn to use computers and calculators and probably iPods and PDAs. But hold back. Children are not mini adults.

How to Promote a No-Battery Zone

- Provide toys that allow variety—balls, a sandbox, building blocks, art supplies, etc.

- Change it up by encouraging all types of play: high-energy and physical play, quiet games, arts, crafts, music, building, and imaginative play. Relax. Unplugged play is *fun*. Children don't need to know that it's often educational. Look for *small* windows of opportunity that can flow seamlessly into your day—set your toddler up for a ten- or fifteen-minute game of Shake, Rattle-n-Roll while you do chores, start a silly guessing game at the dinner table, tell a story in the car on the drive across town. Keep it casual. Keep it short.

- Make your home a place that other children enjoy visiting. It's easier to control what kinds of games kids play on your own turf.

- Don't hover, and don't micromanage your child's play. Let him explore matters on his own. Simply offer a quick demo about using a toy or a new material (if needed), and then back off.

- If your child looks stumped, toss out a play-inducing challenge: "What sort of fort could you make with these boxes and blankets?"

- Don't be afraid to let grandparents, friends, and gift givers know you prefer low-tech or *no*-tech toys for your child. And until your child is in school, try to keep him away from high-tech *anything*.

- As kids get older, set up a Family Electronic Play Plan. You—not your child—should decide how much time is allowed for electronic play each week, and when to fit it into your routine. Some families limit electronic toys and play to weekends. You'll know best what works for you. (See what the American Academy of Pediatrics recommends to curb electronic play, page 16.)

- Create a regular time that is Family Game Night—once a month or once a week—and put it on your calendar so you don't forget. (See *Family Game Night* ideas, page 359.)

DIBS: A Three-Step Action Plan

My best advice is to treat high-tech play like a hot fudge sundae—perfectly fine for now and then, but not for every day. Easy for me to say! And not so easy for you to do. But here's a three-point action plan called DIBS that may help.

1. *Delay* introducing your child to high-tech toys, computers, and electronic games during the infant, toddler, preschool, and kindergarten years, when your child's brain is growing rapidly, and incorporating all the social, emotional, and physical development that goes with that. Educational psychologist Jane Healy, author of *Your Child's Growing Mind,* has studied children's use of computers for years and has concluded that they will *not* be disadvantaged if they are not introduced to computers until age seven or eight.

> **"** By the time children are seven, there have been enormous changes in the brain. Then, the kids are really able to do very interesting and very important things with a computer. **"**
>
> **—Jane M. Healy, Ph.D.**
> educational psychologist and
> author of *Your Child's Growing Mind*

2. *Introduce* your child to the habit of having fun without plug-ins. That's what this book is for! Let the pleasure of good old-fashioned play win your child's heart.

3. *Be Selective* and deliberate about how much time you allow for electronic play in your older child's week and which games are okay. Make a specific Electronic Play Plan for your family and stick to it. See suggestions from other families below.

Make an Electronic Play Plan

Time for another reality check: The American Academy of Pediatrics recommends that children three years or older get no more than one or two hours a day of *quality* screen time. This includes any time spent in front of a video game, computer, or television. The AAP recommends that children two years of age and younger have no screen time.

So, what's a parent to do? Here are some specific plans that other real families have used to limit electronic play and screen time:

- Consider a No Video Games rule during the week for school-age children. On weekends, offer a rich assortment of unplugged play opportunities with family and friends, but also allow your child some freedom to choose electronic play.

- Create two distinct bins or boxes for toys—one for electronics and another for all unplugged toys and games—so that you're better able to put time restrictions in place for toys chosen from the electronic toy bin.

- Connect chore time with electronic game time for older children who clamor for extra electronic playtime (beyond the family limit). The idea is that your child can do household chores for a set amount of time and then trade in for a certain, fixed amount of video game time. (Parents report that this system, while not for everyone, gives the child the power to decide how much effort he is willing to put into earning video playtime.)

- Create a Reading Bank in your family. Encourage your child to read for pleasure. For every thirty minutes of reading time banked during the week, your child can engage in an equal amount of screen time on the weekend.

The bottom line is that the most effective way to limit electronic play in the early years is to embrace other sorts of play. And the good news is that the habits and preferences your child forms during the toddler years will carry through to adolescence and beyond. As your child moves into the preteen years (typically a time of increased pressure for high-tech play), he will begin to play with more independence. You won't be able to prohibit the electronic play that goes on at friends' houses or the high-tech learning tools he's likely to encounter in school, nor should you; in today's world, many of us need some degree of technological aptitude. But if you've laid a groundwork of unplugged play, I can guarantee that your child will be more likely to gravitate toward unplugged games—simply because he knows firsthand the pleasure of creating, doing, and playing without plug-ins.

> **“** *The very brain circuits that are activated during play are also activated during joyous, happy moments in our lives, and the more you exercise a brain circuit, the stronger it gets. So letting kids have a good time in play is one of the healthiest things you can do for them.* **”**
>
> **—Daniel Goleman, Ph.D.**
> psychologist and author of
> *Emotional Intelligence* and *Social Intelligence*

UNPLUGGED PLAY

Make Yours an Unplugged Community

Parents who set limits for their children about electronic toys sometimes feel as though they are swimming upstream. To tackle this problem, find other parents who are also swimming upstream and include them in your social circle. Plan potluck dinners with the parents and playdates with the children (or parent and child play parties). Also, organize informal Unplugged Play Parties for small groups of two to four children, with each family involved taking a turn hosting a playdate at their home once a month. There's no need to make these playdate parties especially elaborate or terribly structured. Just provide a little bit of kid-friendly food and opportunities to play indoors and outdoors.

> **❝**The more you can involve others in the effort to lead a simpler, saner, slower life, the better. It's as easy as, 'Come on over Saturday and bring a dish, and we'll all play in the backyard.' What matters is that you get together and enjoy each other's company. People will thank you.**❞**
>
> **—Edward Hallowell, M.D.**
> psychiatrist and author of *Driven to Distraction* and *CrazyBusy*

Know Your Video Games

Your child likely knows a lot more about the vast selection of video and computer games available than you do. Your job is to become educated about what's out there, both good and bad. Here are several websites that will give you a quick start on your video game education:

- *www.parentschoice.org* Look for current and past child-friendly, award-winning computer software and video games for children of various ages.

- *www.mediafamily.org* National Institute on Media and the Family is a nonprofit organization that has video and computer game reviews for parents who want both a description and rating system for children's electronic videos. (Look for the Kidscore section of the site for complete reviews.)

- *www.esrb.org* Look up specific video and computer games on the Entertainment Software Rating Board site to find a brief description and rating for a game.

Become a Ratings Reader

When you think about purchasing or renting a video or computer game, take a look at the Ratings System for video and computer games provided by the Entertainment Software Rating Board (ESRB):

EC (Early Childhood): Suitable for ages three and over, with no inappropriate materials or content.

E (Everyone): Suitable for children ages six and over. This product may possibly contain minimal violence or crude language.

E+10 (Everyone Ten Years and Over): May have content with mild violence, language, or minimally suggestive themes.

T (Teen): Suitable for children thirteen years of age and over. These games may contain violence, suggestive themes, crude humor, minimal blood, or infrequent use of strong language.

M (Mature): Suitable for ages seventeen and over. May contain intense violence, blood and gore, sexual content, and strong language.

A (Adults Only): Suitable only for adults. May contain prolonged scenes of graphic sex or violence. Not intended for rental or sale to anyone under the age of eighteen.

Rating Pending: The game has not yet been rated. (This symbol appears only in advertising prior to the game's release.)

> 66 Right now, there's an enormous number of toys that have little computers in them that make sounds and lights and sing songs. I am not a fan of those toys because, from my point of view, there are two problems. One, they tend to make the world too frenetic and busy for young children. The other thing about those toys is they teach children to bond with a machine. I don't think that's a good lesson to teach three-month-old, six-month-old, or two-year-old children. 99
>
> **—Mary Pipher, Ph.D.**
> psychotherapist and author of
> *Reviving Ophelia* and *The Shelter of Each Other*

And What About the Internet?

I'm a hard-liner on this one, since I don't think *any* children under ten should have independent access to the Internet. And, then, even if you are sitting next to your child, use the child-protection features to visit only those sites that are appropriate. And here's a novel idea: If your child wants to "chat," he can invite a friend over to play! End of story!

Additionally, there is one very good website to know about from the American Library Association (www.ala.org/greatsites). This site is actually a portal that will connect you and your child to seven hundred great websites and search engines for kids that have been carefully scrutinized by the staff at the ALA. Another section of the site presents resources about safety guidelines for children on the Internet: www.ala.org/ala/oif/foryoungpeople/ childrenparents/especiallychildren.htm.

How to Use This Book

To begin, check out the section of the book that matches your child's age—toddler, preschooler, or six- to ten-year-old. Once you're there, you'll find that the games are organized by situation. Who's playing? Just your child? Look in the *Solo* games. You and your child? Flip to *Parent and Child*. For two to four children, check out the *Playing with Others* pages; and lastly, for foolproof party plans, the *Birthday Party* games will have you covered.

There are games for rainy days and sunny days, games that last five minutes and games that can stretch on for hours. Do you need a solo game to amuse your toddler while you cook dinner tonight? If so, a quick skim through the *Busy-Body* pages will give you lots of ideas for those moments when you have only a bit of time or when you need to keep your toddler occupied while you're busy with some activity nearby. (Try Hallway Bag-Ball; all you need is a paper bag and a few tennis balls.) For longer chunks of time, *Spontaneous Solo Play* provides plenty of ideas for ways to get your child moving, inventing, and creating on her own.

If you have a preschooler in the family and a playdate planned for tomorrow, flip to the *Playing with Others* pages in the Preschool section; within those pages, if rain is on the way, you'll find plenty of exciting options in the *Indoor Play* portion. How about a couple rounds of Musical Socks? When the sun peeks out and the children scramble outdoors, turn to the *Outdoor* pages to find ideas for sandbox play.

And let's not forget the *Arts and Crafts* activities. Nothing can replace the tactile pleasure of working with paper, crayon, glue, and glitter, or the satisfaction of making something yourself.

Using your child's age as a starting point, and then pinpointing the play circumstances—one child or two, indoors or out, active or creative play—will help you navigate through this book and find games that are just right for your child (and his playmates) and just right for this moment of play.

This might mean sampling games in younger age sections too. Some games in the *Toddler Play* section will appeal to your preschool child, and some games in the preschool section will capture your six-to ten-year-old's interest. Enjoy the freedom to move through the pages of this book to discover games that will engage your child. And then encourage your child to tweak the games to suit his style, interests, and abilities.

If your child has a physical delay or disability, or cognitive, social, or speech delays or disabilities, you'll find hundreds of games in these pages that offer fabulous opportunities for your child to have fun and at the same time work on targeted goals, such as increasing muscle strength, cardiovascular endurance, or motor or speech development. Perhaps, for example, your child has trouble flexing his arms or reaching and grasping. There are loads of catching and tossing activities to help

Toys for Children with Special Needs

Specialized toys are available for children with motor delays or impairment, visual or hearing impairment, language delays, and a range of other special needs. Here are a few parenting resources to help you find toys and play suggestions tailored to your child's abilities:

National Lekotek Center A nonprofit organization and resource on toys and play for children with special needs. Their website, www.lekotek.org, features a toy rating system that reviews many specialized toys and includes where-to-buy information, along with many play tips and articles to help you tailor play to your child's needs.

Beyond Play Toys An online source for toys and products for children with special needs. Their website, www.beyondplay.com, features over 1,000 toys and products you can order directly, along with useful articles and play tips. The Search by Product feature helps you find toys suited to your child's abilities and developmental stage.

fine-tune those skills. Some of these games use balls of various sizes, others use beanbags, which may make tossing, catching, and grasping a bit easier for a child with motor delays or disabilities. (You can even substitute a silk neck scarf for a ball or beanbag to invent a new variation of catch that allows extra time for catching the floating scarf.) As in all cases, you know your child best. Select games (and invent variations) that allow just the right balance of challenge and success. When you discover a game that hits this mark, you'll know—your child will want to play again and again.

> **"**We underestimate the simple little things. When a baby learns to shake a rattle and hear the sound and be pleased with it, he's learning that he can affect his environment. And he's learning that there's a cause-and-effect mechanism at work here, which is going to be the basis of the thinking in science and physics and algebra and important kinds of school learning later on. So what he's doing, basically, is twofold: he's learning habits of mind that say, Okay, I am a problem solver. Okay, I can work and enjoy it, and I can be motivated from inside, and I can pay attention. The other thing he's learning is a whole lot of skills in terms of physical movement. And he's also, in fact, learning that he feels good about all this and that it's pleasurable for him. **"**
>
> **—Jane M. Healy, Ph.D.**
> educational psychologist and author of *Your Child's Growing Mind*
> and *Failure to Connect: How Computers Affect Our Children's Minds*

If your child has difficulty picking up on social cues, many of the *Playing with Others* games are perfect to practice speaking, listening, and watching. When it comes to progress through play, the key element that seems to grease the wheel is engaging your child in a way that his interest is in high gear. And when he is interested, he is also motivated.

I am inspired time and time again by the commitment parents bring to adapting play to a child's individual needs, whether or not that child has special needs. You as a parent are first and foremost focused on your child's abilities (rather than disabilities) and you can use these abilities as the starting point for play. If you are a creative thinker, you are constantly brainstorming ways to enhance and adapt your child's play. And, believe me, a can-do, infectious attitude will get passed along to (and absorbed by) your children.

And don't think the opportunities to "seize the play" end here. One of my favorite play traditions has its own special section in this book. I'm talking about Family Game Night, a wonderful way to put your own seal of approval on the importance of play. In the *Family Game Night* appendix, you'll find 120 different ideas for activities and games for the entire family to play together. This might mean Mom or Dad and the kids, or maybe even Grandma, Grandpa, and cousins too. There are silly games, challenging quizzes, high-energy antics, and quiet kitchen table games you can play while digging into a big tray of lasagna. You'll find everything you need to plan your very own family tradition of playtime, once a week or once a month. These special times will be remembered long after that rousing round of Animal Charades is over.

So what are you waiting for? Go forth and seize the play!

Part I:
Toddler Play
(age 1 to 2)

Teaching a toddler "how to play" is a little like trying to teach Einstein how to think. Toddlers are wired to play! Every object they encounter becomes a potential toy. Every action they see you do, they imitate as a form of play. Using their hands and arms and moving around is play. Looking inside a box, moving the cardboard flaps back and forth, and dumping its contents on the floor is play. Hearing the songs you sing and listening to the words you read is play. Splashing hands and feet in a dishpan of water is play.

Your toddler's play takes shape as he experiments and explores. His desire to make things happen directs his play! He pushes a toy car across the

wooden floor and it crashes into the couch with an impressive sound and flips up in the air. What sweet satisfaction for a little being who likes to make things happen! The play is fluid and flexible, with one good idea or action leading to another. From your toddler's perspective the world exists so that he can play, with new and interesting opportunities literally around every corner.

The backstory to all this fun and excitement is that your child is learning and growing with each stroke of play. What an amazing package of self-reliance: I play, therefore I grow.

Here's a snapshot of the specific ways your toddler grows as he plays:

Physical Development Large-muscle control, strength, and stamina develop as toddlers walk, run, climb, jump, kick a ball, scoot on ride-on toys, and roll and toss a ball.

Small muscle control (fingers and hands) and hand–eye coordination improve as toddlers turn knobs, string large beads, play with blocks, use crayons, markers, toy tools, maneuver push toys and pull toys, and transfer an object from one hand to the other with confidence.

Intellectual Development A toddler's brain grows and thinking skills develop through play. Toddlers typically learn about cause and effect (if I do *x*, then *y* happens); learn to understand words and simple instructions; identify objects by pointing (and understand that pictures in a book represent three-dimensional, "real" objects); begin to recognize letters and colors; start to count; experiment and discover how things work (open/close, inside/outside, etc.); and build memory by recognizing stories, songs, and rhymes.

Social/Emotional Development Toddlers develop important social skills as they play. They learn that a conversation consists of listening and talking (and taking turns); to use words to express their wants and needs; to imitate the actions of others; to start to feel empathy for others in distress (who are crying); to offer toys to another child as a token of friendship (for brief moments of time).

The toddler section of this book was created with two important, related themes in mind. One, that toddlers are the masters of their own play, inventing their own clever play scenarios, often on the spot. (For that reason, the *Play* heading under many of the toddler activities in the book doesn't imply a rigid set of rules for play as it may for older child activities. Instead it's important that you think of the "rules" simply as basic ideas for play, because, once again, teaching a toddler "how to play" is a lot like trying to teach Einstein how to think!) And two, your job as a parent is to support and encourage your child's play. You provide safe toys and supervision, offer toddler-friendly play ideas, and give short demos on how to work the toys, props, games, or materials, simply to get things started or help when things get bogged down.

> **"**I think the conclusion we've come to is that people are really a baby's best playmate, and unhurried, sensitive interactions are the best stimulation for the developing brain.**"**
>
> **—Ross Thompson, Ph.D.**
> Professor of Psychology, University of California, Davis

Younger Toddler Play vs. Older Toddler Play

Toddlers twelve to twenty-four months have very different interests and capabilities than older toddlers, twenty-four to thirty-six months. The youngest toddlers are in the early stages of learning to walk; they are trying to gain control over their hands and their toys. These are huge physical tasks, and to a great degree, a young toddler's play is all about mastering these skills. Young toddlers tend to explore most toys and objects by putting them in their mouths. (So you must be diligent about their safety each minute of the day.) In short, these toddlers don't have the same physical or cognitive skills that the older ones have, which is important to keep in mind when selecting toys and activities. Toddlers can get overwhelmed with frustration if given a toy to manipulate that is far beyond their capability. And when toddlers have a meltdown, no one is happy.

> "Hands-on, three-dimensional, physical play really matters. Between one and two, already this child can start to invent games. She can figure out new ways to do things; and it's coming from inside her own mind. This is what's very important."
>
> **—Jane M. Healy, Ph.D.**
> educational psychologist and
> author of *Your Child's Growing Mind*

Any toys and play activities that are best suited for children twenty-four to thirty-six months are noted throughout. Older toddlers typically have better hand–eye coordination, can manipulate toys more easily, have steadier balance, and have a better understanding of language. All of these leaps in skills and abilities open up a whole new way of playing.

The Well-Stocked Toddler Toy Cupboard

Just as any chef needs gadgets and supplies in the kitchen, so too does a toddler need toys, props, and materials for a daily life filled with creative, active play. In the back of this book (page 365), you will find an easy-to-navigate list of age-appropriate toys and household items that are marvelous for freewheeling solo play and playing with others too. The list identifies every single item needed to play every single game or activity in the toddler section.

By no means do you need to go out and buy every item in order for your child to have a happy life of playing. Once you've stocked your toy cupboard with just *several*, you'll be in a wonderful position to suggest new and exciting games to hold your toddler's attention—on the spot. So select a few items, as your budget allows, to start creating your toddler's unplugged toy cupboard!

Solo Play

It's safe to say that your toddler isn't going to be old enough to go play outside by herself anytime soon. For one thing, your child needs your constant supervision; for another, she loves to be near you. But she will still be engaged in her own version of solo play, exploring and directing her play independently for brief moments each day.

There are two types of solo play for toddlers covered in this section of the book. The first is what I call *Busy-Body Play*. The play ideas in this category are perfect for the many occasions when you need a few minutes of concentration to make dinner or work at your desk while your toddler plays happily nearby. (Or perhaps you're looking for a way to keep your child occupied in a waiting room or on a plane.) These games require very simple, basic props or toys and only minimal setup, and can typically be played in one designated play area.

The second category of solo play in this section is *Spontaneous Solo Play*. This type of play is more freewheeling and self-directed; it unfolds naturally as your child explores toys or simple props. With this type of play, your child is on the go, moving from place to place as she investigates and plays. She may pick up a baby doll and begin to feed the baby a bottle and a minute later discover a shoe box across the room that gets incorporated into this ad-lib style of play. Self-directed play is ideal for the times when your child can enjoy freedom to move about, from one area to the next, and decide on her own what to play and how long to play it.

Busy-Body Play

Sometimes a child can become bored and restless when he sees your attention wandering away from him. These activities are designed to captivate your child's attention for a few minutes while you are busy with a task only a few feet away. To get things started, give your toddler a quick demo or show him one or two good ideas for solo play. Many times he will begin by copying you

before discovering other ways to play on his own. With busy-body play, he will be using hands and fingers and feet and toes, his eyes and ears and thinking skills too. Of course these activities keep your child busy while you work, but each activity was designed first and foremost to delight and entertain your toddler and put his curiosity and capabilities to work. Most of these play ideas incorporate familiar toys or household items, but offer specific play possibilities that are interesting or challenging to your toddler.

Toddlers like to be where the action is, which means they naturally gravitate to the kitchen, where there is a buzz of excitement a significant part of each day. Let them join in! The kitchen floor or table can be easily transformed into an ideal place for toddler play. Just gather up a few of the simple props and toys used for the games in the following pages (many of which you can find right in your kitchen cupboard), show your child how the game works, and your child will take over from there. As he explores, your child will enjoy your occasional encouragement, and you will have the pleasure of watching a joyful toddler at play. It's a recipe for cozy, casual, comfortable fun that makes for a happy play routine and wonderful memories too.

The Kids' Cupboard

Toddlers love having their very own kitchen cupboard. And you will love that it can be filled with safe playthings for solo busy-body play. Ideally, this should be a low cupboard that your child can open and close himself while you work in the kitchen nearby. For toddlers, dragging all the gadgets out of the cupboard is like hunting for treasure, and experimenting with the objects themselves is a captivating form of wizardry. This serious toddler science consists of stacking containers, putting one item inside the other, putting lids on and taking them off, and seeing what noise can be made with pots and pans. Here are some toddler-safe playthings to include in your happy playtime kids' cupboard. (Remember to add new gadgets and toys to the cupboard from time to time to spice things up a bit.)

Cake pans	Metal roasting pan	Plastic empty squeeze bottles* (mustard, ketchup, or syrup)
Cardboard egg cartons	Muffin tins	
Dish towels	Unbreakable plates and cups	
Funnel		Plastic water bottles*
Measuring cups and spoons	Plastic buckets and tubs (with lids)	Plastic yogurt containers with lids (large)
Metal or plastic mixing bowls (stacking)	Plastic colander	Pots and pans with lids

*SAFETY ALERT: Remove small lids or caps to prevent choking hazard.

Toddler Play (age 1 to 2)

1 Kitchen Soccer

Place a laundry basket on its side, propped up against the wall in the kitchen, to create several rolling and tossing games that are just right for toddlers.

QUICK & EASY

AGE: 1–2 YRS

CATEGORY:
SOLO PLAY/BUSY-
BODY PLAY

NUMBER OF
CHILDREN: ONE

Materials:
- Pack of plastic Wiffle golf balls
  (22 balls to a pack)*
- Unbreakable mixing bowl
- Medium to large plastic laundry basket

Setup:
Place all of the Wiffle balls in the bowl. Put the laundry basket on its side on the floor, propped up against the wall or cupboards. (The basket now resembles a soccer goal.) Squat down to your toddler's height and give your child a quick demonstration: Bounce the ball on the floor about 20 inches away from the basket and watch it bounce inside the goal. (If you use a square, plastic mesh laundry basket, the ball will be less likely to bounce back out.)

Where Can I Find Beanbags?

Toddler-safe beanbags can be purchased at teacher supply or educational supply stores. You'll find sturdy round or square canvas beanbags decorated with colors, numbers, and alphabet letters. These can be used for tossing and are also great during the preschool years for games involving colors, numbers, and letters.

Play:
Position your toddler 2 to 3 feet away from the basket, and place the bowl of balls nearby. As you've demonstrated, the player gives each ball a hearty bounce and watches as it bounces into the basket to score a goal. When all the balls have been bounced inside the goal one by one, your toddler gathers the balls up, puts them back into the bowl, and starts over again. (If you're feeling particularly energetic, you can call out "Two points!" every time your toddler bounces a ball into the basket—or just give your nerves a break and let him play on his own!)

2 Romper Roll

Set up the laundry basket in the same way described above, but have your child sit on the floor 2 to 3 feet away to roll (rather than bounce) a small or medium playground ball into the basket. Part of his time will be spent rolling the ball, and part of his time will be spent retrieving it (or chasing after it if it meanders around the room) before sitting back down to roll it again.

3 Beanbag Basket Toss

For older toddlers (nearing thirty-six months), set up the laundry basket in the same way described above. Create a "tossing line" on the floor by placing a long piece of painter's tape (masking tape) across the kitchen floor a short distance away from the laundry basket. Give your child a bowl of toddler-safe beanbags and challenge her to toss each of the beanbags inside the goal (laundry basket).

*SAFETY ALERT: Be certain to use plastic Wiffle golf balls (or Ping-Pong balls) rather than hard, regulation golf balls.

4 Tunnel Tube

This simple downhill rolling game involves a cookie sheet, a towel, a short mailing tube, and Wiffle balls—no baking involved!

QUICK & EASY

AGE: 1–2 YRS

CATEGORY:
SOLO PLAY/BUSY-BODY PLAY

NUMBER OF
CHILDREN: **ONE**

Materials:

Bath towel

Metal cookie sheet

Cardboard mailing tube (18"–20" long works best)

Duct tape

Invisible tape

Pack of plastic Wiffle golf balls (22 balls to a pack)

Plastic sandbox bucket with handle

Setup:

Fold the towel in half lengthwise and then roll it up tightly, like a fruit roll-up. Place the rolled towel on top of the cookie sheet and slide it to one end. (This creates the "lift" for one end of the mailing tube to create a tube-slide for the ball.) Place the cardboard mailing tube lengthwise on the cookie sheet, with one end propped up on the towel, as shown below.

Secure the high end of the tube in place using a big piece of duct tape. Tape the other end of the tube to the cookie sheet using the invisible tape (to avoid sticky residue after cleanup). Dump all of the Wiffle balls into the bucket. Place the cookie sheet on the floor.

Play:

Show your toddler how to insert one ball into the high end of the tube, listen to it roll, and watch it come out the other end. Let your child play on his own, taking one ball after another from the bucket and dropping it into the tube. For added excitement, place the cookie sheet (with tube attached) on the seat of a sturdy kitchen chair, place a roasting pan on the floor underneath, and watch as some of the balls bounce inside the pan and others bounce onto the floor. Finding all the balls scattered around the room and putting them back in the bucket is part of the fun.

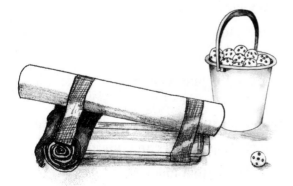

> **"**It's not so easy being a toddler. They're weaker than us, they're slower than us, they can't speak as well. They feel like they're losing all day long. They just want to win a few. And what works the best with toddlers is to allow them to win little tiny things just to feel triumphant in little moments all throughout the day.**"**
>
> **—Harvey Karp, M.D.**
> pediatrician and author of
> *The Happiest Toddler on the Block*

UNPLUGGED PLAY

5 Job-Jar

One of toddlers' favorite types of play is imitating grown-up chores. Create a Job-Jar filled with toddler-friendly cleanup ideas and you'll be surprised by how playful chores can be.

QUICK & EASY

AGE: **2 YRS**

CATEGORY:
SOLO PLAY/BUSY-BODY PLAY

NUMBER OF
CHILDREN: **ONE**

Materials:

Marker

Colored construction paper

Giant plastic jar with a lid

Washcloth or dish towel

Setup:
Think of a few toddler-safe cleanup or setup

ideas that your child can do in the kitchen with you there. Jobs may range from washing the outside of the fridge or kitchen cupboards with a damp washcloth to dusting the kitchen chairs or baseboards (steer clear of feather dusters, as feathers have an uncanny way of winding up in toddlers' noses). Write one job on each piece of paper and fold it in half. Put the papers in the jar.

Play:
Pull one piece of paper from the jar and read the chore out loud. Give a quick demonstration of what needs to be done, and give your child a damp washcloth (or dish towel) for the job. Let him improvise his own special way to do this chore. (And remember: This is playtime, so keep the focus on fun rather than spotless cleaning!)

Toddler-Safe Playtime

A parent's *number one* job is to keep her child safe. With a toddler in the family, this job requires planning, commitment, and constant supervision. Though curiosity is a wonderful thing, remember that toddlers don't yet understand the concept of danger, so you must be their eyes and ears to keep them safe. (Clearly convey safety rules and the need for constant supervision to all of your child care providers and teenage babysitters too.) The very first step is to take a realistic look at your surroundings, with an eye toward your toddler's capabilities, reach, and interests. Here are some general guidelines to keep in mind regarding toddler play and safety:

• Toddlers need constant adult supervision when they play indoors and outdoors.

• Keep older siblings' toys and games with small parts out of reach.

• Install safety gates to protect your child from falls on stairs.

• Remove or cover all furniture with sharp edges or corners and remove small tables and chairs that can easily tip over.

• Keep safety latches on cabinets that store chemicals, cleaning supplies, and medicine.

• Carefully supervise all play that involves water, including buckets and tubs of water.

• Balloons pose a serious choking hazard; keep them away from toddlers.

6 | Pillowcase Surprise

Toddlers are delighted to discover toys and objects hidden inside something else. Here's a mystery-object game that will awaken their universal love of surprise. Scour through your kitchen cupboard for containers and other safe kitchen gadgets to explore.

QUICK & EASY

AGE: 1–2 YRS

CATEGORY:
SOLO PLAY/BUSY-BODY PLAY

NUMBER OF CHILDREN: ONE

Materials:

Pillowcase or 6–10 athletic socks (adult size)

Wooden blocks and/or

Plastic toys and/or

Plastic lids and/or

Plastic measuring cups and/or large plastic bowl

Setup (for toddlers 1 to 2 years old):

Young toddlers are still trying to gain mastery over their hands and fingers, so you'll use a large pillowcase, rather than a sock, for their version of this game. Put 10 to 12 toddler-safe mystery items in the bottom of the pillowcase.

Play:

Your one- or two-year-old looks through the pillowcase to see what he can find. He might pull one item out at a time; he might dump the contents on the floor. This is a great way of holding your child's attention, especially if you put brand-new, unknown, and of course, toddler-safe items in the pillowcase.

Setup (for toddlers 2 years and older):

For your two- or three-year-old, gather up 6 to 10 clean, adult-size athletic socks. Hide one toddler-safe mystery object or toy in each sock by pushing it down firmly into the toe. Once you have filled all the socks with one mystery item, toss them in the giant bowl.

Play:

Challenge your child to find all the mystery items by wiggling the items out of the socks. Or, she can guess what's inside by reaching in and touching the object. If wiggling her hand inside the sock is too difficult, your child may discover she can hold on to the toe section of the sock and spill the contents out onto the floor quite easily. After all the mystery objects have come out, line them up in a row so your child can give a little commentary about what she has found.

" Play is so important to healthy brain development, not just later in life, but starting very early in babyhood. Why? Because play is what allows kids to manipulate their environment. And how you manipulate your environment is about how you begin to take control, how you begin to develop your senses, how you view the world. "

—Kenneth Ginsburg, M.D.
pediatrician and coauthor of the American Academy of Pediatrics report on *The Importance of Play in Promoting Healthy Child Development and Maintaining Strong Parent-Child Bonds*

Toddler Play (age 1 to 2)

7 Scrub-A-Dub

Toddlers love to imitate what you do, and they love to play around in water. Mix these two things together for a game of Scrub-A-Dub.

QUICK & EASY

AGE: 1–2 YRS

CATEGORY: SOLO PLAY/BUSY-BODY PLAY

NUMBER OF CHILDREN: **ONE**

Materials:

Beach towel

Small plastic dishpan

Plastic lids from food containers

Baby-size washcloth (or regular washcloth, cut into 4 pieces)

Setup:

Fold the beach towel in half and place it on the floor. Put 1 inch of water in the dishpan and place the dishpan on top of the towel. Toss the plastic lids and small washcloth inside the dishpan.

Play:

Young toddlers will enjoy playing around with the water and plastic lids. Older toddlers will get a kick out of scrubbing the lids "to make them really clean."

> ❝Any object in your household is a toy to a baby. So you can be doing laundry and sorting socks, and your child can just be putting the laundry in and out of the hamper. And you know what? To a child, that's a perfectly fun way to learn up and down, and high and low, and in and out, and eventually reds and whites, and counting. ❞
>
> **—Maureen O'Brien, Ph.D.**
> child development specialist and author of *Watch Me Grow: I'm One-Two-Three*

8 Scrubbing Baby's Dishes

Ask your toddler to help you scrub all the baby utensils while you work in the kitchen. A little plastic tub with only an inch of water can provide a good stretch of fun. Put a collection of safe infant spoons and bowl, spill-proof infant cups, baby-bottle rings, and nipples into the water. Provide a tiny sponge or small washcloth for soap-free scrubbing!

9 Spoon Scrub and Sort

Rummage through your silverware drawer and create an odds-and-ends collection of teaspoons that aren't in use or don't match and designate them for regular Scrub and Sort playtime for your older toddler. Buy an inexpensive plastic utensil-organizer with four or five compartments; store these special spoons in the tray in a low cupboard so that your toddler can get to them. Ask your toddler to scrub and sort these spoons for your family while you are in the kitchen working. Fill the small plastic tub with an inch of water and the washcloth and have your child dump all the spoons into the water and give them a scrub. Have a dish towel standing by so he can dry the spoons and place them one by one in the tray's compartments.

10 Rock Scrub

Medium to large rocks (the size of a potato) from a creek bank are good fun for a toddler with a vegetable scrubber or large sponge. (Caution: Do not let your child play with small stones or rocks, which could be a choking hazard.)

*SAFETY ALERT: Always supervise toddlers when they are playing with water. Also, if your child likes to put things in his mouth, sponges can pose a choking hazard, so use a washcloth instead.

11 Shake, Rattle-N-Roll

Movement and noise come alive with one transparent pack of tennis balls.

AGE: 1–2 YRS

CATEGORY: SOLO PLAY/BUSY-BODY PLAY

NUMBER OF CHILDREN: ONE

Materials:

Plastic tennis-ball container with lid

3 new tennis balls

Play:

With the three tennis balls inside, secure the lid on the plastic tube. Children one to two years old will enjoy placing the tube on its side on the floor and giving it a shove to see how far it will roll. They also like shaking the tube with both hands and listening to the racket the balls create. Last but not least, lifting off the lid, dumping the balls on the floor, and chasing after them makes for excellent sport.

*Safety Alert: Tennis balls are not intended to be tasted by toddlers, so provide careful supervision.

12 Hallway Bag-Ball

The next time the cashier asks, "Paper or plastic?," pick the paper sack so your toddler can play Hallway Bag-Ball!

AGE: 1–2 YRS

CATEGORY: SOLO PLAY/BUSY-BODY PLAY

NUMBER OF CHILDREN: ONE

Materials:

Paper grocery bag

Plastic balls or tennis balls (use toddler-safe balls to avoid choking hazard)

Setup:

Have your toddler sit on any uncarpeted floor. Fully open the paper grocery bag and place it on the floor on one of its long sides, several yards away from your child. (Give the bag a little stretch to keep it open.) Squat down next to your child and roll the ball so that it goes inside the paper bag.

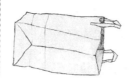

The Honorable, Humble Paper Bag

A paper grocery bag is a versatile prop for toddler play. It can be a lightweight, carryall container for your toddler, ideal for moving a favorite toy from place to place. It is easily transformed into a hiding place for peekaboo items—close the flap, Teddy is gone, open the flap and he appears once again. A stiff new grocery bag placed on its side becomes a goal for a ball rolling along the floor (see Hallway Bag-Ball above). Or remove the bottom of the bag with a pair of scissors and place it on its side with a bit of invisible tape and you've created a terrific tunnel. (Zoom a push-and-go car through the tunnel and your child will squeal with delight; roll a ball through the tunnel once and let your child take over.)

Play:

Once your child sees how to play, he'll simply roll the balls and retrieve them from inside the bag. Both parts of the game, hitting the target and retrieving the balls, are equally enjoyable.

*SAFETY ALERT: Because of the fuzz and dye used in manufacturing, tennis balls are only appropriate for children who no longer put things in their mouth.

13 Muffin Sorter

Just pinching items with fingers, picking them up, and putting them inside little containers is pure and exhilarating play for toddlers.

AGE: 1–2 YRS

CATEGORY:
SOLO PLAY/BUSY-
BODY PLAY

NUMBER OF
CHILDREN: ONE

Materials:

Assorted toddler-safe objects
    for sorting:
    Plastic Wiffle golf balls, giant pop beads,
    tiny colorful sock-balls (made using 1 or 2
    toddler-size socks)
    Plastic or wooden toy figures or animals
    Unbreakable mixing bowl
    Muffin tin

Setup:

Place all of the objects in the plastic bowl. Put the muffin tin and bowl on the floor next to your child. The object of the game is to place the various materials inside the muffin compartments, take them out, put them in again, and perhaps to dump the contents onto the floor and watch the action as the items scatter. So simple, yet so satisfying! (If your child seems more enamored with taking things out than with arranging them in the muffin tins, start by filling each muffin compartment with objects and place the empty bowl nearby.)

14 Duckie-Dip

Rubber duckies from the bathtub find their way into the kitchen in this game.

AGE: 2 YRS

CATEGORY:
SOLO PLAY/BUSY-
BODY PLAY

NUMBER OF
CHILDREN: ONE

Materials:

Beach towel
Plastic dishpan
Ping-Pong balls (or floating
    tub toys, such as plastic ducks)
Small kitchen strainer or tiny fishnet
    (used for fish tanks)
Large plastic food-storage container
    or giant plastic mixing bowl

Setup:

Fold the beach towel in half and place it on the floor or kitchen table. Put 2 inches of water in the dishpan and place it on top of the towel. Add the floating Ping-Pong balls or tub toys to the dishpan.

Play:

Give your child the strainer to use as a net, and see how many ducks or floating plastic balls he can "catch." The catch goes into the mixing bowl. When all the critters have been caught, the player plops them back in the water and starts all over again.

*SAFETY ALERT: Stepping on a Ping-Pong ball can create sharp edges and points that could cause a hazard to children. Supervise so as to avoid any hazards.

15 | Box Ball

Question: What's thin, flat, and lifeless and can be transformed into a ball with the squeeze of two hands? Answer: a piece of paper!

AGE: 1–2 YRS

CATEGORY:
SOLO PLAY/BUSY-BODY PLAY

NUMBER OF
CHILDREN: ONE

Materials:
Medium-size cardboard box
(or large plastic colander)
Sheets of colored construction paper
or copy paper

Setup:
Set up the cardboard box a few feet away from your child.

Play:
Your child crumples the colored paper into balls, tosses the balls into the cardboard box to score a basket, and dumps all the paper-balls back onto the floor to start all over again.

SAFETY ALERT: Best for older toddlers who won't eat paper.

16 | Outdoor Box Ball

For older toddlers, create your own game of outdoor box ball for a few minutes of high-energy fun. First, work with your child to make an assortment of paper-balls; then, find an appropriate container to act as the catching basket. (A kitchen colander, child's sand bucket, plastic sieve, or wastebasket all work well.) You hold the container, your child tosses the ball in your direction, and you chase and catch it in your container. For more paper-ball fun out in the yard, create a tossing line on the lawn with masking tape (roll out the tape, sticky side down, pressing your feet as you go to secure it). Stand back a few feet and toss the balls over the line.

Peekaboo with Boxes

Young toddlers love to play open-and-close and now-you-see-it-now-you-don't games with boxes. Your sixteen-month-old son might drop a tennis ball inside a shoe box, put the lid on, and see that the ball has vanished from sight. When he opens the lid, the ball is there once again. Toddlers repeat this routine again and again and again as they play, and fascinating discoveries are being made along the way. Your child begins to realize that just because an object can't be seen in the moment doesn't mean it is gone forever. This bit of wisdom later gets applied to other aspects of your toddler's life. For example, he will discover that important people (Mom, Dad, siblings, caregivers) vanish from sight for a while but reappear later. According to early childhood development specialists, a child is learning about object permanence when he plays in this way.

Toddler Play (age 1 to 2)

17 Edible Finger Paint

Here's a way to allow your child the pleasure of smearing edible finger paint around and around, with an easy cleanup built into the play.

AGE: 1–2 YRS

CATEGORY:
SOLO PLAY/BUSY-BODY PLAY

NUMBER OF CHILDREN: **ONE**

Materials:

Small mixing bowl (unbreakable)

Flour

Water

High chair (with plastic tray)

Optional: tiny drop of food coloring

Setup:

In a small mixing bowl, stir a small quantity of flour and some warm water together until the substance reaches the consistency of runny pudding or baby food. Add a drop of food coloring if you want color. Allow the mixture to cool before your child plays with it.

Busy-Body Play
High and Low

Many of the busy-body activities in this book can be adapted for the high chair or the playpen so you can keep your child in one place for a few minutes while you work nearby. My friend Kiki calls her child's high chair his "desk" when he wants to play "office"; at other times it is miraculously transformed into a chef's "table" when her child wants to play "cook." This is a splendid way to keep your child close, within eyesight, and safe.

Play:

Place your toddler in her high chair and snap the tray in place. Dump the contents of the goop on the tray and let your child finger paint to her heart's content. (Place newspapers on the floor beneath the high chair for easy cleanup.)

NOTE: If your child prefers to sit at the kitchen table, you can also contain the mess by placing the edible finger paint in the middle of a cookie sheet with sides.

18 Bake Me a Cake

Can you tolerate a little orchestrated mess today? If so, here's an activity that is goopy fun for toddlers!

AGE: 2 YRS

CATEGORY:
SOLO PLAY/BUSY-BODY PLAY

NUMBER OF CHILDREN: **ONE**

Materials:

Water

Small plastic margarine tub

Flour or cornmeal

Spoon

¼ cup size measuring cup(s)

Toy cake pan or loaf pan

Setup:

Put your child in her high chair. Put about ½ cup water in the plastic tub. Add several tablespoons of flour or cornmeal to make a soupy, runny mixture—the cake batter! Be prepared for some spills.

Play:

Hand your child a spoon and ask her to mix up a "cake" with these goopy ingredients. Mixing is good fun, and so is spooning the goop into the cake pan using the small measuring cup.

*SAFETY ALERT: Please supervise your child carefully so that none of the ingredients

creates a choking hazard. This food play activity is about mixing and stirring (the goop should not be eaten), and may not be appropriate for younger toddlers (who put everything in their mouths).

19 Pizza-Pizza

A toddler-inspired pizza pie that might or might not be eaten but is deliciously fun to make.

AGE: **2 YRS**

CATEGORY:
SOLO PLAY/BUSY-BODY PLAY

NUMBER OF CHILDREN: **ONE**

Materials:

Dry, toddler-safe cereal

Raisins (soft)

Small plastic bowls

Waxed paper

Small cardboard pizza box

¼ cup flavored yogurt

Flour tortilla

Spoon

Setup:
Set up the pizza-making station at the kitchen table or by spreading a tablecloth on the floor to create a toddler-friendly work space. Put a few tablespoons of cereal and raisins, to be used as "pizza toppings," in each of the bowls. Put a piece of waxed paper in the bottom of the pizza box. Spread about ¼ cup yogurt on the flour tortilla, put it inside the pizza box, and hand it to the "pizza chef."

Play:
Your toddler uses the spoon to spread the "sauce" around on the pizza a little more. Then he adds the pizza toppings one at a time. (Provide only healthy, toddler-safe "toppings" for this activity so that you don't have to worry if your toddler eats as he plays.) When he finishes his pizza, your child may close the box and play pizza delivery next.

Note: This pizza is not intended to be cooked, but can be eaten.

*Safety Alert: This activity is not appropriate for younger toddlers or toddlers who may choke on the ingredients.

How Things Work

Toddlers are all about exploring to figure out how things work. Something as simple as a cardboard box with a flap top and a doll can provide exciting discoveries for your child. She uses her hands to discover how the box changes when a flap is moved back and forth; now it's open, and now it's closed. Over and over again your sixteen-month-old child manipulates the lid of the box and watches what happens. Next, she puts her doll inside the box and closes it, and the doll disappears. She opens it again, and her baby doll reappears! You can almost see the gears in her mind turning. The mental notes she is making now will be revised and expanded further as she plays another day.

Why "No TV or Videos" Is Best for Your Toddler

The American Academy of Pediatrics recommends completely avoiding screen time (that means both TV and videos) for children under two years of age. I usually want to know why when I hear a rule like this, and perhaps you do too. Here are some concrete reasons why these AAP recommendations make perfect sense for toddlers:

- Toddlers are wired to be active learners who explore and experiment through play. The passive viewing encouraged by a video is quite different from the hands-on approach to which toddler brains are naturally prone.

- Toddlers want and need to develop their physical selves through movement (it's the path to large and small muscle development). Television and video viewing is sedentary and discourages the very movement their growing bodies crave. (The AAP says that childhood obesity is clearly linked to lack of physical play and exercise.)

- Hands-on active play promotes growth for the whole child (physically, socially, emotionally, and intellectually). When toddlers play *physically*—with balls, blocks, and toys—they develop thinking skills too. By hauling blocks around or stacking them, for example, they begin to understand cause and effect and discover the properties of matter, shape, and size. Social skills come into active play as well; toddlers learn to get along with others and resolve conflicts as they play.

- Toddlers are wired to learn language through everyday interactions. Language acquisition relies upon having many spontaneous, back-and-forth conversations with others. Mom asks a question and toddler answers, which causes Mom to say something more. This two-way conversation is very gratifying to a toddler. He asks for more milk and he gets it. Machines project sound in your child's direction, but even a toddler quickly learns that you can't have a true conversation with a television. When toddlers play with parents, language blossoms.

- Toddlers practice patience and learn to tolerate frustration as they play. The boy who gets mildly upset when his three-block tower tumbles down has a chance to persevere in the face of a disappointment. He tries again and again and may eventually get the blocks to do just what he wants. This lesson of perseverance plants a seed in the toddler's mind: Mastering something new takes time. Many videos, with their alluring special effects and fast-paced action, send quite a different message to toddlers, and educators worry that they set the stage for a shortened attention span and the expectation of instant gratification.

- Toddlers form expectations and habits through their everyday routines. When your child has the freedom to play and explore with open-ended toys that allow for many ways to play, he comes to believe that he can make things happen through his own actions. This is a powerful discovery with lifelong repercussions.

Busy-Body Play on-the-Go

Keeping your toddler busy in your own home is one thing; passing time happily while you are out and about, especially when there is waiting involved, is quite another. Because toddlers are so curious, they often want to run around and explore any new and exciting environment (which means that almost any outing, from a visit to the doctor to a meal at a restaurant, might be tackled with the zeal of a Martian explorer). In order to compete with the excitement of a new place, you must carry a few new and exciting playthings in the diaper bag to hold your child's attention while you wait. (And they'll be all the more fascinating if you reserve them for these busy-body on-the-go times.) On the other hand, there may be days (and environments) when your child will seek the comfort of a familiar, soothing activity while you wait. The best plan is to be prepared with props for both situations. Here are some portable games that may serve you well when you find yourself in the waiting mode in various settings away from home.

PARENT TIP

20 Creativity in the Examining Room

❝When my kids were toddlers, I got into the habit of carrying crayons with me whenever we had an appointment at the pediatrician's office. During the long waiting time in the examination room, they would draw pictures or scribble with crayons on the white paper pulled out to cover the exam table. This kept my children busy, and sometimes our doctor would even spend a few minutes drawing with them.❞

—Peggy from Maryland

UNPLUGGED PLAY

21 Scribble-Scrabble Notebook

Toddlers love having their very own vinyl notebook with pages to flip and a plastic crayon-filled pocket.

AGE: 1–2 YRS

CATEGORY:
SOLO PLAY/BUSY-BODY PLAY

NUMBER OF CHILDREN: **ONE**

Materials:

½"-thick three-ring binder with clear plastic sleeve on cover

Notebook paper for three-ring binder

Plastic (zip-style) pencil pouch with three holes to fit inside three-ring binder

Toddler-size crayons

8½"-by-11" piece of paper with a color photo of your toddler (print this photo from your computer or take a 4"-by-6" photo to your local copy center to make a color copy on 8½"-by-11" paper)

Setup:
Fill the notebook with paper, put crayons in the plastic pencil pouch, and insert the 8½"-by-11" photo of your child into the clear sleeve on the front of the notebook. Keep the notebook in your tote bag for whenever boredom strikes!

Play:
This is a special notebook that should only be brought out for drawing and scribbling when you are on the go. Your child may prefer to do all her own coloring, or she may like opening the notebook so that you can draw on one page and she can draw on the other. Follow her lead.

22 Polka-Dot Hat to-Go

Work with your toddler to put sticky "dots"(or shapes) all over a clear sherbet tub and you've created a colorful hat while waiting. The finished hat is not much for grown-up eyes to look at, but it sure is cool to make!

AGE: 1–2 YRS

CATEGORY:
SOLO PLAY/BUSY-BODY PLAY

NUMBER OF CHILDREN: **ONE**

Materials:

Color dot stickers (available at office supply stores, or use scissors to create your own dots and shapes from the sticky parts of Post-it notes)

Empty sherbet tub with lid

Setup:
Put the stickers inside the plastic tub, snap on the lid, and toss in your diaper bag.

Play (for toddlers 1 to 2 years old):
Remove the lid from the tub and take the stickers out. Turn the plastic tub upside down on the floor, peel off a sticker, and apply it to the surface of the tub. Quickly hand another sticker to your child and show him how to stick it on the tub. Continue to hand stickers to your child as he decorates the entire "hat." If you run out of room on the hat, hand your child the lid and let him decorate that as well.

Play (for toddlers 2 years and older):
Your older toddler may be able to peel the stickers off the sheet of paper on his own, and that action becomes part of the play. (If your child has trouble peeling, use your fingernails to loosen just the top edge of all the stickers on the page.) Older toddlers may take time to create some sort of "design"–using all the red dots on one section and then applying all the blue dots to another.

23 | Scarf Magic

Long silky scarves stuffed inside a big cup appear to grow longer and longer with every tug. It really looks like magic!

QUICK & EASY

AGE: 1–2 YRS

CATEGORY: **SOLO PLAY/BUSY-BODY PLAY**

NUMBER OF CHILDREN: **ONE**

Materials:

Scissors (for adult use only)

Large, rigid plastic or paper beverage "to go" cup with sturdy plastic lid

3 or 4 long, narrow silk scarves

Setup:

Cut a big hole (the size of a silver dollar) in the lid of the large to-go cup. Tie the scarves together end to end (by knotting the corners) to create one humongous, long scarf. Stuff the giant scarf into the cup, leaving one end of the scarf on top. Put the lid on the cup and toss it in your diaper bag for the moment your toddler gets a little bit impatient or bored.

Play:

When your child is ready to play, thread the end of the first scarf through the big hole in the top of the lid. Help your toddler grab the end of the scarf and begin pulling it out of the cup. (You will need to hold the lid in place while she pulls the long scarf all the way out of the cup.) Your toddler will delight in the perception that her tugging action seems to make the scarf "grow" right before her very eyes.

24 | Simple Magic

For a simpler version, remove the cup lid and layer three or four scarves on top of one another inside so your child can search for and pull out each scarf from the cup one by one.

Tip: If your child has trouble finding the end of the scarf, knot one corner of each scarf before you stuff it in the cup. Then instruct her to "find the knot." Your child may also enjoy stuffing and mashing all the scarves back into the cup which will extend the play for several extra minutes.

*Safety Alert: Supervise toddlers carefully so they do not get tangled in the scarves.

PARENT TIP

25 | Mommy's Cart

❝*My son is two and a half and loves to go grocery shopping with me—as long as he gets to push his own grocery cart through the aisles. I take his toy cart along and he proudly pushes it around the store while I push the regular cart. He's old enough to understand the basic idea that only Mom is allowed to get items off the shelf, so I hand him any item that is small enough to handle (and unbreakable), and he puts these items in his cart. When there is a meat item or something messy, I simply say, 'This is meat for Mommy's cart,' and he's perfectly content. When it's time to check out, we head for the lane without candy, and I always let him push his cart up to the register in front of my cart. Then he hands me each item from his cart and I place it on the conveyer belt. He's a bit slow in doing this, which works out fine, because I have time to unload one or two items from my cart in between his items and we check out pretty quickly.*❞

—Diana from Connecticut

Toddler Play (age 1 to 2)

26 | Lunchbox Art

Waiting for the food to arrive at a restaurant is one of the more difficult waiting times for a child. But it doesn't have to be!

AGE: 1–2 YRS

CATEGORY: SOLO PLAY/BUSY-BODY PLAY

NUMBER OF CHILDREN: ONE

Materials:

Lunch box

Large crayons

Stack of plain white copy paper (rolled width-wise and secured with a rubber band) or 4"-by-6" index cards

Roll of invisible tape

Sheets of round, colorful stickers (available at office supply stores)

Setup:
Pack a lunch box full of simple, toddler-safe art supplies that your child can pull out during those waiting times.

Play:
Let your child scribble, draw, and sticker right at the table, and then stow it away easily when the food comes.

SAFETY ALERT: Supervise your toddler carefully so that she doesn't put any of the art supplies or materials in her mouth.

27 | Slot Machine

Breathe new life into a ho-hum deck of playing cards to create this portable coffee can game.

AGE: 1–2 YRS

CATEGORY: SOLO PLAY/BUSY-BODY PLAY

NUMBER OF CHILDREN: ONE

Materials:

Scissors and duct tape (for adult use only)

Empty coffee can with lid

Deck of playing cards

Setup:
Use scissors to cut a slit in the lid of the coffee can long enough so that one playing card can slip through. Use small pieces of duct tape to cover the inside rim of the can to cover any potentially sharp edges. Put the deck of cards inside the coffee can, put the lid on, and put this "toy" in your diaper bag.

Play:
Remove the deck of cards from the can and replace the lid. Hand your child one card at a time and ask him to put each card through the slot. Once all the cards are in, open the lid and let him dump them out and start all over again. He may play another round on his own.

PARENT TIP

28 | Hold on to Your Coupons

"I rescued my husband's worn-out leather wallet from the wastebasket a few months ago and created 'money' to put inside it by cutting colorful coupons from the pharmacy insert in the Sunday paper. I keep this wallet in my purse for my twenty-one-month-old son, Joshua, to play with whenever we find ourselves waiting someplace. In a sit-down restaurant, I'll pull out Josh's wallet and he has a good time dumping all the money on the table and sorting through it. Then I help him put it in a stack and fit it back inside the wallet. It's amazing how much amusement he's gotten out of this old, beat-up wallet."

—Lynn from Ohio

Clapping and Counting Games

When your child is not feeling well (or even if her mood is just a bit subdued), traditional clapping and counting games might be just the ticket to pass the time in a waiting room. The rhythms are comforting, and the finger play creates a bit of added interest to hold your child's attention.

Developmentally, your toddler will be able to hold his hands open, but he may not be able to clap on his own just yet. You can help him clap by holding his hands and gently clapping them together or by letting him hold on to your hands while you clap. The repetitive nature of the action and language of the rhymes will delight your toddler (who will ask you to repeat them again and again) and help develop his hand–eye coordination and language skills as he plays.

29 Pat-a-Cake

Patty cake, patty cake,
baker's man,
(clap baby's hands together)

Bake me a cake as fast as you can.

Roll it and pat it and mark it with a *B*,
(move baby's hands in a circle, clap them together, and write an imaginary B on baby's hands)

And put it in the oven for baby and me!
(put baby's hands together, move them toward your mouth, and kiss, or pretend to nibble tops of baby's hand.)

QUICK & EASY

AGE: 1–2 YRS

CATEGORY:
PARENT &
CHILD/INDOOR

NUMBER OF
CHILDREN: **ONE**

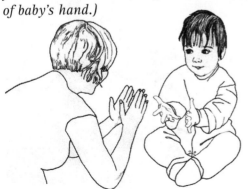

30 Two Little Blackbirds

Two little blackbirds
(wiggle your two index fingers)

Sitting on a hill
(wiggle two fingers again)

One named Jack *(crook one finger)*

One named Jill
(crook the other finger)

Fly away, Jack! *(wiggle the "Jack" finger as you move it behind your back)*

Fly away, Jill! *(wiggle the "Jill" finger as you move it behind your back)*

Come back, Jack *(bring the "Jack" finger back as you wiggle it)*

Come back, Jill *(bring the "Jill" finger back as you wiggle it)*

Two little blackbirds *(wiggle both index fingers)*

Sitting on a hill *(wiggle both fingers again)*

(repeat the entire verse and movements)

QUICK & EASY

AGE: 1–2 YRS

CATEGORY:
PARENT &
CHILD/INDOOR

NUMBER OF
CHILDREN: **ONE**

Toddler Play (age 1 to 2)

31 Peas Porridge Hot

Clap your hands while reciting this rhyme. Clap your hands on your legs. Clap your hands on your baby's knees. Or cross your hands to your chest between each clap.

AGE: 1–2 YRS

CATEGORY:
PARENT & CHILD/INDOOR

NUMBER OF CHILDREN: **ONE**

Peas porridge hot,
Peas porridge cold,
Peas porridge in the pot
Nine days old.

Some like it hot,
Some like it cold,
Some like it in the pot
Nine days old.

My mommy likes it hot,
My daddy likes it cold,
But I like it in the pot
Nine days old.

> ❝ When you're thirty years old, you should be able to sing a lullaby to your baby; you should be able to dance at your wedding; you should be able to sing 'Happy Birthday' to your kids; you should be able to sing in worship services; you should be able to clap your hands in time to the beat with everybody else at the football game. And all that stuff depends on what happens in the first five years of life. ❞
>
> **—John Feierabend, Ph.D.**
> Professor of Music Education at the Hartt School at the University of Hartford, and author of the *First Steps in Music* series

32 Eensy Weensy Spider

(Also called the "Itsy Bitsy Spider")

The eensy weensy spider
went up the waterspout
(place tip of right thumb on left forefinger; while these fingers are joined, swivel both hands so that the left thumb

AGE: 1–2 YRS

CATEGORY:
PARENT & CHILD/INDOOR

NUMBER OF CHILDREN: **ONE**

joins up with the right forefinger; release the bottom pair of fingers and swivel them back to the top; continue to alternate joining and releasing each pair of fingers)

Down came the rain
and washed the spider out!
(hold your hands in the air and wiggle your fingers to imitate rain)

Out came the sun
and dried up all the rain
(hold your arms in the air in the shape of a circle)

So the eensy weensy spider
went up the spout again
(create a brief climbing action with your fingers and thumbs)

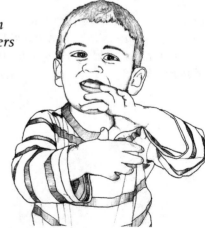

33 Hickory, Dickory, Dock

Hickory, Dickory, Dock

The mouse ran up the clock.
(use two fingers to gently "walk" up baby's arm)

The clock struck one
(kiss baby's head)

And down he run. *(use two fingers to gently walk down baby's arm)*

Hickory, Dickory, Dock! *(hug and kiss baby)*

AGE: 1–2 YRS

CATEGORY: **PARENT & CHILD/INDOOR**

NUMBER OF CHILDREN: **ONE**

34 Pitty Patty Polt

Pitty, patty, polt,
(tap on child's foot)

Shoe a little colt,
Here a nail, there a nail,

Pitty, patty polt.
(tap on child's foot)

AGE: 1–2 YRS

CATEGORY: **PARENT & CHILD/INDOOR**

NUMBER OF CHILDREN: **ONE**

35 Higglety Pigglety

Higglety Pigglety Pop!
(clap hands)

The dog has eaten the mop.

The pig's in a hurry,
(roll arms with hands in fists)

The cat's in a flurry,

Higglety Pigglety Pop!
(clap hands)

AGE: 1–2 YRS

CATEGORY: **PARENT & CHILD/INDOOR**

NUMBER OF CHILDREN: **ONE**

36 One Potato, Two Potato

Clap while reciting this rhyme, or make a fist and knock the tops of other player's fists on each count.

One potato, two potato,

Three potato, four;

Five potato, six potato,

Seven potato more.

(repeat the entire verse and movements again)

AGE: 1–2 YRS

CATEGORY: **PARENT & CHILD/INDOOR**

NUMBER OF CHILDREN: **ONE**

37 One, Two, Three

One, two, three
(tap on baby's knee)

Tickle your knee
(tickle baby's knee)

Four, five, six
(tap on baby's tummy)

Pick up sticks
(tickle baby's tummy)

Seven, eight, nine
(tap on baby's chin)

You're all mine!
(big hug!)

AGE: 1–2 YRS

CATEGORY: **PARENT & CHILD/INDOOR**

NUMBER OF CHILDREN: **ONE**

NOTE: *For more counting rhymes, see also "One, Two, Buckle My Shoe" and "This Old Man" on page 177 (in Preschool Play section).*

Spontaneous Solo Play

Toddlers are inventors and explorers, and it shows in their play. When your child grabs a new dump truck for the first time, it's as though a little voice inside his brain calls out, "This really is something! How does it work? What can I do with it?" Then your child uses his hands and whole body to answer these questions as he plays. This is what I call "self-directed solo play." If you join in the play, it's usually best to let your child lead the way—though he may need just a wee bit of a demonstration to see how to manipulate a new toy or object. For example, you may pick up a small wooden mallet and pound a peg on the new pounding toy so your child gets the idea of one way to play. When all of the pegs have been pounded through, turn over the toy so your child sees the next round of pegs for pounding. In this manner, you provide a quick how-to and then let your little play-master invent his own play. Some of the play ideas in this section of the book involve classic toys like dolls, trucks, and wagons. Other games use simple, safe kitchen or household gadgets that are transformed into toys when placed in the hands of your curious, active toddler. Since this style of play is all about exploring in a spontaneous way, many of the play ideas appear without "how to play" instructions.

> **"** Babies love dropping spoons off the high chair so much. They're dropping the spoon and making a prediction that it's going to fall to the ground. And sure enough, it does. And Mom picks it up and puts it on the high chair. And baby says, 'You know, I think I'll make a little physics prediction here—I bet if I drop it, it's gonna fall again.' And they drop it and it does. The baby is going: 'YEAH! The world works! It's predictable; I understand it.' **"**
>
> **—Andrew Meltzoff, Ph.D.**
> professor of psychology and coauthor of *The Scientist in the Crib*

38 Ride a Wagon

Wagons let you transport lots of things from place to place. Indoors, toddlers can fill up a wagon with cars, trucks, blocks, and books. Outdoors, rocks, leaves, dolls, and stuffed animals are taken for a (somewhat bumpy) ride.

QUICK & EASY

AGE: 1–2 YRS

CATEGORY:
SOLO PLAY/
SPONTANEOUS

NUMBER OF
CHILDREN: ONE

Materials:

Safe, small (toddler-size) plastic wagon

Assorted items to haul indoors: *blocks, books, assorted plastic food containers and lids, junk mail, all the hats in the house, sock-balls (athletic socks rolled into balls), small cardboard boxes, toddler-safe shoes and sandals*

Assorted items to haul outdoors: *large rocks and stones, leaves, water, sand, dirt, measuring cups, floating toys (small ducks, boats, etc.)*

Setup:

Indoors, designate one low, kitchen cupboard to hold all the toddler-safe containers for wagon loading. Or add dolls or stuffed animals to transform the wagon into a portable dollhouse or barn. Outdoors, fill the wagon with an inch or two of water and expect a bit of splashing

and wet clothes. Add floating toys and measuring cups for portable water play, or add a washcloth and use the wagon as a "bathtub" for dolls. Create a giant "car wash" for your child's plastic cars, trucks, or plastic balls, with plastic cups for rinsing. Add seashells or rocks that need a good bath, and provide a baby toothbrush for some soap-free scrubbing.

*SAFETY ALERT: Supervise water play carefully, and don't provide items that pose a choking risk to children who are prone to putting things in their mouths.

PARENT TIP

39 Beat the Buzzer

" Every weekend, my two children (ages two and three and a half) drag out nearly every toy they own. By the end of the day our home looks like a war zone. I wanted the children to learn to help put all these toys away, so I came up with a 'game' that we play called Beat the Buzzer. Basically, I just announce that it's time to play Beat the Buzzer, and get the kitchen timer (which has a rather loud 'buzzer sound' rather than a beep). I give each child a big box to put all their toys in. Playing this cleanup game has taken me out of the nagging role. And our older child enjoys the challenge of trying to get all her toys in the box before the buzzer sounds. My two-year-old son mainly likes to play because his sister is playing, so I have to help him pick up some of his toys so he can 'win' before the buzzer sounds. "

—Tom from California

UNPLUGGED PLAY

40 Cars and Trucks

Toddlers love brightly colored dump trucks, push-and-go cars, and every transportation toy in between! After making these easy tunnels and garages out of shoe boxes, show your toddler how to zoom his car through a tunnel or park it in the garage.

QUICK & EASY

AGE: 1–2 YRS

CATEGORY:
SOLO PLAY/
SPONTANEOUS

NUMBER OF
CHILDREN: ONE

Materials:

Shoe boxes and small to medium cardboard boxes

Marker (for adult use only)

Ruler

Scissors (for adult use only)

Plastic or wooden trucks, cars, and toddler-safe trains

Setup:

Create a series of "garages" and "tunnels" for your child's cars and trucks. To make the tunnels, place a shoe box or a cardboard box upside down on a table and draw a large upside-down *U* in the center of each of the two long sides of the box. (Your *U*s should match up exactly, so use a ruler to make sure.) Use scissors to cut out the tunnel openings. To make a garage, make the same cutout but on only one side of a shoe box. Put the lid on the top of the box so the garage has a dashing roof!

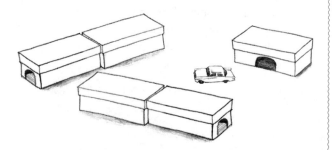

Ramp It Up!

A large sheet of foam board (poster board with foam backing) makes a terrific ramp for zooming small cars and trucks down a hill. Prop the foam board up against your couch or easy chair at an angle. This ramp will stay in place when positioned on carpeting; if you have a hard floor, use strips of invisible tape to hold it in place. Stuffed animals have been known to take a ride down this slippery slide too.

41 Stuffed Animals

Many children have one special, beloved stuffed animal that plays the role of a quiet, lovable playmate.

QUICK & EASY

AGE: 1–2 YRS

CATEGORY:
SOLO PLAY/
SPONTANEOUS

NUMBER OF
CHILDREN: ONE

Materials:

Tablecloth

Stuffed animal(s) and/or plastic (toddler-safe) people or action figures

Optional:

Plastic laundry basket (cage)

Shoe box (bed)

Dump truck or small wagon (car for teddy)

Tea set

Dish towel

Setup:

Drape an extra-large tablecloth over one end of the kitchen table or a card table and secure in place so that it creates a fort or house for the stuffed animal. (Young toddlers may simply enjoy crawling into "Teddy's" house; older toddlers may like outfitting the house with a shoe box for Teddy's bed and plates for Teddy's dinnertime.) Help organize a tea party.

42 | Dolls

A baby doll can be washed and fed and put to bed by your toddler. This is a fun way for your toddler to imitate Mom or Dad caring for baby.

AGE: 1–2 YRS

CATEGORY:
SOLO PLAY/
SPONTANEOUS

NUMBER OF
CHILDREN: **ONE**

Materials:

Baby dolls

Simple, toddler-safe baby accessories: tiny hairbrush with extra-soft bristles and short round handle; baby bottle; plastic spoon and bowls; tiny toy high chair; baby clothes; shoe box to use as baby bed; baby blanket or dish towel; small plastic tub and damp washcloth (no water needed); doll stroller or tiny plastic wagon

Setup:
Assemble a few simple props and give each prop a name (*"Here's a bathtub for baby. Here are baby's bed and blanket."*) Show your child how to brush the baby's hair or wash the baby's face with the damp washcloth.

43 | Bumper Ball

A large plastic ball and two makeshift "bumpers" on the floor set the stage for brilliant ball play—rolling the ball and watching it bounce back each time.

AGE: 1–2 YRS

CATEGORY:
SOLO PLAY/
SPONTANEOUS

NUMBER OF
CHILDREN: **ONE**

Materials:

2 cardboard mailing tubes

Roll of painter's tape (masking tape)

Large, toddler-safe plastic ball with plenty of bounce

Setup:
Designate a playing area in the kitchen that is free from foot traffic. Your child will need approximately 4 feet of uncluttered floor space (uncarpeted floor is best) and a wall without furniture to serve as the "backboard" for play. Place the two mailing tubes side by side on the floor, perpendicular to the wall, then angle the tubes to create a "V," with 1 foot of space between the tube ends near the wall, and 2 feet of space between the tube ends farthest from the wall. Tape them in place. These create "bumpers" (similar to those used at the bowling alley for young bowlers). Provide a quick demo for your child to start the play: Stand a few feet back from the bumpers and roll the ball into the "V" so that it hits the wall (backboard) and comes rolling right back to you. Now let your toddler take over.

> **"**The closer the contact between parent and child at the earliest stages, the better the relationship and the better the outcome for the child.**"**
>
> **—John Evans**
> psychotherapist and author of *Marathon Dads*

44 Blocks

Toddlers love to pile up blocks, knock them down, put them in a wagon, and haul them around. (And sometimes they stack them up to make a fine tower too.) Once they begin to show an interest in pretend play, blocks can become a wonderful prop for more elaborate scenarios.

AGE: 1–2 YRS

CATEGORY: SOLO PLAY/ SPONTANEOUS

NUMBER OF CHILDREN: ONE

Materials:

Blocks (wooden, cardboard, interlocking plastic)

Cardboard boxes

Plastic laundry basket or bucket

Small plastic wagon

Setup:

Show your younger toddler how to stack blocks end to end or on top of one another in stacks of two or three. Show your older toddler how to create simple patterns using the different colors.

> **"** Stacking blocks or trying to put one thing inside another, rolling something, or playing in clay or mud or with sticks or boxes—all of those things are teaching toddlers important principles about the three-dimensional physical world. **"**
>
> **—Jane M. Healy, Ph.D.**
> author of *Your Child's Growing Mind*

45 Ride-on Toys

Toddlers are keen on scooting from place to place on their ride-on toy; unknown to them, it's a marvelous way to build muscles and develop coordination. If yours needs a little encouragement and you happen to have an office chair handy, you might just want to display the principle of scooting and riding!

AGE: 1–2 YRS

CATEGORY: SOLO PLAY/ SPONTANEOUS

NUMBER OF CHILDREN: ONE

Materials:

Plastic or wooden ride-on toys that your child propels by scooting his feet. Here are a few of my favorites:

Fire truck

Farm tractor (seat lifts up to reveal farm animals inside)

Motor scooter (nonelectric)

Jeep

Race car

Plane

School bus (seat lifts up to reveal plastic people inside)

Pony

The Joys of Pulling and Pushing

I'm talking about pull toys and push toys—terrific fun for toddlers. Pull toys are exciting for older toddlers who have mastered walking and are able to maneuver toys around furniture and doorways. It takes a bit of skill for a toddler to walk forward while glancing backward every now and then to see what's happening as he pulls along that duck on wheels (toddlers are keen observers, so they find pull toys fascinating to watch). As he glances back, he's watching the wheels go round and round, seeing the toy in relation to objects it passes along the way, noticing something is wrong when the wheel gets hung up on the sofa and suddenly stops. Whew, that's a lot of multitasking while your child plays with his simple little pull toy! For younger toddlers, large, sturdy ride-on toys with a high, upright handle or grab bar in back can be used to help them walk. Other, smaller push toys are just plain fun to zoom around with—and "just plain fun" is a concept any parent and child can get behind. Here are a few of my favorite pull and push toys:

Pull Toys

Classic pull-along telephone

Duck on a string (waddles and quacks)

Pull-along wooden block set (in wooden wagon)

Pull-along wooden stacking animals

Train on a string

Wooden pull-along zoo animals

Push Toys

Doll stroller

Mini (plastic) grocery cart

Mini (plastic) lawn mower

Mini (plastic) vacuum cleaner

Musical roll-along toy with safe, rounded handle (so child won't get hurt if she falls)

Popcorn popper

Push-along trains, cars, trucks, boats, tractors, airplanes

Push-and-go vehicles (depress the plastic passenger and the car zooms forward)

Wooden giraffe walker (shape sorter attached)

PARENT TIP

46 Turning "No" into "Yes"

❝My two-year-old's favorite word seems to be 'no.' He really seems to get a kick out of saying it! What I try to do, whenever possible, is find the reverse thing that we can say yes to when he digs in his heels with a no. So, for example, if my son does not want to get his coat on when it's time to go outside, I lightheartedly say, 'Yes, you do get to go outside and play when you put your coat on.' Then I enthusiastically add, 'I wonder what fun things we will discover outside together today; maybe a caterpillar, maybe a squirrel, maybe another big red rock.' Usually by this time in the conversation, he's thinking about the outdoor adventures I'm describing and the word 'no' has just faded into the background.❞

—Rebecca from New Jersey

Role-Play and Pretend Play

Children one to two years old are just starting to show an interest in role-play and pretending. Your toddler may imitate the things she sees you doing–talking on the phone, stirring a spoon in a pan, feeding the dog, or mowing the lawn. As your toddler moves from the second to third year of life, her imitations and pretending may become much more involved. Your thirty-month-old daughter, for example, may play "grocery store" by placing boxes and cartons in a toy shopping cart, opening her purse to find money, or unloading her groceries at the kitchen table.

Here are some favorite play activities that incorporate imitation, role-play, or imagination. Toddlers love to imitate and pretend in their own way, so all the help your child may need to get started is having a few good props and toys available. Note that because children one to two years old typically have a different way of "pretending" than children two to three years old, you'll find play ideas for each of these age groups in this section.

> ❝Kids observe—they watch what you do, and their brain takes it in. And that becomes a model for how they're going to behave. Language is learned this way, and how to operate in the social world is learned that way too, so it's very, very important—this connection, this invisible brain-to-brain connection—in how kids learn and how they mature and grow up. ❞
>
> **—Daniel Goleman, Ph.D.**
> psychologist and author of
> *Emotional Intelligence* and *Social Intelligence*

47 Mailbox

Mail is just one of those life mysteries that fascinates children. It's a winning combination of the written word, an adult in a uniform, and a little box with a now-you-see-it-now-you-don't slot.

AGE: 1–2 YRS

CATEGORY: SOLO PLAY/ PRETEND

NUMBER OF CHILDREN: **ONE**

Materials:
Scissors (for adult use only)
Cardboard shoe box (with lid)
Deck of laminated child-size playing cards
Junk mail envelopes
Rubber stamp without ink
Stuffed animals or dolls (pretend pals)

Setup:
Use the scissors to cut a long, wide slit in the lid of the box for your child to drop each letter inside the mailbox. (Make this slit 10 inches long and ½ wide so that business-size envelopes can go in easily.)

Play (for toddlers 1 to 2 years old):
Young toddlers should put each playing card in the slot of the shoe box mailbox. Spread the cards out on the floor and supervise and help as needed to get all the cards inside the box. When all the cards are inside, take off the lid and let your child explore the cards, dump them out, and start all over again.

Play (for toddlers 2 years and older):
Older toddlers can arrange the letters in piles, use the rubber stamp to "stamp" the letters with "ink," mail the letters, and even deliver the mail to parents, siblings, or the stuffed animals seated around the room.

48 Telephone

Telephone designs change with each passing year, but a toddler's fascination with this grown-up gadget never wanes. Give your older toddler a notepad and ask him to take a very important call from the office. Tell your younger child to call a relative or a friend.

AGE: 1–2 YRS

CATEGORY: SOLO PLAY/ PRETEND

NUMBER OF CHILDREN: **ONE**

Materials:
Toddler-safe toy telephone or toy cell phone
Notepad and crayons, or toddler-safe office supplies (optional)

The Amazing Telephone

What a funny perception your toddler must have of the telephone. He knows only what he sees with his own eyes or hears with his own ears, so he doesn't realize that you are actually talking to another person as you chat into the phone. Instead, your child simply sees a shiny object on the kitchen counter that rings from time to time (or a smaller ringing object in Mom's purse). When it rings, Mom and Dad stop what they are doing and run to the phone, pick it up, and talk and laugh into it. It's easy to see why a telephone holds so much interest.

Toddler Play (age 1 to 2)

49 Office

If you work from home or if you've taken your toddler along on a visit to the office, you know that the concept of adult work is a source of endless fascination and a subject for emulation. A high chair can serve as an "office" space for a younger toddler; older toddlers can be set up at the kitchen table with their own special set of office supplies. An old shoe box makes a good "in-box."

QUICK & EASY

AGE: 1–2 YRS

CATEGORY: SOLO PLAY/ PRETEND

NUMBER OF CHILDREN: ONE

Materials:
  Paper
  Crayons
  Junk mail envelopes
  Telephone
  Plastic wastebasket
  Shoe box
  Recycled phone book (pages will get torn)*
  Index cards*

*NOTE: Starred materials are best for older toddlers.

★ CLASSIC ★

50 Dress-up

Items like purses and wallets have a precious grown-up quality for toddlers, of course, who invent their own special uses for them.

QUICK & EASY

AGE: 1–2 YRS

CATEGORY: SOLO PLAY/ PRETEND

NUMBER OF CHILDREN: ONE

Materials:
  Plastic tub with lid (for storage)
  Hats: sailor hats, baseball caps, stocking caps, straw hats

  Toddler-safe purses, wallets, backpacks, tote bags
  Child-size sunglasses (with lenses removed)
  Mittens or gloves
  Shoes*
  Adult-size vests*

Setup:
Collect items at thrift stores to keep your toddler interested. Store in the "dress-up box." An old baseball cap and vest may transform your child into a busy construction worker on a big job. A wide-brimmed hat and the perfect purse makes for a very fancy lady.

*SAFETY ALERT: Be sure to remove any small objects (like buttons or clips) that could come loose and pose a choking hazard.

Box Play

Introduce your toddler to a cardboard box and he's likely to climb inside for a test drive! Cardboard storage boxes are wonderful crawl spaces, scooting machines, and receptacles for flying beanbags. Gift boxes can become a holding place for outdoor treasures like shells and leaves. Recycled pudding, cake, muffin, or cereal boxes make realistic props for "grocery store" play. Use the lid of a shirt box to create a zoo for plastic animals, a house for plastic people, a truck to slide across the carpet . . .

51 | Grocery Store

Younger children may enjoy simply putting pretend groceries (containers) inside the shopping bag and dragging them from place to place, while an older child might want to emulate the entire food selection and preparation process (in that case you might provide a wallet to encourage paying at the checkout line!).

AGE: 1–2 YRS

CATEGORY:
SOLO PLAY/
PRETEND

NUMBER OF
CHILDREN: ONE

Materials:
Cloth tote bag with handles (shopping bag)
Juice boxes and/or
Cake mix or pudding boxes* and/or
Plastic milk jugs with handle (remove lid)* and/or
Cardboard egg carton* and/or
Small plastic bottles
(remove lids to prevent choking hazard)* and/or
Plastic honey bears and/or
Yogurt or margarine tubs and/or
Diaper wipe tubs and/or
Petroleum jelly containers and/or
Unbreakable peanut butter jars

Setup:
Try a prompt like, "Do you want to go to your grocery store in the cupboard and buy some things for Mommy to make for dinner tonight?" Your child's version of "grocery store" will be under way in no time.

SAFETY ALERT: Starred props and toys are intended for older toddlers (typically two to three years old) who no longer put objects in their mouths.

52 | Story Time/ Library

Books are nice to read, but they're great props for role-play too.

AGE: 1–2 YRS

CATEGORY:
SOLO PLAY/
PRETEND

NUMBER OF
CHILDREN: ONE

Materials:
Plastic bin full of board books
Cloth tote bag
Older children's or grown-up
books (ones you won't mind
getting a little beat up)
Stuffed animals and dolls
(the children for story-time reading)

Setup:
Put together a bin of board books that your toddler can handle on her own. Turning pages, pointing to objects in the book, and emulating parents reading are all part of the fun. Older toddlers may "read" stories to a favorite teddy bear. Or perhaps they will become the children's librarian, reading stories to imaginary children gathered in a circle and later checking out books and slipping them inside a book bag.

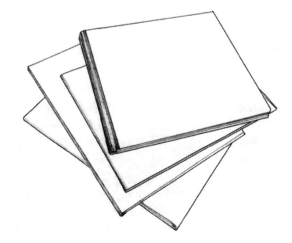

53 Cook

Oh, the thrilling things that go on in a kitchen! The sounds (bacon frying in a pan, blenders whirling, dishes clinking), the smells, the sights, the action. . . . With an assortment of kitchen-related materials, the play will come naturally as your child imitates everything that's happening.

AGE: 1–2 YRS

CATEGORY:
SOLO PLAY/
PRETEND

NUMBER OF
CHILDREN: ONE

Materials:

Plastic measuring cups and spoons

Unbreakable salt and pepper shakers (empty)

Plastic or stainless steel mixing bowls

Plastic cookie cutters (no small parts)

Squeeze bottles

Unbreakable muffin tins

Child-size rolling pin

Plastic cups and plates

Plastic containers with lids

Pie pan, cake pan, cooking pot, or cookie sheet

Spatula and safe cooking utensils

Setup:

Put the little chef on the floor or in a high chair. Then place a request! Favorite dishes are good options, but so are those with funny names—pineapple upside-down cake, for example.

54 Restaurant

Restaurants are action-packed places. Waiters scurry around with big platters and pitchers filled with ice, pouring water into glasses, while sound effects abound!

AGE: 1–2 YRS

CATEGORY:
SOLO PLAY/
PRETEND

NUMBER OF
CHILDREN: ONE

Materials:

Unbreakable bowls, cups, and
small spoons

Empty juice boxes

Food or pretend foods

Plastic soda bottles (partially filled with water for
pouring)*

Notepad and crayon (for writing down orders)*

Cloth napkins*

Setup:

You'll need to set up the temporary restaurant for your child. Help her fold the napkins and show her how you set the table. Your younger toddler's restaurant play may end up looking more like the feast of a caveman than that of a four-star diner, but banging the bowls with a spoon and moving things from place to place are all part of the exploratory play experience. Older toddlers might get the hang of folding cloth napkins and pouring water as they "serve" their patrons.

*SAFETY ALERT: Starred materials are best for older toddlers.

35

55 Fixer-Upper

Tools are what separate us from other animals; a toddler's first experience with tools is an important developmental step. They're also the ultimate mechanism for discovering how things work—something toddlers love to do.

AGE: 1–2 YRS

CATEGORY:
SOLO PLAY/
PRETEND

NUMBER OF
CHILDREN: ONE

Materials:

> Plastic children's tools (hammer, saw, wrench, screwdriver, garden tools, etc.)
> Plastic toolbox or carrying case with a handle
> Objects that require "fixing"
> Ride-on toys
> Toy shopping cart, wagons, doll stroller, toy lawn mower
> Kitchen chairs, kitchen table
> (legs can be "sawed" and "tightened")

Play (for toddlers 1 to 2 years old): Young toddlers will enjoy hauling the tools around from place to place in a toolbox that they can open and close on their own. Dumping the tools out and putting them back in the box again is a big (temporarily messy) part of the fun. They may do a bit of enthusiastic banging and pounding with these tools too, so get ready for a bit of noise.

Play (for toddlers 2 years and older): Older toddlers love to pretend to fix any toy that has wheels. (This is particularly true if your child has ever seen you fixing a car, bike, or lawn mower.) They may also use their tools to repair the hinges and handles on low kitchen cupboards, and other safe furniture around your home. A set of wooden blocks can easily be incorporated into fixer-upper play to fix or build things in your child's "shop" as well. Busy toddlers don't stay in one place very long, so it's likely that everything in sight will be "fixed" in very short order!

*SAFETY ALERT: Be sure to provide soft plastic tools with rounded ends and no sharp edges whatsoever.

56 Taking Care of Baby

Rocking a sweet, tiny plastic baby to sleep is a very responsible way of playing grown-up. And imaginary responsibilities are wonderful, because the possibilities are limitless—one minute your toddler could be putting baby down for a nap, and the next, they could be flying a plane together!

AGE: 1–2 YRS

CATEGORY:
SOLO PLAY/
PRETEND

NUMBER OF
CHILDREN: ONE

Materials:

> Toddler-safe baby doll and baby bottle
> Shoe box (for baby bed)
> Baby blanket
> Plastic cup, bowl, and baby spoon
> Small plastic dishpan and sponge
> Board books

Setup:

If your child seems to be establishing a regular nurturing routine with Baby, you may want to set up the "bed" (shoe box) in a permanent place. The only time your older toddler might need assistance is if it becomes necessary to give Baby a bath (hygiene is very important to toddlers too). Set her up with a dishpan with just a slight amount of water in it and a sponge (no soap).

Toddler Play (age 1 to 2)

Play Ideas for Parent and Child

Whenever I read a promo for an electronic toy that uses the word *interactive*, I have to chuckle. Interacting with a machine pales in comparison to interacting with a living, breathing human being. All the bells and whistles in the world can't change that.

Parents (and caregivers) are fabulous play partners for toddlers. Mom rolls a ball, and her nineteen-month-old son rolls it back with a squeal. Dad hops up and down and makes a monkey sound, and his thirty-month-old daughter joins in with a game of Follow the Leader. These interactions create a package deal that can't be beat. The toddler gets Mom's or Dad's undivided attention, which she adores. And she learns new skills and builds up stamina and muscle power in the most playful, delightful way.

Indoor Play

Setting aside time to play indoors together makes for fun times, but also sends the message early on that play can (and should) be a part of everyday life. Toddlers learn that home is a safe place to explore and navigate—where living and playing are indistinguishable.

Rhyming Games

Have some fun creating your own simple rhyming games. Incorporate your child's name or favorite toy, or familiar family activities you experience together. Here are a few of my own rhymes and rhyming games to serve as a sample. To get started, just sit on the floor facing each other and use the simple props listed below to create action as you play.

57 | Doggie, Doggie

A small beanbag masquerades as a "doggie bone" in this game of lost and found.

AGE: 1–2 YRS

CATEGORY:
PARENT &
CHILD/INDOOR

NUMBER OF
CHILDREN: ONE

Materials:

Small beanbag (the bone)

Toy telephone

Unbreakable bowl

Stuffed animal (preferably a dog)

Rhyme:

Before you get started, tuck the beanbag in your back pocket or waistband.

Doggie, Doggie where's your bone?

Underneath the telephone?
(pick up the phone to look)

No sir, no sir, it's not there. *(shake your head no)*

Tell me, tell me, tell me where.
(turn up both hands to show your palms)

Did the kitty take it, and put it in her bowl?
(look inside bowl)

Did your mama hide it, deep down in a hole?
(look at ground, hands in lookout position)

Doggy, Doggy, where's your treat?
(keeping the "bone" [beanbag] hidden in your hand, slide it under "Doggy's" feet)

I declare, it's at your feet!

58 | Busy As Can Be!

The kitchen is a busy, bustling little world to enjoy together.

AGE: 1–2 YRS

CATEGORY:
PARENT &
CHILD/INDOOR

NUMBER OF
CHILDREN: ONE

Materials:

2 spoons (1 for parent, 1 for child)

Rhyme:

(Substitute your child's name for "Lucy.")
Working in the kitchen, Lucy and me,
(point to child, then to self)

Stirring, stirring, busy as can be,
(stir around and around with the spoon)

One spoon for Lucy, one spoon for me,
(have a quick taste from the spoon)

Working in the kitchen, happy as can be.

(Invent more verses, using your child's favorite foods and kitchen gadgets.)

59 | Through and Through!

Learn a rhyming song that teaches the senses, the parts of the body, and unconditional love.

AGE: 1–2 YRS

CATEGORY:
PARENT &
CHILD/INDOOR

NUMBER OF
CHILDREN: ONE

Rhyme:

(Insert "Mommy" or "Daddy" as appropriate.)

I'm your Mommy through and through,

Let me take a look at you.
(hands over eyes in lookout position, looking from side to side)

I see you with my eyes, *(point to your eyes)*

Big as pumpkin pies.

I hear you with my ears, *(pull out your ears)*

Hanging here for many years.
(tug on your earlobes)

I'm your Mommy through and through,

Let me give a kiss to you! *(kiss baby)*

(Invent similar rhymes about a favorite doll, teddy bear, or family pet!)

Toddler Play (age 1 to 2)

Songs and Lullabies

Singing is a lovely gift to give to your child and introduces music into your child's life in a natural and comforting way. It offers a dose of fun for both the singer and the listener. Here are some classic children's songs that may inspire you to recall music memories from your own childhood. You'll have the opportunity to create charming stories, too, as you invent silly rhymes for your child's own version of "Hush Little Baby" (see Personal Lullaby variation, page 39). The joyful musical experiences that you share with your toddler help make music a familiar and expected part of daily life. A splendid gift, indeed.

60 Twinkle, Twinkle

Twinkle, twinkle little star,
How I wonder what you are!

Up above the world so high,
Like a diamond in the sky.

Twinkle, twinkle little star,
How I wonder what you are.

AGE: 1–2 YRS

CATEGORY:
PARENT &
CHILD/INDOOR

NUMBER OF
CHILDREN: ONE

61 Are You Sleeping?

**English version:
("Are You Sleeping?")**

Are you sleeping,
are you sleeping,
Brother John, Brother John?

Morning bells are ringing,
morning bells are ringing.

Ding, ding, dong, ding, ding, dong.

AGE: 1–2 YRS

CATEGORY:
PARENT &
CHILD/INDOOR

NUMBER OF
CHILDREN: ONE

French version: ("Frère Jacques")

Frère Jacques, Frère Jacques,
Dormez-vous, dormez-vous?
Sonnez les matines, sonnez les matines
Ding, deng, dong, ding, deng, dong.

62 Baa-Baa Black Sheep

Baa, baa, black sheep,
Have you any wool?
Yes sir, yes sir,
Three bags full.

One for the master,
One for the dame,
And one for the little boy
Who lives down the lane.

Baa, baa, black sheep,
Have you any wool?
Yes sir, yes sir,
Three bags full.

AGE: 1–2 YRS

CATEGORY:
PARENT &
CHILD/INDOOR

NUMBER OF
CHILDREN: ONE

63 | Hush Little Baby

Hush, little baby, don't say
a word,
Papa's gonna buy you
a mockingbird.

AGE: 1–2 YRS

CATEGORY:
PARENT &
CHILD/INDOOR

NUMBER OF
CHILDREN: ONE

If that mockingbird don't sing,
Papa's gonna buy you a diamond
ring.

If that diamond ring turns brass,
Papa's gonna buy you a looking glass.

If that looking glass gets broke,
Papa's gonna buy you a billy goat.

If that billy goat won't pull,
Papa's gonna buy you a cart and bull.

If that cart and bull turn over,
Papa's gonna buy you a dog named Rover.

If that dog named Rover won't bark,
Papa's gonna buy you a horse and cart.

If that horse and cart fall down,
You'll still be the sweetest little girl (boy) in
town.

64 | Personal Lullaby

*Use favorite family words to invent your own
special verses for classic lullabies. Here is a
sample from my friend Kiki Walker:*

Hush little baby, don't you cry,
Papa's gonna find you a butterfly,

And if that butterfly won't light,
Papa's gonna buy you a big red kite.

And if that big red kite does break,
Papa's gonna make you a chocolate cake.

And if that chocolate cake won't keep,
Papa's gonna sing you fast asleep!

> "The mother and father and other caretakers are really the baby's favorite playthings. Toy manufacturers are desperately trying to make a toy that lights up, makes sounds, and moves, all in synchrony with one another. This is really what parents and caretakers naturally do when they interact with babies."
>
> **—Andrew Meltzoff, Ph.D.**
> professor of psychology and coauthor of
> *The Scientist in the Crib*

Reading Aloud

Reading aloud is a beautiful way for grown-ups and toddlers to play. Think of books as toys; you are a special playmate who can make these toys come alive for your child. You open the book to a page with colorful pictures and you begin to read aloud. As you do so, you activate your child's sense of hearing, sight, and touch as you explore the book. When you read the first line in *The Runaway Bunny,* your child listens intently. She notices that your voice is different now than it was a few minutes ago at the dinner table, and this is fascinating. She examines the colorful pictures on the page as the melodic rhythm of your voice continues. A few minutes later, when you mention the word "carrot," her eyes move across the page to the large, orange carrot. She uses her fingers to point when you ask, "Where's the bunny?"

All of these small moments of active listening, looking, and touching help make reading books together a playful experience. But the magic doesn't stop there. Your child is getting comfortable seeing letters and words in print and turning pages of the book. These early experiences set the stage for learning letters, recognizing words, and eventually learning to read. Reading picture books together during the toddler years is truly a very important way for your child to grow through play! You'll discover your own favorites, but here are some of my picks to add to your list. Keep in mind that the age classification system for books is flexible. Your one-year-old may still enjoy the books you read when he was an infant. As he gets closer to three, the books in the Preschool section may become favorites too. (See list of recommended Preschool books for read-aloud on page 130.)

> " When you're playing with a toddler with a book, the important thing is the interaction between the parent and the child. So if your toddler is more interested in pointing to the pictures and naming them, or making the animal sounds, or flipping the pages, then that's what you should be doing. "
>
> **—Betty Bardige, Ph.D.**
> developmental psychologist and coauthor of *Poems to Learn to Read By*

Are You My Mother?
by P. D. Eastman

Barnyard Dance!
by Sandra Boynton

Big Dog, Little Dog series
by Dav Pilkey

Brown Bear, Brown Bear, What Do You See?
by Bill Martin Jr.,
illustrations by Eric Carle

Each Peach/Pear/Plum
by Janet Ahlberg,
illustrations by Allan Ahlberg

The Everything Book
by Denise Fleming

Freight Train
by Donald Crews

Goodnight Moon
by Margaret Wise Brown,
illustrations by Clement Hurd

Guess How Much I Love You
by Sam McBratney,
illustrations by Anita Jeram

Have You Seen My Duckling?
by Nancy Tafuri

I Can
by Helen Oxenbury

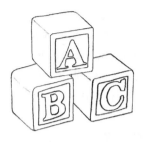

The Itsy-Bitsy Spider
by Rosemary Wells

I Went Walking
by Sue Williams,
illustrations by Julie Vivas

Little Gorilla
by Ruth Lercher Bornstein

Max's First Word
by Rosemary Wells

Maybe My Baby
by Irene O'Book,
illustrations by
Paula Hible

Moo Baa La La La
by Sandra Boynton

My Very First Mother Goose
by Iona Opie, illustrations
by Rosemary Wells

Old Macdonald Had a Farm
by Pam Adams

Owl Babies
by Martin Waddell,
illustrations by Patrick
Benson

Pat the Bunny
by Dorothy Kunhardt

The Runaway Bunny by
Margaret Wise Brown,
illustrations by Clement Hurd

Sheep in a Jeep by Nancy Shaw,
illustrations by Margot Apple

Silly Little Goose!
by Nancy Tafuri

Sleep Tight, Little Bear
by Martin Waddell,
illustrations by Barbara Firth

The Snowy Day
by Ezra Jack Keats

The Teddy Bears' Picnic
by Jimmy Kennedy,
illustrations by
Alexandra Day

Three Little Kittens
by Paul Galdone

Toes, Ears and Nose
by Marion Dane Bauer,
illustrations by Karen Katz

Welcome, Baby! Baby Rhymes for Baby Times
by Stephanie Calmenson,
illustrations by Melissa Sweet

Whose Mouse Are You?
by Robert Kraus and
Jose Aruego

Toddler Play (age 1 to 2)

Action Games

Toddlers love to show you what they know and what they can do. And with movement and fun blended together, the excitement is contagious. You don't need a big block of time to play—just find 10 minutes in your day to play one of these indoor games with your child.

65 Teddy Says . . .

It's a variation on the classic "Where are your ears, your eyes, your nose?" with a touch of Simon Says thrown in for good measure!

QUICK & EASY

AGE: 1–2 YRS

CATEGORY:
PARENT &
CHILD/INDOOR

NUMBER OF
CHILDREN: ONE

Materials:
   Favorite teddy bear or
      stuffed animal

Play (for toddlers 1 to 2 years old):
Young toddlers will learn to point to their head, eyes, nose, ears, elbows, feet, etc. Bring in the furry third party by starting each request with "Teddy" ("Teddy says touch your eyes," "Teddy says show me your nose"). As toddlers become a bit older, they will understand many more words and be capable of more physical movements. Extend this game to more complex physical actions by saying, "Teddy says jump up and down," or "Teddy says turn around."

Play (for toddlers 2 years and older):
Your older toddler can play a more elaborate version of Teddy Says. To start the game, prop up the stuffed animal and announce that Teddy wants to see some of the things that your child has learned to do for herself. Create a series of requests: "Teddy says rub your tummy"; "Teddy says pat your head"; "Teddy says touch the ground." Let your child's understanding of language and her physical abilities lead the way as to which commands from Teddy are

included in the game. Add some silly requests to make this game lively and fun. Once your child is familiar with the game, let her become the voice of Teddy and take a turn making Teddy requests that you must perform: "Teddy says hop"; "Teddy says touch your mouth"; etc.

★ CLASSIC ★

66 Beanbag Toss

Beanbags have a good feel and are easy for small hands to hold, so they are a good choice for early tossing games.

QUICK & EASY

AGE: 2 YRS

CATEGORY:
PARENT &
CHILD/INDOOR

NUMBER OF
CHILDREN: ONE

Materials:
   Dishpan
   Toddler-safe beanbags
      (available at teacher supply stores)

Setup:
Place the dishpan in the center of the room with the beanbags on the floor nearby.

Play:
Toss one beanbag inside the dishpan to give your toddler the idea of how to play. Young toddlers won't need much distance to enjoy this game. Older toddlers can stand a foot or 2 away to toss the beanbags inside the plastic bucket.

*SAFETY ALERT: Discard or repair any beanbags with tears, which can present a choking hazard.

67 Find the Beanbag!

There is a young detective lurking in every toddler, and this type of game brings it right out.

AGE: 1–2 YRS

CATEGORY: PARENT & CHILD/INDOOR

NUMBER OF CHILDREN: ONE

Materials:

Toddler-safe beanbag
 (available at teacher
 supply stores)

4 or more quart-size plastic tubs
 (ice cream or yogurt containers, for example)

Setup:

Place the ice cream tubs upside down on the floor in a straight line. Have your toddler close her eyes (or wait until her attention wanders for a moment) and slip the beanbag under one of the tubs.

Play:

Tell your child that you've hidden a beanbag under one of the tubs. Now it's time to "find the beanbag!" Encourage her to turn over each tub until she finds it. After you've played for a few minutes in this way, your older toddler (two to three years old) may enjoy hiding the beanbag and turning the tables. In this case, cover your eyes during the hiding phase. When she's done hiding she calls out, "Find the beanbag!"

68 Find the Animal!

Shoe boxes are terrific for hide-and-seek object play—toddlers love taking the lids off and on and looking inside. You can play a similar game using shoe boxes and a small stuffed animal. Or, as your child nears three years old, you could vary the game by adding an element of color identification. Use red, yellow, green, and blue beanbags and ask your toddler to find a specific color.

69 Color Pockets

A color matching game for older toddlers who are starting to recognize colors.

AGE: 2 YRS

CATEGORY: PARENT & CHILD/ INDOOR

NUMBER OF CHILDREN: ONE

Materials:

Library pockets
 (available at teacher
 supply stores)

Foam board or cardboard (20" by 30")

Invisible tape

Scissors (for adult use only)

Construction paper
 (green, blue, yellow, red, white, orange)

Glue stick

Small bucket or bowl

Setup:

Arrange the library pockets in two rows on the foam board and tape them firmly in place. Cut a square of each color (green, blue, yellow, red, white, and orange) and glue one color to each of the pockets. (Toddlers love to use glue sticks—with supervision of course—so if there's time, let your toddler help with the gluing.) Next, cut squares from the remaining construction paper to match each of the six colors on the library pockets. (Fold these squares in half or quarters for easier handling for your toddler.) Place all the color squares in the bucket and mix them around.

Toddler Play (age 1 to 2)

Play:

Your child pulls a colored paper square from the bucket and tucks it inside the library pocket of the same color, continuing the matching process until all the colors have been used. (You may need to give a little assistance to get the paper squares out of each pocket.) As your child gets older and knows more colors, add more library pockets with new and different colors to the foam board to expand this game.

Favorite Toys for Bathtub Play

Of course the classic rubber duck and floating fish are fun, but here are a few other toys and gadgets just right for toddler tub play:

Giant sponges
Nontoxic bubbles and wand
  (for grown-up use)
Ping-Pong balls
Plastic funnel
Plastic measuring cups
Plastic sprinkling can
Rubber animals that squirt
Sandbox sieve
Small squeeze containers
Toddler-safe boats
Waterwheel tub toys
Waterproof dolls

SAFETY ALERT: Never, ever leave your child alone in the tub. Constant supervision is required for all water play.

70 Money Search

Toddlers notice each time you exchange money with a cashier in a store; the interaction involves such abstract concepts (barter, currency) that it often mesmerizes toddlers. Here's a quick hiding game that allows toddlers to collect their own dollars and put them inside their very own wallet or purse.

AGE: **2 YRS**

CATEGORY: **PARENT & CHILD/ INDOOR**

NUMBER OF CHILDREN: **ONE**

Materials:
  Pretend (paper) money (available at toy stores)
  Invisible tape
  Oversize blank playing cards (available at teacher supply stores) or large index cards
  Scissors (for adult use only)
  Wallet or purse from the dress-up bin

Setup:

Tape one toy dollar to a blank playing card or index card and trim the excess card and dollar so they are the same size. "Hide" these dollars around the room, leaving half of each dollar in plain sight.

Play:

Give your child the wallet or purse to hold. Find the first dollar together and encourage your child to put it away in the wallet or purse. Walk around the room with your child and nudge him in the right direction (if needed) to find all the remaining hidden dollars.

71 Color Dot Hide-and-Seek

Color recognition is an exciting phase in a child's development. Suddenly, the world comes alive with red fire trucks, bright green apples, blue skies. . . . Here's a game that celebrates your toddler's first stabs at color sorting.

QUICK & EASY

AGE: **2** YRS

CATEGORY:
PARENT & CHILD/ INDOOR

NUMBER OF
CHILDREN: **ONE**

Materials:

Sheets of peel-off color dot stickers
(available at office supply stores)

Pack of index cards or blank
make-your-own flash cards
(available at teacher supply stores)

Paper lunch bags

Invisible tape

Setup:

Select two or more colors that your child recognizes, say red and yellow. Peel and stick one yellow dot in the center of each of six of the blank cards. Peel and stick one red dot on the remaining six blank flash cards. Open two paper lunch bags and tape one of the yellow-dot cards on the outside of one bag and a red-dot card on the other bag. Place the two bags on the floor.

Play:

Have your child sit on a chair or on the floor while you "hide" the cards faceup, in very visible places around the room. Now give your child the yellow-dot bag and ask him to "find" all the cards with yellow circles and put them inside. Once all these cards have been found, give your child the red-dot bag and have him do the same with the red-dot cards. Expand this game with more colors, or add cards with shapes, numbers, or alphabet letters when your child gets a bit older.

❝There are a lot of scientific principles involved in some of the simpler activities of early childhood. We have to actually have experiences to understand cause and effect, and we have to have experiences in order to understand a sequence of things. . . . We have to have experiences of touching and feeling and manipulating to get the concepts of bigger and smaller, more and less— all the concepts that will later be important in mathematics, in science, in reading. As adults we take those things for granted, but those are really complex understandings for a little child.❞

—Jane M. Healy, Ph.D.,
educational psychologist and author of *Your Child's Growing Mind* and
Failure to Connect: How Computers Affect Our Children's Minds

Arts and Crafts (With Lots of Parent Help and Setup)

Toddlers are enthusiastic artists. What fun to have a crayon and paper when you are fourteen months old and making your creative mark for the very first time! Making art as a young toddler is all about experimentation—and the joy of messing around with art materials is no small prize.

Though art making does not necessarily entail collaborative play, I have included *Arts and Crafts* for toddlers in the *Parent and Child* play section of this book because grown-up setup, supervision, and cleanup are required. Having said this, you'll find a mix of messy play ideas (best to try when you're both in good moods!) and no-fuss (no-mess) ideas like scribbling on paper. Knowing that parents sometimes like to get creative too, at the end of this section I've included a few craft projects that the two of you can do together. Some toddlers love seeing the end product that they've created, others are more enthralled with the process. Either way, there's good stuff going on as you scribble, paint, paste, and glue together.

Ode to Drawing

Scribbling and drawing are simple, natural, self-directed ways for toddlers to experience the joy of making art. Toddlers will draw in their own way, sometimes with tentative marks, other times in robust scribbles that cover the page. Just show your child how to get started and let him enjoy the process. This "anything goes" approach, which doesn't focus on the results, sets the stage for creative self-expression that blossoms at each stage of childhood. And the humble action of drawing on paper is powerful: Learning to hold and manipulate crayons is a wonderful way to develop the fine motor skills needed to write letters and numbers in the next couple of years. An early familiarity with making (and seeing) letters and words on paper promotes a love of reading too. Your job is simply to provide some chunky crayons (or nontoxic markers), assorted paper (tape it to the table to help the youngest ones), and stand aside to let the magic begin. And be forewarned, toddlers will just as happily draw on the table, floor, and wall as they will on paper!

*SAFETY ALERT: Always supervise carefully to keep kids safe with crayons and markers.

72 Scribble Lunch Bags

Toddlers like to scribble on flattened lunch bags; there's great fun in turning an everyday object into a piece of art. Post-transformation, the flattened bag can be opened up and used as a receptacle for all sorts of things.

AGE: 1–2 YRS

CATEGORY:
**PARENT & CHILD/
ARTS & CRAFTS**

NUMBER OF
CHILDREN: **ONE**

Materials:

Paper lunch bags

Crayons

Setup:

Place a stack of flattened paper lunch bags and an assortment of chunky crayons on the table.

Play:

Select a crayon to begin making your own drawing, or scribble on a bag, and your toddler will soon follow suit. Once you've finished coloring a few bags, set them aside to save for lunch, or open one or more bags and stand them up in the middle of the table. Then put a few items inside (a flower, a cookie, or a small stuffed animal), and fold a 2-inch or 3-inch flap down to make it easy to carry the bag. Some toddlers will continue coloring and some will redirect their attention to their new colorful accessory.

If your toddler gets going and starts to produce in any quantity, you might want to decorate a shoe box to hold all the fancy lunch bags.

73 Fancy-Schmancy Cookie Plates

While the cookies are baking (and the excitement is building), your little artist creates special cookie-serving plates with colorful drawings and designs. Use thin paper plates and crayons.

TIP: Be sure to let the cookies cool completely before placing them on the colorful plates so the crayon design doesn't melt.

Nontoxic Art Supplies

Seek them out! You'll find a wide assortment of nontoxic art supplies—finger paints, watercolors, washable paints, chalk, crayons, glue, ink pads, and more—at your local school or teacher supply store. Look for the nontoxic symbol on these products: AP (Approved Product seal) surrounded by the words *ACMI Arts & Creative Materials Institute Certified.*

74 Scribble Bookmarks

Toddler art isn't just for hanging on the wall! These easy-to-make bookmarks are perfect homemade gifts for Grandma, Grandpa, and other extended family members, and since the surface area is small, they might be less intimidating to a toddler than a full piece of paper.

AGE: 1–2 YRS

CATEGORY:
**PARENT & CHILD/
ARTS & CRAFTS**

NUMBER OF
CHILDREN: **ONE**

Materials:

Recycled vinyl or cloth tablecloth
   (that you don't mind getting scribbles on)

Invisible tape

Pack of blank make-your-own flash cards
   (available at teacher supply stores)

Nontoxic, washable markers

Toddler Play (age 1 to 2)

Setup:

Put the tablecloth on the floor or kitchen table as a protective layer for toddler scribbling and drawing. Put the art supplies on the work area. Use invisible tape to tape one of the flash cards to the table so it stays in place while your child decorates and draws on it. Tape another card in place for you to draw on. Start drawing on your own flash card and provide markers for your toddler to scribble on his. (Use a marker to write your child's name and the date the drawing was created on the back of each bookmark. Collect these bookmarks in a shoe box or special envelope and send them out to loved ones on birthdays and holidays.)

Homemade Glue-Paste for Toddlers

Whether you're in a pinch or you're looking for a way to make sure your glue is 100 percent nontoxic, you can whip up this easy glue-paste from flour and water. It won't have exactly the same "sticking" properties as store-bought glue, but it's a good bet for toddlers, who just enjoy the process of gluing. Here's how to make it:

1/3 cup all-purpose unbleached white flour

2 tablespoons sugar

1 cup water

Mix the flour and sugar together in a small pan. Pour the water in slowly, stirring and mixing as you pour. Cook over low heat for a few minutes, continuing to stir. Allow to cool thoroughly before your child uses for gluing.

75 | Torn Paper Collage

This is a swanky name for an activity that lets toddlers tear paper (which they love to do) and mess around with glue (which they also love to do)!

QUICK & EASY

AGE: 1–2 YRS

CATEGORY:
PARENT & CHILD/
ARTS & CRAFTS

NUMBER OF
CHILDREN: ONE
OR MORE

Materials:

Old bedsheet or newspapers

Nontoxic white glue
(or homemade glue-paste,
see box, this page)

Small plastic mug or spill-proof paint pot

Paintbrush

Washcloth

Ziplock bag

Colored construction paper

Colored tissue paper or small pieces
of wrapping paper

Setup:

Spread the old bedsheet or newspapers on the kitchen table (for easy cleanup). Pour a small amount of glue into the spill-proof container or mug, and add just enough water to thin the glue so it's easily spreadable with a paintbrush. Wet the washcloth and place it inside the ziplock bag. Put it on the table to use as a wipe when hands get sticky.

Play:

You and your child each get a few pieces of construction paper, tissue paper, and/or wrapping paper, and begin tearing various size

pieces. When you've gathered a pile of colorful shreds of paper, begin assembling your Torn Paper Collage on a fresh piece of construction paper. Use the paintbrush to dab little bits of glue on the construction paper and select pieces of torn paper to lay on top of the glue. Continue working together (or each on your own separate sheets of paper) to glue lots of shreds of paper on the page to form a multicolor collage. (Some parents find that their child loves to specialize in slopping glue on the page while the grown-up adds scraps of paper. Use whatever teamwork plan seems best for you.)

Safety Alert: Please supervise your child so that neither the glue nor the ziplock bag creates a safety hazard.

76 Sticky Paper

Here's another activity that celebrates the joy of smearing glue on paper.

QUICK & EASY

AGE: 1–2 YRS

CATEGORY:
PARENT & CHILD/
ARTS & CRAFTS

NUMBER OF
CHILDREN: ONE

Materials:
- Colored construction paper
- Large (nontoxic) glue stick
- Masking tape or painter's tape
- Large cookie sheet

Setup:
Place a stack of construction paper on the table along with the glue stick. Tape a sheet of paper to the cookie sheet. (This holds the paper in place for vigorous gluing and contains the mess.)

Play:
Offer a little demo to get things moving for the youngest toddlers. First, use the glue stick to smear some glue on the paper stuck to the cookie sheet. Add a clean sheet of paper and use your hand to rub the top sheet of paper so the pages

stick together. Let your toddler use the glue stick to apply glue to the new top sheet of paper and continue to add more layers of paper to the paper-sandwich. The finished product is simply a stack of colored papers, but the joyful process of learning to glue is worth the mess. (For cleanup, remove the paper and tape from the cookie sheet and wash it to remove all the glue.)

Safety Alert: Please supervise your child carefully so he doesn't eat the glue or the paper!

★CLASSIC★
77 Painting

Are you having a good day today? Then there's no time like the present to introduce your toddler to painting for the very first time!

AGE: 1–2 YRS

CATEGORY:
PARENT & CHILD/
ARTS & CRAFTS

NUMBER OF
CHILDREN: ONE
OR MORE

Materials:
- Newsprint paper or butcher paper
- Nontoxic, washable children's paints
- Plastic nonspill paint pots (available at school supply stores)
- Artist's or painter's brushes with short, stubby handles
- Large adult-size T-shirt or dress shirt (to use as a painter's smock)

Setup:
Clip paper to an easel or set up a painting area at a plastic play table. (See "A Special Painting Place" on page 50 for paper setup and easy cleanup ideas.) Pour a little paint in a paint pot and add one brush. There really are no rules and no "how-to" about it, just let your child dip his brush in the paint and start putting paint on the paper. (Young toddlers may prefer dabbing to making brush strokes.) Don't expect to see

pictures or representational artwork. This is all about learning to handle paint and brushes and having a bit of fun.

NOTE: To make things easier, designate one color of paint for beginning painters and provide one spill-proof pot of paint and one brush! (Today's color is RED!) As your child gets used to painting, you can incorporate more colors.

A Special Painting Place

Painting is a fun but messy business for toddlers, so designate a special area and setup for toddler painting that includes a system for easy cleanup. A plastic or wooden preschool easel with a trough to hold a spill-proof container of paint is one way to ease cleanup woes. Since the process of dipping brushes in paint is what's most exciting to your child, limit your setup to one pot of paint. That one pot will provide loads of fun and will make cleanup easier, too. Clips at the top of the easel hold large sheets of paper in place, but use tape along the sides to secure the paper more firmly to the easel. Another idea is to use a small, sturdy, toddler-size plastic table or picnic table for artwork: Tape butcher paper together to cover the entire table (creating one giant painting surface), and use tape to secure the paper to the table too. And always spread out a painter's drop cloth or old vinyl tablecloth underneath your little artiste's painting area!

78 | Paint Dabber

In little dibs and dabs, your toddler applies paint to paper using a painter's sponge (on a stick). This art play is a cross between painting and printmaking.

QUICK & EASY

AGE: **2 YRS**

CATEGORY:
**PARENT & CHILD/
ARTS & CRAFTS**

NUMBER OF
CHILDREN: **ONE**

Materials:
Newspapers or old tablecloth
   (to cover kitchen table)
Nontoxic, washable children's paint
Plastic picnic plates or disposable pie pan
   (for paint pallet)
Newsprint paper or construction paper
Small painter's sponge (with a wooden or
   plastic handle to hold)

Setup:
Spread newspapers or an old tablecloth on the kitchen table to ensure an easy cleanup. Pour a little of one color of paint in a plastic plate. Place a large sheet of newsprint, drawing paper, or construction paper on the table.

Play:
Help your toddler dab the sponge into the paint for the first time (apply a little pressure to saturate the sponge). Then move the sponge to the paper and dab paint on the page. Let your child experiment with repeated dabs all over the paper from that first dollop of paint. When the sponge gets dry, your child dips it into the paint again and continues to make dabs all over the page. After a while, you may want to pour another color of paint in a second plastic plate to add a second color to the painting. Rinse out the sponge and dip it into this second color.

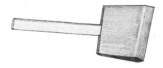

79 DIY Art Box

PARENT TIP

❝I bought a sturdy cardboard file box with handles from the office supply store and turned it into a toddler art supply box so all our art stuff is in one place. I gave my daughter, Lucy, sheets of yellow poster board to draw on. Then I cut these drawings to fit the sides and lid of the file box, used clear packaging tape to stick them on, and now her art supply box is decorated beautifully.❞

—Julia from Michigan

80 Roller-Painting

Grab your beret (or better yet, a shower cap), and let the good times roll! As anyone who's dabbled in house painting knows, a paint roller is good, squishy fun. Since this activity requires some dexterity, it's best for older toddlers.

AGE: **2 YRS**

CATEGORY: **PARENT & CHILD/ ARTS & CRAFTS**

NUMBER OF CHILDREN: **ONE OR MORE**

Materials:
Roll of butcher paper (or large sheets of drawing paper or newsprint)

Painter's tape or invisible tape

Nontoxic, washable children's paint (available at teacher supply or art stores)

Disposable pie pan or plastic picnic plate

Mini paint roller for interior house painting (available at hardware stores)

Large adult-size T-shirt or dress shirt (to use as a painter's smock)

Setup:
Cover a plastic play table (or outdoor picnic table) with butcher paper. Use tape to secure the paper to the table. Pour a small quantity of paint in the pan.

Play:
Dip the roller in the paint pan and let your child roll it back and forth across the paper. (Be ready to descend with the cleanup supplies as soon as it appears your child has taken his last stroke across the paper!)

81 Puppet on a Stick

If a craft session is called for and your art cupboard is bare, a paper plate, crayons, and scraps of fabric can save the day!

AGE: **2 YRS**

CATEGORY: **PARENT & CHILD/ ARTS & CRAFTS**

NUMBER OF CHILDREN: **ONE**

Materials:
Paper plates (regular size or small dessert plates)

Clear, wide packaging tape or wide masking tape

Wooden paint stir sticks or giant wooden craft sticks

Nontoxic, washable markers

Crayons

Glitter glue or white liquid glue

Scraps of yarn, ribbon, fabric

Directions:
Turn the plate over (with eating side facedown) and securely tape the wooden stick to the back of the plate with several strips of tape. (The wooden stick becomes the handle, so make certain it is positioned so your child can easily hold it.) Help your child get started drawing a face on the front side of the plate using markers and crayons. Add glitter glue, and scraps of yarn, ribbon, or fabric for the hair, beard, or mustache.

Toddler Play (age 1 to 2)

82 Paper Plate Mitten Puppet

Place two sturdy paper plates together, so that the undersides of the plates are facing outward. Use masking tape to attach the outside edges. (Leave a space about 4 inches across the bottom of the plates unsecured, so that a child's hand can slip inside this mitten-style puppet.) Help your child decorate one side of the plate with a girl's face and the other side with a boy's face so that your child has two pretend characters.

83 Animal Photo Puppets

Clip color photos of animals or of people's faces from magazines. Help your toddler glue these photos to the paper plate, use yarn for hair, beard, or mustache. Add a wooden stick for a handle, or make the mitten-style puppet above.

> **"** When children take their first physical steps, parents get so excited. But at exactly that same time, children make their first marks on paper, which is the beginning of drawing, writing, and reading, and all forms of literacy. So, parents need to be thinking not only 'Oh, my child's a year old—he or she is probably going to walk soon,' but 'My child's a year old, and my child's going to draw soon—I have to get crayons and paper and make sure that I make that a positive experience.' **"**
>
> **—Susan Striker**
> founder of Young at Art
> and author of *The Anti-Coloring Book* series

84 Sock Puppet

If an elaborate craft proves a test for your motor skills (or patience and time), here's a very simple activity even the least crafty parent can put together. All you need is a sock and a marker!

AGE: 1–2 YRS

CATEGORY: PARENT & CHILD/ ARTS & CRAFTS

NUMBER OF CHILDREN: **ONE**

Materials:

White tube socks

Nontoxic, washable markers

Setup:
Simply slide a tube sock over your child's hand and arm and have him place his thumb opposite his other fingers inside the tip of the sock. As he opens and closes this grip, help form a big mouth at the end of the sock. Take notice of approximately where the eyes and face should be while the sock is on your child's hand.

Play:
Take the sock off your toddler's hand, and use the washable markers to let him draw the eyes and mouth in the appropriate location on the sock.

85 Advanced Sock Puppet

For a more elaborate puppet (and more parent involvement), purchase wiggly eyes (sold at craft and fabric stores) and sew them on the sock with thread. Draw eyebrows and a mouth with the washable markers for a complete face. Sew on strands of yarn so that they fall down along both sides of the face to create hair.

Outdoor Play

When you go outside to play, you've put your stamp of approval on the great outdoors, where the stimulus is abundant. Leaves don't need batteries to sway in the wind; birds don't need remote controls to fly. And best of all, they're free! Take your toddler outside, and any game you play becomes alive to all the unexpected possibilities of the great outdoors.

86 Roll It, Toss It

Is there a game more timeless than catch? There's something about its utter simplicity—the rhythm, the repetition, the trying, and failing, and trying again—that conjures up idyllic visions of family life. This toddler version of catch is a warm-up that uses rolling or tossing to instill the concept.

QUICK & EASY

AGE: 1–2 YRS

CATEGORY:
PARENT & CHILD/ ARTS & CRAFTS

NUMBER OF
CHILDREN: **ONE**

Materials:
> Beach ball (slightly deflated for better handling by the youngest toddlers)

Play:
Young toddlers will enjoy a simple game of rolling or throwing the ball back and forth with you; some nudging and demonstrating may be needed in order to get the game going. Older toddlers (with more advanced motor skills and language comprehension) will enjoy a game similar to Simon Says, where you call out "roll it" or "toss it" and your child follows along.

Anatomy of a Mud Puddle

Sure, mud is messy and a kid's muddy play clothes do need to be washed, but mud puddles are so much fun! A quick look at a puddle's properties gives a hint as to why little kids like to mess around in them. First, there's the thrilling surprise of splashes that leap up as you stomp. Then, there's the tactile pleasure of squishing the oozing mud between your fingers, and letting drops of it drip, drip, drip, and splash, splash, splash down into the puddle. The visual attraction of the puddle captures your child's attention too: The surface looks like a mirror, with flashes of color and moving images (the sun shining down on it after the rain, clouds passing overhead).

Of course toddlers don't *think* about mud in this way, but they do *experience* it with all their senses. So next time there are some good mud puddles calling your child's name, grab her rubber boots and old play clothes (have a clean towel waiting at the back door), and go meet that puddle.

UNPLUGGED PLAY

87 Ringer-Ball

Stand the Hula-Hoop upright to create a toddler-friendly tossing target. (And while you're at it, a quick hula demonstration never hurt anyone!)

AGE: 2 YRS

CATEGORY:
PARENT & CHILD/
OUTDOOR

NUMBER OF
CHILDREN: **ONE**

Materials:
  Newspaper (or Nerf balls, tennis
    balls, or beanbags)
  Large Hula-Hoop

Setup:
Crumple up sheets of newspaper to make a pile of newspaper balls for tossing.

Play:
Standing, hold the Hula-Hoop alongside your leg (about a foot off the ground) while your child tosses balls through the hoop from a short distance away.

88 Ring-a-Ding-Soccer

Once your older toddler has mastered the art of elementary Ringer-Ball, you might introduce a playground ball and have him try to kick it through the Hula-Hoop (this time, hold it so it's resting on the ground).

89 Toddler Basketball

This game requires a little help from a grown-up basket-tender (holder) in the beginning, but older toddlers will squeal with delight when they get a "basket" on their own.

AGE: 1–2 YRS

CATEGORY:
PARENT & CHILD/
OUTDOOR

NUMBER OF
CHILDREN: **ONE**

Materials:
  Plastic tub
    (or small laundry basket)
  Soft, medium-size ball
    (easy for your child to grab and handle)

Play:
Hold the basket at toddler height. Don't forget that part of your job as basket tender is moving the basket to help catch the ball! As more skills and interests in ball games develop, vary the game a bit by having your toddler bounce the ball on the ground while you move in with the basket to catch the ball on the bounce.

90 Bouncy Ball

A bouncing ball is an endless source of fascination for a toddler. Here's a game that relies on simple teamwork between child and grown-up to bounce and catch the ball with a dishpan.

AGE: 1–2 YRS

CATEGORY:
PARENT & CHILD/
OUTDOOR

NUMBER OF
CHILDREN: **ONE**

Materials:
  Small playground ball (available in 2 sizes—
    look for the small one)
  Large plastic colander or
    dishpan with handles

Setup:
Get your toddler excited about this game with a simple solo demonstration to set the stage for play. Hold the colander in one hand and bounce the ball on an uncarpeted floor. Quickly grab the colander with two hands and position it to catch the ball off the bounce.

Play:
Your child uses two hands to bounce the ball (as hard as he can) on the floor, and you catch the ball off the bounce using the colander. (As your toddler gains more bouncing skill and power behind each bounce, you can stand a fair distance away and run to scoop the ball with drama, flair, and sound effects!)

91 Zoom, Zoom, Zoom!

No, it's not a car commercial! This feisty game has a name that is fun to say over and over again.

QUICK & EASY

AGE: 1–2 YRS

CATEGORY: **PARENT & CHILD/ OUTDOOR**

NUMBER OF CHILDREN: **ONE**

Materials:

6 or more tennis balls

Small bucket with handles

Plastic slide (with rounded edges for safety)

Setup:
Place all the balls in the bucket.

Play:
Stand on one side of the slide, holding the bucket of balls; have your toddler stand on the other side near the sliding board's midpoint. Hand your child one ball at a time and encourage him to release the ball onto the slide and watch it zoom down onto the lawn or playground. When all the balls have zoomed down the slide, your child plays "pick up" and puts all the balls back in the bucket. Most young toddlers love this game and will want to play again and again.

92 Zoom Up

Families with a big-kid slide in the backyard or access to a big-kid slide can play this rolling game uphill. Stand at the very end of the slide and roll the tennis ball up the slide with a hearty thrust to see how far *up* it will go before it rolls right back down to your feet. Have your toddler join you in this riotous physics experiment. To add a bit of a challenge, position a small basket at the top end of the slide for a game of Zoom Up basketball. (Place a towel inside the basket to prevent erratic bounces.)

> ❝For children with cerebral palsy who have problems opening and closing their hands quickly enough to catch a ball, take an oven mitt and put a couple of rough pieces of Velcro on it. Then attach the opposite (soft) pieces of Velcro to a lightweight child-size ball. Toss that ball to the child while she's wearing the mitt that has the Velcro on it. And, as long as the ball touches the Velcro, she's going to catch the ball. It's a good game for children between eighteen months and up.❞
>
> **—Kristi Sayers Menear, Ph.D., CAPE**
> Assistant Professor of Human Studies
> at the University of Alabama at Birmingham

93 Follow the Leader

This classic game has three great ingredients that toddlers love: lots of physical play, an opportunity to imitate, and (last but not least) the joy of seeing a grown-up act silly!

QUICK & EASY

AGE: 2 YRS

CATEGORY: **PARENT & CHILD/ OUTDOOR**

NUMBER OF CHILDREN: **ONE**

Setup:
Think of all the physical skills (including making sounds) that your child has mastered before you start this game. Examples might include walking with hands in the air, hopping, clapping, galloping, barking like a dog, meowing like a cat, running to the fence, touching it, and running back again, etc.

Play:
Play the part of the leader and make up a series of movements and sounds for your child to imitate.

Toddler Play (age 1 to 2)

94 One-Two-Three, Hop Like Me

Make up your own counting rhyme and add some actions to match:

"One, two, three . . . Hop like me.
(hop, hop, hop)

Four, five, six . . . Pick up sticks.
(bend down, pretend to pick up sticks, and pop back up again)

Seven, eight, nine . . . Do the monkeyshine.
(somersault, roll around, etc.)

And then there's ten . . . Cluck like a hen. *(invent a funny "chicken walk" and add sound effects)*

> " *Parents are more important to their child than any program or any other thing is, particularly in early childhood. So that time spent with them, reading, playing, talking, singing—that's the most valuable experience they can give their children.* "
>
> **—David Elkind, Ph.D.**
> Professor of Child Development
> at Tufts University and author of
> *The Hurried Child* and *The Power of Play*

95 Portable Sandbox

This mini sandbox in a dishpan is just right for first-time sandbox play for toddlers.

AGE: **2 YRS**

CATEGORY:
PARENT & CHILD/ OUTDOOR

NUMBER OF
CHILDREN: **ONE**

Materials:
Small plastic tub with lid
Clean play sand
(available at toy stores)
Sandbox toys (sieve, sprinkling can, cups, rounded sand tools)

Setup:
Fill a plastic tub with clean, fine sand and take it outdoors on the porch or patio.

Play:
Fill containers with sand and dump out! Rake the sand into patterns and put it through a sieve. A sandbox is like a miniature garden for a toddler. Add a bit of water to the sprinkling can and let him experiment with watering the sand.

*SAFETY ALERT: Supervise your child to make sure he does not eat the sand or rub sand in his eyes.

96 Animal Patrol

It's quite magical for a toddler to scoop up some sand with a strainer, give it a few gentle shakes, and discover an animal hiding inside the strainer.

AGE: **2 YRS**

CATEGORY:
PARENT & CHILD/ OUTDOOR

NUMBER OF
CHILDREN: **ONE**

Materials:
Small plastic tub with lid
Clean play sand (available at toy stores)
Toddler-safe plastic animals
Small kitchen strainer with handle
Small bowl

Setup:
Fill the tub with clean play sand and take it outdoors to the porch, patio, or stoop. Hide a handful of plastic animals (or figures) throughout. (Hide them close to the top, or bury them way down deep to increase the level of challenge according to your child's age, ability, and patience.)

Play:
Show your child how to use the strainer to scoop sand; gently shake to unearth hiding animals. When your child finds an animal, he places it in the bowl and continues to look for more.

*Safety Alert: Supervise your child when playing with sand. Sand play is best for toddlers who no longer put everything in their mouth and also for children who won't throw sand.

97 Picnic-Plate Float

Splashing, squishing, and squealing—oh, my! Take your toddler's shoes off for this wading-pool Nerf-toss.

AGE: **2 YRS**

CATEGORY: **PARENT & CHILD/ OUTDOOR**

NUMBER OF CHILDREN: **ONE**

Materials:
Wading pool
Plastic picnic plates with raised rims
Nerf balls

Setup:
Fill the wading pool with several inches of water. Place the empty picnic plates in the pool. (The more plates in the pool, the greater the chance your toddler will land the ball inside the floating target!)

Play:
Stand along the outside of the pool and toss the Nerf ball into one of the plates.

*Safety Alert: Constantly supervise all water play and drain the pool when the game is over.

★ CLASSIC ★
98 Toddler Tag

Never underestimate the fun of a good game of chase!

AGE: **2 YRS**

CATEGORY: **PARENT & CHILD/ OUTDOOR**

NUMBER OF CHILDREN: **ONE OR MORE**

Setup:
You only need to modify this classic slightly for your toddler. The format is simple: Ask your child to run after you as you zigzag around the yard or park.

Play:
When she catches you, she touches you, and then you give chase and run after her. This toddler version is enhanced with silly movements, detours, and sound effects from Mom or Dad. If two adults are both willing to play, the three of you can take turns chasing one another around the lawn. The more the merrier, and it's good exercise for you too!

PARENT TIP
99 Running Around to Let Off Steam

❝Some days my twenty-month-old son gets really frustrated playing with his giant LEGOs. When one of these moods strikes, I announce it's time for a game of chase outside and we move outdoors for a couple minutes of run-around play. It gives him a chance to let off a little steam, and the change of scenery helps to reset his mood. This is a quick-fix idea for frustration that almost always works with my toddler.❞

—Jonathan from Tennessee

Beach Day

Being near the ocean is a beautiful and powerful experience for people of every age, so imagine how exciting a toddler's first encounters with the vast expanse of salty water and grainy sand will be—it's like a giant bathtub or swimming pool right next to the world's biggest sandbox! The sights and sounds (squawking gulls and crashing waves) may be sensory overload for a two- to three-year-old, so wait until low tide to introduce him to the beach's many play opportunities.

100 Beach Puddle

Splash in a shallow tidal pool and dig into the giant sandy beach!

QUICK & EASY

AGE: **2 YRS**

CATEGORY: **PARENT & CHILD/ OUTDOOR (BEACH)**

NUMBER OF CHILDREN: **ONE**

Materials:
- Plastic sand bucket and shovel
- Plastic sprinkling can
- Floating (bathtub) toys

Play:
Head to the beach shortly after high tide, with the plan to play in the shallow tidal pools created in the sand. (Or dig a shallow reservoir in the sand, several inches deep, and fill it with buckets of seawater to create a play-pond.) Plop yourselves into the tidal pool, begin filling the bucket and sprinkling can with water, and float toys alongside the small pond. When this repetitious play wears thin, a little splashing and stomping in the water extends the excitement.

101 Big Water, Little Water

A pond appears as you and your child scoop buckets of "big water" from the ocean.

QUICK & EASY

AGE: **2 YRS**

CATEGORY: **PARENT & CHILD/ OUTDOOR ((BEACH)**

NUMBER OF CHILDREN: **ONE**

Materials:
- Plastic shovel
- Plastic cup
- Buckets

Play:
Dig a small pond (2 feet across and several inches deep) about 10 feet from the ocean or lake's edge. Give your child a plastic cup to dip into the water, and encourage her to carry it back to the pond and dump the water into the hole. Back and forth from the ocean (big water) to the pond (little water), filling and dumping. The pond takes shape quickly if you help by filling a bucket and dumping it each time your toddler empties her cup. Carrying and dumping water accounts for the first stage of play. Before long, your child will be splashing or stomping in the pond, creating a second round of play. Add a few tub toys and more fun unfolds.

*SAFETY ALERT: These activities are best for older toddlers who won't put sand in their mouth or eyes. Always supervise all toddler water play.

Toddler Play (age 1 to 2)

Let It Snow!

Imagine for a minute the excitement your toddler experiences when introduced to snow for the very first time. He'll hear the crunch, crunch, crunch with each step he takes. His eyes will discover an entirely new outdoor world that is blanketed in white. And the *feel* of the snow is remarkable—it's cold, then wet, and then it begins to melt! All these discoveries are part of your child's play experience. A snowsuit, boots, and waterproof mittens keep the warmth in and the moisture out, allowing for an extended play day in the snow. Here are a few activities for outdoor, frosty fun together.

102 Buckets and Shovels

Plastic sand buckets and small shovels are perfect for older toddlers who will enjoy filling the buckets with snow, dumping it out, and stamping the snow mounds with their feet.

AGE: **2 YRS**

CATEGORY: **PARENT & CHILD/ OUTDOOR (SNOW)**

NUMBER OF CHILDREN: **ONE**

Materials:
Plastic sand buckets of
  various sizes
Small plastic shovels

Play:
Bring along a few buckets and shovels while playing outdoors, and cue your child to shovel the snow into the bucket and to dump it out,

creating mounds of snow. Both of you can stand atop the little hills to see what happens.

103 Train Tracks

If your child loves trains, or is simply mesmerized by the designs his feet make in the snow, he will thrill at this game.

AGE: **2 YRS**

CATEGORY: **PARENT & CHILD/ OUTDOOR (SNOW)**

NUMBER OF CHILDREN: **ONE OR MORE**

Play:
Shuffle your feet through the snow, making "train tracks" as you go. First you are the locomotive in front, chug, chug, chugging along the tracks (a few sound effects for this special winter express), with your child making his own tracks behind you. Then, switch places and let your child be the engine car, with you chug, chugging behind as the caboose.

> **"**One of the things a parent can do is really watch the baby. Pay attention to what the baby is touching or looking at or listening to, and take advantage of that. Let the baby be your partner and lead you into a natural everyday game.**"**
>
> **—Sharon Ramey, Ph.D.**
> Professor of Child and Family Studies and coauthor of *Right from Birth*

Toddler Play (age 1 to 2)

104 Sledding

There is nothing more fun or memorable for a parent and child than a day of sledding in a winter wonderland. Pull your toddler around the park or your own backyard in a baby-safe sled.

AGE: **2 YRS**

CATEGORY:
**PARENT & CHILD/
OUTDOOR
(SNOW)**

NUMBER OF
CHILDREN: **ONE**

Materials:
Baby sled with rope pull

Play:
Place your child in the sled and pull her around the park or yard. Although your toddler isn't ready for coasting downhill at top speed, she will still be absolutely delighted to have you pull her through the snow, safe and sound on flat ground.

105 Snowball Drop

Make a sport out of creating snowballs and watching with delight as they drop to the ground and disappear!

AGE: **2 YRS**

CATEGORY:
**PARENT & CHILD/
OUTDOOR
(SNOW)**

NUMBER OF
CHILDREN: **ONE**

Materials:
Baby sled with rope pull

Play:
Pack a snowball and hold it in your hands. Let your toddler explore this fascinating "ball" by holding it in his own hands. Make another snowball, hold it high above your head, and drop it on a snowy patch of the lawn or on the sidewalk while your toddler looks on. Create more and more snowballs for your child to lift overhead and drop to the ground with delight. (What an amazing little ball that shatters or disappears when it is dropped, then more and more snowballs magically appear!)

106 Snowball Stomp

Line up a row of 10 snowballs on the ground. Use your boot to stomp one of the snowballs in the line and chances are your toddler will continue an enthusiastic game of Snowball Stomp going with the other snowballs in the lineup.

Playing with Others

During your child's early years, development happens at such a quick pace; these changes affect the way your child plays. When one- to two-year-olds play around other toddlers, they are likely to play with their own toy in a solitary way. From time to time these little playmates might glance at each other, but they will quickly move their attention back to their own toy. The early childhood development specialists call this parallel play.

I call this type of play "side by side" because toddlers often warm up to each other by just coexisting in the same space. These favorite toys are a good bet for those times (it's best if each child has similar toys to play with and the freedom to direct his own play). You may need to get the play started by stacking blocks or rolling a ball down the slide or ramp. Be ready to step in to help resolve issues surrounding toys, turn-taking, and territory, which are the three sticky points when toddlers play together.

Here are some terrific toys that I recommend for side by side toddler play:

Balls (see page 84)

Barn and farm animals
 (see page 56)

Blocks and giant LEGOs
 (see page 84)

Cars, trucks, and ramp (see page 26)

Dolls and doll accessories
 (see page 27)

Dress-up props and toys (see page 32)

Kitchen set and plastic foods
 (see page 34)

Paper and crayons (see page 46)

Plastic people or action figures
 (see page 26)

Plastic toddler slide (see page 84)

Pots, pans, mixing bowls, and
 plastic containers (see page 5)

Ride-on toys, wagons, and shopping
 carts (see page 28)

Stuffed animals (see page 26)

> **"**The best toys are the toys that have a lot of possibilities, as opposed to toys that do one thing. **"**
>
> **—Alicia F. Lieberman, Ph.D.**
> Irving B. Harris Professor of Psychology at the
> University of California, San Francisco,
> Director of the Childhood Trauma Research Project,
> and author of *The Emotional Life of the Toddler*

As toddlers get a bit older, they may continue to play side by side, but each child takes a bit more notice of what the other playmate is doing, perhaps imitating or incorporating those actions into his own play. Older toddlers may truly play together for short bursts of time. One child may be piling his blocks in a heap on the floor, and another might be pushing a cardboard box on the ground nearby. The block builder might drop a block or two into the box-driver's cart as he passes by. Seconds later, both resume their solitary play. If a friendly mood prevails, these fleeting moments of playing together might expand into honest-to-goodness cooperative play. On another day, these same little fellows might shun joint play for solitary play, drawing firm boundaries around their possessions. And so it goes when toddlers get together to play.

Indoor Play

Read through the selection of indoor ideas to see what activities might be just right for your child's next playdate. Keep in mind that because toddlers tend to play separately when they play together (side by side), it's best to have multiple props so there's plenty to go around—two chairs, two boxes, two stuffed bears! Conflicts will arise, but here are some strategies you can initiate to make playdates more harmonious:

- Accept the fact that your toddler doesn't like the idea of sharing (or giving up) his favorite toys when a playmate comes over. Move these special stuffed animals or toys to another room so that conflict doesn't arise.

- Expect a few disputes about possessions as toddlers play together. As you supervise, be ready to step in to redirect play and deal with hurt feelings.

- Include some larger toys and equipment (such as a toddler slide) that can't be grabbed by one child, so the children have some small opportunities to experience sharing and taking turns.

> **"**A really important and positive rule children learn in playgroups is that fighting with each other, biting each other, pinching each other, does not mean the end of the relationship. One child can say 'I'm sorry' and can do something to appease the other, and things can again get better from there. **"**
>
> **—Alicia F. Lieberman, Ph.D.**
> Irving B. Harris Professor of Psychology at the
> University of California, San Francisco,
> Director of the Childhood Trauma Research Project,
> and author of *The Emotional Life of the Toddler*

- As toddlers get older and show interest in truly playing together, offer toys that can be mixed together for short moments of cooperative play.
- Provide older toddlers with interesting props, playthings, and dress-up clothes for pretend play.

Pretend Play

You'll see the very first hints of pretend play when your child imitates something he has seen others do. Perhaps your one-year-old tap-tap-taps his toy mallet on the wall, imitating Mom or Dad hanging a framed photo on the wall the night before. He might pick up one of your sneakers and shake it upside down on the ground, imitating what you do at the back door to remove wet grass clippings from your shoes. (This imitative play offers a fascinating window onto how many things your toddler notices.) Eventually, these single actions morph into more elaborate pretend play where your child is acting out a sequence of events pieced together from recent experiences or created from his imagination. Your thirty-month-old son may pretend to pump gas into his ride-on truck, ride to the "store," and load up some "lumber" (wooden blocks). Much of this type of pretend play is created spontaneously when your child plays alone.

> *"With little ones, you may want to get on the floor and really set the stage for sharing by saying: 'It's your turn. Now it's my turn. Now it's Johnny's turn.' So you're actually taking a ball or the toy and you're passing it around."*
>
> **—Michele Borba, Ed.D.**
> former classroom teacher and author of
> *Parents Do Make a Difference* and
> *12 Simple Secrets Real Moms Know*

Some toddlers, particularly older toddlers, enjoy pretending with other children. Though pretending is often a spontaneous event, you can help set up pretend play for two or more toddlers. Some favorite pretend play scenes and accessories for two or more toddlers include: Dress-up; Restaurant; Grocery store; Kitchen, (cook); Tool-play and fixing; Transportation (cars, trucks, trains) and ride-on toys; and House (with dolls).

See pages 30–35 for suggested props and play ideas.

Toddler Play (age 1 to 2)

106 Box-Cars for Two

Boxes are among the very best toys for freewheeling, open-ended play. Add two boxes and two kids and it's double the fun.

QUICK & EASY

AGE: 1–2 YRS

CATEGORY: **PLAY WITH OTHERS/INDOOR**

NUMBER OF CHILDREN: **TWO OR MORE**

Materials:

Shoe boxes or small cardboard boxes (1 or more for each child)

Blocks, toys, or stuffed animals

Play:

Toddlers fill their shoe boxes with their personal cargo, then push or pull their box-car along the carpet or smooth floor.

107 Colorful Box-Cars

For customized, colorful box-cars, cover the outside of each box with colored construction paper and invisible tape. This way, each child has a distinctly different-colored car.

108 Shoe Box Garages

See page 26 for turning shoe boxes into garages and tunnels just right for plastic cars and trucks. (Make a garage for each playmate, to keep things happy.)

109 Airplane, Rocket Ship, or Campout Cave

For your older toddler, turn an appliance box (the size of a TV) into a Campout Cave. Simply turn the box on its side and provide blankets or sleeping bags, pots and pans and gear for a pretend campout adventure inside. Or stand the box upright and let the toddlers step inside for a pretend rocket ship or airplane journey.

(Let the children use crayons or markers to add color and designs to decorate the outside of the Rocket Ship.)

See page 4 (*Solo Play*) for more creative play ideas for one or more toddlers!

110 Hoops

A tossing game that is noncompetitive fun for two or more toddlers. This game uses the simplest of props and can be set up quickly.

QUICK & EASY

AGE: 1–2 YRS

CATEGORY: **PLAY WITH OTHERS/INDOOR**

NUMBER OF CHILDREN: **TWO**

Materials:

2 kitchen chairs (without any sharp edges or corners)

Hula-Hoop

Wide roll of painter's tape (or invisible tape)

Balls (different colors, 1 for each child works best) or a bucket of beanbags

Setup:

Place two kitchen chairs in the middle of the room, with the seats facing each other, spaced about 22 to 25 inches apart. Rest the Hula-Hoop across the seats of the chairs; it should create a low hoop in which to toss the ball or beanbags. Use the painter's tape to secure the hoop to the chairs.

Play:

Each child takes a turn tossing the balls or beanbags into the hoop. Encourage the children to stand as close to the hoop as needed to launch the ball successfully. Alternately, have two buckets of balls or beanbags—one bucket for each child. In this game, half the fun is launching all the balls into the hoop. The other half is carrying the bucket to the hoop to collect all the balls.

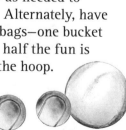

Dump and Fill

Adults may wonder why repetitive, seemingly futile dump-and-fill activities capture a toddler's attention, but there's actually a lot going on for one- to three-year-old children. On the simplest level, it's great fun to watch the action when you tip a tub of giant LEGOs on a wooden floor and they scatter about the room. Not to mention the resulting sound: an auditory exclamation point to the play! Dump-and-fill games are a good type of activity for two or more toddlers because each child can work independently with his own set of materials, while having the joy of watching another toddler do those same interesting motions. Young toddlers are typically attracted to the dumping, whereas older toddlers are often more interested in the filling action. Toddlers are also soaking up preliminary lessons about volume, gravity, cause and effect; and let's not forget the concepts of empty and full.

III Solid Object Dump and Fill

This free-form play may seem repetitive to you, but for your toddler, it never gets old.

AGE: 2 YRS

CATEGORY:
PLAY WITH OTHERS/INDOOR

NUMBER OF CHILDREN: **TWO OR MORE**

Materials:

Plastic containers and bins

Shoe box with lid

Oatmeal tub (cylindrical container)

Half-gallon juice or milk cartons
    (top cut off)

Plastic mix-and-pour bowls
    (with handle and pouring spout)

Stainless steel mixing bowls and pans

Blocks

Giant-size LEGOs

Toy animals and people

Wiffle golf balls

Plastic food container lids

Large puzzle pieces

Nesting cubes

Play:
Your toddler may drag the empty container from place to place, put objects inside (and then drag it from place to place), tip the container upside down, or fill the bucket with all the objects and dump them out on the floor. There are no rules, but your toddler may need a few quick demonstrations of what can go inside, or how items can be stacked in order to get started.

112 Water Dump and Fill

Plop, drip, splash—the sounds from bathtime transplanted to playtime.

AGE: 2 YRS

CATEGORY:
PLAY WITH OTHERS/INDOOR

NUMBER OF CHILDREN: **TWO OR MORE**

Materials:
Cotton area rug with nonslip
    backing or recycled bathroom
    rug or vinyl tablecloth to place
    under the play area

Medium to large plastic tub or dishpan
   (or a portable plastic infant bathtub or
   large stainless steel roasting pan)
Plastic measuring cups
Kitchen funnels
Plastic ice-cream scoop (one-piece, no small parts)
Plastic cups, bowls
Tub toys
Small plastic colander, sieve, or strainer
Squeeze bottles
Waterwheel

Setup:

Spread an area rug or vinyl tablecloth on the floor to create a confined play area. Put 1 or 2 inches of water in the plastic tub and place it on top of the rug. Add toddler-safe tub toys and cups for scooping and dumping inside the tub.

Play:

Turn bathtime into playtime by using these same water toys in the mini tub.

SAFETY ALERT: Supervise water play carefully and put only a small amount of water in the plastic tub.

PARENT TIP

113 I Spy Good Sharing

"A really fun way to reinforce positive sharing between toddlers is a game I call 'I Spy Good Sharing.' It does two things; it helps the very young kids realize that they can take charge and control their own behavior, which is a new concept for them. It also gives them a chance to notice what other people are doing and to step outside of that all-about-me phase that happens to the two- to four-year-olds. So, the next time your child or his playmate is doing a pretty good job sharing or taking a turn, remember to say, 'I Spy Good Sharing' as a quick and playful way to say, 'good job.'"

—Lauri from New Hampshire

The Joys of Water Play

Toddlers haven't been in this world long enough to take their five senses for granted. They are fascinated by the touch, taste, sound, sight, and smell of everything around them. It's easy to see why a small dishpan of water with a few floating toys and a couple of measuring cups offer great appeal and great fun for your toddler. Plunging little hands into the water alerts your child to its special cool, wet feel. This may prompt a few tastes to see what that wet stuff tastes like too. Tossing a rubber duck into the tub makes an impressive plop sound, accentuated by a surprising splash in your child's face (all the more surprising if that splash also reaches the family dog, who was sniffing around nearby, and who goes scurrying away with a yelp). "What's next?" that little toddler brain might ask. How about dipping a measuring cup into the water, lifting it out, and pouring its contents back into the tub? All these actions and reactions create quite a thrilling playtime for your toddler.

Art Play for Two or More

I absolutely love to watch two or three toddlers sitting side by side, engaged in simple art-play. One child picks up a chunky crayon and makes a few marks on paper. The other child watches intently. That second child picks up a crayon, and now it's the first child's turn to watch. Back and forth they go, creating, watching, and imitating one another. And just when things seem to settle in, with both artists scribbling away at the same time, one child reaches over and grabs a crayon from the other. This is the way that all budding artists and collaborators get their start.

114 Giant Toddler Drawing for Two

Turn your kitchen table into an enormous canvas, with lots of elbow room for each child to scribble. What a thrilling way to spend an afternoon!

QUICK & EASY

AGE: 1–2 YRS

CATEGORY:
PLAY WITH
OTHERS/INDOOR

NUMBER OF
CHILDREN: TWO
OR MORE

Materials:
Roll of butcher paper or
    4 to 5 paper grocery bags
Invisible tape
Assortment of chunky (preschool type) crayons
Large unbreakable bowl

Setup:
Completely cover your kitchen table with butcher paper. (If using paper bags, cut off the bottoms and make one lengthwise cut on each bag to create large flat pieces of paper. Completely cover the table with the brown paper.) Tape over all the seams so you end up with one giant coloring surface. Loosely tape the ends and sides to the table to hold it in place. Place a large bowl filled with crayons in the center of the table.

Play:
Sit down with the children, grab a crayon, and begin drawing on any part of the paper; the children will follow suit and create their own scribbles and drawings. For added excitement (and as the paper gets covered with scribbles), tape a fresh piece of butcher paper in front of each artist. (If the toddlers want their own picture to have and hold when scribble time is done, carefully remove the tape from the paper so that each child gets his very own drawing to take home.)

Tip: When all the scribbling is done (and your little artist is napping), remove these first "masterpieces" and store them in a drawer for later use. These drawings make wonderful homemade wrapping paper for grandparents or aunts and uncles who live far away.

Toddler Play (age 1 to 2)

115 Circle Prints

Toddlers like to watch shapes appear on the paper and they like the repetition of this activity too.

AGE: 2 YRS

CATEGORY:
PLAY WITH
OTHERS/INDOOR

NUMBER OF
CHILDREN: TWO
OR MORE

Materials:

Recycled tablecloth
(to devote to messy
art projects) or newspapers

Construction or newsprint paper

Tape

Nontoxic, washable paint
(available at teacher supply stores)

Plastic picnic plates

Empty trial-size (1.5 ounce) round plastic lotion or
shampoo containers

Wet washcloths (for cleanup)

Setup:

Spread the tablecloth or newspaper over the kitchen table for easy cleanup. Place a piece of paper in front of each child. (For young toddlers, tape the paper to the tablecloth to keep in place.) Pour 1 or 2 teaspoons of paint in each plastic plate. Each child gets his own paint.

Play:

Each child gets his own plastic bottle. He dips the bottom of the container into the paint and presses on the paper to create circle prints. Most toddlers are happy with single-color printmaking. If you want to expand this art-play, provide two or three plates of paint with containers for each child, designated to each specific color so the paint colors don't get mixed. Have wet washcloths on hand to move in quickly when print-time is over.

SAFETY ALERT: Supervise carefully and use containers large enough to not pose a choking hazard to infants or toddlers.

116 Giant Printmaking for Two

It's impressive for a toddler to be given the green light to scribble on such a giant surface. This is a wonderful relief from the common phrase "No, you can't do that," which every toddler hears from time to time!

AGE: 2 YRS*

CATEGORY:
PLAY WITH
OTHERS/INDOOR

NUMBER OF
CHILDREN: TWO
OR MORE

Materials:

Roll of butcher paper or
4 to 5 paper grocery bags

Scissors (for adult use only)

Invisible tape

2 large nontoxic ink pads

Rubber printing stamps (with handle)
in large circles, squares, other shapes,
and an assortment of large letters
(available at teacher supply stores)

Setup:

Completely cover your kitchen table with butcher paper. (If using paper bags, cut off the bottoms and make one lengthwise cut on each bag to create large flat pieces of paper. Completely cover the table with the paper.) Tape over all the seams so you end up with one giant printmaking surface. Loosely tape the ends and sides to the table to hold it in place. Place one nontoxic ink pad within easy reach of each child.

Play:

Press one of the rubber stamps firmly into the ink pad and press it on the paper as a quick demo. Let the children create designs all over the paper, while you provide supervision to keep things safe and also settle minor disputes.

SAFETY ALERT: Best suited for older toddlers who

do not put things in their mouth. Supervise infants or toddlers carefully and do not offer them any small stamps that could pose a choking hazard.

117 Play Dough

I love the smell of play dough! It's also cheap, colorful, and easy to share.

AGE: 1–2 YRS

CATEGORY:
PLAY WITH
OTHERS/INDOOR

NUMBER OF
CHILDREN:
TWO OR MORE

Materials:

Vinyl tablecloth or recycled bedsheet or tablecloth for easy cleanup

Lots of play dough (play clay) in one color

Plastic animals, figures, etc., to stand up in the play dough

Small margarine tubs

Tiny rolling pin for each child

Plastic cookie cutters, baby jar lids, or large LEGOs for making imprints (or set of play dough tools)

Setup:

Place the tablecloth or sheet on the table or floor to designate the play area. Take the play dough out of the containers and place it in the center of the table or floor area. Give each child roughly the same (or similar) clay toys (rolling pin, cookie cutter, etc.) to work with. Children will enjoy sticking the plastic figures in the dough and discovering that they "magically" stand up. These toys also make interesting impressions in the dough. The margarine tubs make wonderful molds. A toddler hand makes a fine, individual stamp (and so does a foot!).

See page 125 in the *Preschool Play* section for making your own fabulous play dough.

> " You want to give children practice with solving their anger and frustration without you. Give them a start, but then move away and see if they can solve them on their own."
>
> **—Rebecca Kantor, Ed.D.**
> Professor of Early Childhood Education at Ohio State University

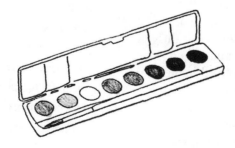

Toddler Play (age 1 to 2)

Musical Play

Musical play for toddlers is more about experimenting with sounds and rhythm than it is about fine music making. But now that I've offered this disclaimer to prepare your ears and steady your nerves, let me also say that messing around with musical instruments (and banging on pots and pans) is a terrific way for your toddler to become acclimated to the idea that he has the power and potential to make "music."

118 Musical Cake Pan

Watching the ball go round and round and listening to the "music" it makes is fascinating and fun for toddlers.

QUICK & EASY

AGE: 1 YR

CATEGORY:
PLAY WITH
OTHERS/INDOOR

NUMBER OF
CHILDREN: TWO
OR MORE

Materials:

1 or 2 plastic Wiffle golf balls

*Small, round metal cake pans
(1 for each child) or cookie tins
without lids (about 5" diameter
is the perfect size for small hands)*

Setup:

Put one plastic golf ball in the cake pan or cookie tin.

Play:

Show the children how to hold both sides of the pan firmly. Have them move their hands and the pan from side to side (ever so slightly) to cause the ball to circle round and round the edge of the pan. The faster each child moves her hands from side to side, the faster the ball goes around and the more "music" she can make. It takes a little practice, but once she gets the hang of it, she'll be able to make a variety of sounds. (If her hands are holding on to the sides *and* the bottom of the pan, the sound is a bit softer or muffled. If she grabs only the sides, a clear, louder sound is created.) Once each child has

perfected the movement needed to create the action and sounds, add a second Wiffle ball. Watch the two balls chase each other around the rim of the pan, and listen to a slightly deeper musical sound.

119 Toddler Band

Shake, rattle, 'n' roll! Toddler band practice always makes for a noisy good time. And who knows—maybe one day your grown-up musical genius will be able to say, "It all started in my parents' kitchen with a cowbell and a couple of baby rattles."

QUICK & EASY

AGE: 1–2 YRS

CATEGORY:
PLAY WITH
OTHERS/INDOOR

NUMBER OF
CHILDREN: TWO
OR MORE

Materials:

Baby rattles

Cong-ltas•

Hand drums

Large wooden train whistle*

Maracas (toddler-style)

Musical shakers*

Rhythm sticks*

Sand blocks*

Tambourine*

Triangle*

Wooden clackers

Three wonderful sources for musical shakers and instruments for young children are Hearthsong (www.hearthsong.com); Music for Little People (www.musicforlittlepeople.com); and Little Hands Music (www.littlehandsmusic.com).

Play:

Sing a familiar toddler or preschool song (clap along to add a beat) or play favorite music, and give each musician an instrument to shake or tap. (See favorite songs in the *Toddler Play* section, page 38, and Favorite Preschool Songs, page 176.) Most toddlers will need some adult direction for musical play with others, so be prepared to sing songs and demonstrate how to tap or shake each musical instrument to get things started. Embellish your child's musical play by adding simple hats or costumes and encouraging a march around the living room, parade style, for some spontaneous musical fun.

*SAFETY ALERT: Instruments marked with an asterisk are best for toddlers older than two.

<table>
<tr><td>

120

Rattle 'Round the Room

</td></tr>
</table>

Toddlers will shake, shake, shake all the way around the room with this engaging game that encourages kids to explore all the different sounds they can make.

QUICK & EASY

AGE: 2 YRS

CATEGORY:
PLAY WITH
OTHERS/INDOOR

NUMBER OF
CHILDREN: TWO
OR MORE

Materials:
 Assorted baby rattles and shakers*
  (2 for each child, 2 for parent demo)

Setup:
Give each child her own toddler-safe musical shakers (claim 1 or 2 shakers for yourself to give a little demo).

Play:

Since toddlers are marvelous imitators, show them a few of your best music-making moves: Shake the rattle high in the air, loud and fast. Then hold the shaker at waist level and move it slowly to make a quieter sound. Encourage the children to shake their arms or twirl in circles. To change things up, sing some favorite songs for a round of toddler-style dancing *and* music. Older toddlers (who understand the concept of "stop and go") may enjoy a version of Stop and Go Dancing (page 88) in which they shake, shake, shake while a song is sung or played, and hold the shakers still and silent when the music stops.

TIP: Animal shakers, vegetable shakers, or fruit shakers are a few cleverly shaped, toddler-safe shakers for children two years and older—yes, some of them are decorated to look like cucumbers, peppers, eggplants, carrots, apples, oranges, lemons, and bananas!

<table>
<tr><td>

121 **Teddy Bear Waltz**

</td></tr>
</table>

Let Teddy join in the fun by taping a small rattle or musical shaker to his arm (using invisible tape) so the children can make more music together by dancing with their toys.

Outdoor Play

Outdoor play is active, providing fun and fitness for toddlers. Here are a few activities to keep two or more children playing happily side by side outdoors. Some of these games work best when each child has his own toys or props to play with (since toddlers are not yet masters at sharing). And, of course, your supervision is needed to help keep things on an even (and safe) keel as the children play together.

122 Water Painter

One of my son's favorite playtime activities when he was two was "painting" the sidewalk and porch steps with water. This can be fabulous summertime fun for toddlers.

AGE: 1–2 YRS

CATEGORY:
PLAY WITH OTHERS/ OUTDOOR

NUMBER OF CHILDREN:
TWO OR MORE

Materials:

Small plastic buckets
(1 for each child)

Water

Paintbrushes with short, rounded handles and 2" to 3" bristles

Paint tray and small paint rollers (alternative to buckets and brush)

Bathing suits (optional)

Setup:
Fill each bucket with about 2 inches of water. Prop up a paintbrush inside each bucket. (Or put 1 or 2 cups of water in a plastic paint tray and add a small paint roller to each tray.)

Play:
Toddlers love to paint the deck, sidewalk, patio, railings, or deck furniture with water and paintbrush. In fact, they are very persistent painters, no matter that the designs evaporate in minutes from the sun overhead.

123 Multicolored Water Painter

Pour water into several plastic margarine tubs and add a few drops of food coloring to each. Let your little H_2O artiste paint only the concrete sidewalks (rather than the decks, railings, and furniture mentioned above). The color can be easily washed off concrete with a hose or will disappear naturally with rainwater.

124 Shining the Grass

Give the grass a squirt to make it shine and help it grow! (Trees like a drink too.) Toddlers love to "wash" outdoor furniture, porches, and railings, too, with these pint-size squirt bottles.

AGE: 2 YRS

CATEGORY:
PLAY WITH OTHERS/ OUTDOOR

NUMBER OF CHILDREN: TWO

Materials:

Small plastic squirt bottles (1 for each child, available at beauty supply shops)

Water

Setup:
Fill bottles with water.

Play:
Use the water bottle to squirt and "shine" the grass, as well as other outdoor items that might need watering. You might find that your toddler decides that she—or you—needs watering too!

125 Leaf Buckets

Searching for fallen leaves in autumn is a gratifying endeavor. Can you spot a yellow leaf?

AGE: 1–2 YRS

CATEGORY: PLAY WITH OTHERS/ OUTDOOR

NUMBER OF CHILDREN: TWO OR MORE

Materials:
- 2 small plastic buckets
- Leaves on the ground

Play:
Toddlers love to carry their very own little buckets for leaf gathering. When you get home, start a leaf collection on your mantel so your toddler can admire her treasures year-round.

★ CLASSIC ★

126 Sidewalk Chalk

Toddlers are trying hard to figure out all the rules of life. And then, out of the blue, you introduce your child to sidewalk chalk and you say it's okay to draw on the sidewalk! Life is full of rules, and happy surprises too.

AGE: 2 YRS

CATEGORY: PLAY WITH OTHERS/ OUTDOOR

NUMBER OF CHILDREN: TWO OR MORE

Materials:
- Sidewalk chalk*
- Small plastic containers (margarine tub, Tupperware containers, etc.)

Setup:
Place a few pieces of sidewalk chalk in each container. Give each toddler her own tub of chalk.

*SAFETY ALERT: Sidewalk chalk is not safe for toddlers who still put things in their mouths.

127 Wading Pool Water Play

Splash around and grab at toys bobbing in the water. Use a sprinkling can to take a shower or wash a plastic doll. Find out what floats and what sinks! Warm weather water play is wet and riotous fun.

AGE: 1–2 YRS

CATEGORY: PLAY WITH OTHERS/ OUTDOOR

NUMBER OF CHILDREN: TWO OR MORE (plus one adult per child for safety)

Materials:
- Plastic tub, large dishpan, or wading pool
- Toddler-safe tub toys
- Toy sprinkling can
- Plastic balls (for floating)

Setup:
If using a tub or dishpan, pour in 4 to 6 inches of water to create a toddler-size wading pool.

*SAFETY ALERT: Supervise your child vigilantly while he is playing in the wading pool. If your attention is required elsewhere even for a moment, take your toddler out of the pool and keep him in your arms so he does not go near the water unattended. Also note that plastic tubs are slippery, so help your child in and out of the tub with care.

Toddler Play (age I to 2)

128 Laundry Basketball

A giant laundry basket is just the right prop for a happy game of toddler basketball. Though it's tempting to cheer your toddler on every time he makes a goal, I try to temper this instinct so as not to frustrate a toddler who's having difficulty with his slam dunk.

AGE: 1–2 YRS

CATEGORY:
PLAY WITH
OTHERS/
OUTDOOR

NUMBER OF
CHILDREN: TWO
OR MORE

Materials:
Large plastic laundry basket, or multiple smaller baskets (1 for each child)

Medium- to large-size plastic balls (or small playground balls) in varying colors (1 for each child)

Setup:
Place the laundry basket on the lawn. Use your own ball to demonstrate how to toss the ball in the basket. Each child plays with his own colored ball.

129 Scooper Duper

Mix together two unlikely play props: plastic balls and an ice-cream scooper and you have a flexible game called Scooper Duper.

AGE: 1–2 YRS

CATEGORY:
PLAY WITH
OTHERS/
OUTDOOR

NUMBER OF
CHILDREN: TWO

Materials:
Ping-Pong balls

2 plastic gallon-size ice-cream tubs

One-piece, molded plastic ice-cream scooper (without sharp edges or small parts)

Setup:
Put the balls in one of the tubs. Put 1 or 2 inches of water in the other tub and place it a few feet away on the lawn.

Play:
The object is to scoop the balls from the tub one at a time using the ice-cream scooper and drop them (plop!) into the empty tub. Children one to two years old will probably end up using their hands. When the transfer has been completed, the process can be reversed. (It's a bit more of a challenge because of the water.)

130 Toddler Soccer

There are no rules in Toddler Soccer. All you need to play are a couple of kids, a lawn, some playground balls, and a bit of stamina!

AGE: 2 YRS

CATEGORY:
PLAY WITH
OTHERS/
OUTDOOR

NUMBER OF
CHILDREN: TWO
OR MORE

Materials:
Playground balls, with a different color for each child (trust me on this one!)

Setup:
Distribute the balls and playfully demonstrate kicking a ball a little ways, running after it, and kicking it again, from one end of the lawn to the other.

Play:
Some children will switch to rolling the ball or carrying the ball around the lawn, and that's fine too!

131 Wash the Baby— or the Cars!

Toddlers love to wash things on their own. They see Mommy and Daddy doing household chores all the time, and they want to do their part too! When two or more toddlers are splashing and scrubbing, "washing" something takes on a whole new dimension.

AGE: 1–2 YRS

CATEGORY:
PLAY WITH
OTHERS/
OUTDOOR

NUMBER OF
CHILDREN: TWO
OR MORE

Materials:

Plastic cups

Plastic dishpan (1 for each child)

Washcloth or small sponge or plastic vegetable scrubber (1 for each child)

Plastic dolls or plastic cars and trucks

Setup:
Pour a couple of inches of water into each child's plastic dishpan. Add a plastic cup and sponge, washcloth, or vegetable scrubber to each tub. Be sure to give each child the same washing tools and cups (for rinsing and pouring) to avoid squabbles. To spice things up, add a floating toy to each dishpan to see what happens next. Scrubbing, pouring, and splashing will ensue.

Don't Bite Back!

Often, the biggest toddler playtime problem doesn't have to do with grabbing, not sharing, or shyness—it's biting. Rather than go the old-fashioned approach ("just bite the child back so he'll see what it feels like"), you'll find far better results if you respond with a stern "no, you cannot do that." Immediately remove the child from the situation to speak with him alone about how biting hurts and that it's a no-no. Until he's ready to be brought back to the group, allow him to work on a solo activity. Remind him that biting is not permitted and then reintroduce him to the group.

Birthday Party Play

Your toddler's first or second birthday is a marvelous occasion to celebrate—but it can also be a bit nerve-wracking. Short of hiring a fire engine or having a group of astronauts come by, how are you going to keep all those toddlers happily occupied? Look no further! Everything you need is in this section. But before you begin planning your child's party, here are a few key elements of the most successful toddler birthday parties to keep in mind:

- Low-key fun
- Toys for independent play
- Space to move about (indoors or outdoors)
- Group activities involving side-by-side play
- A few brief cooperative play ideas (ring-around-the-rosy, etc.) that children can join in or watch
- One adult to supervise every toddler
- Keep it short (sixty to ninety minutes at most)

You can design a splendid party for your child's first or second birthday by incorporating play ideas from the three main birthday activity categories you will find in this section—*Mom & Me or Dad & Me Party Activities, Play Stations,* and *Group Play Activities.* With a little mixing and matching of the play ideas in this section, you can create a terrific sixty- or ninety-minute party. Immediately following this list of categories, you'll see a sample First Birthday Party Play Itinerary and a Second Birthday Party Play Itinerary to give you suggestions of how to mix and match games and activities to create a successful party. (But keep in mind that only you will know how to pace the party to suit the moods, interests, and abilities of the toddlers present, so by all means let your own judgment determine how many toys and games to offer to keep your crowd happy.)

Mom & Me or Dad & Me Party Activities are very short activities and crafts for parents and toddlers to enjoy together—decorating prebaked sugar cookies with frosting and sprinkles or making very simple birthday crowns from precut scalloped borders, for example.

Play Stations are play areas set up indoors or outdoors with appealing toddler toys and props (enough so that each child winds up with the same materials), including an assortment of balls, cardboard boxes, and plastic dishpans.

Group Play Activities are favorite activities for all the children to play together (side by side)—chasing bubbles on the lawn, pouring cups of water in a wading pool, using big paintbrushes or rollers to "paint" the sidewalk with water.

Create a Party Itinerary

Before the party begins, preselect activities from the three birthday party categories in the following pages that you think will fit the abilities and interests of your partygoers. Since kids can be so unpredictable, create a rough draft itinerary rather than a rigid schedule for the day. Gather all the necessary materials and supplies, set up the play stations, and designate a play area for the *Mom & Me or Dad & Me* activities. It's smart to assume that the children will play each activity only for a brief time (mere minutes!), so be sure to provide multiple play opportunities to keep things moving. Start your child's party with an arrival activity that is appealing and easy for each toddler to understand at a quick glance.

Sample First Birthday Party Itinerary (60 minutes)

Arrival Activity (5+ minutes):
Birthday Mural

Play Stations (15 minutes):
Buckets of LEGOs or Blocks, Cars Go Zoom, Let's Play Ball

Time for Cake or Cupcakes (5 to 10 minutes)

Mom & Me or Dad & Me Activity (10 minutes):
Super-Simple Toddler Crowns, Crumpled-Paper Toss, Sock Toss

Repeat Play Stations Games Again

Sample Second Birthday Party Itinerary (60 to 90 minutes)

Arrival Activity (5 to 10 minutes):
Party Play Dough

Play Stations (20 minutes):
Cars Go Zoom, Music Makers for All, Teddy Bear Picnic, B.Y.O. Scooter, Buckets of LEGOs or Blocks, Dress-up

Time for Cake or Cupcakes (10 minutes)

Mom & Me or Dad & Me Activity (10 minutes):
Treasure Boxes

Group Play (15 minutes):
Paint Party, Walking the Plank, Bubble Clapper, Stop and Go (Sit Down) Dancing, Butterfly in the Garden

Toddler Play (age 1 to 2)

Mom & Me or Dad & Me Party Activities

One great thing about toddler parties is that each child is accompanied by a parent or caregiver who will probably stay during the entire party. This means that all the children will be well supervised; it also provides opportunities for activities that toddlers and adults can do together. That way, each toddler gets individual attention and reassurance from someone special in his life, at the same time getting a taste of group play and excitement at the party. Here are some short, first-rate party play activities for parent (or caregiver) and child.

132 Super-Simple Toddler Crowns

Use premade scalloped cardboard borders to make instant toddler crowns. The children will scribble and decorate and, just when their attention span is coming to an end, an instant crown appears on their heads.

QUICK & EASY

AGE: 1–2 YRS

CATEGORY:
BIRTHDAY PARTY/
MOM & ME or
DAD & ME

NUMBER OF
CHILDREN: **THREE
OR MORE**

Materials:
Butcher paper
Pack of precut cardboard scalloped borders
   (available at teacher supply stores)
Invisible tape (for adult use only)
Crayons and nontoxic markers
Color dot stickers (available at
   office supply stores)

Setup:
Cover your entire kitchen table with the butcher paper and secure with tape to hold it down. Place a length of scalloped

border on the table for each child, and use invisible tape to secure it to the butcher paper (making it easier for toddlers to color). Note that since the entire table will be scribbled on, the butcher paper becomes a lovely creative by-product from this craft.

Create:
The children decorate their crowns using crayons, markers, and stickers. (Grown-ups can help by peeling a corner of each sticker from the paper for easy toddler handling, or by holding the scalloped border in place while their child scribbles.) When the decorating is done (or the child's good humor begins to disappear), the parents peel off the tape to remove the border from the table, cut the scalloped border to crown length, and tape the two ends together.

*Tip: The first time around, the toddlers probably won't understand what they are decorating. When they see one of the parents turning that masterpiece into a "hat" or crown that can actually be worn, the level of excitement will rise. For this reason, it's a good idea to have enough material for each child to make two crowns—one for Mom or Dad and one for herself!

133 Treasure Boxes

This is a fun activity with a bonus—a take-home prize for each child. Why spend money on party favors when you can have the children handcraft their own?

AGE: 1–2 YRS

CATEGORY:
BIRTHDAY PARTY/
MOM & ME or
DAD & ME

NUMBER OF
CHILDREN: **THREE OR MORE**

Materials:

Child- or adult-size shoe box
   (with lid, 1 for each child)

Construction paper

Color dot stickers
   (available at office supply stores)

Nontoxic glue sticks

Crayons and nontoxic markers

Scissors and tape (for adult use only)

Setup:
Prior to the party, collect enough shoe boxes so that each child gets his own. (Visit your local shoe store to find recycled shoe boxes and repair with tape if needed.) Cut each piece of the construction paper into fourths. Fill each shoe box with one or two sheets of sticker dots, a glue stick, quarter sheets of construction paper in multiple colors, and three to four chunky crayons (make sure the contents of each shoe box are identical).

Create:
Have the children scribble on or decorate their construction paper; when they're finished, the adults tape the pieces to the inside and outside of the shoe box lid. Cut additional drawings to decorate the sides of the box. When the decorating is over, this becomes a terrific take-home party prize.

A Party Plan for Your Child's First Birthday

Have simple expectations, try to make it fun, be flexible, and read your audience as the party gets under way. This is my very best advice about hosting a successful first birthday party for your child. Think of the party as a short, sixty- or ninety-minute playgroup with cake and a few photos thrown in for good measure, and you get the basic idea about what is achievable.

The unique challenge of planning a one-year-old's party revolves around the fact that some children won't yet be walking; others can walk but not run; and some are better at using their hands to maneuver and play than others. In short, you have quite a range of abilities, interests, and play styles to contend with. Here are a few First Birthday Party tips:

• Schedule the party early in the morning or after the afternoon naptime (so all children are in good humor).

• Keep the party short (sixty to ninety minutes is best).

• Rely on each parent (or caregiver) present to help supervise and play.

• Have a short birthday cake break during playtime, but realize that many of the children won't sit still for long.

135 Hidden Stars

The moon and stars are magical, faraway wonders to a child. With a tiny bit of nudging from Mom or Dad or a caregiver, each child can find the hidden stars and pack them away inside their very own party favor bags.

AGE: 1–2 YRS

CATEGORY: BIRTHDAY PARTY/ MOM & ME or DAD & ME

NUMBER OF CHILDREN: THREE OR MORE

Materials:

- Brightly colored poster board (or purchase precut cardboard stars at teacher supply stores)
- Pencil and scissors (for adult use only)
- Colorful gift bag with handles for each child (available at party supply stores)
- Optional: glitter glue, stickers, markers

Setup:

Before the party, cut out one large, 6- to 8-inch cardboard star. Use it as a pattern to trace more stars onto the poster board. Cut out enough stars so that there are four to eight for each child. Set aside one star per child. Write each child's name on a star, decorating with glitter glue, stickers, and markers if time permits. Deposit these personalized stars into the gift bags and write each child's name on the outside of the bag. Hide most of the other stars all over the lawn (or throughout the house), with at least part of each star in plain sight. Keep a bag of extra stars that can be quickly hidden while the hunt is wrapping up, so that if some children have had less success in their searches, you can nudge them and their parents toward these remaining stars.

Play:

Give each child his star-collecting bag. Each child's parent acts as the guide through the "finding" process. Since this game is not a competition—every child should find roughly the same number of stars—be prepared to give parents a few "hints" about where to look next or when their child is getting hot or cold.

134 Party Play Dough

The tactile quality of this play will keep the children absorbed and content for a while. With parents in the wings to help mop up the mess, it's an easy favorite for birthday parties.

AGE: 1–2 YRS

CATEGORY: BIRTHDAY PARTY/ MOM & ME or DAD & ME

NUMBER OF CHILDREN: THREE OR MORE

Materials:

- Container of play dough (1 for each child)
- Tiny rolling pin (for play dough)
- Toddler-safe play dough tools
- Colored gift bag (with handles) for each child
- Old tablecloth or large sheets of butcher paper and tape

Setup:

Prior to the party, put one can of play dough and a set of play dough tools in each gift bag, making sure the contents of each match exactly. Write each child's name on the outside of their bag. Completely cover your table with butcher paper and secure with tape. (Or, cover a large area of your kitchen floor to create a giant play dough station.) Give each child a gift bag and a space at the table, and set them on the road to spontaneous play.

*SAFETY NOTE: This activity is best suited to children who no longer put things in their mouths.

136 Cookies with Sprinkles

This can be a bit messy, but it's yummy, gooey, creative fun for toddlers!

AGE: 2 YRS

CATEGORY:
BIRTHDAY PARTY/
MOM & ME OR
DAD & ME

NUMBER OF
CHILDREN: THREE
OR MORE

Materials:

Frosting:
  2 cups confectioners' sugar
  Tablespoon
  Milk
  Food coloring (optional)
  Medium-size mixing bowl
Small bowls (1 for each child)
Small spoons (1 for each child)
1 or 2 jars of edible sprinkles
Large sugar cookies (prebaked or store bought)
Small ziplock bags
Party bags with handles (1 for each child)

Setup:

Make your own simple frosting a few minutes before the party begins. Place 2 cups of confectioners' sugar in your mixing bowl. Stir in milk one tablespoon at a time until you've created a runny frosting about the consistency of gravy. (Add a drop of food coloring if you like.) Spread a tablecloth on the table and scoop a small amount of frosting into each of the small bowls.* Place a bowl and a spoon at each setting, and a jar of sprinkles nearby.

*NOTE: After about 30 minutes, the frosting will begin to harden in the bowls; right before the party, thin it with a bit of milk.

Play:

Seat the children. Each child gets to decorate one or two large sugar cookies. Parents and toddlers work together to drizzle a spoonful of frosting on their cookie. Then the toddlers go to work shaking sprinkles on top. (Obviously, some of the children will sample their cookies or frosting as they create—it's all part of the game!) When cookie time is over, leave the cookies out on the table to dry. Have one adult helper come back later to put each cookie in a ziplock bag to go in each cookie artist's treat bag at the end of the party. One word of caution: Make sure to keep the family pet away from the cookie table, or you'll have some disappointed toddlers on your hands at the end of the party!

137 Animal Cookies Stuck in the Mud

Use brown food coloring (red and green food coloring mixed together) in the frosting, and have each child drizzle it over a giant sugar cookie. Before it sets, stick a few animal crackers in the frosting (the mud!). Sprinkles are the final touch in this elaborate cookie creation.

138 Crumpled-Paper Toss

Parents make the paper ball and toddlers do the tossing. It's a super-simple game, but the children get a big charge out of watching, listening to, and mimicking all the action going on—the sound of paper being scrunched, the sight of paper balls flying and the busy bodies all around.

AGE: 1–2 YRS

CATEGORY:
BIRTHDAY PARTY/
MOM & ME or
DAD & ME

NUMBER OF
CHILDREN:
THREE OR MORE

Materials:

2 or 3 medium-to-large cardboard boxes (or a few laundry baskets) placed around the room

Package color copy paper (100 sheets)

Setup:

Place a cardboard box in the middle of the room. Parents and children should sit on the floor, scattered around the room. Give each parent a short stack of colored paper.

Play:

Begin by having the parents scrunch the copy paper into balls (tightly squeezed so they're easier to handle). Parents demonstrate by either tossing the ball into the box or handing the ball to their child and helping them carry or drop it into the box. From this starting point, the game takes on a life of its own. The parents continue to make paper balls, and the children toss the balls into the box. Some children may want to scrunch up the balls on their own. Some may want to turn the box upside down or climb inside for a ride! (That's why it's a good idea to have a couple extra baskets or boxes on hand as spares.)

Tip: A little toddler-happy background music adds a nice touch while this activity is under way.

A Party Plan for Your Child's Second Birthday

I offer this mantra for a successful second birthday party: "Appealing toys and the opportunity to move about." Think of these little playmates as land rovers who move about to briefly investigate whatever strikes their fancy, stay a few minutes to play, and then move on again. This is why the play station idea is tailor-made for toddler birthday parties.

The second distinctive feature about two-year-old toddlers is that they love to walk, run, skip, hop, and dance. Physical movement of every sort *is* play for them. Build on this idea by including group games that encourage the children to romp around the room or lawn.

Second Birthday Party Tips

• Schedule the party for sixty to ninety minutes only and select a time of day when everyone is well rested.

• Enlist the help of a few of the parents present when getting each game under way and corralling the children.

• Plan one arrival activity for toddlers and parents (or caregivers) to do together. (This helps the children adjust to the "group" in a secure way and is a good waiting activity as latecomers arrive.)

• Assemble toys and props to create a few play stations, and perhaps plan one or two short group games during the party. Plan to have birthday cake sometime in the middle or at the end of the party.

• Monitor the mood of the children and add high-energy play ideas to let off steam, or quiet-time activities to allow them to settle down as needed.

Play Stations

I love the idea of having "play stations" at a toddler birthday party—designated play areas indoors or outdoors that have been set up (or stocked) with safe, enticing toys. My toddler play station motto is, *If you offer it, they will play.* If you offer four large playground balls in one area of your backyard at a party with four toddlers, you can bet the children will begin playing with the balls.

The play that unfolds from these play stations will likely be a combination of solitary play (with each child tapping, swatting, rolling, and kicking the ball) and fleeting moments of joint play. Toddlers will follow the same model in their itineraries—they'll most likely move individually from station to station, rather than as a group. So children and parents may wind up scattered among several play stations, experimenting and playing.

Here are some toddler-friendly play stations (areas) to include in your child's birthday party.

139 Teddy Bear Picnic

Materials:

Assortment of stuffed animals (or
  B.Y.O.T.—Bring Your Own Teddy)

Giant picnic blanket

Miniature plastic cups, plates,
  and spoons

Small containers (with lids)
  of safe finger foods for each child/teddy

Shoe boxes and doll blankets (1 for each teddy)

AGE: 1–2 YRS

CATEGORY:
BIRTHDAY PARTY/
PLAY STATIONS

NUMBER OF
CHILDREN:
THREE OR MORE

Play:
Lay the blanket down and arrange the place settings and snacks on top. The shoe boxes can be used as chairs to prop up the teddy bears for the picnic. Later, Teddy can also curl up with his blanket and take a nap inside his shoe-box bed. If he wants to go for a drive, Teddy can also ride around in his fancy shoe-box Cadillac. While children are eating, you might read a quick teddy bear story or recite a rhyme.

140 Dress-Up Box, aka Hats Galore

Materials:

Large hatbox

Children's and grown-ups' hats

Wallets, purses, capes

Sunglasses (with lenses removed)

Large hand-held mirror for
  parent(s) to hold while the children check out
  their new looks

Blanket (to spread on the ground)

Teddy bears and stuffed animals

AGE: 1–2 YRS

CATEGORY:
BIRTHDAY PARTY/
PLAY STATIONS

NUMBER OF
CHILDREN:
THREE OR MORE

Play:
Start out with the hats in the hatbox. This simple dress-up station will come to life when toddlers put hats on their own heads, on the teddy bears, or on their parents. And when they behold the magical transformations in the mirror, more glee ensues.

Toddler Play (age 1 to 2)

141 Let's Play Ball

Materials:
Soft, medium-size balls for indoor play; playground balls for outdoors (1 for each child)
Slide
Cardboard boxes, plastic baskets, or crates

AGE: 1–2 YRS
CATEGORY: **BIRTHDAY PARTY/ PLAY STATIONS**
NUMBER OF CHILDREN: **THREE OR MORE**

Play:
Toddlers will tap, roll, kick, chase, and toss the ball (alone or with grown-ups or other toddlers), send it down a slide, or drop it in a box.

142 Music Makers for All

Materials:
Cowbells, rattles, shakers (see page 178 for finding toddler and preschool music makers)
Crowns or party hats (1 for each child)
Capes (1 for each child)
Streamers

AGE: 1–2 YRS
CATEGORY: **BIRTHDAY PARTY/ PLAY STATIONS**
NUMBER OF CHILDREN: **THREE OR MORE**

Play:
Musical experimentation; add props so older toddlers can create a musical parade.

> ❝The best advice is to keep the birthday plans simple, especially when children are young. An elaborate or expensive birthday party is not going to be more fun or go more smoothly than just a simple party at home.❞
>
> **—Shelley Butler**
> coauthor of *The Field Guide to Parenting*

143 Water Play

Materials:
Plastic dishpan or large disposable roasting pan (1 for each child)
Plastic cups and containers
Tub toys (rubber duck, fish, or boat—1 for each child)
Towels (for spills or drying wet children)
Optional:
Bathing suits
Large wading pool with a few inches of water*

AGE: 1–2 YRS
CATEGORY: **BIRTHDAY PARTY/ PLAY STATIONS**
NUMBER OF CHILDREN: **THREE OR MORE**

Play:
Place each of the small plastic pans on the deck or patio or lawn (with beach towels or washable blankets underneath) and fill with a few inches of water. Provide plastic cups and tub toys, and each toddler will invent his own fun.

SAFETY ALERT: Always supervise toddler water play.

144 Buckets of LEGOs

Materials:
Giant LEGOs or wooden blocks
Small buckets with handles or shoe boxes (1 for each child)

AGE: 1–2 YRS
CATEGORY: **BIRTHDAY PARTY/ PLAY STATIONS**
NUMBER OF CHILDREN: **THREE OR MORE**

Play:
Place LEGOs or blocks in the buckets or boxes. Hauling, dumping, tower building, and tower crashing will ensue. Allow for enough elbow room so that each child can build and knock down his blocks. At the end of the party the blocks stay at your house, but send the box or bucket home with the children with small party favors inside.

145 Cars Go Zoom

Materials:

Sheets of 20"-by-30"
foam board (poster board
with foam backing)

Note: 1 sheet makes 2 ramps;
buy enough so each child has
a ramp

Yardstick

Scissors or utility knife to cut foam board
(for adult use only)

Invisible tape

Small, toddler-safe toy car (1 for each child,
or B.Y.O.C.—Bring Your Own Car)

AGE: 1–2 YRS

CATEGORY:
BIRTHDAY PARTY/
PLAY STATIONS

NUMBER OF
CHILDREN:
THREE OR MORE

Setup:

Before the party begins, cut each piece of foam
board in half lengthwise to create individual
10"-by-30" ramps for each of the attendees.
Use the yardstick as a guide to score and cut
one side; then flip it over, fold it in half, and
cut along the crease to create two ramps. (It's a
good idea to create one or two extra ramps, for
a quick exchange, in case one of the ramps gets
bent.) Prop the foam board ramps against
a sofa or chair at an angle. These ramps will
stay in place when positioned on carpet; if
you're placing them on a hard floor, use strips
of invisible tape to hold them in place.

Play:

Give each child one or more toddler-safe cars
and a quick demo showing them how to zoom
the car down the ramp. These ramps and cars
are marvelous take-home party prizes too.

146 B.Y.O. Scooter

Materials:

Ride-on toys (1 for each child,
provided by child's parents)

Small buckets of water

Washcloths or sponges
(1 for each child)

AGE: 1–2 YRS

CATEGORY:
BIRTHDAY PARTY/
PLAY STATIONS

NUMBER OF
CHILDREN:
THREE OR MORE

Play:

Supervise the children while they play
on their ride-on toys indoors, in a
large playroom, or outdoors on the
lawn or sidewalk. Give each child a
small bucket of water and washcloth
to create their very own "car
wash" for their ride-on.

Safety Alert: Provide
constant supervision to
ensure that the children
stay clear of cars.

Twirling Scarves and Streamers

Older toddlers might enjoy waving
scarves or streamers around to
music. Provide each child with a long
silk scarf or crepe-paper streamer and
show them how to wave their arms up
and down and side to side to make the
streamer dance.

UNPLUGGED PLAY

Group Play Activities

When things are going well, it's so interesting to sit back and watch a group of toddlers play. They have a funny little group dynamic. Some children focus exclusively on their own toys and scarcely notice other playmates. Others relish short moments of playing with other children and imitating their hilarious play ideas.

In this section you will find noncompetitive, open-ended group play activities that allow lots of room for individual tastes. There's a little something for everyone. There's a time to join in and a time to watch. A time to run, clap, dance, and sing, all to the beat of a different drummer. These "games" really don't have rules, and they don't require everyone's participation. Simply think of these activities as "play opportunities," and keep an open mind about the various ways the play might evolve.

147 Bubble-Clapper

I'll bet there is at least one or two bubble-clappers in the crowd just waiting to chase those elusive bubbles around the lawn.

QUICK & EASY

AGE: 1–2 YRS

CATEGORY:
BIRTHDAY PARTY/
GROUP PLAY

NUMBER OF
CHILDREN: **THREE
OR MORE**

Materials:
Small jar of bubbles and bubble wand (for each grown-up)

Play:
You use the wand and bubble solution to blow bubbles, and your toddler tries to catch the bubbles (using her hands) or she claps them between two hands to make them pop. This is a simple but captivating activity to play with toddlers. (Older toddlers will enjoy playing outdoors and chasing the bubbles around the yard.)

148 Walking the Plank

This game combines the joys of physical and pretend play. Maybe there's a giant mud puddle surrounding the plank (excellent for stomping and jumping!), and maybe that puddle is filled with turtles and frogs, and who knows what else. . . .

QUICK & EASY

AGE: **2 YRS**

CATEGORY:
BIRTHDAY PARTY/
GROUP PLAY

NUMBER OF
CHILDREN: **TWO
OR MORE**

Materials:
Wooden board (no nails or jagged edges)
2 or 3 old beach towels

Setup:

In a safe, flat, grassy area, place the board on the ground. (For older toddlers with better balance, roll or fold the beach towels and place them underneath the board at intervals to raise the plank by a couple of inches.)

Play:

Ask (or show) the children to "walk the plank" without falling off the edge and see what happens!

149 Birthday Mural

Your child doesn't need to wait until college to join an artistic cooperative; start her off early with this fun and easy group drawing project. If you've got good adult helpers in the mix, drawing is a great way to keep the toddlers focused and out of the way while you set up the cake in the kitchen.

AGE: 2 YRS

CATEGORY:
BIRTHDAY PARTY/
GROUP PLAY

NUMBER OF
CHILDREN: **THREE
OR MORE**

Materials:

*Roll of butcher paper or
    4 or 5 paper grocery bags*

Invisible tape

Large, unbreakable bowl

Big assortment of chunky crayons

Setup:

Completely cover your kitchen (or picnic) table with butcher paper. Tape all the seams together to create one giant coloring surface and loosely tape the ends and sides to the table to hold it in place. Place the large bowl in the middle of the table and fill it with an assortment of crayons. (If you prefer, the activity can also take place on the floor. Start off the mural by drawing a birthday

cake with one or two candles in the center of the paper, or a wrapped present (don't forget the bow!), or your child's name.

Play:

Scribble-fest! If attention starts to wander and the party is in need of some direction, have the parents trace their child's hand on the mural and write their child's name near the hand. After the party, this will make a nice keepsake for you and your birthday boy or girl.

150 Ring-Around-the-Rosy

Songs are a great way to bring people together (large and small). And in the sometimes overwhelming chaos of a birthday party setting, the children will find comfort in a familiar song.

AGE: 2 YRS

CATEGORY:
BIRTHDAY PARTY/
GROUP PLAY

NUMBER OF
CHILDREN: **TWO
OR MORE** (plus
one adult helper)

Play:

The adult and all the children stand around in a circle holding hands. As you sing the song (below), everyone begins to move the circle in a clockwise or counterclockwise direction. When you sing the last line of the song, "We all fall down," you all suddenly sit down on the floor. This is always a very giggly moment for the toddlers, who'll insist on playing again and again.

Ring around the rosy,

A pocket full of posies,

Ashes, ashes,

We all fall down!

151 Paint Party

Don't panic—the "paint" in this game is actually water! Paint Party is always a crowd-pleaser, and cleanup is over in the blink of an eye.

AGE: 2 YRS

CATEGORY: BIRTHDAY PARTY/ GROUP PLAY

NUMBER OF CHILDREN: THREE OR MORE

Materials:

Plastic buckets or dishpans

Chunky, round-handled exterior paintbrushes (1 for each child)

Small paint rollers (1 for each child)

Setup:

This game takes place on a concrete patio or sidewalk. Fill the buckets or dishpans with a few inches of water. Place all the brushes and rollers on the ground near the buckets. Show the toddlers how to pick up a brush and begin "painting" the patio surface or sidewalk; have another grown-up demonstrate how to use the roller.

Play:

Put your birthday party to work painting and rolling away.

SAFETY ALERT: Supervise all water play constantly and dump out the water once you're through playing. Stay in a safe area, away from cars and traffic.

152 Stop and Go Dancing

Start the music and everyone dances. Stop the music and all the dancers sit down. A great way to get a dose of dancing and an element of Simon Says into your party.

AGE: 2 YRS

CATEGORY: BIRTHDAY PARTY/ GROUP PLAY

NUMBER OF CHILDREN: TWO OR MORE (plus an adult helping with music)

Materials:

Music player and music

Play:

When you start the music, all the little dancers should begin to wiggle, shake, and twirl. (To get everyone going, you'll need to be a dancer too.) About 20 seconds later, stop the music and call out, "All the dancers sit down!" Repeat. As the children get the idea, stop and start the music at shorter intervals to create a stronger element of surprise.

153 Musical Runaround

Create a similar game with music that might include waving hands, clapping, jumping, or hopping to the music. All the action stops as soon as the music stops.

154 Sock Toss

That large heap of socks in your living room isn't a load of unfinished laundry—it's the main ingredient in this active, risk-free game of indoor tossing and dumping. And if your socks don't match, no one will be the wiser!

AGE: 1–2 YRS

CATEGORY:
BIRTHDAY PARTY/
GROUP PLAY

NUMBER OF
CHILDREN: **TWO
OR MORE**

Materials:
Lots and lots of socks
Large cardboard box or laundry basket
Phone book or dictionary
Shoe boxes (1 for each child)

Setup:
Create several dozen sock-balls. (Roll each sock or pair of socks into a tight ball.) Position the cardboard box on the floor, propped up against the sofa. (Put a large phone book or dictionary under the back edge of the box so it is propped at an angle for easier tossing.) Put all the sock-balls in a large heap a few feet away from the box.

Play:
The children grab balls and toss them into the basket. When all the socks have been tossed, they dump the box over on its side and toss all the balls back into a heap in the center of the room. (You might also want to set up a shoe box for each child, providing an alternate tossing target so some toddlers can play solo style; the shoe boxes are also terrific for spontaneous use as "cars" to be pushed around the room.)

155 Hoop-Dee-Do

A Hula-Hoop is a perfect target for a game of beanbag toss. And if you've got any hula experience under your belt, you might want to cap the afternoon with a demonstration of your prowess.

AGE: 1–2 YRS

CATEGORY:
BIRTHDAY PARTY/
GROUP PLAY

NUMBER OF
CHILDREN: **TWO
OR MORE**

Materials:
Large Hula-Hoop
Beanbags
Small plastic buckets or bowls (1 for each child)
Whistle on a string or a bell (for adult use only)

Setup:
Place the Hula-Hoop on the ground on a safe grassy playing area. Put beanbags in each bucket or bowl so that every child has his own bags to toss.

Play:
The toddlers stand around the outside of the hoop, a few feet away, and toss the beanbags into the center. Blow the whistle as a signal for all the children to go inside the circle and retrieve their beanbags.

> **"**Rises in screen time have led to the rise of a sedentary lifestyle for our children. In 1982, the childhood obesity prevalence in the United States was actually less than 4 percent. By 2004, that number had grown to about 30 percent. It really is a huge problem.**"**
>
> **—Henry Joseph Legere, M.D.**
> pediatrician and author of *Raising Healthy Eaters: 100 Tips for Parents of Children of All Ages*

Toddler Play (age 1 to 2)

156 | Butterfly in the Garden

Easy butterfly cocoons, arms, and legs are all you need for this simple and active game. Directed pretend play is a fun and underused element to bring to a toddler party.

QUICK & EASY

AGE: 2–3 YRS

CATEGORY:
BIRTHDAY PARTY/
GROUP PLAY

NUMBER OF
CHILDREN: THREE
OR MORE

Materials:

Medium- to large-size cardboard boxes (boxes 12" by 18" are ideal, 1 for each child)

Beach towels or blankets (1 for each child)

Scissors (for adult use only)

Setup:

Remove box flaps and trim the sides of the boxes down to about 6 inches to create a little butterfly bed that each butterfly can easily climb into. Place a crumpled beach towel inside each box to create a cozy bed. Or, if you are playing indoors (or very young toddlers are playing), create little beds on the floor using only the blankets (so that the butterflies don't have to climb into their beds).

Play:

When the butterfly fairy says, "Fly, little butterflies, fly," the toddlers run and flap their "wings" (arms); when the fairy says, "Butterflies go to sleep," the toddlers pretend to go to sleep in their butterfly beds. Start the game by giving a little demo to show how to fly like a butterfly (run around flapping your arms). Give another demo to show how a butterfly goes to sleep. After the children get the idea and know where their own butterfly beds are, call out, "Fly, little butterflies, fly!" and let the flapping begin.

> **"** Some great research at the University of Illinois shows that kids with symptoms of ADHD (Attention Deficit Hyperactivity Disorder) find their symptoms decreased with any kind of direct exposure to nature. We're beginning to learn that playing outdoors in nature increases the ability of a child to pay attention. **"**
>
> **—Richard Louv**
> author of *Last Child in the Woods: Saving Our Children from Nature-Deficit Disorder*

Part II:
Preschool Play
(age 3 to 5)

Three- to five-year-old play oozes with energy and excitement: While toddlers are just learning to walk and maneuver in the physical world, preschoolers have refined large and small motor skills, enabling them to run, skip, jump, chase, and use their hands with confidence. They love to create—building roads and bridges in the sandbox, making up silly songs, painting, and drawing. And their imaginations are in high gear too. Preschoolers are marvelous pretenders, inventing elaborate play using only a few simple props. They are keen observers who notice the tiniest of details about what grown-ups and workers wear and do—these observations are cleverly worked into their pretend-play scenarios.

Preschoolers are thrilled to have playmates and are happy to play *with* a friend in a collaborative or cooperative way (as opposed to the toddler style of playing with others that often involves playing *alongside* another child). Even the shy child is curious and excited to play with another child, once he gets warmed up to the new situation. Since children three to five are capable of following simple rules and instructions, group games suddenly become a big hit too.

And beneath all the excitement of running, building, creating, and pretending, preschoolers are making huge leaps and bounds in development as they play. Here is a glimpse at some of the ways children grow as they play from three to five.

Physical Development Large motor skills surge during the preschool years as children run, hop, skip, jump, dance, climb, kick a ball, ride tricycles, and learn about balance.

Small motor skills are mastered as children use their

hands and fingers for pouring and sifting, digging in sand, throwing a ball, coloring, cutting, pasting, turning pages, manipulating clay, paint and chalk, threading objects on strings, and using toy tools.

A tremendous sense of power also comes through physical play. You can see it in your child's expression (that says, "Look what I can do all by myself!") when she is swinging on a swing, sliding down the slide, or maneuvering a playground ball around the lawn.

Cognitive Development Preschoolers expand their brainpower and thinking skills exponentially through ordinary play. They understand quantities (more or less), begin to count, recognize shapes, match and sort, and understand categories. They learn about plants, animals, the natural world, try to figure out how things work, and recognize cause and effect. And they learn about letters and words (and the ideas and objects they represent), and move into making representational art.

Social and Emotional Development When children play, connecting with others and managing emotions and behavior happens in many small but meaningful ways. Social learning takes place gradually, through a preschooler's social successes and missteps. They learn about taking turns, sharing, and recognizing the needs and perspective of another child. Preschoolers use language to express their own wants, needs, and ideas, and to settle disputes with others. They even begin to use language in creative and humorous ways in their pretend play, by telling jokes and

> "When they get to school, the teachers tell us today's children can't negotiate; they're having trouble with social conversations. They're having trouble because they're accustomed to just pushing a button and the machine they're on just reacting to them. The other thing that's declining now is fantasy play, the ability to imagine, the ability to think up new scenarios, new stories, new ideas, and new concepts in your own head. Kids are having all these stories brought to them so vividly on the screen that they're not playing imaginatively themselves; and this has got to be a great loss in terms of the future of creativity of the people in this country."
>
> **—Jane M. Healy, Ph.D.**
> educational psychologist and author of *Your Child's Growing Mind*

inventing stories. And they will create elaborate pretend-play scenarios in order to understand or gain control over events in their lives. Group play creates opportunities to learn about playing fairly; as they discover what it means to collaborate with other children, they'll invent exciting play ideas by working together. Quite simply, they experience the joy of being a friend and having a friend.

The Well-Stocked Preschool Toy Cupboard

Many of the best playthings for preschoolers are either classic toys (like playground balls, blocks, beanbags, trucks, dolls, sandbox toys, and art supplies) or a mixture of toys and safe household items that become props for pretend play. These toys are well suited to the spontaneous, ad-lib style of play that is the hallmark of the preschool stage. Because preschoolers are not apt to put harmful things in their mouths, they now have access to a wider assortment of toys (art materials, bubbles, and objects and games with small parts). Since they have mastered large and small muscle control, their toys for physical play (from tricycles to swings) are different from those for toddlers too. On the other hand, many of the tried-and-true classic toddler toys still have appeal for a preschooler, but they will play in very different ways than during the one-to-two stage.

You certainly don't need to buy all of the toys on the Well-Stocked Preschooler Toy Cupboard list in Appendix II. In fact, you may be surprised to find how many household play items you already have. The important thing is to select toys geared to your child's age, capabilities, activity level, and interests. You know best what will light your child's fire. If, for example, your child is a rough-and-tumble little guy who loves the outdoors, then naturally he'll gravitate toward a dump truck and a mix of outdoor toys that encourage boisterous, run-around styles of play. But no need to stop there. Provide other toys to give your child a taste of additional types of play. For example, that rough-and-tumble preschooler may also love to make drawings, paintings, and music, if given the chance. Choose wisely to allow diverse play opportunities for your child. Flip to the Appendix to peruse the list of many toys and materials for encouraging fun, imaginative, and active play or head straight to the games and activities in the following pages.

Preschool Play (age 3 to 5)

Safe Preschool Play

Keeping your preschooler safe is a job that requires diligence, good thinking, and planning—but not obsession. You can't prevent every single scraped knee, but you can work to sidestep serious injuries and danger. The challenge is to strike a balance that allows you to keep an eye on safety while also allowing your child freedom to explore, play, and have a happy childhood.

The first step toward finding this balance begins with knowing your child well enough to see where her innocent perceptions and ideas might lead her astray. Next, take a realistic look at your surroundings and the safety concerns they present. It also helps to have a general understanding of what children at the preschool age are typically developmentally capable of—and what fascinations might draw them toward danger. Here are some ideas to keep in mind regarding preschool play and safety.

66 *Playgroups are a great opportunity for a child with a physical disability to gain a little more motivation to move and to mimic the movements of other children. The child with a physical disability may need some Velcro to keep his hands on the handlebars of the tricycle and maybe his feet on the pedals, and then, certainly, a caregiver should be very close by while the child is riding on the ride-on toy. A child may need Velcro on a glove to help her catch a ball. Or a particular size paddle to help her bat at a beach ball. The idea is that the adult thinks ahead about the equipment so the child with the disability will be able to participate.* 99

—Kristi Sayers Menear, Ph.D., CAPE
Assistant Professor of Human Studies at the
University of Alabama at Birmingham

• Preschoolers need constant adult supervision when they play outdoors. While they may have a superficial understanding that a passing car can hurt them, this thought can easily be overridden by their enthusiasm or excitement about chasing that rolling ball. Likewise, they may know about "stranger danger," but this does not mean they can be trusted 100 percent of the time to make sound decisions on their own about strangers. (This is particularly true for preschoolers, who have a high regard for adults and aim to please them.)

• Supervise all sidewalk and driveway play continuously. Accidents happen when a child strays onto the driveway or bends down to retrieve something fascinating from under the tire of a parked car. Even when standing upright, children can't necessarily be seen by drivers. Establish an iron-clad rule in your family that no one (even visitors) moves their car forward or backward before a head count is done to determine the whereabouts of all the children.

- Keep matches and lighters locked up and out of reach at all times. Preschoolers do not understand the dangers of fire and tend to be fascinated by it.

- Be close at hand to supervise when your child plays indoors and frequently check in with your child when he is playing in an adjacent room.

- Be aware when your child is playing with a toy that has wheels, especially around stairs. Preschoolers love to imitate, so an older sibling's skateboard may present a risk. (It's best to keep skateboards and other teenage toys out of sight, and make a rule that those toys are only to be used by the older child.)

- Supervise your child on swing sets, slides, and jungle gyms.

- Protect your child from head injuries by insisting she wears her bicycle helmet (even with training wheels, bikes have been known to tip over on tight curves and turns). It's a good habit to get into during these early years.

- Continue to keep safety latches in place on cabinets with chemicals and cleaning supplies throughout the preschool years.

- Carefully supervise all play involving water. Even buckets or tubs of water pose a danger to preschoolers, who might slip and fall or who don't fully understand the dangers of drowning.

- Be aware of the "dare you" factor, where a sibling or playmate presents a dare that preschoolers are willing to try. (My five-year-old daughter ate nearly a half dozen pats of real butter in kindergarten on the dare of a friend. Thank goodness it wasn't a more dangerous dare! Needless to say, there was quite a mess to clean up immediately thereafter.)

- Clearly convey safety rules and the need for constant supervision to all of your child care providers or teenage babysitters.

Preschool Play (age 3 to 5)

Solo Play

There are three main types of solo play covered in this section of the book. First, you'll discover what I call *Busy-Body Play.* Busy-body games and activities are ideal for the many occasions when you need a few minutes of concentration to make dinner or work in the kitchen while your child plays nearby. These games are designed for engaging your child's attention for ten or fifteen minutes and require only minimal setup and occasional adult help.

The second category, *Self-Directed Play,* is a freewheeling, unstructured style of play that unfolds rather naturally for your child when you provide the playthings and offer a bit of help to get things started. The last category is *Arts and Crafts,* which includes *Spontaneous Arts* and *Creative Crafts* ideas. These activities plunge your child into the world of imagination, experimentation, and invention.

Busy-Body Play

Busy-body play is ideal for the many times when you need a little time to accomplish a task and your child wants to play nearby. These are the times when parents typically are tempted to let electronic games or television keep children occupied. So in this section, I've provided you with unplugged play ideas for those times, very often using materials you'll already have on hand. The games and activities listed here require very little setup time, so you can get this play going in an instant.

The kitchen is an inviting place for preschool play. First, there are kitchen gadgets

What Good Things Happen When Your Child Plays Alone?

She learns to direct her own fun and exploration. She discovers new things and challenges herself. She is allowed to play at her own pace. She starts to learn persistence and how to deal with frustration. She turns on her imagination, invents pretend scenarios, and makes up stories. She learns how to entertain herself without Mom, Dad, or machine (electronic toys), and gives you a few minutes of quiet time.

and supplies that lend themselves to marvelous preschool-style activities (Sticker Sorter, Apple Polish, Spicy Soup for Hungry Caterpillars). A designated area on the smooth kitchen floor becomes a perfect spot for games with a little bit of action (Ping-Pong Roll-Along, Junior Bowling, or Beanbag Color Toss). The kitchen table or island is a natural place for your child to sit and ponder, sort, or create (with games like Supper Search, Button Bonanza, or Greetings for Grandma). But probably most important of all, your child loves the pleasure of your company, and the kitchen is where you are for a part of each day. So you'll find games in this section that you can play with your child while you work when time permits and the mood is right (Griddle Riddles and Knots and Numbers).

But I Don't Want to Stop Playing!

Preschoolers are notorious for having a bit of trouble making transitions from one activity (or place) to another. This is true in part because preschoolers truly live in the moment. If your child is happily engaged in playing with his dump truck, for example, all his attention is focused on that. He's enjoying the moment and just doesn't want to quit. And yet, the reality of family life is that sometimes your child's play will need to be interrupted. Here's a respectful way to move your child from one activity to another. A few minutes before it's truly time to stop playing, give your child a firm but friendly warning—"It will be time to put the truck away and have lunch in just a few minutes." This short announcement gives your child advance warning that one activity is about to end, and another one is about to start. For many children three to five, it helps them shift gears and make the transition from one activity to the next in good humor.

UNPLUGGED PLAY

Preschool Play (age 3 to 5)

★CLASSIC★
157 Kitchen Table Fort

As long as there are kitchen tables and blankets in the world, this one's a classic that will never go out of style. A kitchen table, magically transformed, becomes a stage for discovery where familiar toys and gadgets take on a new twist.

AGE: 3–5 YRS

CATEGORY:
SOLO PLAY/
BUSY-BODY

NUMBER OF
CHILDREN: ONE
OR MORE

Materials:

1 or 2 large bedsheets
  (to cover table and table legs completely)
Extra-wide packing tape
Toys
Stuffed animals
Safe kitchen gadgets, etc.

Setup:

Drape the sheet or sheets over the table so that the edges reach the floor on all sides. (If using two sheets, overlap them on the top of the table and tape them together.)

Play:

Collect toys and props from around the house, put them inside the fort, and let your child explore them in his new hidden place.

158 Dining Room Campout

Creating a private little world for your child is a wonderful way to give her time alone in her own mysterious world. All too often, we and our children get caught up in the frenzy of our lives; what a treat to be able to steal some time away for a campout!

AGE: 3–5 YRS

CATEGORY:
SOLO PLAY/
BUSY-BODY

NUMBER OF
CHILDREN: ONE
OR MORE

Materials:

Sleeping bag
Safe outdoor camping gear
Small cardboard box (for pretend camp stove)
Pots, pans, spatula, bowls, and cups
Teddy bear and dolls

Setup:

Gather all the camping gear into the dining room or living room and close the window blinds to make it "nighttime."

Play:

Encourage your child to cook a campout meal and serve it to her camp buddies (the teddy bear and dolls), and to sing songs by the "campfire" before settling down inside the sleeping bag.

❝The more complicated the toy, the more expensive the toy, the less imaginatively the child will use it. A child will play unbelievably with a ball or a stick or an old rag. But you give them some complicated thing that has to be assembled and costs a thousand dollars, you know . . . the toy does it all.**❞**

—Edward Hallowell, M.D.
psychiatrist and author of *Driven to Distraction* and *CrazyBusy*

159 Spicy Soup for Hungry Caterpillars

Would caterpillars really eat this spicy brew? Who knows, but it's a good way for little cooks-in-training to get creative in the kitchen.

AGE: **3–5 YRS**

CATEGORY: **SOLO PLAY/ BUSY-BODY**

NUMBER OF CHILDREN: **ONE OR MORE**

Materials:

Large plastic mixing bowl

Plastic spice jars filled with assorted, outdated spices

Large wooden spoon

Plastic or metal soup ladle

Small plastic cereal bowls

Kitchen chair

Apron

Small paper cook or chef's hat (available at paper supply stores)

Note: If you don't have many extra spices to spare, take a couple of empty spice jars and fill one with flour and one with parsley.

Setup:

Place the mixing bowl in the sink and fill it halfway with water. Arrange the collection of spice jars, utensils, and cereal bowls on the counter next to the sink. Pull up a chair to the sink for your child to stand on. If the sink is full of dishes, make Spicy Soup at the kitchen table instead. Simply place the bowl of water on top of two folded beach towels. There may still be a few water mishaps, but no need to cry over spilled soup! The peace and quiet during playtime may be worth a possible cleanup.

Play:

Ask your child to mix up some Spicy Soup to "feed" all the hungry caterpillars in the neighborhood. Let her ladle soup into bowls and dump it back into the mixing bowl time and again. When playtime is nearly over, ask your child to ladle a little soup into one bowl and place it outside on the porch for any hungry caterpillars who pass by at night!

*Safety Alerts: Never give your child any type of pepper or hot spice; young children may get spice in their eyes if they rub them while playing. Use a kitchen chair without sharp corners and supervise your child carefully. Make a family rule that your child must ask for your help anytime he wants to get up and down from the chair.

PARENT TIP

160 Tell Me About It!

❝*I get such a charge out of the things my son tells me each time I say, 'Tell me about what you're building.' He nearly always describes something he recently saw in real life that made a big impression. Last week, his preschool took a field trip to a fire station. Yesterday, when I asked what he was building with his blocks, he told me it was a firehouse and the man inside pushes a button and a really, really BIG bell rings a noise. I loved his rendition of that big bell ringing a noise. I've learned that if I ask the right question at the right moment, I hear all about his ideas and his imagination while he plays.* ❞

—Stan from Oregon

Preschool Play (age 3 to 5)

UNPLUGGED PLAY

161 Griddle Riddles

The family cook says, "I'm thinking of a food that is Dad's favorite thing to eat on Sunday morning. What is it?" Your observant preschooler makes guesses to try to get an answer. Broccoli? No! Waffles and sausages? Yes!

QUICK & EASY

AGE: **3–5 YRS**

CATEGORY: **SOLO PLAY/ BUSY-BODY**

NUMBER OF CHILDREN: **ONE**

Play:

Your child selects one of the following categories and you provide a series of clues to help him guess: A Person I Know; Something to Eat; An Animal I Have Seen (this can be a type of animal or a familiar pet in the extended family or neighborhood). Once the category is requested, the cook thinks of a person, a food, or an animal and gives one initial clue to describe it. For example, if the category is food (Something to Eat) and the cook is thinking of pizza, she might offer this first clue: "It's something our family eats every weekend after Jed's soccer game." The child takes a guess. If he guesses incorrectly, the cook offers another clue: "It's the food that Anna's dog ate right off my plate when I left the table." Once the correct guess is made, the child picks another category and the process is repeated.

> **❝** There are so many things that you can do that encourage play for your child. And then to see the child come up with things that you hadn't even thought of; that's the best of all! **❞**
>
> **—Fred Rogers**
> Emmy award–winning creator and host of
> *Mister Rogers' Neighborhood*

162 Knots and Numbers

For children who've learned how to tie knots, this is a nice quiet-time activity—well, sort of quiet. The object is to tie a ribbon into as many knots as possible before the kitchen timer goes off.

QUICK & EASY

AGE: **3–5 YRS**

CATEGORY: **SOLO PLAY/ BUSY-BODY**

NUMBER OF CHILDREN: **ONE**

Materials:

Grosgrain ribbon (3' to 4' in length)

Kitchen timer

Large die

Setup:

Tie the ribbon (at its midpoint) to a handle or knob on a kitchen cabinet so that you have 2 long strands of ribbon hanging down that can be used for the tying part of this game.

Play:

Challenge your child to tie as many knots as possible in the ribbon before the buzzer sounds. (Set the timer for 3 to 4 minutes the first time, to gauge how much time your child might need to fill the ribbon with knots, and adjust the timer accordingly for future rounds of play.) When the buzzer sounds, count the knots with your child.

163 Knots and Numbers on a Roll

For an extra challenge, create a variation of this game, where your child rolls a die and ties the number of knots indicated on the die, then rolls the die again and ties more knots, all with the kitchen timer ticking. He repeats this rolling of the die and tying knots without stopping until the buzzer sounds. Then you both count the total number of knots on the ribbon. (Hint: This game is not about winning, so give your child a realistic goal at the start of the game.)

164 Ping-Pong Roll-Along

Here's how four-year-old Dominic described this game: "You sweep the ball with the flyswatter around the cans and stuff." That's a perfect description of this indoor, miniature golf–like game, in which you'll construct the obstacle course for your budding preschool golfer.

AGE: 3–5 YRS

CATEGORY: SOLO PLAY / BUSY-BODY

NUMBER OF CHILDREN: ONE

Materials:

- 6 to 10 soup cans
- Markers (for adult use only)
- Index cards
- Large plastic cup
- Invisible tape
- Ping-Pong balls (or plastic Wiffle golf balls, which are easier to control)
- Brand-new, clean flyswatter

Setup:

This game can be played on wood, linoleum, or carpet, preferably in a large room. Let your child select the surface area on which it seems easiest to control and maneuver the ball around. Using soup cans, set up an obstacle course of sorts in the center of the room. Place two cans side by side with 4 inches between them, for example, and the ball

will be aimed between the cans. Other cans are placed alone in the center of the room, the idea being to send the ball in a circle around the can. Write a number on an index card corresponding to each can's intended order in the obstacle course. Place each numbered card on the ground near its can. Create a finish line by placing the plastic cup on its side and taping it to the carpet or floor.

Play:

Your child taps the Ping-Pong or Wiffle ball with the flyswatter and directs the ball through the obstacle course to the finish line.

165 Expand Your Course

Use the entire first floor of your house to create a miniature golf–type obstacle course.

166 Beanbag Color Toss

Color recognition, hand–eye coordination, and movement are all involved in this simple kitchen tossing game. For all you multitaskers, this is a game you can easily get (and keep) going while tending to household chores.

AGE: 3–5 YRS

CATEGORY: SOLO PLAY/ BUSY-BODY

NUMBER OF CHILDREN: ONE

Materials:

- Invisible tape
- A variety of colored construction paper
- Beanbags

Setup:

Use a strip of tape to create a line across the kitchen floor and tape pieces of colored construction paper to the floor about 3 inches away from the line. The papers should be spread out in a semi-random fashion.

Preschool Play (age 3 to 5)

Play:

Select a color and challenge your child to hit the corresponding paper target with a beanbag. If you say, "Three red squares," your child keeps tossing until he lands a beanbag on the red square three times. He might prefer to play on his own, choosing his own color targets.

167 Bowl Toss

Put a variety of plastic bowls or pans in the center of the floor; your preschooler tries to toss the beanbags into the bowls. Just like in billiards, the player can either predict which bowl he plans to hit or randomly try his luck.

168 Hats Ahoy

Place two kitchen chairs across from each other; take two yardsticks and lay them side by side across the chairs, extending from one seat to the other. Line the yardsticks with various hats. Mark a line a short distance away and try to knock the hats off with the beanbags.

> **"**As parents, we often move to a default position of turning on the TV, and we don't even care what's on—it's just something to occupy us. Whereas if we approach kids in an active way and say, "Tell us what you really like doing. What would you like to do instead of watching TV?," chances are they will generate a very long and interesting list for you. **"**
>
> **—Michael Rich, M.D.**
> Director of the Center on Media and Child Health, Children's Hospital–Boston, and Assistant Professor of Pediatrics, Harvard Medical School

169 Too Many Pizzas!

A wacky game of mixed-up numbers and way too many pizzas! This is a splendid numbers game to play when your child is nearby while you are making dinner or doing the dishes.

AGE: **3–5 YRS**

CATEGORY:
**SOLO PLAY/
BUSY-BODY**

NUMBER OF
CHILDREN: **ONE
OR MORE**

Materials:
Deck of playing cards

Setup:
Remove the aces, kings, queens, and jacks from the deck. Also remove any high numbers that your child might not yet recognize. (For a five-year-old, you may be able to leave all the remaining cards; for a three-year-old, you may wish to play only with a few low numbers like 2, 3, and 4.)

Play:
Start off this game with the following lines: "I called [insert name of your favorite pizzeria] to order one pizza. But, when I went to pick up my pizza, they mixed up my order. How many pizzas do you think they *really* gave me?" Your child draws a card from the deck and announces the number indicated on the playing card—*"Ten pizzas!"* Continue by ad-libbing other silly number questions involving people, animals, favorite foods, trips to the grocery store, birthday presents—whatever you can think of to delight your child.

170 Sticker Sorter

Sorting is the type of busybody activity preschoolers love. They get to peel and stick, work with their understanding of shapes and sizes, and be Mommy or Daddy's little helper in the kitchen. Most of all, as all good teachers know, colorful stickers can make anything appealing—even homework!

AGE: **3–5 YRS**

CATEGORY:
**SOLO PLAY
BUSY-BODY**

NUMBER OF
CHILDREN: **ONE
OR MORE**

Materials:
Canned goods from your pantry

Color dot stickers (available at office supply stores)

Setup:
Arrange all your canned goods in a low kitchen cupboard.

Play:
Have your child put stickers on the lids of all your canned goods to help you sort and organize. Here are three possible ways to sort with stickers:

1. Green dots on green veggies, red dots on tomatoes and tomato sauces, yellow for corn and beans.

2. Blue dots on large cans and red dots on small cans (for stacking and sorting, to make more room in the cupboard).

3. Red dots on the top of the can, yellow dots on the bottom (the picture on the can helps show which end is up).

4. Yellow dots on the foods your child loves.

5. Pink dots on the cans for the family pet.

171 Apple Polish

Preschoolers get serious about their apple-polishing, and the assembly-line setup makes their work all the more official. You'll have gleaming apples in your fruit bowl in no time.

AGE: **3–5 YRS**

CATEGORY:
**SOLO PLAY/
BUSY-BODY**

NUMBER OF
CHILDREN: **ONE
OR MORE**

Materials:
Beach towel

Small mixing bowl

Fuzzy kitchen towel

Thin soft kitchen towel

Large mixing bowl

Large bag of apples

Setup:
Fold the beach towel in half and place it on the kitchen table, where your apple polisher will be working. Fill the small mixing bowl with several inches of water and put it on top of the folded beach towel. Place the two polishing cloths (kitchen towels) on one side of the bowl and the large empty bowl on the other to create your assembly line. Open the bag of apples and give a quick polishing demonstration.

Play:
Your child dips the apples in the water, dries and shines them, and places them in the large empty bowl.

Preschool Play (age 3 to 5)

172 Bigfoot

QUICK & EASY

AGE: **3–5 YRS**

CATEGORY:
**SOLO PLAY/
BUSY-BODY**

NUMBER OF
CHILDREN: **ONE**

Though your child can play this one on her own, you might not be able to resist the temptation to leave your "adult" duties behind to watch her conquer your house with her huge, scary paws. (And she might not be able to stop herself from throwing a few growls in for good measure!)

Materials:

Kitchen timer

Large die

Play:

Set the kitchen timer for 7 to 10 minutes. Your child rolls the die on the floor. The number shown on the die dictates the number of giant steps she's allowed to take as she travels from room to room. (She takes the die with her as she travels about the house. Once she reaches each step-counting destination, she throws the die again, picks it up, and clomps along on her merry way.) The object is to see how many rooms your child can make it through before the kitchen timer buzzes.

173 Junior Bowling

QUICK & EASY

AGE: **3–5 YRS**

CATEGORY:
**SOLO PLAY/
BUSY-BODY**

NUMBER OF
CHILDREN: **ONE**

Buy a team bowling shirt from the local thrift store to make this watery bowling game really official. The bottles make a really satisfying "plop" when they go over.

Materials:

Small plastic water or soda bottles, with screw-on lids (dig into your recycling bin)

Playground ball or tennis ball (depending on child's ability and challenge level)

1-minute egg timer

Setup:

Partially fill the plastic bottles with water. (The more water added, the harder the bowling pins will be to topple. For the youngest children, fill the bottles a third full.) Screw the caps back on tightly. Line up the bowling pins on a hard floor surface, in a V formation.

Play:

Your child stands several feet back from the bowling pins and rolls the ball toward the pins to see how many can be knocked down. Putting the pins back up can be part of the fun too. Use a one-minute egg timer and challenge your child to put the pins up before the timer stops.

❝Ladies' neck scarves are wonderful playthings because children can throw them up in the air, and they're slow to come down and catch. So if the child has some challenges with visual tracking skills or opening and closing his or her hand, that scarf is going to float in the air a lot longer than, say, a beanbag or a ball is.❞

—Kristi Sayers Menear, Ph.D., CAPE
Assistant Professor of Human Studies
at the University of Alabama at Birmingham

174 Puzzler Matchup

Help your child create her own puzzle on the spot! This homemade challenge is a good way to get some use out of all those old magazines you've got lying around.

QUICK & EASY

AGE: 4–5 YRS

CATEGORY:
SOLO PLAY/
BUSY-BODY

NUMBER OF
CHILDREN: ONE

Materials:

4 to 6 interesting full-page color photos
cut from a magazine

Scissors (for adult use only)

Nontoxic white glue

Construction paper

6 paper grocery bags

Setup:

When you're cutting up your magazines, try to select pages with children, animals, or other colorful items that might be of interest. Glue each large image to a full sheet of construction paper (if you have a little time, your child can help). After the glue is dry, take a minute and cut each photo into four, six, or nine equal pieces, depending on your child's ability and age. No need to get fancy by creating complexly shaped puzzle pieces—simple rectangles, squares, and triangles work well. Each magazine page becomes a puzzle to solve! Put the pieces for each puzzle in separate paper bags and mix them up a bit. (If you are able to preplan, you could do these steps ahead of time and set the bags aside until the right moment presents itself.)

Play:

Your child works to solve the puzzles on her own, reaching into each bag and taking the pieces out one at a time, matching the pieces together, and moving along to the next puzzle.

175 Puzzler Mix-up Matchup

Create more of a challenge by combining the pieces from three or four puzzles inside one bag. Your child will sort through the pieces and may discover some silly matchups along the way.

176 Greetings for Grandma

It's so nice to make something for someone else. And homemade greeting cards far outshine commercial cards in the eyes of grandparents across the land—you'll be surprised at how long treasures like these will stay in the family.

QUICK & EASY

AGE: 3–5 YRS

CATEGORY:
SOLO PLAY/
BUSY-BODY

NUMBER OF
CHILDREN: ONE

Materials:

Package of colored construction paper
(20 to 30 sheets)

Nontoxic markers

Glitter glue

Small scraps of ribbon

Buttons

Standard white greeting card envelopes

Setup:

Fold each piece of construction paper in half width-wise, and fold it in half again to create a standard greeting card.

Play:

Your child decorates the outside of each card with a lovely design created with markers, glitter glue, ribbons, and buttons. On both inside flaps, she prints numbers and letters she has learned or creates another design. When she is finished, she should print her name as well.

177 Dunkin' Ducks

While you're cooking at the stove or chopping on the counter, set your preschooler up for some dunk-a-licious play at the sink. The ducks won't stand a chance.

AGE: **3–5 YRS**

CATEGORY: **SOLO PLAY/ BUSY-BODY**

NUMBER OF CHILDREN: **ONE**

Materials:
  Food coloring
  Plastic squeeze bottles (empty mustard or
    mayonnaise container) filled with water
  2 or 3 floatable plastic ducks or tub toys
  Kitchen chair

Setup:
Fill your kitchen sink with a few inches of water. Add a few drops of food coloring to the water in each plastic squeeze bottle. Place the plastic tub toys in the sink, and position a sturdy kitchen chair right up to the sink for your child to stand on.

Play:
The dunker aims the squirt bottle at the toys to try to move them from side to side with water pressure. (The ducks won't truly be dunked under the water, but moving them around the sink pond is lots of fun.) When the squirt bottle is empty, the lid comes off and the bottle is easily refilled by submerging it in the water.

178 Dunkin' Ducks Outdoors

Use a baby pool or plastic dishpan on the lawn or on the porch for an outdoor version of this game.

SAFETY ALERT: Always provide supervision during water plays and dump the water out of the pool as soon as playtime is over.

179 Supper Search

This great predinner game will visually whet your child's appetite. And since flipping through magazines is usually a quiet, grown-up activity, your preschooler will be excited to see it modified into this fast-paced, picture-finding pastime.

AGE: **3–5 YRS**

CATEGORY: **SOLO PLAY/ BUSY-BODY**

NUMBER OF CHILDREN: **ONE**

Materials:
  Magazines
  Kitchen timer
  Nontoxic marker
    or pencil
  Paper

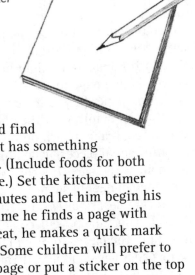

Play:
Challenge your child to flip through a magazine and find every page that has something to eat or drink. (Include foods for both pets and people.) Set the kitchen timer for 5 to 10 minutes and let him begin his search. Each time he finds a page with something to eat, he makes a quick mark on the paper. (Some children will prefer to tear out each page or put a sticker on the top corner.) When the buzzer sounds, it's time to count all the marks and come up with the grand total.

180 Theme-Based Search

Call out a common object or animal (dog, cat, shoe, car), depending on the magazine.

181 Macaroni Mix-up

Once you see that this sorting game buys you a few minutes of time, you'll be searching for every pasta shape known to humankind. And never underestimate the pleasure of saying the word macaroni!

QUICK & EASY

AGE: **3–5 YRS**
CATEGORY:
SOLO PLAY/ BUSY-BODY
NUMBER OF CHILDREN: **ONE**

Materials:
Mixture of various dried pasta shapes (elbow, ziti, bow tie, spiral, penne, shells, wheels, etc.)
Dried kidney beans
Dried navy beans
Plastic tub with lid
Muffin tin
Plastic grocery bag

Setup:
Create a mixture using a large variety of dried

pasta shapes and dried beans and place it in the plastic tub. Put the lid on the container and shake to mix the ingredients.

Play:
Ask your child to help you cook by sorting the ingredients in the tub and separating them in the muffin tin.

Tip: When the sorting is finished, place the muffin tin inside a plastic grocery bag, tip the ingredients into it, and then pour the contents back into the plastic tub and secure the lid. (If you tip the contents directly from the muffin tin into the tub, the final step of this game will involve *you* on hands and knees picking the macaroni and beans from the floor.)

Note: If you think your child might be reluctant to see her work undone, simply provide a little extra time, and some small storage bags, so she can store each type of pasta in its own bag.

Preschool Play (age 3 to 5)

Favorite Toys for Busy-Body Play

The best toys will invite your child to explore and invent his own way of playing. Every child is wired differently, so know that some will hold your child's attention better than others. Here's a list of classic toys for busy-body solo play—experiment to see which toys strike *your* child's fancy.

Plastic grocery cart and grocery props
Dress-up clothes
Blocks
Kitchen set (with pots, pans, bowls, and plastic food or cardboard boxes)
Toy tools and tool belt

Trains, cars, trucks, and ramps
Dolls and doll accessories
Stuffed animals and props (boxes, tea set, picnic set, wagon)
Farm animals and people (plastic or wood) with props

Toy cash register and play money
Puzzles
Doctor's kit
Books
Art supplies (markers, crayons, paper, scissors, glue stick)

182 | Story Basket

A basket and some old magazines become brainstorming fodder in this kitchen-table activity. Let your child be the storyteller, and listen to her while you cook. It'll make for some interesting conversation during dinner too!

AGE: 3–5 YRS

CATEGORY: SOLO PLAY/ BUSY-BODY

NUMBER OF CHILDREN: ONE

Materials:
1 or 2 magazines (with color photos and photo ads)
Scissors (for adult use only)
Medium-size basket

Setup:
Select one or two popular magazines containing many color ads and photos featuring people in various scenarios. (Find people doing things indoors and out, people with happy expressions and serious expressions, children at play, etc.) Cut out the most interesting of these photos and put them in the basket.

Play:
Your child sorts through the picture basket to find a photo that interests her and creates a story about the people or animals in the picture. To help your child get started, encourage her to give the person (or animal) a name and tell a story about what he is doing and who his friends are. Some parents enjoy taking a turn telling their own tall tale about a different picture in the story basket.

183 | Button Bonanza

Years ago, a four-year-old boy asked me why we didn't put a button on the banana so we could "close it up and save it for later." To this day, whenever I see a button box, I am reminded of this wonderful question.

AGE: 3–5 YRS

CATEGORY: SOLO PLAY/ BUSY-BODY

NUMBER OF CHILDREN: ONE

Materials:
Large button box filled with assorted buttons
Muffin tin

Setup:
Help your child select buttons in different colors, one color for each muffin compartment. Put your button box with the rest of the buttons in the center of the table.

Play:
Your child matches and sorts the buttons as he drops the buttons in their compartments in the muffin tin.

184 | Large and Small

Mix in some very large buttons and designate one cup for large buttons and one cup for small, and sort by size instead of color.

185 | Two, Three, or Four Holes

Sort the buttons into three cups by separating the buttons according to the number of holes each has.

Self-Directed Play

Preschool children are truly in their element when they direct their own play. Child development experts say that self-directed play allows your child to create play scenarios to perfectly suit his curious mind, his interests, and his physical capabilities. Still, preschoolers sometimes need someone to jump-start an idea or challenge to get solo play moving. When the play really gets under way, one clever idea usually leads to another. You can almost see your child's brain at work: "I wonder what would happen if I put this thing on top of that thing?"

To encourage self-directed solo play, your job is to provide playthings that your child can manipulate (perhaps with a bit of a challenge) and that capture his attention and imagination. These are often inexpensive toys and household items that can be adapted for all sorts of play possibilities. Second, think of yourself as a supporting actor who has a bit part in the theater of your child's self-directed play. Most of the time you are in the wings, quietly observing the action. Every now and then, especially in the beginning to get things started, you may be needed to utter a short line like, "Can you build two different kinds of buildings from these LEGOs?"

Following are some of my favorite preschool toys and props for inspiring open-ended solo play. Because it's true that children sometimes need brief, adult help, you'll notice that each play activity has several ideas for parents to help jump-start the play or extend the play. You'll see that the "Play" directions have been omitted. That means once you've done the setting up, your child's imagination takes over—no directions necessary! For some games, you'll see a section called "Jump-start," which contains ideas for getting the play started or for keeping it going.

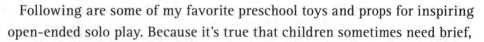

> " Pretend play is telling stories, in a way. If you look at the development of pretend play, it very much parallels the development of language. As language develops, the sorts of things that they can play become more elaborate. So by two they're playing slightly more elaborate pretend games; by three they've expanded; and by four, four and a half, we've really gotten into the realm of real storytelling. "
>
> **—Dorothy Einon, Ph.D.**
> author of *How Children Learn Through Play*

Preschool Play (age 3 to 5)

Preschool Play (age 3 to 5)

★CLASSIC★

186 Dress-Up

There's an actor inside every child, and setting your child loose on a wacky assortment of cast-off clothing is just the way to awaken her. Dress-up never, ever, goes out of style.

QUICK & EASY

AGE: **3–5 YRS**

CATEGORY:
**SOLO PLAY/
SELF-DIRECTED**

NUMBER OF
CHILDREN: **ONE
OR MORE**

Materials:
Men and women's hats of every
   type: hard hats, fancy hats,
   baseball caps, ski caps, straw hats

Other accessories: old reading glasses
   (remove lenses), work gloves, scarves,
   ski goggles, sunglasses, sun visor, neckties,
   briefcases, backpacks, old wallets, purses,
   beaded evening bags, bandanas

Jewelry: broken watches, clip-on earrings,
   bracelets, necklaces, rings

Shoes: work or snow boots, shoes, slippers, sandals

Clothing: shirts, pants, vests, skirts, dresses,
   jackets, sweaters, slips, pajamas, robes, snow
   pants, ski pants, raincoats, ponchos, capes
   (with a hair clip to hold it in place), shawls,
   mesh curtains (for brides and ghosts),
   Hawaiian shirts, lab coats, bowling shirts,
   sports shirts, swimming trunks, leotards

> ❝I think favorite tried and tested games
> depend a little on the child. You need to
> watch your child carefully and see what
> it is that your child enjoys, because your
> child's an individual and not necessarily
> like everybody else's. ❞
>
> **—Dorothy Einon, Ph.D.**
> author of *How Children Learn Through Play*

Setup:
Gather up old clothes in advance and add to the collection from yard sales, thrift stores, and Grandma's attic. Store all the dress-up props in an old suitcase on wheels for easy maneuvering. Encourage your child to gather up other household items and props (nonbreakable, of course) that she can use in her play, such as kitchen items, office and school supplies, calculators, dolls, books, riding toys, etc. Small wagons or toy shopping carts are ideal for gathering and hauling these props.

Jump-start:
- **Secret Identity** Challenge your child to pick out an outfit, put it on (complete with accessories and props), and come over to wherever you are working, so you can "guess" at her identity or occupation. With many outfit changes, this play can go on for quite some time.

- **Dress for the Occasion** Suggest a person your child might imitate, such as Grandma, and a place she might go, such as church, and challenge your child to dress like Grandma would for this occasion. Some children find it overwhelming to sort through a pile of random dress-up clothes. With this in mind, you can create "outfits" that have some theme (Mom, Dad, farmer, bowler) and put each one in a giant ziplock bag. (Store all these bags inside the dress-up suitcase.)

187 Blocks and Building Toys

Don't give those wooden toddler blocks away just yet. Preschoolers will use these and other blocks in new, inventive ways!

QUICK & EASY

AGE: 3–5 YRS

CATEGORY:
SOLO PLAY/
SELF-DIRECTED

NUMBER OF CHILDREN: ONE OR MORE

Materials:

Blocks: wooden blocks, interlocking logs, LEGOs, Tinkertoy Classic Jr. Building Set (wooden, no small parts), large cardboard or plastic brick blocks (hollow)

Vehicles: cars, trucks, trains, airplanes
People and animals: action figures, farm or zoo animals, dolls, stuffed animals
Furniture: doll furniture, small plastic tubs and containers, shoe boxes and other small cardboard boxes and tubes, miniature toy ladder, fences, trees, road signs

Jump-start:

Preschoolers love a challenge. If things get bogged down, get creative with a loose request: "Can you make a circle all the way around your teddy bear using these wooden blocks?"

Containers for Storing Blocks

Children love to mix and match all sorts of blocks into their building creations. With a little bit of planning, you can create a storage system to keep blocks tucked neatly away when they're not in use. Designate a bin for each type of building block, so that wooden blocks, LEGOs, and cardboard bricks each have their own stackable container. Here are some suggested containers:

Clear plastic shoe box (with lid) for small blocks

Colorful, plastic milk crates (available at office supply and multipurpose stores)

Underbed storage tubs with lid and wheels (designed to slide under the bed)

Oversize plastic food-storage tubs with lids

Wicker baskets

Heavy-duty, clear plastic bag with large zipper (comforters and quilts are sold in these bags)

Small carry-on suitcase or recycled child's suitcase on wheels (often available at thrift stores)

Cardboard file box with lid and handles (from office supply store), covered in butcher paper (or fabric) and decorated with markers

Preschool Play (age 3 to 5)

Prescool Play (age 3 to 5)

188 Sand-Cake Impressions

Awaken the little sculptor in your preschooler by setting her up to make "impressions" in damp sand. Children love seeing how images appear and disappear naturally in the sand.

QUICK & EASY

AGE: **3–5 YRS**

CATEGORY:
**SOLO PLAY/
SELF-DIRECTED**

NUMBER OF
CHILDREN: **ONE**

Materials:

Clean play sand (available at toy stores)

9" cake pan (unbreakable)

Spray bottle filled with water

Objects for creating impressions in the sand: empty soda or water bottles (the bottom surface has contours that make a flower pattern when pressed), empty thread spools, seashells, hands, fingers, feet, corks, plastic spice jars, forks, spoons

Setup:

Pour several inches of clean play sand into the cake pan and set it on a clean patch of grass or sidewalk. Spray it with a fine mist of water so the sand becomes wet enough to hold impressions.

Jump-start:

Your child directs this play by lightly pressing the objects listed above (and others you discover in your kitchen) into the damp sand. Handprints are easily made too. After each impression is finished, show your child how to smooth out the image for another round of play by using her hand or by gently shaking the pan back and forth. (When play is done, bring the pan inside and store the sand inside a large ziplock bag for another day.)

189 Indoor Sand-Cake Impressions

You can move this activity indoors if you are willing to risk a little bit of sand on the kitchen floor. Simply place a large bathroom rug with nonslip backing on the hard floor; your child can play with the sand-cake pan on top of this rug. When play is done, gather up the four corners of the rug and take it (and your child) outside for a little dusting off.

SAFETY ALERT: Supervise carefully to prevent children from eating or throwing sand.

Treasures and Toys at Teacher Supply Stores

A couple of years ago, I discovered the most amazing assortment of pretend-play props, toys, and arts and crafts supplies at our local teacher supply store. I've since learned that most cities have one or more teacher supply or school supply stores—yet many parents have not yet had the pleasure of visiting one! You won't find the latest electronic toys or video games, but you *will* find hundreds of items that are just right for unplugged play: wooden toys, kitchen sets, zoo animals, cooking utensils, dump trucks, bulldozers, building blocks, play tool kits, science kits, and many small, inexpensive props that will inspire your child to create her own unique way to pretend. To find a teacher supply store in your area, do a quick search at the National School Supply Equipment Association website: www.teacherstores.com.

190 | Tools and Fix-It Play

This is a beloved form of pretend play for children playing alone. And the commentary your child offers while he plays makes for marvelous eavesdropping.

AGE: **3–5 YRS**

CATEGORY: **SOLO PLAY/ SELF-DIRECTED**

NUMBER OF CHILDREN: **ONE OR MORE**

Materials:

Catalogs or magazines

Sheet or blanket

Preschool-style toy hand tools (for indoor play) and child's garden tools (for outdoor play)

Small bench (for workbench)

Toolbox

Giant cardboard box or table fort (for workshop)

Extras: safety goggles, wooden blocks, scraps of lumber, fine sandpaper or sanding blocks, large paintbrushes, paint rollers and paint tray, plastic plumbing pipe, fixtures, riding toys (for mechanical fix-it play), wagon, work gloves, hat, carpenter's apron, ruler, tape measure, yardstick, level, carpenter pencil and paper, small squeeze bottle (pretend oil), wheelbarrow, watering can, rags

Jump-start:

Tear pictures from catalogs or magazines of all the household items that need to be "fixed" (the wagon, stroller, tricycle, hinges on the suitcase, etc.). Set up a "fix-it" area for your little worker so he has his own makeshift repair shop. Place a sheet or blanket on the floor and encourage him to keep all equipment and tools in this spot. Make clear that your child is just "pretending" to fix real household items, so nothing gets plugged in or taken apart during these play fix-it activities. When your child is finished "fixing" everything, he writes up a "bill" to show how much you owe for all his work!

191 | Kitchen Set Play

Your child may pretend to be a short-order cook at a diner, a mom cooking dinner for her child, a cafeteria cook, or a street vendor making chili dogs. A play kitchen set is just the toy to get this splendid solo play going!

AGE: **3–5 YRS**

CATEGORY: **SOLO PLAY/ SELF-DIRECTED**

NUMBER OF CHILDREN: **ONE OR MORE**

Materials:

Large plastic kitchen stove, sink, and fridge combo (or your child makes her own imaginative kitchen set combo by using medium-size cardboard boxes turned upside down)

Kitchen items (plastic mixing bowls, small pots and pans, wire whisk, spatula, picnic blanket, plastic plates and cups, cookie sheet, cake pans, plastic pitcher, apron, chef's hat, dishpan, sponge, and water for washing dishes)

Empty food boxes and cartons (from eggs, cake mixes, pudding, rice, or pizza)

Plastic or wooden fruits, vegetables, cookies, pizza (available at toy stores)

Baby doll with high chair, stuffed animals

Toy shopping cart or basket

Jump-start:

Ask your child to go to the "grocery store" (kitchen pantry or cupboard) with her shopping cart or basket and pick out four foods to make a special dessert for the family. (This is all "pretend" of course, but it's good to have a couple of low shelves in the pantry with cans and boxes of food that are okay for kitchen play.)

Preschool Play (age 3 to 5)

192 Trains, Trucks, Cars, and Ramps

Your child can drive the subway train, moonlight as a garbageman, or drive a huge truck filled with circus animals, all in one day. There are endless possibilities, and only simple props are needed to set the stage.

QUICK & EASY

AGE: **3–5 YRS**

CATEGORY: **SOLO PLAY/ SELF-DIRECTED**

NUMBER OF CHILDREN: **ONE OR MORE**

Materials:

Vehicles: toy trucks of every kind, cars, buses, trains, motorcycles, airplanes, helicopters

For ramps: cardboard boxes, cookie sheets, boards, books

For tunnels: big books propped open and laid upside down so cars can pass underneath, blocks stacked up on both sides of the "road" with paper or cardboard taped to the top

For lanes, roadway, and racetrack: pipe cleaners (to make lanes), wooden blocks, poster board and markers (to make racetrack or obstacle course)

Kitchen timer (for races)

Miscellaneous props: shoe boxes (parking garage), straws for water hoses or gas pumps, plastic tubs, water and rags for car wash, small toy animals and people, doll furniture (moving-van play)

Jump-start:

• **Car Lot** Set up a car show or create a car lot where cars and trucks can be bought, sold, and traded.

• **Small Haul** Large car carriers or trucks can haul small cars from one room to the next (the fix-it shop) for various repairs.

• **Truckin'** Give your child the kitchen timer so he can "time" how many passes the truck can make around the room, how quickly he can line up the vehicles in some sort of order (big to small), or how quickly he can dump 4 loads of blocks.

• **Lineup** Collect every car in the house and line them up along windowsills or in a long line across the floor.

• **Racetrack** Challenge your child to set up roads or racetracks, complete with ramps, and put on a "race," testing out every car in the house to see which ones go the fastest. After each race, set up new ramps and test out the speed again.

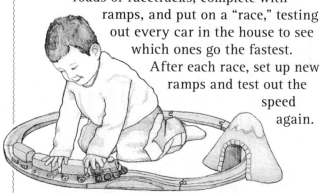

Parents Are Pretenders Too

While it's true that preschoolers are masters at pretend play (and like to be the boss of their play), they also enjoy pretend play with parents. There's something thrilling for your child about seeing grown-up, organized, all-knowing Mom or Dad down on the floor, pretending to be a race car driver at the speedway and racing miniature cars around the track. These moments of play are pure pleasure for your child; and what a lucky thing for you to be invited into your child's magical world of pretend.

193 Doll Play

Most children won't need much encouragement to take an interest in their dolls (baby dolls hold a special interest for preschool children). As they play, preschoolers incorporate familiar family routines or invent elaborate fantasy play.

QUICK & EASY

AGE: 3–5 YRS

CATEGORY: SOLO PLAY/ SELF-DIRECTED

NUMBER OF CHILDREN: **ONE OR MORE**

Materials:

A variety of dolls

Extras: stroller, high chair, baby pack (carrier), wagon, toy grocery cart, baby bottles, cups, plates, utensils, diapers, blankets, clothes, empty shampoo bottles, washcloth, towels, plastic tub and soap for bathing, comb, brush, mirror, shoe boxes (to turn into house, bed, car, school bus), pretend doctor set, storybooks, baby rattles and toys, small wading pool

Jump-start:

Challenge your child to use a wagon to take all the dolls on a field trip (to a museum, aquarium, zoo, baseball game, etc.). Gather up a few props so your child can create the "field trip" scene—zoo animals, tent, chairs, etc.

> **"** Children are constantly creative. They're constantly trying out things to see how they work, fiddling around with things. They're always, always investigating. I think they are being creative whenever they're playing. So we shouldn't just think of creativity in terms of arts and crafts. **"**
>
> **—Dorothy Einon, Ph.D.**
> author of *How Children Learn Through Play*

194 Stuffed Animals

Playing with stuffed animals has its own special allure. These furry critters might become a friendly little play pal one minute and magically transform into wild and ferocious creatures in the next moment of play.

QUICK & EASY

AGE: 3–5 YRS

CATEGORY: SOLO PLAY/ SELF-DIRECTED

NUMBER OF CHILDREN: **ONE OR MORE**

Materials:

Stuffed animals of every kind

Extras: tea set, wagon, riding toys, hats, scarves, recycled baby clothes, books, puppets, small- and medium-size cardboard boxes (to make beds, cars, home, cave, etc.), bells, cymbals, kazoo, tambourine, tablecloth or sheet (to make a picnic or fort), camping gear, school setup and supplies, stroller, child's umbrella

Jump-start:

• **Stuffed Animal Circus** Stuffed animals act out stories from favorite children's books. Create a puppet show for stuffed animals. Make a tent (drape a tablecloth or sheet over a table) where animals can perform circus acts, or tape a pillowcase across the bottom of the doorway to create a "curtain."

• **Stuffed Animals on Tour** Challenge your child to take his favorite animals on a trip to visit a special place that the bears (or bunnies) have never seen before. Props will be helpful to set the stage for that "special place"—a beach, a big city, etc.

Preschool Play (age 3 to 5)

Preschool Play (age 3 to 5)

195 Farm (or Zoo) Animal Play Set

There is something magical about setting up a farm or zoo environment and tending to the animals. This open-ended play is exciting for children who have visited a real farm or zoo, or who have become familiar with these fascinating critters in a favorite storybook.

QUICK & EASY

AGE: 3–5 YRS

CATEGORY:
SOLO PLAY/
SELF-DIRECTED

NUMBER OF
CHILDREN: ONE
OR MORE

Materials:

Set of preschool-style plastic or wooden farm (or zoo) animals

Plastic people (farmer and his family or workers to help on the farm)

Farmhouse (or create your own with a cardboard box turned on its side)

Plastic barn or habitat (or create a barn from a shoe box)

Barnyard props: small margarine tubs for food and water troughs for the animals, a metal pie pan with a splash of water makes a good pond, a few grains of oats or scraps of yellow yarn (hay) to feed the animals, scraps of ivory yarn for straw to make soft animal beds in the barn

Storybook, with a farm or zoo theme and colorful illustrations (to show what goes on during a typical day on the farm)

Jump-start:

To help get play started, encourage your child to create the farm environment, or suggest she do the morning farm chores to care for the animals.

NOTE: If your child has a favorite book with farm or barnyard characters, look at the pictures before the play begins as a quick way to see where the animals sleep and eat and what the farmers must do to tend to their animals.

PARENT TIP

196 Family Fun Book

❝When my son was little, my mother said to me, 'Write those funny stories down. You'll never remember them later and you'll be sorry you forgot them.' So I wrote all the adorable moments down, and at the end of the year, I printed out the whole year's collection of hilarity and saved them in a three-ring binder. We have kept this book now for nine years, and have gone through some interesting stages with this book. I actually didn't mention it to my son for some time because I thought he might be sensitive about some of the funny little episodes recorded in the book from his earliest years. Now that he's older, he enjoys reading from our 'funny book' of family stories. He is very proud that I have kept this book celebrating his childhood. It is his own personal history, kept lovingly in a worn, reused three-ring binder, and one of our greatest possessions.❞

—Els from New Jersey

Arts and Crafts

There are two types of art-play activities for preschoolers covered in this section. The first is *Spontaneous Art* ("Art")—young children are given safe art materials to create whatever their hearts (and little hands) desire. This is a no-rules style of art-play providing loads of fun and valuable opportunities for experimentation and expression.

Creative Crafts ("Crafts") is the second category of art-play. Preschoolers are thrilled to make something clever, creative, and useful: a simple necklace, bowl, or greeting card. These ingenious treasures go hand in hand with the preschooler's proclamation, "I made this all by myself for you!"

The Artist's Tools

An Easel for Your Budding Artist A child-size wooden or plastic easel feels like something made for a real artist! Unless you have a lot of space and a room that can handle the spills (basement or playroom with a vinyl floor), you might want to reserve easel painting for outdoor art-play. Consider your porch, deck, or patio your "outdoor art space" and spend time enjoying the weather outdoors while your child paints nearby. For easy cleanup, just hose down the deck and messy hands and feet when the artwork is finished.

Every Artist Needs a Smock I can still remember the artist smock I wore in kindergarten many years ago. These smocks were recycled from our dad's oversize (and tattered and torn) dress shirts. Our teacher simply cut off the sleeves to fit each child's arms (with a rolled cuff at the bottom). You can also use the same technique with oversize long-sleeved T-shirts or jerseys, available at your local thrift store.

Look for Nontoxic Art Supplies At your local school or teacher supply store, you'll find a wide assortment of nontoxic art supplies: finger paints, watercolors, washable paints, chalk, crayons, glue, ink pads. Be sure to look for the nontoxic symbol: AP (Approved Product Seal) surrounded by the word ACMI (Arts & Creative Materials Institute). This nonprofit organization sponsors a voluntary nontoxic certification program for children's art materials.

One Big Art Portfolio When my children were preschoolers, I purchased one oversize artist's portfolio for each child. All the special drawings, paintings, prints, and stories they made have been saved in these portfolios. From the start, my children knew that the very large artwork suitcases with the huge zippers meant that what they had created was "real" art that deserved a special keeping place! The other upside is that, though it's been many years now, their early artwork has been perfectly preserved.

UNPLUGGED PLAY

Containing the Mess

Art can be messy, it's true, but that should never discourage you or your child from making it. I can say that the benefits of creative play far outweigh a stain here or there, but I do still get a knot in my stomach each time I remember the day I spilled an entire container of India ink on my mother's new living room carpet, oh so many years ago. (And the well-intentioned home remedies that my grandmother offered on the phone—like boiled milk—did nothing to help me out of the mess!) Needless to say, when my mother arrived home from work that day, she was livid. So here are a few ideas for containing the mess of spills and splatters that might help you avoid the "boiled milk" solution.

• Create a designated art space for your child's painting projects in a room with a tile, vinyl, concrete, or wood floor.

• Use only washable paints, available at teacher or school supply stores.

• Have a bucket and large sponge handy for cleanups.

• Preschoolers are happy experimenting with three to four colors of paint, so limit the number of paint containers, and put a short-handled brush in each container to reduce the number of spills and splatters.

• Purchase nonspill paint pots with lids (available at teacher or art supply stores) or use a cardboard drink-holder (from the fast-food restaurant or coffeehouse).

• Allow your child the pleasure of painting outdoors with an easel, when weather permits.

• Designate one large vinyl or oilcloth tablecloth with a nonslip backing or a recycled painter's drop cloth for all painting projects done on the floor.

• When using a paint roller or sponge for printmaking, have a couple of extra pie pans or trays as "resting places" for rollers and sponges when they're not in use.

> *" I once gave my son a black satin evening bag and gold paint and said, 'I'm going out tonight. Will you decorate this for me?' I still have that handbag, and my son's now twenty-six. And I love it! It's just a black satin handbag with gold scribbles on it. "*
>
> **—Susan Striker**
> founder of Young at Art and
> author of *The Anti-Coloring Book* series

Spontaneous Art

Open-ended, unstructured dabbling with art materials, freedom to explore and express, get your hands in goop, and see what masterpiece might result—this is preschool art at its best. Children are experimenting with color, shape, and texture and expanding their understanding of the world around them as they do so. The fine motor skills they learn as they manipulate materials will pave the way for writing skills later. As they mix and match, trying this and that, they are practicing problem solving. Open-ended art-play can be messy, but from your child's perspective, that's half the fun.

197 Fabric Scrap Collage

One of my favorite works of art on the walls of my home is a small fabric scrap collage my daughter made when she was four. Old scraps or cast-off clothing can be reborn in these unusual and easy-to-make collages.

QUICK & EASY

AGE: 3–5 YRS

CATEGORY:
SOLO PLAY/ART

NUMBER OF
CHILDREN: ONE
OR MORE

Materials:
Scraps of silk, linen, or wool
Nontoxic white glue
Construction paper or heavy drawing paper

Setup:
Cut small rectangles and squares of solid-colored silk, linen, or wool fabric (or other fabric with an interesting assortment of textures).

Create:
Your child glues the scraps to the paper in a design of her own choosing. At the very end, suggest that she write her name with a fine-tipped nontoxic marker or crayon anywhere she likes on the paper.

Five Tips to Encourage Spontaneous Preschool Art

1. Expect a bit of a mess.

2. Plan spontaneous art for a time when you and your child are in a good mood.

3. Let your child's imagination determine how to use the art materials.

4. Don't ask "What is it?" Preschoolers are often creating without any object in mind.

5. Honor your child's creative spirit when you see it in action.

★ CLASSIC ★

198 Painting

Preschoolers are enthusiastic and flexible painters; they get a thrill out of standing at an easel and paint happily at the kitchen table too.

QUICK & EASY

AGE: 3–5 YRS

CATEGORY:
SOLO PLAY/ART

NUMBER OF
CHILDREN: ONE
OR MORE

Materials:

Newsprint paper or other large
   paper

Easel or vinyl tablecloth

Artist brushes with short handles

Nontoxic, washable paints
   (in nonspill paint pots)

Small piece of damp sponge

Cotton swabs

Narrow paint roller and disposable pie pan

Crayons and/or nontoxic markers

Setup:

Clip paper to an easel (and place the easel in a place that can handle paint spills), or place a large vinyl tablecloth over the kitchen table to create a work space. If possible, it's best to have one brush for each color of paint, so your child doesn't have to rinse the brush every time he wants to work with a new color.

Jump-start:

- **Painting with a Sponge** Give your child a small sponge-applicator (available in paint or hardware stores) to experiment with different ways to apply color to paper. Sponges can be dabbed or wiped on the paper to create streaks of color. Dipped in water, they'll create a light "wash" effect.

- **Painting with a Cotton Swab** Have your child dip a cotton swab in paint and use this "brush" to create small patterns on paper.

Cotton swabs are perfectly sized for small hands. And since they come in such large supply, you can assign one cotton swab to each color (don't worry about rinsing the same one in water between each use!).

- **Painting with a Small Roller** Pour a generous dab of color into a disposable plastic plate. Give your child several small rollers (available at art supply or hardware stores) each dipped into a different plate of paint, so she can roll them onto a large piece of newsprint or poster board. Be sure to put a large vinyl tablecloth down before beginning this project, or better yet, take the whole thing outside so you can hose down the mess after.

- **Mixed Media Painting** After the paint dries, have your child switch to crayons and markers for all sorts of interesting effects.

> **"** *A five-year-old comes running up to a parent and says, 'Oh, look at my picture. I drew a picture. Do you like my picture?' Instead of gushing and praising and saying, 'Oh, it's beautiful. It's the best picture you've ever done,' try saying, 'What do you think about your picture?' Then stop and listen to their story. Kids will tell you why they like their work. And then all you have to do is reflect that back and say, 'Wow, you look so excited, you're so proud of yourself.' When you reflect that back to your child, they internalize those good feelings; they internalize their self-pride and that is always there for them to draw from.* **"**
>
> **—Tim Jordan, M.D.**
> behavioral pediatrician and author of
> *Keeping Your Family Grounded When You're Flying*
> *by the Seat of Your Pants*

★ CLASSIC ★

199 Drawing

Drawing can be done nearly anywhere, anytime, with very little mess. For most children, pencils and crayons are easier to control than paintbrushes, so drawing is a more manageable way for them to enjoy the pleasure of creative expression and work on their representational skills.

QUICK & EASY

AGE: 3–5 YRS

CATEGORY:
SOLO PLAY/ART

NUMBER OF
CHILDREN: ONE
OR MORE

Materials:
Drawing instruments: crayons, nontoxic markers, colored pencils, artist's drawing pencils, white or colored chalk, and white grease pencils (great on black paper)

Paper: construction paper, newsprint, rolls of butcher paper, copy paper, note cards, drawing tablets, blank playing cards, index cards, file folders, poster board, tracing paper, envelopes, brown paper bags, paper plates, blank journals, waxed paper, aluminum foil, thin cardboard gift boxes

Jump-start:
- **Scratch Drawings on Aluminum Foil** Tear a stack of small pieces of heavy-duty aluminum foil. Have your child use a pencil to draw on the foil.

- **Scratch Drawings on Waxed Paper** Tear a sheet of waxed paper and place a piece of black construction paper behind it so your child can see the lines and images he is creating. Place on a hard surface and use the handle end of a teaspoon or a pencil point to scratch a drawing on the waxed paper. When the waxed paper drawing is finished, your child may enjoy holding it up near a lamp to see the design clearly.

> **❝**I always encourage parents to buy blank, bound books and just carry them around in a backpack or in Mom's handbag. Then, when you're in a restaurant and your child's bored, you can tear up some scraps and make a collage, you can draw, you can use a pencil or a pen if that's the only thing handy. I always used to carry a little stamp pad and stamps too, or you can even carry watercolors into a restaurant and use a water glass for the water source. My son did dozens of those books over the years. They would really take a period of months to complete, just working one page at a time, sometimes at a restaurant, sometimes on an airplane. **❞**
>
> **—Susan Striker**
> founder of Young at Art
> and author of *The Anti-Coloring Book* series

- **Rubbings** Take the paper off of a crayon, and use the broad surface of it to create a rubbing of a textured object. You might place a leaf or a poker chip on a hard surface and lay a thin piece of paper on top. Your child can rub the crayon over the paper and watch an image of the object magically appear.

- **Eraser Drawings** Let your child use a pencil to scribble all over a note card, then use the eraser to "draw" a picture.

- **Gift Box Masterpieces** Purchase a variety of white gift boxes at your local paper store. (The tops and bottoms will be flat when purchased and will need to be popped up to create the sides of the box later.) Preschoolers love to use crayons and markers to draw on the shiny surface. (Shiny white gift bags make for fun drawing too.)

Preschool Play (age 3 to 5)

> "Believe it or not, when your children are building with blocks or using finger paints or any kind of manipulative hands-on play—anything where they're using their imaginations—they're actually building connections inside those little brains. You can almost look at them and see those synapses growing and all those neurons reaching out to make important connections!"
>
> **—Jane M. Healy, Ph.D.**
> educational psychologist
> and author of *Your Child's Growing Mind*

★ CLASSIC ★

200 Finger Painting

Sometimes art means permission to make a mess! (Don't worry, it's a snap to clean up.)

AGE: 3–5 YRS

CATEGORY:
SOLO PLAY/ART

NUMBER OF
CHILDREN: **ONE
OR MORE**

Materials:
Newspaper

Washable, nontoxic finger paints

Paper (shiny, finger painting paper or plain drawing paper) or a cookie sheet

Jump-start:
Put newspapers down for easy cleanup. Give your child finger paints to spread around on finger painting paper. For short-lived, messy painting fun, have her use finger paints on a cookie sheet at the kitchen table.

Simple Homemade Finger Paint

Using ordinary kitchen ingredients you most likely already have on hand, you can easily make an assortment of inexpensive finger paints:

2 tablespoons sugar

1/3 cup cornstarch

2 cups cold water

1/4 cup clear dishwashing liquid

Serving spoon

Food coloring

Small yogurt containers with lids

Mix the sugar and cornstarch together in a small saucepan. Add the water and stir until all the lumps dissolve. Cook over very low heat, stirring constantly to avoid sticking or burning. Continue to cook and stir until the mixture becomes clear and thick like gelatin. Remove from heat and let cool to room temperature. Add the dishwashing liquid. Spoon a small quantity into each container and add a few drops of food coloring to create the desired colors. (Mix the primary colors to create colors like turquoise, purple, brown, and orange.)

SAFETY ALERT: These paints contain a generous amount of dish detergent and are therefore not appropriate for toddlers or other children who put everything in their mouths.

201 Paint-Blot Magic

This project leaves some of the art-making up to fate—another word for this is "magic." And here's a plus: As the paint-blot technique lends itself to high-speed production, your preschooler will be the proud designer of dozens of blot paintings in no time at all.

AGE: 3–5 YRS

CATEGORY: SOLO PLAY/ART

NUMBER OF CHILDREN: ONE OR MORE

Materials:
Construction paper
  (or other heavy, slightly textured paper)
Short-handled artist's paintbrush
Washable, nontoxic paint (assorted colors)

Create:
Help your child fold the sheet of construction paper in half, make a firm crease, and then open it back up. Show her how to use the paintbrush to put two or three dabs of paint on one side of the paper, creating interesting designs by using several colors. While the paint is still wet, place the paper on a firm surface and fold at the middle crease so the two halves touch. Run your hand over the whole surface so the painted side transfers to the unpainted side. Open up the paper and voilà! A symmetrical surprise. Once dry, these creations can also be recycled into colorful, original gift wrap.

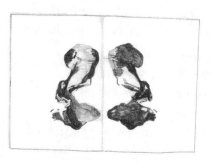

202 Blot-Magic Creatures

Once your child gets the hang of this process, suggest that he cluster his dabs of paint close together. Once the paint transference is complete, ask him what sorts of critters and creatures he can find in his painting. Display these finished prints on the fridge and let everyone in the family call out what sorts of creatures they see.

203 Indoor Chalk Art

There's something healthily subversive about using chalk for art. It is, after all, the teacher's special tool. Let your child reclaim it, in the house on the pavement!

AGE: 3–5 YRS

CATEGORY: SOLO PLAY/ART

NUMBER OF CHILDREN: ONE OR MORE

Materials:
Assortment of small colored
  chalk pieces
Construction paper
Chalkboard and eraser
Cotton balls and swabs

Jump-start:
Your child can use chalk to draw on paper or a chalkboard and experiment with cotton balls, cotton swabs, or a chalk eraser to move the color around, or use fingers for smudging and smearing. Have him experiment by using the broad surface of the chalk to make rubbings on paper (with a textured object like a coin underneath).

204 Saltwater Chalk Drawings

Mix ¼ cup of water and 1 teaspoon of salt in a small bowl. Stick the chalk in the salt water for a short time (30 to 60 seconds). Using the wet chalk on paper will give you a distinctly different effect.

Preschool Play (age 3 to 5)

205 PARENT TIP — Commercial Break Creativity

> When my son was between the ages of one and five, we lived in Africa. When we went to Africa, we took some videos featuring Public TV programs for children. These were the only videos our young son had seen, so when we moved back to this country, he had never seen a commercial on television. One day he heard from his kindergarten classmates about the existence of other channels and asked if we had those on our TV. It was a dilemma, because I did not want him to become bombarded with commercial messages about toys and junk food. The deal we came up with for my son was that if he was going to watch a program on a channel with commercials, he had to make interesting drawings and artwork during the commercial breaks in the program. He had to complete two pictures every time he watched something on a channel other than Public Television. We started a gallery of his artwork on my guest bedroom walls. This worked for some years, and I still have a lovely collection of my son's artwork made during these TV commercial breaks. "

— **Mohua from Maryland**

206 Outdoor Chalk Art

Take chalk time outside to add some drizzle to the chalk dust.

QUICK & EASY

AGE: **3–5 YRS**

CATEGORY:
SOLO PLAY/ART

NUMBER OF
CHILDREN: **ONE
OR MORE**

Materials:
Chunky pieces of colored sidewalk chalk

Small bucket filled with water or plastic spray bottle filled with water

Jump-start:
Trace shadows of people and objects on the sidewalk or patio. Spray a mist of water over the drawings to "melt" them.

SAFETY ALERT: Designate a safe place to draw on the sidewalk or patio and supervise your child carefully. (He will be enthralled with his artwork and not paying any attention to cars, so you must be vigilant.)

★CLASSIC★

207 Play Dough

There's something so earthy and satisfying about playing with clay. We're so unaccustomed to getting our hands dirty these days; it's nice for your child to have a chance to really get in there and mold something with her very own hands.

AGE: **3–5 YRS**

CATEGORY:
SOLO PLAY/ART

NUMBER OF
CHILDREN: **ONE
OR MORE**

Materials:
Play dough (see recipe on opposite page for homemade variety)

Recycled vinyl or oilcloth tablecloth

General tools: small rolling pin, spoons, Popsicle sticks, disposable plastic picnic knife

Jump-start:
Any household item could potentially be called in for service. Here's a list of creative tools your child can use to make imprints in her play dough: coins, giant buttons, small strainer, small comb, forks, corks, safety scissors, ABC blocks, keys, key rings, hairpins and barrettes, poker chips, potato masher, lids from spice jars, slotted spoons, giant plastic paper clips, wooden clothespins, rigid plastic hair curlers, small tomato paste cans (unopened). For the more sculpture oriented, many items can be used as molds: melon-ball scoopers, assorted cookie cutters, measuring spoons, plastic cups, small muffin tins, assorted plastic lids, plastic Easter eggs, etc.

Homemade Play Dough

You can go out and buy play dough in containers or you can mix up a batch right at the kitchen counter. Here's what you need:

1 cup flour	1 tablespoon vegetable oil	1–2 teaspoons food coloring
1 cup water	2 teaspoons cream	Saucepan
¼ cup salt	of tartar	Cookie sheet

Combine all the ingredients in the saucepan and mix well. Stir the ingredients over low to medium heat for about 5 minutes. When the mixture forms a ball, remove from heat. Turn the ball of goop onto the cookie sheet and let it cool. Once cool enough to handle, add food coloring and knead with your hands for several minutes until it becomes smooth. Store the play dough in an airtight plastic container.

Note: Play dough can make trouble when it gets ground into the carpet, so creating a play dough place that offers easy cleanup is recommended. The kitchen table or breakfast counter works well. (Or, an inexpensive yard sale coffee table placed in the playroom can be reserved especially for messy crafting.) Here are some smooth surfaces, just right for rolling and cutting the play dough, that will also contain the mess:

Giant-size cookie sheets without sides

Lids from giant plastic storage tubs

Large vinyl place mats or oilcloth tablecloths (shake the dough crumbs into the sink)

A large plastic cutting board (designated exclusively for play dough)

Preschool Play (age 3 to 5)

Creative Crafts

Though it's true that when young children engage in craft making, they start out with a preconceived end goal in mind, they'll be putting their own creative spin on everything they make. Don't impose your own rules about what something should look like. A purple blob on a greeting card might be a random design or might represent a grizzly bear. Either way, this is a good way for children to explore their creativity.

When preschoolers make crafts, they discover that they can make useful things themselves and that not everything of value has to be purchased from a store. I've talked with many adults over the years who remember the Christmas ornament they made thirty-five years ago, or the homemade treasure box given to Mom on Mother's Day. These humble crafts obviously can make a long-lasting impression on the artist and the recipient of the handmade treasure.

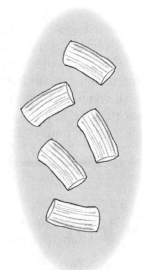

★ CLASSIC ★

208 Noodle Necklace

It's fun to say and fun to make. Quite the fashion statement too!

QUICK & EASY

Materials:

Extra-large uncooked rigatoni

48"-long shoelace (new)

AGE: 3–5 YRS

CATEGORY:
SOLO PLAY/CRAFTS

NUMBER OF
CHILDREN: ONE
OR MORE

Setup:

Start off the project by threading one piece of rigatoni through the shoelace, looping the lace through the pasta a second time, and knotting it off to create a "stop gap." Place a cup or two of noodles on the table.

Create:

Your child threads the end of the lace through one piece of rigatoni at a time. When the lace is nearly filled with noodles, help your child tie the ends of the shoelace together to create a long necklace. Some preschoolers will do best by placing one noodle on the table, steadying it briefly with an index finger, and using their other hand to thread the lace through its center.

209 Striped Noodle Necklace

Stretch this craft over into a second day by providing a variety of washable, nontoxic paints, several small paintbrushes, a disposable pie pan (for use as an artist's pallet), and a small container of water. Put some newspapers down on the table to contain the mess before your child begins painting. Paintbrush in hand, your child will decorate the pasta beads with multicolored stripes.

210 How Long Is One Cup of Pasta?

Gather up a box of rigatoni, one or two long shoelaces, and a yardstick. Challenge your child to find out how long a cup of pasta is. (If you have a very persistent child, you can ask, "How long is a *box* of pasta?" When he's threaded the cup or box of pasta, the two of you can measure the strand of pasta with the yardstick and write the measurement down on the pasta box. Dump the pasta back in the box once you're done, and save it to reuse for future projects.

211 Cereal Necklaces

For a child with good manual dexterity and a patient personality, use a bowl of dried cereal such as Cheerios to create a small bracelet or necklace. Froot Loops make a colorful creation too, and some children will enjoy sorting colors and making patterns (three red, two yellow, one green). Threading these small pieces is slow, careful work, and you'll be needed to briefly demonstrate in the beginning and again at the end how to tie a knot.

Scissor Safety

Preschool scissors, available online and at teacher and art supply stores, are just right for beginners. These special scissors with oversize handles (or double loops) allow your child to use more fingers for extra control. There are scissors that will cut paper and nothing else. Look for scissors that will work for both left- and right-handers, since children begin to show their preference during this stage. Even with safety scissors, supervise closely and teach your child these scissor-safety rules:

- Scissors are "tools" to be used in designated work areas—they are not toys for jabbing!

- Walk carefully (no running) when carrying scissors—tips down—from place to place.

- Store scissors in your art box, out of reach of little brothers and sisters.

- Check out an assortment of safe scissors at www.fiskarsschool.com.

212 My Name

Celebrate your child's identity with colorful scrap collage.

Materials:
  Safety scissors
  Colored construction paper
  Pencil
  Large sheet of colored poster board
  Nontoxic glue stick

AGE: **3–5 YRS**

CATEGORY:
SOLO PLAY/CRAFTS

NUMBER OF
CHILDREN: **ONE OR MORE**

Create:
Your child cuts a few sheets of the construction paper into little scraps. When the cutting is complete, use a pencil to write his name in big letters on the poster board. Working on one letter at a time, your child smears glue on the pencil outline and sticks the scraps of paper over it to fill in the letters of his name.

213 Confetti Design

Sprinkle confetti like fairy dust and see what patterns emerge.

Materials:
  Confetti (available at party supply stores)
  Ziplock bags
  Recycled bedsheet or washable tablecloth
  Nontoxic white glue
  Plain white paper plates

AGE: **3–5 YRS**

CATEGORY:
SOLO PLAY/CRAFTS

NUMBER OF
CHILDREN: **ONE OR MORE**

Setup:
Pour the confetti into color-coded ziplock bags for easy handling. Place the sheet or washable tablecloth over the kitchen table for easy cleanup.

Preschool Play (age 3 to 5)

Create:

Your child squeezes glue on the plates to create blobs or shapes, then pinches small amounts of confetti and sprinkles it over one section of glue at a time. When all the glue is covered, gently tip the plate and let the excess confetti fall onto the tablecloth. If spots of glue still show, repeat. (For easy cleanup, gather the corners of the tablecloth and pour the confetti into a garbage bag.)

214 Lunch Bag Puppet

This is a very easy craft to make, and since it's a toy, you'll find that you'll get good mileage out of it.

Materials:

Construction paper

Scissors

Paper lunch bags

Glitter glue or nontoxic white glue

Nontoxic markers

Crayons

AGE: 3–5 YRS

CATEGORY: SOLO PLAY/ CRAFTS (with help from parent)

NUMBER OF CHILDREN: ONE OR MORE

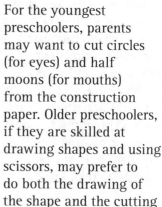

Create:

For the youngest preschoolers, parents may want to cut circles (for eyes) and half moons (for mouths) from the construction paper. Older preschoolers, if they are skilled at drawing shapes and using scissors, may prefer to do both the drawing of the shape and the cutting by themselves. Let your child do as much of the drawing and cutting as he is capable of and help out as needed. Leaving the lunch bag with its original folds, lay it on the table with its folded-up bottom facing up. Create a face on this bottom flap, gluing on your construction paper cutouts and decorating with markers and crayons. Let the glue dry thoroughly before playing with the puppet. Show your child how to manipulate the puppet with your hand inside the bag to make the puppet head move and "talk."

Friday Evening Art Show

In many cities across the country, Art Walks are organized once a month on a Friday evening, and the entire community is invited to walk from gallery to gallery, taking a peek at the art work. Many galleries offer drinks and appetizers to create a festive atmosphere for this event. If you have a preschooler who makes lots of drawings, paintings, and sculptures, you can borrow this Art Walks idea to highlight your child's most recent artistic creations. Simply designate a box, suitcase, or portfolio where your child can store her artwork. Select a night for a Family Art Show, complete with food and treats. Before the show begins, help your child hang her work on the walls in her bedroom or throughout your home. (Hang the drawings and paintings at your child's eye level using invisible tape.) To preserve the moment, take a photo of the artist standing in front of her display of artwork. Encourage older siblings to join the fun and establish fair and friendly rules that honor and encourage your child's creative spirit.

Play Ideas for Parent and Child

For preschoolers, parents are still the most important people in the world. And it's a good thing too, because grown-ups have a lot of playful and surprising tricks up their sleeves. Making time to play with your child is essential at this stage, when your child's imagination, sense of humor, ability to remember and to recognize letters, colors, numbers, and shapes are all developing; suddenly thinking, talking, and guessing games are possible. And playing with someone at a more advanced developmental stage (you!) will encourage all of that. He will soak up the subtleties of language as you play, tell stories, riddles, and jokes, and read books together. So pick a game, any game, listed in this section and take a step into your preschooler's wonderful world of play.

Reading Aloud

Reading aloud is a very important part of playtime for your child. Of course, there's the fun of snuggling up on the couch, looking at the pictures, and enjoying the plot; the playful use of words and the rhythm of language come alive as you read. But the magic of the story continues in your child's mind long after you close the pages of the book. It's as though these cherished stories and characters are like tiny seeds scattered into your child's imagination. The characters and events from favorite books will likely crop up in your child's pretend play, creative ideas, and drawings and paintings. It's also a nice, low-key activity for you to do when you feel like you're running on empty.

Here are some of my favorite read-aloud books for preschoolers. I hope you will invite some of these charming characters into your child's world.

Preschool Play (age 3 to 5)

Preschool Play (age 3 to 5)

Alexander and the Terrible, Horrible, No Good, Very Bad Day by Judith Viorst, illustrations by Ray Cruz

A Baby Sister for Frances by Russell Hoban, illustrations by Lillian Hoban

Bark, George by Jules Feiffer

Blueberries for Sal by Robert McCloskey

Brown Bear, Brown Bear, What Do You See? by Bill Martin Jr., illustrations by Eric Carle

Bunny Cakes by Rosemary Wells

Caps for Sale by Esphyr Slobodkina

The Cat in the Hat by Dr. Seuss

Chicka Chicka Boom Boom by Bill Martin Jr. and John Archambault, illustrations by Lois Ehlert

Cloudy with a Chance of Meatballs by Judi Barrett, illustrations by Ron Barrett

Corduroy by Don Freeman

Curious George by H. A. Rey and Margret Rey

Dandelion by Don Freeman

Don't Let the Pigeon Drive the Bus! by Mo Willems

Each Peach Pear Plum by Janet Ahlberg, illustrations by Allan Ahlberg

Goldilocks and the Three Bears by Jan Brett

Green Eggs and Ham by Dr. Seuss

Harold and the Purple Crayon by Crockett Johnson

Harry the Dirty Dog by Gene Zion, illustrations by Margaret Bloy Graham

The Hello, Goodbye Window by Norton Juster, illustrations by Chris Raschka

I Went Walking by Sue Williams, illustrations by Julie Vivas

Julius, the Baby of the World by Kevin Henkes

Leo the Late Bloomer by Robert Kraus, illustrations by Jose Aruego

Lilly's Purple Plastic Purse by Kevin Henkes

Little Bear by Else Holmelund Minarik, illustrations by Maurice Sendak

The Little Engine That Could by Watty Piper, illustrations by George and Doris Hauman

Madeline by Ludwig Bemelmans

Make Way for Ducklings by Robert McCloskey

Mike Mulligan and His Steam Shovel by Virginia Lee Burton

Millions of Cats by Wanda Gag

My First Little House Books (series) by Laura Ingalls Wilder

The Napping House by Audrey Wood, illustrations by Don Wood

Olivia by Ian Falconer

Once There Was a Bull . . . (Frog) by Rick Walton

One Gorilla by Atsuko Morozumi

Pete's a Pizza by William Steig

The Polar Express by Chris Van Allsburg

The Real Mother Goose by Blanche Fisher Wright

The Runaway Bunny by Margaret Wise Brown, illustrations by Clement Hurd

Snowflake Bentley by Jacqueline Briggs Martin, illustrations by Mary Azarian

The Story About Ping by Marjorie Flack, illustrations by Kurt Wiese

The Story of Ferdinand by Munro Leaf, illustrations by Robert Lawson

Swimmy by Leo Lionni

The Tale of Peter Rabbit by Beatrix Potter

The Very Hungry Caterpillar by Eric Carle

Wheels on the Bus by Raffi, illustrations by Sylvie K. Wickstrom

Where the Wild Things Are by Maurice Sendak

Winnie the Pooh by A. A. Milne, illustrations by Ernest H. Shepard

Tell Me a Story!

I'm convinced that every parent has the potential to become a first-rate storyteller. As luck would have it, you couldn't ask for a better audience than your preschool child. She will be thrilled and enthralled by the stories you weave if you let your imagination lead the way.

I do know from experience that not all grown-ups feel confident that they have what it takes to tell a good story. With this in mind, here are a few tried-and-true suggestions to help you create characters and stories to captivate your child's attention and turn on her imagination.

Creating One Main Character for Your Story

Your child will especially enjoy stories about a familiar person, animal, or a particular type of worker he finds fascinating. If your child visited the zoo in recent memory and was particularly mesmerized by one animal, make the animal the main character in your story. Or perhaps the local baker with an interesting accent offers your child a cookie from time to time when you visit the bakery. Use this friendly, intriguing man as the central character in your story, embellishing with great fanfare.

With my children, I used our own family dog, Cocoa, as the basis for the stories of Cocoa the Wonder Dog. Cocoa the Wonder Dog was a magical dog who traveled around the world doing all sorts of clever things, from painting pictures in Paris to attending culinary school in England.

Creating the Adventures and Action in Your Story

I've discovered two things that make for good plot and action when creating stories for children. First, take something ordinary, like going to the grocery store, and let something truly extraordinary occur. (My friend Meg Cox created stories for her son about Max the Polar Bear, who lived inside the grocery store freezer, right next to the tubs of ice cream.)

Second, ideas for a plot often flow spontaneously when you begin with what you know and love. Cocoa the Wonder Dog became an artist and went to Paris in my very first Cocoa story simply because painting and drawing are a part of my life. Making art was also something that both of

my children seemed interested in. So this tale was woven with ease and enthusiasm because it started with an idea near and dear to my own heart. Every parent has something from his or her adult life or childhood that holds special appeal. Use these heartfelt interests to bring your story to life.

Expanding the Story with Sequels

Here's the thing: Preschoolers enjoy hearing the same story over and over again. In fact, they often pay such close attention to the details that if you forget to mention the purple hat the Wonder Dog was wearing on the airplane in the second telling of the story, you will quickly be reminded. From your child's perspective, there is something nurturing and reassuring about hearing the very same story or details over and over again. This said, however, there will come a time when you just can't bear another repeat of the exact same story. When this happens, no need to invent a new main character—simply create a sequel adventure for the character your child has come to know and love. Retain your beloved character's trademark antics but move him to a new location to continue the story. So perhaps the polar bear living in the grocery store hops a ride on the ice cream delivery truck and ends up in a ski town in Vermont in February. (I'll bet you could think of several funny plots involving a polar bear on the ski slopes at a posh resort in Vermont.)

Creating an Ending for Today's Chapter

I always like to end a chapter in a children's story with some sense of accomplishment or discovery. Perhaps some new challenge was met and the character is pleased with his achievement.

Cocoa the Wonder Dog had never actually held a paintbrush before the first installment

---

PARENT TIP

215 Storytelling on Wheels

❝When my kids were very little, we often drove to my mom's house about thirty-five minutes away. After one too many are-we-there-yets, I started making up stories. We called them Benji and Betty stories, about brother and sister bears who had lots of fun and sometimes got in trouble. I could make them as long or short as I wanted (or needed!). I would try to make the stories about things my kids would be going through, like losing a tooth or going to playgroup; I could share what I wanted my children to know through the bear family's experiences. My children have gotten older and we don't do it as much—but I tell Benji and Betty stories to my nephew now.❞

—Margaret from Maryland

of my story (rather difficult with paws). But lo and behold, through sheer determination, by the end of the first story she learned to paint by holding the paintbrush between her teeth. And she discovered how much fun it was to make a painting that no one else had ever made before. The End. Now this spontaneous ending may never win a prize in literary circles, but it was just right for a natural ending to my preschool story. Though your child does love imaginative adventures, she also likes to grab onto concrete conclusions that she can understand.

Your Storytelling Routine

The first time I told the Cocoa story, it was 3:00 A.M. and my daughter had just awoken from a nightmare. The story relaxed us both and replaced the unhappy pictures in my child's mind with a happy adventure about an extraordinary dog. Other stories emerged during long car trips. Each family can find its own regular time for stories—bedtime, breakfast time, dinnertime, or after school. Of course, some days your brain won't feel in gear to invent a new story for your children; you should be able to substitute reading aloud without much resistance.

I Believe I Saw a Little Cheating Going on There!

Children four and five years old may get carried away by their desire to win and slip in a bit of cheating to improve their chances. If your child tries this tactic, don't assume that she's going to grow up to be an embezzler. But do calmly let her know that you saw what she did and give it a name: It's cheating. A very short chat about why cheating isn't fair to the other players usually does the trick. Follow up with a comment like, "We'll play again tomorrow and I know you'll want to play fair next time, without jumping ahead extra squares on the board."

Indoor Play

The kitchen table is transformed from a dull piece of furniture into a fabulous play arena when parent and child sit down for a friendly game of Matchmaker, Hearts & Spades, or Chutes and Ladders. The living room can become a trove of secret, hidden treasures. Here are some splendid playtime activities just right for parents and preschoolers at home.

Preschool Play (age 3 to 5)

216 Same Card Game

The name of the game is "same." Preschoolers are learning to take in the world's infinite contents and organize them into categories. Each time they plop something into one of those categories, they gain a little sense of mastery.

AGE: **3–5** YRS

CATEGORY:
PARENT & CHILD/ INDOOR

NUMBER OF CHILDREN: **ONE**

Materials:
  Scissors (for adult use only)
  2 identical garden catalogs or 2 identical store fliers with small color photos of various items
  Nontoxic glue stick or tape
  3"-by-5" index cards

Setup:
Your child helps you create 24 playing cards by cutting and pasting identical duplicate photos of 12 items from the two catalogs. Glue the photos to index cards to create two matching decks of 12 cards each. Keep these two decks separate.

Play:
Place all the cards from one deck faceup in a rectangle. Mix or shuffle the second deck and place it facedown. Your child draws one card at a time and finds its match on the table. (Each time a match is made, your child sets it aside so the group of faceup cards gets smaller and smaller.) The game ends when all cards have been matched.

217 Hearts & Spades

If older brothers or sisters play cards, preschoolers will want a card game of their own.

AGE: **4–5** YRS

CATEGORY:
PARENT & CHILD/ INDOOR

NUMBER OF CHILDREN: **ONE OR MORE**

Materials:
  2 decks of playing cards

Setup:
Remove all the hearts and all the spades from each deck of cards. You will use only 26 cards from each deck (52 total). Keep the cards from the two decks separate.

Play:
Shuffle each of these small decks of cards. Place one deck facedown in the middle of the table. Using the second deck (dealer's deck), deal four cards faceup in front of each player. Players take turns turning over a card from the deck on the table and matching the cards in their hand. When a match is made, the player puts these two cards facedown on the table and is dealt one more card from the dealer's deck so that each player has a hand of four cards at all times. (If no match is made, the child may place this matchless card facedown at the bottom of the dealer's deck and take another card.) The game continues until all the cards (in both players' hands) have been matched.

NOTE: Use a full deck of cards for older children, who are skilled at discerning the difference between spades and clubs or hearts and diamonds.

218 Matchmaker

Matchmaker, matchmaker, make me a match! When you create your child's own deck of cards, you'll find tons of simple and satisfying sorting and memory games to play together.

AGE: 3–5 YRS

CATEGORY: PARENT & CHILD/ INDOOR

NUMBER OF CHILDREN: ONE OR MORE

Materials:

Pencil

Blank flash cards
  (available at teacher supply stores)

Nontoxic markers

Ink pad and block-print stamps
  (available at teacher supply stores)

Small ziplock bag

Setup:

The charm of these games comes in part from using homemade matchmaker cards. You'll be working with the following shapes: squares, rectangles, circles, ovals, triangles, diamonds, octagons, stars, and hearts. Use a pencil to draw an outline of each shape on two of the blank playing cards. Write the name of the shapes at the top of each card.

Have your child color code the cards by coloring in the shapes, designating one color per object (red for squares, blue for circles, for example). The reverse side of the card can be decorated using the stamp. (To increase the number of possible games to play, create additional pairs of cards for each shape.)

Play:

Line up one card of every shape, faceup on a table. Shuffle the remaining cards and deal them to your child one at a time. He finds the matching cards and puts like with like. Store the new playing cards in a ziplock bag for the next round of play.

219 For Older Children Learning the Alphabet

Using blank flash cards, create a deck of alphabet cards. Use these to play various simple games: lining up cards in the correct order from *A* to *Z*, turning over one letter and thinking of a person, place, or thing that starts with this letter, etc.

220 Story Detective

This game challenges your child to sift through her accumulated knowledge of fairy tales and books.

AGE: 3–5 YRS

CATEGORY: PARENT & CHILD/ INDOOR

NUMBER OF CHILDREN: ONE OR MORE (with an adult)

Play:

This guessing game begins with you telling the plot of a familiar story, omitting the names of characters involved. For example, if you were describing a little bit of the plot from *Goldilocks and the Three Bears,* you might say, "This book has a little girl with blonde hair" as the first clue. Pause and let your child take a guess. If her guess is not correct, add another clue: "She went into someone else's house one day and sat down in a chair." Keep adding clues (based upon your child's guessing abilities) until she guesses the correct story.

It's a marvelous game for memory and also a fun way to incorporate details of favorite stories and characters into spontaneous play.

221 Storytelling Notebook

Set aside a special time and place for writing in your child's storytelling notebook each week.

AGE: **3–5 YRS**

CATEGORY:
PARENT & CHILD/ INDOOR

NUMBER OF CHILDREN: **ONE**

Materials:
Nontoxic glue stick
Recent photo of your child
Construction paper
Pen
Scissors (for adult use only)
Spiral notebook
Clear contact paper

Setup:
Glue your child's photo to a sheet of construction paper. Help your child print his name beneath the photo. Cut to fit to the outside of the spiral notebook, and wrap this personalized notebook cover using clear contact paper; secure with glue.

Play:
Have your child tell you a story of his own while you write it down in his story-telling notebook. (Write down exactly what your child dictates.) Some children will chose to tell a story about a favorite stuffed animal, the family pet, or a character in a much loved book. Other children may simply want to tell you something they did that day with a friend. There are no rules for these stories, which blossom and grow as this weekly tradition goes on. They are outstanding keepsakes for children to read through in the childhood years and beyond.

222 Letter Scramble

Combining letter recognition with physical activity, this game has a touch of organized chaos.

AGE: **3–5 YRS**

CATEGORY:
PARENT & CHILD/ INDOOR

NUMBER OF CHILDREN: **ONE**

Materials:
Marker (for adult use only)
26 colored index cards
(or a deck of ABC playing cards)
Paper lunch bag

Setup:
Write your child's name on the outside of a paper lunch bag. Print one letter of the alphabet on each index card. Toss the deck of index cards lightly into the air, scattering the cards on the floor in an open area of the room.

Play:
Once the cards are scattered, your child hunts for letters he recognizes. For starters, challenge him to search for the first letter of his name. If he knows a few letters of the alphabet, ask him to find the letters he recognizes, bring them to you, and tell you the letter printed on the card. Each time your child correctly identifies a letter, he places the letter in his paper bag. If he guesses incorrectly, you say the correct letter, ask him to repeat it, and toss that letter back into the pile. Play just long enough for this game to be fun and exciting.

223 Letter Scramble Word Game

Once your older child begins to associate a few words (or names) with specific letters of the alphabet, expand this game a bit so that your child announces the letter *and* tells you a word or name that starts with this letter!

224 Color Coins

Preschoolers like the look and feel of red, white, and blue poker chips. They make terrific pretend coins for this color-coded searching game.

AGE: 3–5 YRS

CATEGORY:
PARENT & CHILD/
INDOOR

NUMBER OF
CHILDREN: ONE
OR MORE

Materials:
Purse or wallet
Red, white, and blue poker chips

Setup:
Hide about 15 poker chips around the room, with half of each chip in plain sight.

Play:
Give your child an old purse (or wallet) and let her search for all the "red" poker chips you have scattered around the room or hidden in plain sight. She'll place the chips she finds in her purse. Have her find each color in turn.

*SAFETY ALERT: This game is only intended for children who won't put play objects in their mouths.

225 Bathtub Bubbles

Early Sunday morning is a good time for an indoor bubble game tradition that gives bath time a boost.

AGE: 3–5 YRS

CATEGORY:
PARENT & CHILD/
INDOOR

NUMBER OF
CHILDREN: ONE
OR MORE

Materials:
Bubble wand
Bubble solution

Play:
Simply add a bubble wand and bubble solution to your child's bath time routine and allow extra time for bubble play.

226 Bathtub Bull's-Eye

Need a playful distraction while you massage some shampoo into your little squirmer's scalp? It's Bathtub Bull's-Eye to the rescue!

AGE: 3–5 YRS

CATEGORY:
PARENT & CHILD/
INDOOR

NUMBER OF
CHILDREN: ONE
OR MORE

Materials:
1 teaspoon salt
Plastic cup
Sidewalk chalk
Bubble solution
Bubble wand
Washcloth

Setup:
Start with a dry tub. Add a teaspoon of salt to a cup of water, soak a piece of washable sidewalk chalk in it for about 30 seconds, then draw a large target on the back of the tub. Start running the water, and add bubble solution.

Play:
Have your child blow bubbles at the target. At the end of the playtime (and bath time), hose down your child and use a soapy washcloth to scrub the chalk bull's-eye from the tub.

Bathtub and Water Play Safety

Don't be fooled into thinking that children three to five are old enough to play in a tub of water on their own. Serious accidents can happen in the blink of an eye. Provide continuous supervision and give your undivided attention whenever your child is near water.

Preschool Play (age 3 to 5)

Board Games and Card Games

Many three- to five-year-olds need help taking turns, keeping hurt feelings in check, and following simple rules, which is why these board games and card games are in the *Parent and Child* section. As a parent, you're in a position to encourage some communal, rule-driven play. Remember that playing by the rules is a concept that takes time and practice for preschoolers to master. Another thing to keep in mind is that many preschoolers do best with activities that are games of chance rather than skill or strategy. The games mentioned below have been selected with these preschool tendencies and abilities in mind. You'll see age recommendations (from the game manufacturers) on the games, but remember that every child develops at his own pace and has his own play preferences. Follow your child's lead in terms of choosing games that suit him.

Animal Rummy card game	Cootie	Hungry Hungry Hippos
Barrel of Monkeys	Don't Wake Daddy	Jenga
Berries, Bugs & Bullfrogs*	Go Fish	Mr. Mouth
Boggle Jr.	Goodnight Moon Game	Old Maid
Candy Land	Guess Who?	Preschool Bingo
Chutes and Ladders	Hi Ho! Cherry-O	Uncle Wiggily**
Clue Jr.	Honey Bee Tree Game	

*For this and other cooperative board games, check out Family Pastimes Inc. (www.familypastimes.com).

**For this and other classic games, check out from Back to Basics Toys (www.backtobasicstoys.com).

Help for the Preschooler Who Hates to Lose

Many children aren't ready to play board games with just one winner until they are four, five, or older. (Let's be honest here, we'd all rather win than lose!) Here are a few guidelines to ease your preschool child into playing board games:

- Select games that rely on *chance* rather than *skill* or strategy.

- Talk to your child about how *you* feel when you lose. (For example, "I know that everyone loses sometimes, so it doesn't hurt my feelings too badly." Or, "I lost this time, but next time I may just win.")

- Keep the focus on the fun of playing; be a good role model and say things like "Good game!" or "It was fun playing together" at the end of the game.

- Have realistic expectations. It takes many young children a long time to get comfortable with the idea of losing gracefully.

In the Car

Things can get hairy during the daily commute (with a child or two in tow)—you're trying to focus on the road and your child begins clamoring for attention, which can quickly morph into chaos. With that in mind, I developed some games your preschooler can play in the car or while you're out and about together.

Do the words "I'm pulling this car over right this minute" ring a bell? With a little attitude adjustment on your part (and a few toys and props along for the ride), this car time can be transformed into brief bouts of happy solo play for your child, mixed with occasional looking and talking games that you both play together.

227 Color Detective

How many big blue objects can your child spot on the drive across town? Challenge her to a game of color detective, and she'll get right on the case!

QUICK & EASY

AGE: **3–5 YRS**

CATEGORY:
PARENT & CHILD/ IN THE CAR

NUMBER OF CHILDREN: **ONE OR MORE**

Setup:
Select a "color of the day" your child is familiar with. For a three-year-old, the challenge may be looking for blue cars. Your four-year-old may be capable of looking for any big blue objects—a blue door, a blue delivery truck, a blue building or bench.

Play:
Your child calls out the chosen objects as she sees them. You might want to keep "score" for your child, keeping a running tally as each item is discovered and announcing the grand total at the end of your commute.

228 Shapes and Colors

For a five-year-old, you may need to up the ante so that your child is looking for both a specific color and shape. A blue circle might sound like a tough assignment, but he will probably surprise you by finding at least one. It could be a blue wheel on a plastic wagon or a billboard with a blue circle in a corporate logo.

229 I Spy A-B-C

Finding your child's initial on a street sign or a license plate is cause for celebration.

QUICK & EASY

AGE: **3–5 YRS**

CATEGORY:
PARENT & CHILD/ IN THE CAR

NUMBER OF CHILDREN: **ONE OR MORE**

Materials:
2 small ziplock bags

Assorted buttons

Color dot stickers in bright colors (available at office supply stores)

Setup:
Spend some time helping your child practice printing the first letter of her name before playing this game; this will help her with letter recognition. Fill one of the ziplock bags with buttons. Stick the dots on the outside of the other ziplock bag in the shape of your child's initial.

Play:
Take the bag with you on car rides. Each time your child spots her initial, she takes a button

from the button bag and deposits it into the letter bag (the bag with her initial stickered on it). At the end of each day of play, your child spills out the contents of the letter bag, and the two of you can count the number of letters you spotted that day. (As time goes by, you can create other letter bags using your child's middle and last initials to expand this game.) You can also play this game at home by flipping through magazines.

230 I Spy 1-2-3

Select a *number of the day,* from 1 to 10, that your child will look for wherever you go.

231 I Spy Piggy Bank

Get rolls of pennies from your bank and use pennies to play these games rather than buttons. At the end of each day, deposit the pennies in your child's I Spy Piggy Bank or create a Giving Bank to save money for a children's charity in your community.

232 Letter Hunt

Make the day more exciting by designating a letter of the day!

Materials:
Alphabet magnets

Play:
Before you leave the house, have your child look at the alphabet magnets on the fridge and select one letter for the day's Letter Hunt. Your child carries the letter in her pocket and searches for it on your commute to preschool or as you walk through the neighborhood. As the Official Letter Spotter, she'll call out the letter whenever she sees it. (To continue this game at home, your child can circle the letter of the day in a magazine or in newspaper headlines.)

AGE: 3–5 YRS

CATEGORY: PARENT & CHILD/ IN THE CAR

NUMBER OF CHILDREN: ONE OR MORE

233 Bus and Truck Tally

Here's a simple and fairly quiet activity that will keep your child happy on short car trips across town, and allow you to keep your eyes on the road. It combines observation skills with letter recognition, with a little counting thrown in at the end of the day.

AGE: 3–5 YRS

CATEGORY: PARENT & CHILD/ IN THE CAR

NUMBER OF CHILDREN: ONE OR MORE

Materials:
Colored index cards
Markers (for adult use only)
2 small ziplock bags
Plastic storage container or shoe box

Setup:
Cut the index cards in half so they are easy to handle. Create 10 to 20 yellow cards with the letter *B* written on them (bus), and 10 to 20 blue cards with the letter *T* written on them (truck). Put all the *T* cards in one plastic bag and the *B* cards in the other. Keep these in the car.

Play:
Each time your child spots a truck, he takes a blue card with the letter *T* out of the bag and places it inside the box. When he sees a bus, he takes a yellow card with the letter *B* out of the bag and places it inside the box. At the end of the day, sit down with your child and count out the cards in the box to see how many times he spotted these impressive, large vehicles.

234 Fire Trucks and Police Cars

As your child gets older, challenge him to look for police cars, fire trucks, motorcycles, or Jeeps, and letter and color-code the cards accordingly.

235 Ten Questions

Tired of being put on the spot with questions from your preschooler that you don't know the answer to? Turn the tables with this sweet and chatty questions game.

AGE: 3–5 YRS

CATEGORY:
PARENT & CHILD/
IN THE CAR

NUMBER OF
CHILDREN: ONE
OR MORE

Setup:
Make this a fun, conversational game that encourages your child's opinions and ideas, not a drill based on extracting "correct" answers.

Play:
Make up 10 questions geared toward your child's age, environment, interests, and observations. Here are some sample questions that I might ask a five-year-old:

1. What is something you like that is white?

2. What is your favorite animal to watch at the zoo?

3. What is your favorite food?

4. What was the hardest thing you ever learned to do?

5. What is your favorite thing to do on a sunny day?

6. Who is your favorite person in a storybook?

7. What would you buy if you had a hundred dollars?

8. What do you think I would buy if I had a hundred dollars?

9. If your family dog or cat (or a dog or cat you know) could talk, what do you think he would say?

10. If you could fly like a bird, where would you fly?

236 Three Questions!

When you are short on time or patience, shorten this game to three or four questions and encourage your child to draw something he mentioned during the game with the remaining time as you drive across town. (Have paper and crayons handy for this game.)

237 Opposites

When children discover the concept of opposites, they love to play around with it. It's one of those things, like learning to tie your shoes, that's really a hallmark of the developmental process. Help your child revel in her amazing new knowledge!

AGE: 3–5 YRS

CATEGORY:
PARENT & CHILD/
IN THE CAR

NUMBER OF
CHILDREN: ONE
OR MORE

Play:
Set up the game with a short explanation of opposites. Use words with easily identifiable opposites and have your child try to guess what they are. You might ask something like, "What's the opposite of hot?" Then continue with concepts of wet/dry, big/little, quiet/loud, fast/slow, tall/short.

> "It really troubles me when I see parents driving to nursery school with kids watching TV in the back of the SUV. That time is precious, when driving the children—to sing songs, to play games, to talk."
>
> **—David Elkind, Ph.D.**
> Professor of Child Development at Tufts University
> and author of *The Hurried Child*
> and *The Power of Play*

Preschool Play (age 3 to 5)

Crafts

I find crafts so relaxing. Unlike high-energy physical games or amped-up time-sensitive games, crafts tend to settle both kids and adults into a place of quiet concentration. So enjoy this rare opportunity for simple, focused activity. Sitting down with your child for some simple cutting and gluing should be rewarding to you both!

★CLASSIC★

238 Life-Size Me

This hand-me-down craft idea is a winner with each new generation of preschoolers.

AGE: **3–5 YRS**

CATEGORY: **PARENT & CHILD/ CRAFTS**

NUMBER OF CHILDREN: **ONE OR MORE**

Materials:

Scissors (for adult use only)

Roll of butcher paper

Crayons or chalk

Nontoxic markers

Create:

Cut a piece of butcher paper approximately 12 inches longer than your child's height. Place the paper on the ground and have your child lie down on top of it. (In order to draw a clear, accurate outline, you may need to tape the ends of the paper to the floor to hold it in place.) Use the crayons or chalk to draw your child's outline. After you've created this template, the real masterpiece begins. Your child now fills in the image by drawing clothes, shoes, eyes, nose, mouth, hair, and accessories to create his very own Life-Size Me drawing. (Or perhaps your child will prefer to create a Life-Size Friend with its own distinct features.) If your child is particularly proud of the outcome, you can use invisible tape to display the drawing on his bedroom door.

★CLASSIC★

239 Macaroni Marvels

These simple pasta plates have been beloved by several generations of budding artists. They also make great wall hangings.

AGE: **3–5 YRS**

CATEGORY: **PARENT & CHILD/ CRAFTS**

NUMBER OF CHILDREN: **ONE OR MORE**

Materials:

Nontoxic white glue

Disposable pie pan

Small paintbrush with short handle

Paper plate

Assorted uncooked pasta (elbow, bow tie, ziti, corkscrew, shells, etc.)

Single-hole punch

Safety scissors

Ribbon

Create:

Squeeze a small amount of glue into the disposable pie pan. Help your child dip the paintbrush in the glue and apply a generous coating of glue to a plain paper plate. Next, she'll gather some pasta pieces and arrange them on the plate to create a unique design. Let the glue dry overnight. Using the hole punch, make a small hole about one inch from the top rim of the plate. Cut a piece of ribbon, thread it through the hole, and tie a knot to create a hanger for your child's art piece.

240 Clothespin People Parade

"What's a babushka?" my little friend asked as I glued the scarf on the wooden clothespin doll.

AGE: 3–5 YRS

CATEGORY: PARENT & CHILD/ CRAFTS

NUMBER OF CHILDREN: ONE OR MORE

Materials:

Nontoxic markers

10 wooden one-piece clothespins (not the clip type), available at craft stores

Nontoxic white glue

Small pieces of yarn or ribbon

Pipe cleaners (assorted colors)

Construction paper

Single-hole punch

Large pack of modeling clay

Create:

Help your child use markers to create a "face" on each clothespin. Attach "hair" by gluing small pieces of yarn or ribbon to the head. Twist one pipe cleaner completely around the body one time, twisting the two ends together tightly in the back and bringing them back around to create arms and hands. Next, cut a small piece of construction paper to wrap around the clothespin to make a dress or pants and shirt. Use the hole punch to create armholes so you can slip the shirt or dress through each pipe-cleaner arm. Use glue to attach the clothes to the body. When you and your child have finished creating your clothespin people, roll a small ball of modeling clay for each doll. Push the tip of each clothespin firmly in place in the clay; flatten the bottom of the clay to create a one-piece shoe so each person can stand upright.

Create a parade of different people in colorful costumes. Line them up and let your child's

imagination take off as she announces who these people are, what their "work" is, and where they are going in the parade.

241 Animal Parade

Using the same materials, create elephants, tigers, cats, dogs, and any other favorite animal. Try positioning the clothespins horizontally and using pipe cleaners and modeling clay to create legs and tails. Yarn or scraps of fabric or paper can be used to create ears, fur, and whiskers.

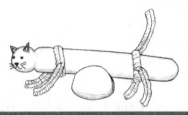

❝By the time kids are three, four, and five years old, their problem solving is getting more complex. I think it's very important for parents and early childhood educators to explicitly use a problem-solving process with them. I think of it as four steps, where you're really asking them out loud, 'What's the problem? What ideas do you have for solving the problem? Which one shall we try first?' And then, 'How did that work?'**❞**

—Marti Erickson, Ph.D.
director of the Harris Training Programs at the University of Minnesota and coauthor of *Infants, Toddlers, and Families*

Preschool Play (age 3 to 5)

Preschool Play (age 3 to 5)

242 Family Mobile

You probably don't have a family crest, but every family is entitled to its own family mobile. It makes a lovely keepsake and also puts some of those excess photos you have lying around to good use.

AGE: 3–5 YRS

CATEGORY: PARENT & CHILD/ CRAFTS

NUMBER OF CHILDREN: ONE OR MORE

Materials:

Scissors (for adult use only)

Several sheets of construction paper or poster board in assorted colors

Photos of individual family members and pets

Nontoxic white glue

Nontoxic markers

Single-hole punch

String or yarn

Wire coat hanger

Create:

Cut out hearts from colored construction paper, one for each member of the family. Vary the colors and sizes, but make sure each heart is large enough to glue a photo on. Take the photographs and cut out heart-shaped photos of each member of the family; if you want to use group photos, cut them to fit on one bigger paper heart. Glue one photo to each colored paper heart. Decorate the hearts with markers or write the names of each family member along the edges of the paper hearts. Punch single holes in the center of the hearts. Thread various lengths of yarn through the holes and tie knots. Tie the hearts to a wire clothes hanger at varying lengths to create a mobile.

243 I Love You Because Mobile

Help your child make a splendid birthday present (or Valentine gift) for someone. Ask your child to come up with four or more things he loves about this special person or four or more fun things they do together. Write each *I Love You Because* message down, just as your child expresses it, on a separate heart. Your child decorates the hearts with glitter glue, stickers, and markers. Assemble these hearts into a mobile for a priceless keepsake.

244 VIP Banner

Tell your child what VIP stands for and make a banner to honor each VIP in the family. Just don't let it go to anyone's head.

AGE: 3–5 YRS

CATEGORY: PARENT & CHILD/ CRAFTS

NUMBER OF CHILDREN: ONE

Materials:

Colored felt rectangles (2 or more colors, 12" by 18" each)

Scissors (for adult use only)

Yarn

Nontoxic white glue

Sequins, glitter glue, buttons, zigzag trim, fabric scraps

Create:

You'll use one piece of felt for the banner, and you'll cut the others into the letters of your child's name and various decorative shapes. Center a 24-inch piece of yarn along the top edge of the felt banner. (Place the yarn about a half inch from the edge.) Squirt a generous line of glue along the edge of the felt and fold the banner over the yarn. Press firmly for a few minutes to let the glue take hold. Allow the glue to dry. Trim the bottom of the banner to create a point. Cut out the letters of your child's name (arrange the letters diagonally, running from the banner's top left corner to its bottom right corner). Decorate with glitter glue, sequins, decorative trim, or felt shapes. Tie the ends of the yarn sticking out from the banner into a bow for easy hanging.

245 Shoe Box Mailbox

Preschoolers love to get their own mail; make it official with a mailbox. (Provide a mix of junk mail and, from time to time, a real note from you.)

AGE: **3–5 YRS**

CATEGORY: **PARENT & CHILD/ CRAFTS**

NUMBER OF CHILDREN: **ONE OR MORE**

Materials:
Shoe box with lid
Construction paper
Nontoxic glue stick
Clear packing tape
Scissors (for adult use only)
Nontoxic markers, crayons, glitter glue

Create:
Help your child cover the shoe box and its lid with construction paper. (Use glue or tape to attach the paper to the box.) Use scissors to cut a slit in the lid of the box for mail delivery. Then have your child decorate the box, using markers, crayons, and glitter glue. Help her write her name and your street address on her mailbox.

Junk Mail Is Good

From a three-year-old's perspective, junk mail is *real mail*. It's got a stamp and postmark and colorful papers with words inside. Why not designate a shoe box for catalogs and unopened junk mail so that your child can have a bit of fun? Here are some of the ways that preschoolers like to "recycle" junk mail:

• Cut open the envelopes

• Use a stamp and ink pad to decorate the envelope or papers inside

• Cut out photos (from catalogs) and glue and paste them on paper

• Cut out coupons

• See how many long strips of paper they can make from each page

• Play post office with the mail

• Play "office" and use the junk mail for their "work"

Preschool Play (age 3 to 5)

246 Waving Hand Greeting Cards

Tracing your child's hand is a way of saying, "Look at the size of your hands and look what they can do!"

AGE: 3–5 YRS

CATEGORY: **PARENT & CHILD/ CRAFTS**

NUMBER OF CHILDREN: **ONE OR MORE**

Materials:
Brightly colored construction paper

Colored pencils

Scissors (for adult use only)

Crayons

Glitter glue

Decorations (short pieces of ribbon, yarn, and lace)

Create:

1. Fold a sheet of colored construction paper in half crosswise and give it to your child.

2. Have your child place her hand on the paper, with her little finger resting against the edge or fold.

3. Trace her hand with a colored pencil, being careful to keep her little finger right up against the edge or fold.

4. Cut along the outline you've created, so that you now have a card that consists of two attached hands.

5. Help your child write a verse on the inside of the card, then have her decorate the outside of the card with glitter glue, sequins, lace, buttons, stickers, and other materials.

247 Homemade Beanbags

When my daughter was a preschooler, she refused to wear what she called "fancy shoes and socks." If you've got neglected dress socks just waiting for a little excitement (or all your beanbags have been mysteriously "lost"), here's an easy way to transform a dress sock into a fun toy.

AGE: 3–5 YRS

CATEGORY: **PARENT & CHILD/ CRAFTS**

NUMBER OF CHILDREN: **ONE OR MORE**

Materials:
4 dress socks (adult or children's)

4 cups of uncooked lentils, split peas, or rice

Small juice cup

Scissors (for adult use only)

Create:
Find four clean dress socks made of thin material (without holes!). Pour 1 cup of uncooked lentils, split peas, or rice into a small juice cup. Stretch the opening of one sock firmly around the cup's rim. Tip the cup upside down to spill all of the lentils into the sock. Tie off the sock in a double knot at the ankle. (Use scissors to trim off the extra length, allowing about 1 inch of sock material at the end of the beanbag so the fabric does not fray.) Repeat this same process with the rest of the socks.

Outdoor Play

There's much to celebrate about the great outdoors, and it's a marvelous place to play together. Because preschoolers are typically such keen observers, the sunshine, wind, sights, and sounds of Mother Nature get mixed into the play experience when you move the play outdoors. What's more, you don't have to be afraid of scuffing the floor or staining the furniture. Whether you are playing a game of Red-Light Roundabout or investigating the critters that share your backyard, the great outdoors is a marvelous place to move about and play.

248 Two-Square

An easy-on-the-rules game that looks a little like Four-Square.

QUICK & EASY

Materials:
Sidewalk chalk
Playground ball

AGE: 3–5 YRS

CATEGORY:
PARENT & CHILD/
OUTDOOR

NUMBER OF
CHILDREN: ONE
OR MORE

Setup:
Use the chalk to draw two large squares a few feet apart on the driveway, or designate two sidewalk squares. Each player stands inside his own square, facing the other player.

Play:
Your child simply tosses the ball, trying to get it to land inside your square. Gently bounce it back into his square so that he can catch the ball (either before or after it bounces). Continue taking turns. Older preschoolers will play a smoother version of this game and may learn to "serve" the ball back into your square right after catching it. This is a flexible game, with no rules about the number of bounces allowed and no worries if the ball lands on the line or outside the square.

*SAFETY ALERT: Supervise carefully. Play in areas where there are no moving cars, and enforce a rule that only you can retrieve the ball if it rolls toward the street or other driveways.

249 Concrete Road-Racer

Test your car-racing skills on an outdoor ramp and roadway.

QUICK & EASY

Materials:
Plastic bucket (turned upside down) or kitchen chair
20"-by-30" piece of foam board (or long wooden plank)
Invisible tape
Sidewalk chalk
Assorted toy cars and trucks

AGE: 3–5 YRS

CATEGORY:
PARENT & CHILD/
OUTDOOR

NUMBER OF
CHILDREN: ONE
OR MORE

Setup:
Turn the bucket upside down on the sidewalk or concrete patio. Lean the foam board up against the bucket (or the seat of the kitchen chair) to create a ramp. Use a few long pieces of invisible tape to loosely attach the foam board to the bucket or seat. Use the sidewalk chalk to draw a finish line a short distance away from the lowest end of the ramp.

Play:
Send the cars down one or more of these ramps and see how far each vehicle travels before it stops, or send two cars down side by side for a traditional race. If you have a child who is

intrigued by numbers and likes the idea of "measuring," have a yardstick handy. Make colored chalk marks on the concrete to indicate where each car or truck landed when it came down from the ramp. Then measure to see how many inches the winning car traveled.

250 Parking Garage

Remove the flaps from one end of a large cardboard box and set it on its side with the opening several yards from the end of the ramp. See how many cars your child can send down the ramp and into the parking garage. You can also use an assortment of lightweight small, medium, and large balls. (Be sure your child is not standing at the low end of the ramp when the balls or cars are released.)

*SAFETY ALERT: Supervise carefully. Play in areas where there are no moving cars and enforce a rule that only you can retrieve the balls or cars if they roll toward the street or other driveways.

251 Red-Light Roundabout

Draw a giant figure eight on the pavement to turn your driveway into a roundabout; you become the traffic cop.

QUICK & EASY

AGE: **3–5 YRS**

CATEGORY: **PARENT & CHILD/ OUTDOOR**

NUMBER OF CHILDREN: **ONE OR MORE**

Materials:
  Sidewalk chalk
  Preschool riding toy or tricycle

Setup:
Draw two giant, adjacent circles on the pavement to create a figure eight roadway for your child to travel around on his tricycle. Position yourself a few feet away from the intersection (where the two circles meet),

directing traffic. Give a little demo of the three hand signals that you will use for this game:

Green light: Your right arm is relaxed at your side, with fingers pointing down.

Yellow light: Your right arm is fully extended to the side at shoulder level.

Red light: Your right arm extends to the side at shoulder level; bend your elbow up at a right angle, facing your palm away from you and spreading your fingers.

Play:
Call out and gesture "green light," and your child begins to ride his tricycle around the figure eight roadway. Each time he approaches the intersection, you give either the green, yellow, or red light command and gesture, and your child responds accordingly.

252 Zigzag Roadway

Position three to five sports cones in a line on the driveway. Leave about 5 feet of space between each cone. Position yourself at one end of this line of cones and play the role of traffic director. Your child uses the cones as an obstacle course.

253 Giant Flying Disc-Toss

Preschoolers typically don't have the skills needed to catch a flying disc, but they sure enjoy tossing one.

AGE: 3–5 YRS

CATEGORY: **PARENT & CHILD/ OUTDOOR**

NUMBER OF CHILDREN: **ONE OR MORE**

Materials:
Flying fabric disc

Setup:
Select a clear open lawn or park for throwing.

Play:
Give a little demo to show how to hold and toss the flying disc, then get out of the way! Help out with the retrieval of the disc as needed.

SAFETY ALERT: Supervise carefully.

PARENT TIP
254 Game Time with Dad

❝We have a play routine in our family that got started by accident. My older son had a friend over to play, and my younger son had no one to play with. On that particular day, I told my younger son that if he'd help me wash the car (the chore I was doing at the time), the two of us would play catch in the backyard together when we finished. This plan was a big hit and now the boys call this arrangement 'Game Time with Dad'; meaning you've got a friend coming over, but I'll be doing something fun with Dad.❞

—Ed from South Carolina

255 Sponge-Blob

Toss around giant, wet, squishy sponges for a blobby-good game on a hot summer day.

AGE: 3–5 YRS

CATEGORY: **PARENT & CHILD/ OUTDOOR**

NUMBER OF CHILDREN: **ONE OR MORE**

Materials:
Large bucket
2 giant sponges
Sidewalk chalk

Setup:
Fill the bucket with water and place the giant sponges inside. Use the chalk to draw a large (5 foot by 5 foot) square on the driveway or concrete patio.

Play:
Standing a few feet away from the square, the first player takes a soaking wet sponge from the bucket and tosses it into the square to create a blob design on the pavement. He quickly retrieves his sponge from the square, and the second player tosses his sponge, creating a second blob of water nearby. (Before you know it, a second game will be under way, in which you each guess what the shape resembles. It's a little like looking at the clouds in the sky!)

256 Sponge-Blob with Numbers

Use the chalk to create nine small squares inside the large box you have drawn on the pavement—three squares across and three squares down. Write a number, one through nine, in each small box, and score corresponding points each time a sponge lands inside one of these boxes.

257 Bucket-Blob

Fill a large plastic tub or dishpan with water and take turns tossing the wet sponges into the tub in a "bombs-away" style. Best for hot summer days when the two of you don't mind getting wet.

Preschool Play (age 3 to 5)

Preschool Play (age 3 to 5)

258 Preschool Kickball

It's a kicking and running game, pure and simple, with Mom or Dad retrieving the ball.

QUICK & EASY

AGE: 3–5 YRS

CATEGORY: **PARENT & CHILD/ OUTDOOR**

NUMBER OF CHILDREN: **ONE OR MORE**

Materials:
Roll of 2"-wide painter's tape
Playground ball

Setup:
Pick a safe grassy area for playing. Designate one area of the lawn as home plate, and mark first base several yards away, off to the side. Mark a power-kick line, 4 inches to 10 inches in front of home plate, by laying a 6-foot strip of tape across the ground. (Roll out the tape, sticky side down, in 12-inch sections, pressing it down with your feet as you go.)

Tip: If the lawn is wet, and your tape lines aren't sticking, see the "Start and Finish" box, page 348.

Play:
Place the ball at home plate and encourage your child to kick as hard as she can to try to cross the power-kick line. Each time the ball crosses the line, your child runs to first base and back and scores a point. (To increase the challenge for older preschoolers, you can roll the ball gently toward home plate so they can take a kick at a moving object.) There are no strikeouts or fouls in this preschool-friendly game, just a spirited round of kicking and running, with Mom or Dad playing in the outfield!

Riding Toys

Plastic or metal ride-on toys are terrific for large muscle development. Most children learn to pedal early on in the preschool stage. First tricycles need to be sized to your child; 12- or 13-inch wheeled trikes will fit most three- and four-year-olds. At five, many children are quite skilled "pedalers," ready for bigger tricycles or a bicycle with training wheels. These toys are also marvelous at inspiring pretend-play scenarios too, so many of the vehicle and pretend-play props and toys will add hours of fun to riding-toy play.

Create a pretend driving scenario with which your child is familiar: become a taxi driver taking visitors to the airport, a bus driver hauling workers to their jobs, a pizza delivery person, or an airplane pilot.

*SAFETY ALERT: When you purchase a tricycle for your child, buy a bicycle helmet with the seal of approval from the Consumer Product Safety Commission (CPSC) at the same time. Make sure the helmet fits properly, and set a helmet rule for any outdoor riding. To avoid falls and serious accidents, provide constant supervision for all tricycle and other ride-on toy play.

Playing with Others

What good things can happen when your preschooler plays with others? He learns what it means to be a friend and have a friend. He learns to cooperate and take turns. He runs, jumps, imitates, learns to lead and follow. He learns that another child has ideas and desires different from his own. He learns to use his words to express his feelings when he is frustrated or angry. He learns how to apologize. He sees what amazing pretend play ideas can be invented when *two* imaginations work together.

Pretend Play

Preschoolers are notorious for their elaborate, creative pretend-play scenarios. Playing fireman, dress-up, and other imaginative games is one of the best ways for two or more preschoolers to have fun together. This is self-directed play at its best, where the children are ad-libbing together to create the action and develop their roles. Your job is simply to gather up props and let them have at it.

Preschool Play (age 3 to 5)

"Pretend play is the greatest thing since squeezed mustard, in my mind. It's a way to learn about symbols, and pretend play is essential for reading. In other words, you have to understand that this little toy car represents a big giant car. You have to understand that this noise represents a car somewhere off on the street. That is no different than having the letter B represent the sound buh, or these letters c-a-r representing a car out on the street. **"**

—Becky Bailey, Ph.D.
developmental psychologist, specialist in early childhood education,
and author of *I Love You Rituals*

UNPLUGGED PLAY

In this section, I've suggested possible props to enrich and help jump-start each theme, but keep in mind that these props are only suggestions. Feel free to improvise, based on the items that are available to you. And by no means do you need every item on these lists in order to proceed! Children can pretend in rooms with four bare walls; they might need only one or two of the items to get started.

The Amazing Cardboard Box!

The cardboard box is the granddaddy of all pretend play props! Stick two children in a room, add a giant box and a few markers, and see what fantastic play unfolds—powered 100 percent by their imaginations. Very often, children will climb right inside a box and only then begin to discover what it is meant to be. A large box may become a house, fort, spaceship, train, cave, castle, pirate ship, or school bus. A medium box might become a stove, dollhouse, hospital, aquarium, parking garage, swimming pool, tea party table, or minicar.

Pretend play with a cardboard box as the centerpiece may be enhanced by mixing in other nontoxic materials and toys:

action figures	life vests
blankets	markers
buckets	pans
crayons	pillows
dolls	stuffed animals
hats and costumes	tools
kitchen utensils	washable paints

But as always, follow your child's lead and you'll be as delighted as she is to see where her imagination will take her.

Where to Find Boxes For large boxes, try appliance, building supply, furniture, plumbing supply, hardware, or bedding and linen stores. If you can't find a free source in your community, consider purchasing giant wardrobe boxes from your local moving company. For small to medium boxes, try grocery stores, liquor stores, shoe stores, discount chains, food co-ops, or office supply stores. Call ahead to see if there's a particular day to stop by for recycled or free cardboard boxes.

Supporting Role for Parents To keep things safe, your main job is to be the one who handles the tools—you cut out any doors and windows in the boxes. Have your child use crayons to outline the areas where she wants the windows and doors. If more than one child is creating something with boxes, it's also important to set up some rules or talk about how long you will "keep" the box creation, so one child doesn't destroy the box and upset another child.

Make an Elaborate Family Playhouse

Start with one giant appliance box (or cut all the end flaps off of two giant boxes and tape them together with wide packing or duct tape to make one giant playhouse). Draw a door and cut it on two sides only, so that it is still attached along the left edge and can be opened and closed to enter. Cut windows out of the box. Tape shoe boxes under each window to create flower boxes. On a sunny day, take the project outdoors and use washable paint to decorate the exterior of the house. Draw flowers where the flower boxes are attached. (Or add plastic flowers inside the window boxes.)

Paint the inside of the house, or paste wallpaper on the interior walls for a truly authentic home-style room. Hang or tape your child's drawings on the inside to add some original paintings to the room. Add a small area rug and an assortment of children's books for cozy reading. When the house is finished, add a medium cardboard box turned upside down for a stove on which to cook the family meals. (Use markers to draw the knobs and burners on the stove.) Bring in a few pots, pans, and bowls so your child can stock the kitchen with utensils to make it seem more "real." Gather up a few cushions or pillows to create a little reading corner to serve as the living room.

Now that is indeed an elaborate playhouse. It'll take a few hours to create, with parent and child working together, but it will lead to many more hours of fun for your child and her playmates.

Preschool Play (age 3 to 5)

259 Family Picnic/Cookout

Hooray for a picnic with no ants, no spills, and no bug bites. Spread out the food, and eat-eat-eat it all up.

AGE: 3–5 YRS

CATEGORY: PLAY WITH OTHERS/PRETEND

NUMBER OF CHILDREN: TWO OR MORE

Possible Props:
Tablecloth
Picnic basket
Paper plates, napkins
Plastic cups, spoons, bowls, pie pans
Large serving spoons, plastic spatula, pie servers
Empty salt and pepper (or spice) shakers
Empty red and yellow squeeze bottles (ketchup and mustard)
Cardboard box (turned upside down for pretend grill)
Pretend foods (made from construction paper)
Stuffed animals, dolls (pretend family and friends)
Frisbee or balls

Characters:
Person Cooking on Grill, Mom, Dad, Children, Grandma, Grandpa, Cousins, Aunt and Uncle

260 Artist's Studio

See how many wonderful paintings we can make when we have our very own studio.

AGE: 3–5 YRS

CATEGORY: PLAY WITH OTHERS/PRETEND

NUMBER OF CHILDREN: TWO OR MORE

Possible Props:

Child's easel

Paper, paint brushes, paints

Painter's rollers and plastic paint pans

Cardboard cut in oval shape for pallet

Painter's smock

Watercolor paints

Cardboard mats or paper frames

Finished artwork to display

Invisible tape to hang artwork on the walls or backs of chairs for display

Dolls and stuffed animals for "models" or customers

Art supply catalog

Cash register and pretend money

Characters:
Painter, Painter's Helper, Framer, Cashier, Customer

261 Office

I'm sorry, Mom, I can't talk right now—I'm very, very busy at the office.

AGE: 3–5 YRS

CATEGORY: PLAY WITH OTHERS/PRETEND

NUMBER OF CHILDREN: TWO OR MORE

Possible Props:

Grown-up dress-up clothes

Boxes (for desks and tables, pretend computer)

Small calculator or old typewriter

Books and magazines

File folders, index cards, stickers, hole punch, paper clips, paper, pencils, nontoxic markers, ink pad and rubber stamps, envelopes

Clipboard

Desk calendar

Wastebasket, wire baskets

Toy telephone and phone book

Office supply catalog

Characters:
Computer Person, Telephone Operator, Report Writer, Filer

★CLASSIC★

262 House

Lunches to make, groceries to buy, babies to change . . . I think I hear the telephone ringing. Hold on—it's for you.

AGE: 3–5 YRS

CATEGORY: PLAY WITH OTHERS/PRETEND

NUMBER OF CHILDREN: TWO OR MORE

Possible Props:

Dress-up clothes (hats, shoes, jewelry, neckties, briefcase, backpacks, purses)

Lunch boxes

Blankets and pillows

Cardboard boxes (for use as cars, beds, tables, washer and dryer, cupboards, microwave)

Dolls, baby clothes, diapers, bottles, pacifier, stroller

Pots, pans, plates, and kitchen gadgets

Simple tools and toy tools

Laundry basket, towels, socks, and sheets

Newspaper, magazines, children's books

Grocery store fliers and coupons

Toy telephone

Alarm clock

Characters:
Mom, Dad, Baby, Sister, Brother, Grandma, Grandpa

263 Shoe Store

Why yes, I do have yellow shoes with red polka dots.

AGE: 3–5 YRS

CATEGORY: **PLAY WITH OTHERS/PRETEND**

NUMBER OF CHILDREN: **TWO OR MORE**

Possible Props:

Shoe boxes

Assortment of men's, women's, and children's shoes, boots, and sandals

Socks

Assortment of purses or evening bags

Shoe horn

Stool and chair

Laundry basket or boxes, turned upside down for displaying shoes

Shoelaces

Empty margarine containers for pretend shoe polish

Small rags for polishing

Shoe catalog

Construction paper

Pencil for tracing customer's foot

Cardboard box for cash register

Play money and coins

Small plain tablet for receipts

Pencils

Paper bags (put shoes inside after customer has paid)

Dolls and teddy bears as pretend customers

Characters:
Shoe Salesman, Store Manager, Cashier, Customer

264 Fishing

Dad, come quick! There's a lake in the living room! Let's try to catch a gazillion-trillion fish today, okay?

AGE: 3–5 YRS

CATEGORY: **PLAY WITH OTHERS/PRETEND**

NUMBER OF CHILDREN: **TWO OR MORE**

Possible Props:

Fishing hat, vest, sunglasses, wind parkas

Shoe box for tackle box

Bobbers and plastic worms (no hooks)

Small pair of pliers

Construction paper (to make fish, minnows)

Life jackets

Large tablecloth for the boat

Small cardboard box turned upside down (motor)

Rubber boots

Yardsticks and rulers for fishing poles (or toy fishing poles)

Large kitchen strainer or small fishing net

Small cooler for fish

Boating/fishing supply catalog

Characters:
Fisherman and Fisherwoman, Captain

265 Farmer's Market

I'll trade you one strawberry for three green beans. And here's a big bag of corn I grew on my farm.

AGE: 3–5 YRS

CATEGORY: **PLAY WITH OTHERS/PRETEND**

NUMBER OF CHILDREN: **TWO OR MORE**

Possible Props:

Table for produce with 1 or 2 chairs

Farmer shirts, clothes, hats

Shoe box and play money for cash box

Preschool Play (age 3 to 5)

Preschool Play (age 3 to 5)

Construction paper and tape for produce signs

Garden seed catalog (cut photos for signs)

Real fruits and vegetables (or plastic produce)

Small plastic containers (pretend jams and jellies)

Bunches of plastic flowers and newspaper for wrapping

Kitchen or bathroom scale

Paper lunch bags and grocery bags

Characters:
Farmer, Cashier and Bagger, Customers

266 Toy Store

In this toy store, you get to open the boxes and play with everything before you pay the money!

AGE: **3–5 YRS**

CATEGORY: **PLAY WITH OTHERS/PRETEND**

NUMBER OF CHILDREN: **TWO OR MORE**

Possible Props:
Stuffed animals, dolls, cars, trucks

Board games, card games

Riding toys

Balls and sports equipment

Cash register (or shoe box for pretend cash register), play money and coins

Large paper bags

Small notepad and pencil for receipts

Toy grocery cart

Toy store fliers and coupons

Paper and plastic bags to wrap purchases

Characters:
Shoppers (Parent, Baby, Child), Cashier, Store Manager

267 Bakery

My dad likes blueberry pie, but this pink cake is the fanciest. And if you want birthday cake, we have the kind with balloons and candles on top.

AGE: **3–5 YRS**

CATEGORY: **PLAY WITH OTHERS/PRETEND**

NUMBER OF CHILDREN: **TWO OR MORE**

Possible Props:
Play dough and rolling pin (or sand for outdoor play)

Cake pans, unbreakable pie pans, muffin tins, cookie sheets

Cookie and candy tins

Plastic measuring cups and spoons

Plastic mixing bowls

Cookie cutters, doughnut or biscuit cutters

Paper cupcake holders

Cake decorating set (empty)

Empty egg cartons, milk cartons, oatmeal boxes

Plastic pie or cake carriers or plates

Metal cooling racks

Wooden or plastic spoons, cake servers, spatula, utensils

Whisk

Birthday candles

Construction paper for making pretend cookies and candies

Small ziplock bags, paper lunch bags

Empty spice jars

Large cardboard box (oven)

Apron, paper chef's hat (available at paper/party stores)

Kitchen timer

Small waxed paper bags to wrap cookies and pastries

Characters:
Baker, Cake Decorator, Cashier, Counter Person, Customer

268 Train

Excuse me, does this train go to the park? Oh, only two stops to the zoo?

AGE: **3–5 YRS**

CATEGORY:
PLAY WITH OTHERS/PRETEND

NUMBER OF CHILDREN: **TWO OR MORE**

Possible Props:

Hat and gloves (for conductor)

Backpacks and small suitcases (for traveler)

Paper to make tickets and signs (or purchase roll of tickets at paper supply store)

Cardboard box turned upside down (ticket counter)

Chairs

Magazines, tour books, maps

Stuffed animals and dolls (passengers)

Table, tablecloth, chairs, and props for the dining car

Characters:

Train Conductor, Ticket Taker, Luggage Helper, Waiter in Dining Car, Passengers

269 Grocery Store

Cleanup on aisle three!

AGE: **3–5 YRS**

CATEGORY:
PLAY WITH OTHERS/PRETEND

NUMBER OF CHILDREN: **TWO OR MORE**

Possible Props:

Canned fruits and vegetables, coffee

Juice cans or boxes

Boxed cake mixes, rice, pasta, beans, puddings

Paper plates, cups, paper towels, sandwich bags, foil

Office supplies and school supplies

Small toys

Magazines and newspapers

Plastic jugs (temporarily rescued from the recycling bin)

Cash register (or shoe box for pretend cash register)

Play money, coins, and coupons

Paper and grocery bags

Toy grocery cart

Dolls and stuffed animals for pretend children

Grocery store fliers and coupons (and scissors for cutting—for adult use only)

Construction paper and tape (make signs and displays with food photos from fliers)

Characters:

Stock Boy/Girl, Cashier, Store Manager, Shoppers (Parent, Baby, Child)

270 Pizza Parlor

Pepperoni-Pineapple is the pizza topping of the day.

AGE: **3–5 YRS**

CATEGORY:
PLAY WITH OTHERS/PRETEND

NUMBER OF CHILDREN: **TWO OR MORE**

Possible Props:

Cardboard pizza boxes (for delivery)

Large cardboard circles to make pretend pizzas

Construction paper to cut out toppings (shredded cheese, pepperoni, green pepper slices, mushrooms)

Plastic pizza cutter

Empty Parmesan and spice shakers

Medium or large cardboard box placed on its side (pizza ovens)

Kitchen timer/buzzer

Small area rug (or large box) for the pizza delivery car

Toy telephone

Pizza coupons and fliers

Small notepad and pencil for phone orders

Paper plates, napkins, utensils, cups

Cash register (or shoe box for pretend cash register), play money and coins

Characters:

Pizza Chef, Telephone Order Taker, Cashier, Pizza Delivery Person, Customer

Preschool Play (age 3 to 5)

UNPLUGGED PLAY

Preschool Play (age 3 to 5)

271 | Superheroes/ Kings/Knights

Storm the castle, we've got to save the knights! (Remember, it's just pretend.)

AGE: 3–5 YRS

CATEGORY: **PLAY WITH OTHERS/PRETEND**

NUMBER OF CHILDREN: TWO OR MORE

Possible Props:

Colorful towels or small cloth (folded) for cape

Hinged hair clip (or safety pin) to fasten the cape

Colored tights or child's long johns

Crown or velvet hat with jewels glued on

Helmet

Eye mask with elastic (the type encircling eyes only)

Belt to hold magic wand or toy sword around the waist

Characters:

Superheroes, Kings, Knights to do the rescuing, one or more persons to be saved from danger

Make a Simple Tunic or Cape

What's a knight without his armor? A heroine without her cape? A king without his tunic? Creating the right costume for your toddler as she prepares to save the world is a quick and easy way to set the stage for first-rate pretend play. Each variation below can be made with household items you are likely to have in your cupboard. It will take a few minutes of your time today to make one of the garments below, but this investment of time will inspire *hours* of splendid fantasy play.

Sweatshirt Tunic:
Begin with an adult small or medium sweatshirt turned inside out. Use pinking shears to cut a V-shaped neck and cut the arms off the sweatshirt, leaving a small cuff of fabric to hang over your child's shoulder. Cut points into the bottom edge of the tunic that hit several inches above your child's knee. Use a silk or twisted yarn cord to create a sash.

Pillowcase Tunic:
Lay a standard-size pillowcase on the table with the end seam positioned at the top and the opening at the bottom. Using pinking shears, cut a V-shaped hole along the top seam for the neck hole of the tunic. Cut a semicircle along each side of the pillowcase to create two oversize armholes. (Be sure to make the neck and armholes large enough so that the tunic slips on and off your child easily.) Cut a scalloped edge or series of points at the bottom of the pillowcase. Use a silk or twisted yarn cord or ribbon to create a sash.

Grocery Bag Tunic:
Cut a V-shaped neck hole from the bottom of the bag (the top of the tunic), and two armholes along the sides. Finish the bottom of the tunic with fringe.

Capes:
Capes can be made using soft blankets, old velvet shawls, large pieces of felt fabric, or oversize towels. Fasten the cape in place with a large safety pin or hair clip.

When Preschoolers Are Obsessed with Weapon Play

Preschool teachers know perhaps best of all that many children three to five are fascinated by violent play themes—pretend knives, guns, bombs, and weapons for hurting or killing others. Try as they might to eliminate this type of play from the classroom, it creeps back in daily. What's going on during these young and tender years that make these violent play themes of such interest?

For starters, many children are seeing violent images on television and in movies and videos, and they are both fascinated and confused by what they see. Preschoolers are notorious for using pretend-play scenarios to work out or get familiar with something perplexing in their lives. They act out the violent play in part as a way to understand what it means. But several problems often occur along the way. First, this sort of violent pretend play can quickly escalate into play that is overwhelming and frightening for some young children. Also, violent pretend play often turns into aggressive play with *real* pushing, shoving, and hurting others. If left unchecked, violent play takes on a life of its own, with small groups of preschoolers preoccupied with this type of play at the expense of other fun and creative kinds of play.

So what's a parent to do to try to manage weapons play or violent pretend play during the preschool years?

- Eliminate your young child's exposure to violent images on television (including news programs), movies, and videos.

- Talk with your child about any troubling violent issues or episodes he hears about from other playmates and use simple, reassuring language to show your child that he is safe.

- Reduce or eliminate toy weapons (knives, guns, grenades, etc.) from your child's toy chest. (Realize that your child will still turn sticks and blocks into his own makeshift pretend weapons on occasion to satisfy his desire to play.)

- Make very clear and specific house rules that real violent play (pushing, hitting, and hurting) are *not* acceptable, and stop this play when you see it in action. You won't have much luck insisting that your child never engage in violent pretend play, but you can set clear, enforceable rules to ensure that there will be no real violent play.

- Before your child has playmates over, ask him which unplugged games his friends might enjoy. And, when friends arrive, be available to help jump-start nonviolent types of play that you know the group will enjoy. Have interesting play props, games, and activities ready to get things moving in a friendly and positive direction.

Preschool Play (age 3 to 5)

272 Beach

Is it freezing outside? What a perfect day to pull on your swimsuit and pretend to go surfing on the really big waves.

AGE: **3–5 YRS**

CATEGORY: **PLAY WITH OTHERS/PRETEND**

NUMBER OF CHILDREN: **TWO OR MORE**

Possible Props:

- Beach blanket or sheet
- Plastic buckets, sieves, shovels, beach balls, toys
- Empty squeeze bottles (sunscreen)
- Bathing suits and sunglasses
- Child's umbrella
- High stool or chair for lifeguard
- Whistle or horn for lifeguard
- Beach hat or visor
- Poster board, cut and rolled to create megaphone for lifeguard
- Construction paper and small dowel rods to make warning flags (Caution, Riptides, Jellyfish)
- Shoe box for first-aid kit; paper towel strips and tape for Band-Aids
- Dolls and stuffed animals

Characters:
Swimmer, Lifeguard, Sunbather, Jogger, Rescue Squad

273 Circus

Look, look! I'm walking the tightrope. And then I'll tame a lion.

AGE: **3–5 YRS**

CATEGORY: **PLAY WITH OTHERS/PRETEND**

NUMBER OF CHILDREN: **TWO OR MORE**

Possible Props:

- Large shirts, pants, and hats for clowns, leotards, animal hats, costumes
- Face paint, wigs, ballet shoes and outfit, child's umbrella
- Stuffed animals and dolls
- Hula-Hoops for animal tricks
- Masking tape (lay on carpet for tightrope)
- Cardboard boxes placed on their side (animal cages)
- Bedsheet or area rug for stage
- Paper for signs and tickets (or purchase a roll of tickets at paper supply store)
- Money box with coins and play money
- Seats for the audience

Characters:
Circus Performer (Clown, Tightrope Walker, Gymnast, Ballerina), Circus Animals (Dancing Bears, Lions, and Tigers), Audience

274 Nursery School

What happens if all the babies start crying or get hungry at the very same time?

AGE: **3–5 YRS**

CATEGORY: **PLAY WITH OTHERS/PRETEND**

NUMBER OF CHILDREN: **TWO OR MORE**

Possible Props:

- Small toy cars, trucks, dolls, blocks, musical instruments, riding toys
- Books for story time
- Pillowcases or area rugs for nap time
- Table, chairs, plates, cups for snack or lunchtime
- Stuffed animals (students)
- Paper and markers for drawing time
- Building blocks
- Toy tools and toolbox for construction play

Characters:
Teacher, Students

275 Airplane

Would you like peanuts or crackers for your snack? Oops, be careful with your tray!

AGE: 3–5 YRS

CATEGORY: **PLAY WITH OTHERS/PRETEND**

NUMBER OF CHILDREN: **TWO OR MORE**

Possible Props:

Backpack, briefcase, luggage

Clothing to create costumes for flight attendant, pilot, and copilot

Large area rug or bedsheet for plane

Seats for pilot and copilot

Communication accessories (pilot headphones, walkie-talkies, pretend flight attendant phone/ microphone, etc.)

Cardboard box and crayons to create cockpit gear

Chairs for passengers

Car seat for baby

Blankets and pillows

Magazines, tour books, maps

Cardboard box (beverage and snack cart)

Doll (baby), pacifier, bottle, baby toys

Characters:

Flight Attendant, Pilot and Copilot, Passengers

276 Bus Ride

Is everybody on the bus? This bus goes really fast, so it's a good idea to sit down in your seat and buckle up.

AGE: 3–5 YRS

CATEGORY: **PLAYIWITH OTHERS/PRETEND**

NUMBER OF CHILDREN: **TWO OR MORE**

Possible Props:

Hat and clothes for bus driver

Walkie-talkie

Poker chips or play money (coins or bus tokens)

Area rug or bedsheet (bus)

Chairs

Backpack, bags of groceries, briefcase

Characters:

Bus Driver, Passengers

277 Post Office

After I stamp them all, I'm going to push this cart full of letters to all the mailboxes in the entire neighborhood. Special delivery!

AGE: 3–5 YRS

CATEGORY: **PLAY WITH OTHERS/PRETEND**

NUMBER OF CHILDREN: **TWO OR MORE**

Possible Props:

Envelopes and stickers (stamps), mailing labels

Junk mail

Magazines and folded newspapers

Small pillowcase (mailbag)

Ink pad and rubber stamps ("first class," etc.)

Rubber bands, pencils, hole punch

Wire baskets for mail sorters

Shoe boxes with labels for packages

Large cardboard box or laundry basket (mailbox)

Twin bedsheet and chair, ride-on toys, or wagon (mail truck)

Uniform for mail carrier

Wall clock

Phone book and zip code book

Cash box and play money, pretend credit cards

Plastic tub or box (stamp vending machine)

Bathroom scale for weighing packages

Characters:

Post Office Clerk, Mail Carrier, Customers

Preschool Play (age 3 to 5)

Preschool Play (age 3 to 5)

278 Kitchen

Everybody get a dishcloth—there are lots of dirty dishes.

AGE: **3–5 YRS**

CATEGORY: **PLAY WITH OTHERS/PRETEND**

NUMBER OF CHILDREN: **TWO OR MORE**

Possible Props:

Pots and pans, colander, plastic mixing bowls

Hand beater, spatula and mixing spoons, plastic measuring cups

Plastic pitcher, cups, plates, utensils, salad tongs, paper towels, and napkins

Plastic tub, empty (squeeze) detergent bottles, dish towels (for washing and drying dishes by hand)

Assortment of empty food boxes and containers, empty spice jars, squeeze bottles

Pretend oven (cardboard box on its side, use crayons to decorate)

Shopping bags, grocery store fliers, and coupons

Play dough, rolling pin, cookie cutters

Characters:

Cooks in the Kitchen

279 Pet Store

Do you want to see the best dog in the history of the universe?

AGE: **3–5 YRS**

CATEGORY: **PLAY WITH OTHERS/PRETEND**

NUMBER OF CHILDREN: **TWO OR MORE**

Possible Props:

Stuffed animals

Wire baskets (cages)

Plastic containers and small strainers for fishbowls

Cans and plastic bowls for pet food

Brushes, combs, collars, leashes

Small pillows (pet beds)

Plastic tubs for shampooing pets

Cardboard boxes or shoe boxes for carrying pets

Pet care books

Poster board, nontoxic markers, tape, magazine photos of pets to make pet store posters

Cash box and play money, credit cards, calculator

Characters:

Pets, Pet Groomer and Caregiver, Cashier, Customer

280 Hardware Store

Do you need a hammer? Some nails? I have just the right tools for your fix-it work.

AGE: **3–5 YRS**

CATEGORY: **PLAY WITH OTHERS/PRETEND**

NUMBER OF CHILDREN: **TWO OR MORE**

Possible Props:

Toy tools and toolbox

Sandpaper, rags, paintbrushes, paint rollers

Buckets, mops, brooms, dustpans

Ruler, yardstick, tape measure

Plastic plumbing pipe, joints

Watering can, small garden trowel

Plastic container full of nuts and bolts, hinges

Small paper and plastic bags for bagging purchases

Construction paper, markers, labels for signs and price tags

Garden seed catalog (cut squares from catalog to make pretend seed packets)

Farm and garden catalog (for ordering)

Cash register and play money, credit cards, calculator (for credit card swipe machine)

Characters:

Store Clerk, Customers (Carpenter, Painter, Plumber)

281 | Firehouse

Snap on your suspenders, and you better cover your ears because this bell makes a really loud noise.

AGE: 3–5 YRS

CATEGORY:
PLAY WITH
OTHERS/PRETEND

NUMBER OF
CHILDREN: TWO
OR MORE

Possible Props:

Giant cardboard box (fire truck)

Markers (to draw tires and steering wheel)

Fireman hat, pants, shirt, boots,
    yellow rain parka

Vacuum cleaner hose or small garden hose

Toy firetrucks with ladders

Toy walkie-talkie, cell phone, telephone

Bell (to call firefighters to action)

Maps, paper, pencils

Toy toolbox and tools

Empty oatmeal canister (fire hydrant)

Poster board and nontoxic markers
    (to make firehouse or safety posters)

Characters:
Firefighter, Firetruck Driver

282 | Police Station

You're under arrest—for talking with your mouth full.

AGE: 3–5 YRS

CATEGORY:
PLAY WITH
OTHERS/PRETEND

NUMBER OF
CHILDREN: TWO
OR MORE

Possible Props:

Police hat, uniform, badge,
    shoes/boots, sunglasses

Ride-on toy (police car or motorcycle)

Toy walkie-talkie, cell phone, telephone, whistle

Large cardboard box (police car)

Poster board and nontoxic markers to make
    safety posters

Dolls

Toy car seat

Paper and pencils for speeding or traffic tickets

Characters:
Police Dispatcher, Police Officer, Motorcycle
Officer, Traffic Director

283 | Farm

My favorite part is feeding the horses.

AGE: 3–5 YRS

CATEGORY:
PLAY WITH
OTHERS/PRETEND

NUMBER OF
CHILDREN: TWO
OR MORE

Possible Props:

Farmer hats, bib overalls,
    boots, work gloves

Toy tractor or large cardboard box

Stuffed animals

Small garden tools

Garden seed catalog (cut small squares
    from seed catalog for garden seed packs)

Buckets for feeding animals

Baskets for collecting vegetables and fruits

Small cardboard box and twine for bailing hay

Small plastic jars, pots, pans, spoons for making
    jams and jellies

Books about farm animals

Characters:
Farmer, Gardener, Animal Keeper, Jam and
Pickle Maker

Preschool Play (age 3 to 5)

Preschool Play (age 3 to 5)

284 Camping

Can you believe it? The bears took our food and then drove our cars away in the middle of the night.

AGE: **3–5 YRS**

CATEGORY: **PLAY WITH OTHERS/PRETEND**

NUMBER OF CHILDREN: **TWO OR MORE**

Possible Props:

Tent (or bedsheet and chairs), sleeping bags, backpack, folding chairs, lantern, flashlight, compass

Hiking shoes, boots, parka, hat, bandana

Cardboard box turned upside down for camp stove or grill

Cooking utensils, pots, pans, tablecloth

Play fishing gear and tackle box

Water jug or thermos, canned foods or packed lunches

Stuffed animals

Characters:
Park Ranger, Campers

285 Library

We have big books, little books, funny books, and storybooks.

AGE: **3–5 YRS**

CATEGORY: **PLAY WITH OTHERS/PRETEND**

NUMBER OF CHILDREN: **TWO OR MORE**

Possible Props:

Table, chairs, area rug for story circle

Assorted books, magazines, newspapers

Index cards and pencils to make library cards

Rubber stamp and ink pad

Paper and nontoxic markers to make "QUIET" sign

Wall clock

Book bags

Characters:
Librarian, Storyteller, Reader

286 Nurse/Doctor's Office

I'm going to give you a shot, but then you can have a really cool sticker. All better!

AGE: **3–5 YRS**

CATEGORY: **PLAY WITH OTHERS/PRETEND**

NUMBER OF CHILDREN: **TWO OR MORE**

Possible Props:

Toy doctor or nurse's kit (stethoscope, needle, medicine, etc.)

Children's books, magazines, and chairs for waiting area

Basket full of Band-Aids, cotton balls, stickers

Clipboard, file folders, labels

Toy telephone, calculator, toy computer

Bathroom scale, small tape measure

Twin bed sheet for examination table

Dolls or stuffed animals

Stretchy cloth bandages for wrapping boo-boos

Characters:
Receptionist, Nurse, Doctor, Child, Parent

287 Restaurant

Order up! If you eat all your supper, I'll bring you some ice cream.

AGE: **3–5 YRS**

CATEGORY: **PLAY WITH OTHERS/PRETEND**

NUMBER OF CHILDREN: **TWO OR MORE**

Possible Props:

Pots, pans, spatula, wire whisk, unbreakable mixing bowl, colander

Chef's hat, apron, uniform for server

Paper, tape, markers, food photos from magazines (to make menus)

Place mats, plates, cups, utensils, napkins

Cookie sheet or pizza pan for serving tray

Pie pan and pie server with plastic lid

Plastic water pitcher

Plastic containers, tongs to create salad bar area

Grocery store fliers for ordering fruits, vegetables, and meats

Toy telephone, notepad, pencils

Plastic bowls and cups with lids and plastic bags for "to-go" orders

Snacks and food

Wall calendar, posters

Cash register, play money, coins, credit card, checkbook, calculator (for credit card swipe machine)

Characters:
Cook, Server, Counter Person, Cashier, Customer

288 Ice-Cream Parlor

Here's the biggest, yummiest banana split you ever tasted. Careful not to drip!

AGE: **3–5 YRS**

CATEGORY: **PLAY WITH OTHERS/PRETEND**

NUMBER OF CHILDREN: **TWO OR MORE**

Possible Props:

A variety of colored tissue paper, rolled into tight balls (scoops of ice cream)

Ice-cream scoops

Tiny paper cups (cones)

Plastic bowls and spoons for ice-cream sundaes

Empty spice shakers to hold pretend sprinkles

Empty squeeze bottles to hold pretend chocolate, strawberry sauce, and whipped cream

Cash register, play money, and coins

Notepad and pencil for taking orders

Kitchen counter with stools or kitchen table

Characters:
Ice-Cream Scooper, Cashier, Customer, Ice-Cream Delivery Truck Driver

289 Auto Repair Shop

What seems to be the problem? If you have car trouble, I know how to fix it.

AGE: **3–5 YRS**

CATEGORY: **PLAY WITH OTHERS/PRETEND**

NUMBER OF CHILDREN: **TWO OR MORE**

Possible Props:

Riding toys, trucks, wagons

Toy tools and toolbox

Flashlight

Plastic funnel

Paper coffee filters

Small tape measure (from sewing kit)

Mechanic's shirt, hat, and work gloves

Bicycle pump

Small paintbrush and water (paint) for touch-ups

Bucket and rag

Auto supply catalog

Cash register, play money, coins, credit card, calculator

Characters:
Mechanic, Tire Fixer, Cashier, Customer

290 Car Wash

Scrub-a-dub-dub! Soap up the cars and then rinse them off (outside is ideal).

AGE: **3–5 YRS**

CATEGORY: **PLAY WITH OTHERS/PRETEND**

NUMBER OF CHILDREN: **TWO OR MORE**

Possible Props:

Buckets, soapy water, spray bottles with water, sponges, old towels for drying

Tricycles, ride-on toys, wagons, toy cars, trucks

Radio, cash register (or shoe box) with toy money, paper, and pencils (to create receipts)

Characters:
Washer, Waxer, Dryer, Cashier, Customer

Preschool Play (age 3 to 5)

291 Taxi Driver

The meter is running, so let's get moving. Where to?

AGE: 3–5 YRS

CATEGORY: PLAY WITH OTHERS/PRETEND

NUMBER OF CHILDREN: TWO OR MORE

Possible Props:
- Giant cardboard box (taxicab)
- Nontoxic markers (to draw steering wheel and tires)
- Map, toy cell phone, walkie-talkie
- Electronic kitchen timer (taxi meter)
- Poster board, paper, markers to make taxicab signs
- Cash box with play money and coins
- Suitcase, briefcase, backpack, shopping bags with shoe boxes inside

Characters:
Taxi Driver, Customer, Tourist

292 Builder

Let's make an elevator that goes up three hundred floors!

AGE: 3–5 YRS

CATEGORY: PLAY WITH OTHERS/PRETEND

NUMBER OF CHILDREN: TWO OR MORE

Possible Props:
- Toy tools and toolbox
- Wooden blocks or scraps of wood
- Ruler, yardstick, small level
- Carpenter's pencil
- Ball of twine
- Stud finder
- Plumbing fittings
- Paintbrushes and buckets
- Small broom and dustpan
- Building supply catalog or newspaper flier
- Paper and pencil (for tallying up the bill)

Characters:
Construction Boss, Carpenter, Plumber, Electrician, Home Owner

293 Babysitter

In a magical land where the babies never, ever cry . . .

AGE: 3–5 YRS

CATEGORY: PLAY WITH OTHERS/PRETEND

NUMBER OF CHILDREN: TWO OR MORE

Possible Props:
- Dolls or stuffed animals
- Small high chair, stroller, changing table, baby swing
- Baby bottle, pacifier, paper towels, tape for diapers
- Bib, blanket, hats, baby clothes
- Toys for baby
- Storybooks
- Play money or old checkbook to pay babysitter

Characters:
Babysitter, Babysitter's Helper, Baby, Older Brother or Sister

294 Laundromat

First, throw everything in a pile. Next, jump in. See how easy?

AGE: 3–5 YRS

CATEGORY: PLAY WITH OTHERS/PRETEND

NUMBER OF CHILDREN: TWO OR MORE

Possible Props:
- Large cardboard boxes (washer and dryer)
- Empty boxes of laundry detergent and fabric softener
- Laundry basket filled with towels, bedsheets, and socks for folding
- Hangers
- Coins, change sorter
- Fruit boxes (vending machine) filled with snacks

Characters:
Laundry Manager, Customer

295 Food Co-op

Lots of grains to scoop into bags, and loads of cereal to put on the shelves.

AGE: **3–5 YRS**

CATEGORY: **PLAY WITH OTHERS/PRETEND**

NUMBER OF CHILDREN: **TWO OR MORE**

Possible Props:

Plastic tubs, food scoops, newsprint paper (wadded into balls for bulk foods)

Unopened boxes of pasta, oatmeal, tea, salt, spices

Canned foods

Water and juice jugs

Unopened packs of paper products (napkins, paper towels, toilet paper)

Cardboard boxes for food bins

Toy fruits and vegetables or pretend food cut from magazines

Paper lunch bags and markers to indicate prices

Kitchen or bathroom scale for weighing foods

Cash register or box with play money and coins

Bags and cardboard boxes for each purchase

Characters:
Customer, Worker

296 Hair Salon/Spa

Ribbons and scarves and clips—oh my, you look pretty.

AGE: **3–5 YRS**

CATEGORY: **PLAY WITH OTHERS/PRETEND**

NUMBER OF CHILDREN: **TWO OR MORE**

Possible Props:

Chairs, stools for haircutting and waiting

Combs, brushes

Toy hair dryer (or plastic utility flashlight, batteries removed)

Curlers, barrettes, bows, headbands, hair combs

Wigs, braids, scarves

Plastic tub for soaking hands and feet

Empty plastic bottles of shampoo, conditioner, lotion, perfume

Shopping bags for purchases

Magazines with hairstyle photos and products

Toy telephone, notepad, pencils

Cash register, play money, credit cards, calculator (for credit card swipe machine)

Dolls (customers)

Characters:

Hairstylist, Manicurist, Cashier, Receptionist, Customer

SAFETY ALERT: Even though there won't be real scissors around, be sure to establish the rule of Hair Salon play: "Absolutely no cutting of anyone's hair, only pretend cutting!"

297 Barbershop

Buzz, buzz, clip, clip—your mustache is funny looking.

AGE: **3–5 YRS**

CATEGORY: **PLAY WITH OTHERS/PRETEND**

NUMBER OF CHILDREN: **TWO OR MORE**

Possible Props:

Play razor, scissors, combs, brushes, and buzz clippers

Plastic or cloth cape

Radio

Poster board and nontoxic markers to make posters

Stools for clipping and chairs for waiting

Magazines and newspapers for hairstyle selection

Cash register and play money, coins, credit cards, calculator (for credit card swipe machine)

Bowl of lollipops

Characters:

Barber, Cashier, Customer

SAFETY ALERT: Even though there won't be real scissors around, be sure to establish the rule of Barbershop play: "Absolutely no cutting of anyone's hair, only pretend cutting!"

298 Yard Sale

That couch is really fancy, so it costs lots of money. I'll throw in the TV for three more dollars.

AGE: **3–5 YRS**

CATEGORY: **PLAY WITH OTHERS/PRETEND**

NUMBER OF CHILDREN: **TWO OR MORE**

Possible Props:

Household and kitchen items

Towels, blankets, pillows, sweaters

Toys, books

Hats, coats, umbrellas, scarves

Easy-to-remove price tags, labels

Poster board, construction paper, nontoxic markers for street signs

Cash box, play money, and coins

Notepad and pencil for receipts

Paper or plastic bags to wrap each purchase

Characters:
Yard Sale Manager, Shopper

299 Spaceship

Ready for takeoff in 10-9-8-7-6-5-4. . . . Are we there yet?

AGE: **3–5 YRS**

CATEGORY: **PLAY WITH OTHERS/PRETEND**

NUMBER OF CHILDREN: **TWO OR MORE**

Possible Props:

Giant cardboard box for spaceship

Nontoxic markers and construction paper to decorate

Toy walkie-talkie (or empty juice cartons—covered with paper and tape)

Binoculars

Helmets

Ski pants or big overalls for space suits

Bags of space food (raisins, Cheerios, crackers)

Characters:
Astronaut, Scientist

300 Animal Doctor

This is an emergency—my doggie has the most awful cold. I don't think he's been taking his vitamins.

AGE: **3–5 YRS**

CATEGORY: **PLAY WITH OTHERS/PRETEND**

NUMBER OF CHILDREN: **TWO OR MORE**

Possible Props:

Stuffed animals

Toy doctor's kit

Clipboard, file folders

Small plastic containers, cotton balls

Wrap bandages or scarves for use as bandages

Card table (examining table)

Used men's dress shirt (lab coat)

Characters:
Animal Doctor, Helper, Pets, Pet Owner

301 Jewelry Store

How many bracelets can you wear all at once?

AGE: **3–5 YRS**

CATEGORY: **PLAY WITH OTHERS/PRETEND**

NUMBER OF CHILDREN: **TWO OR MORE**

Possible Props:

Large wooden or plastic beads

Ribbon or string (for making jewelry)

Assorted dress-up jewelry (clip earrings, bracelets, necklaces, rings)

Decorated shoe boxes and tins (jewelry boxes)

Mirror

Toy magnifying glass

Construction paper, labels, markers for signs and price tags

Jewelry store fliers with photos

Small gift boxes, tissue paper, bows, bags

Cash register, play money and coins, credit card, calculator (for credit card swipe)

Characters:
Store Clerk, Customer

302 Road Construction

Can we build a road in between those two houses? We have to work quickly, or traffic will back up!

AGE: 3–5 YRS

CATEGORY: PLAY WITH OTHERS/PRETEND

NUMBER OF CHILDREN: TWO OR MORE

Possible Props:

Hard hat, work gloves

Orange safety vest

Child's garden tools

Wagon, ride-on toys, trucks

Wooden blocks (barriers)

Poster board, nontoxic markers, wooden paint stir sticks, invisible tape to make construction signs

Crepe paper to mark off construction zone (taped from one piece of furniture to another)

Rolled newspapers or poster board (safety cones)

Masking tape for marking lanes in the road

Toy dump trucks, cement mixers, semitrucks

Characters:
Construction Workers, Pavement Painters, Truck Drivers, Car Drivers, Other Crew Members

303 Dance Recital

No, it's three twirls, one hop, and two skips. Again! (And don't forget to curtsy at the end.)

AGE: 3–5 YRS

CATEGORY: PLAY WITH OTHERS/PRETEND

NUMBER OF CHILDREN: TWO OR MORE

Possible Props:

Leotards, ballet costumes, long skirts with elastic, fancy dresses

Scarves, hats, bandanas, boas, feathers, beaded jewelry

Animal costumes (for dancing animals)

Boys' blazers, ties, pants

Musical instruments, microphone (for musicians performing on the sidelines)

Music

Chairs for the audience

Characters:
Singer, Dancer, Dancing Animal, Audience Members

304 Coffee Shop

So that's fifteen eggs, four pancakes, five-and-a-half slices of bacon, and extra syrup?

AGE: 3–5 YRS

CATEGORY: PLAY WITH OTHERS/PRETEND

NUMBER OF CHILDREN: TWO OR MORE

Possible Props:

Toy coffeemaker or unbreakable coffeepot

Travel coffee mugs, disposable coffee cups

Cardboard drinks carriers

Pizza pan (serving tray)

Plastic containers for pretend sugar and cream

Large plastic coffee thermos (pump style)

Spoons, empty spice shakers for pretend cinnamon

Empty juice boxes for children's drinks

Poster board, nontoxic markers, magazine photos of coffee, tape for posters

Cash register, play money, credit card, calculator (for credit card swipe machine)

Small waxed paper bags to wrap pastries and cookies

Characters:
Coffee Maker, Server, Cashier, Customer

Preschool Play (age 3 to 5)

Preschool Play (age 3 to 5)

305 Photo Studio

No sticking out your tongue when you smile, please.

AGE: 3–5 YRS

CATEGORY: PLAY WITH OTHERS/PRETEND

NUMBER OF CHILDREN: TWO OR MORE

Possible Props:

Chair or stool

Twin bedsheet to drape over chair or hang on the wall with masking tape for backdrop

Toy camera or used disposable camera

Dolls and stuffed animals

Cutout magazine photos of children and families (to be handed out as finished photos)

Lunch bags to hold finished photos

Cash register, play money

Characters:

Photographer, Babies, Children, Families Having Their Photos Taken

★CLASSIC★

306 Tea Party

My grandma says she eats really little sandwiches at teatime. And more cookies, please!

AGE: 3–5 YRS

CATEGORY: PLAY WITH OTHERS/PRETEND

NUMBER OF CHILDREN: TWO OR MORE

Possible Props:

Child's tea set or unbreakable cups and teapot, lukewarm tea

Plastic containers for sugar and cream

Small tablecloth or place mats

Plastic plates and utensils

Snacks, pastries, small tea sandwiches

Dress-up clothes, purses, jewelry, scarves, gloves (for fancy afternoon tea)

Stuffed animals and dolls

Characters:

Friends at an Afternoon Tea Party

Traveling Down the Boredom Highway

When your child learns to wiggle his way through feelings of boredom and eventually seizes upon something fun and exciting to do, it's an "Aha!" moment. He is discovering that he can use his own imagination and interests to amuse himself. Many of the games in this book are designed to help him arrive at that moment, when he can say good-bye to dependence on Mom or machine (electronic games) and say hello to a big idea: *"I can invent a fun way to play on my own."* The long-term benefits of your child learning to entertain himself far outweigh the short-term fix that a video might provide. Now, in truth, the road to self-entertainment involves many tiny steps. To keep your nerves from fraying when you hear your child's familiar whine, remember that boredom is often the essential ingredient that motivates your child to discover creative ways to play.

Musical Play

Musical play should be a part of every preschool child's play routine, and it's especially captivating when two or more children (or an adult and a child) play together. The rhythm, actions, and enthusiasm of one person often energize the others. Music has the ability to soothe and comfort, to energize and motivate, and to bring out feelings that are resting inside us. Once a child gets used to hearing music (yes, this is one time when "plugging in" can be wonderful), or even better, making music, he becomes alert to the sounds of music in his daily life.

307 Musical Socks

"Do those socks sing songs?" Mason asked. "No," I replied, "but they do a pretty good job dancing."

AGE: **3–5 YRS**

CATEGORY: **PLAY WITH OTHERS/MUSICAL**

NUMBER OF CHILDREN: **TWO OR MORE**

Materials:
Socks (variety of sizes, types)
Laundry basket
Cardboard boxes (or baskets)
Music

Setup:
Gather up a collection of socks and turn each one into a ball, rolling the upper part of the sock tightly into the toe. Put the sock-balls in a laundry basket at one end of the room. Position the cardboard boxes around the laundry basket at varying distances, with some of the baskets a few feet away and others six or more feet away.

Play:
Turn on the music. This is the signal for all the players to run to the laundry basket and begin tossing the sock-balls into any of the boxes scattered around the room. Turn off the music, and it's the signal for the children to run and grab the sock-balls, around the room or in the boxes, and toss them *back* into the laundry

basket. The children may take quite a few shots to get all the sock-balls back in the laundry basket. When all the socks are back in the basket, start the music again.

308 Dance Contest

You can get a roomful of preschoolers dancing in the blink of an eye. You'll be hard-pressed to find any wallflowers at this party!

AGE: **3–5 YRS**

CATEGORY: **PLAY WITH OTHERS/MUSICAL**

NUMBER OF CHILDREN: **TWO OR MORE**

Materials:
Music with a good beat for dancing
Boom box or stereo
Silk scarves, hats, costumes

Setup:
Provide a safe environment (and supervision) for moving and dancing around. Help the children outfit themselves with a colorful accessory or two.

Play:
Start the music and challenge the children to show you their most creative, energetic dance moves. The children will have lots of fun copying one another. Expect some high-energy acrobatics!

Preschool Play (age 3 to 5)

Stop the music from time to time and announce the "score" for the group of dancers (I vote "10" every time!) or announce the "winner" of the dance contest. Make sure to single out every child as a winner over the course of the game.

309 Musical ABCs

This game has several elements preschoolers enjoy: secret letters inside a box, the anticipation of waiting your turn to see what's inside, music that starts and stops on a dime.

AGE: **3–5 YRS**

CATEGORY: **PLAY WITH OTHERS/MUSICAL**

NUMBER OF CHILDREN: **TWO OR MORE**

Materials:

Scissors (for adult use only)

Blank index cards

Markers (for adult use only)

Small gift box (or child-size shoe box)

Music

Setup:

Cut several index cards in half or quarters so that each piece will fit inside the small gift box. Write one letter of the alphabet on each piece, then turn all the pieces facedown in a pile. (There's no need to create cards for all the letters of the alphabet—just pick some of the letters the children are sure to know.) Have the children sit in a circle around the pile of cards on the floor.

Play:

Select one card and, without letting the children see it, place it inside the gift box and shut the lid. When you start the music, the children rush to pass the box to one another around the circle. After just a short time, stop the music. The child holding the box opens it, takes out the card, and identifies the letter (the others can help if necessary). Once the letter is identified

correctly, the child holding the box discards the card. She picks another card from the pile (no peeking), places it inside the box, and puts the lid on. That's your cue to turn on the music, and their cue to begin passing the box again.

310 Musical Animals

Use a slightly larger gift box with a lid and a deck of playing cards with animals (and perhaps numbers as well). When the music stops, the child holding the box identifies the animal, gives him a name, and tells the group how old he is, as indicated by the number on the playing card. ("This is a turtle, his name is Freddy, and he is six years old!")

311 Musical Toe Painting

Finger painting to music always brings smiles to preschoolers' faces. Now try it with feet for a few giggles!

AGE: **3–5 YRS**

CATEGORY: **PLAY WITH OTHERS/MUSICAL (OUTDOOR)**

NUMBER OF CHILDREN: **TWO OR MORE**

Materials:

Wading pool (preferably the hard plastic type)

Masking tape

Art paper or newsprint

Washable, nontoxic finger paint in various colors

Disposable plastic picnic plates

A few drops of liquid dish detergent to aid in cleanup

Small stool or washable chair (1 for each child)

Music that parent and child enjoy

Old or easily washable clothes (for wearing)

Water source (for cleanup)

Towel (for cleanup)

Setup:

Put the wading pool on the lawn. Tape some paper to the bottom. Allow the child to choose two to three colors of finger paint (if you throw too many colors in the mix, you'll probably end up with brown). Pour a small amount of each color into its own paper plate. Add a few drops of dish detergent to each of these puddles of paint to ease in cleanup. Place the stools or chairs so that each child's feet can easily touch the paper inside of the wading pool, and position one plate of paint by each of their feet.

Play:

Turn on the music, and let the toe painting begin! Rotate the plates of paint after a few minutes so that each child gets to try out all the colors. Refresh the paper and paint when the artists make a request. After the paintings have dried, hang or give as gifts. Don't forget to sign and date them.

Note: Toe painting sometimes turns into full foot painting!

312 Musical Beanbags

In this musical variation on the classic hot or cold hiding game, group singing becomes a key element in the search and discover mission.

AGE: **3–5 YRS**

CATEGORY:
PLAY WITH OTHERS/MUSICAL

NUMBER OF CHILDREN:
TWO OR THREE

Materials:

Beanbag (see page 146 for Homemade Beanbags)

Play:

Select one child to be the beanbag finder and send her out of the room while the others hide the beanbag. When the finder comes back into the room, the others begin singing a familiar song like "Twinkle, Twinkle, Little Star," starting out softly and then singing louder and louder as the finder gets closer to the beanbag. If the finder heads away from the beanbag, the singers decrease their volume.

313 I've Got Rhythm

The preschool years are a great time for children to discover their own natural sense of rhythm. Children three to five are like little sponges that soak up (and imitate) the actions they see in their world.

AGE: **3–5 YRS**

CATEGORY:
PLAY WITH OTHERS/MUSICAL

NUMBER OF CHILDREN:
TWO OR THREE

Materials:

Any percussive instrument:
Bells
Drums
Shakers

Play:

To help the children create a beat, you can invent simple phrases and clap along with the words as you say them. (Or follow along with shakers, drums, or bells.) You might say, "I Love You" very fast as you clap on each word to show three fast beats. A child might answer you by tapping three quick beats on her drum. Once she can hear the beats and imitate the patterns you make, create your own game of musical Follow the Leader. Clap a simple rhythm for your child to follow. They can imitate this rhythm by clapping back to you, shaking a shaker, jingling a bell, or tapping on a drum.

Preschool Play (age 3 to 5)

Make Your Own Musical Instruments

Preschoolers are fascinated by the sounds they can make! But when they find they can actually make the instruments that help them make those sounds, now that's something to discover. Some, like the Musical Shakers, will even sound nice as you create them: Hear the tap-tap-tap as you pour dried beans into a coffee can, or the clink-clink-clink as you drop coins into a candy tin, or the shoop of the rice into an empty gift box. Here are some preschool-friendly instruments that are easy to make and marvelous for two or more musicians to play.

★ CLASSIC ★

314 Musical Shakers

Shake it up, baby! Shakers are great because they involve the whole body in the music-making.

AGE: **3–5 YRS**

CATEGORY:
PLAY WITH
OTHERS/MUSICAL

NUMBER OF
CHILDREN:
TWO OR THREE

Materials:

Assorted containers:

Toilet paper tube (tape over the ends with giant packing tape)

Small gift boxes with lid (tape closed or secure with a large rubber band)

Plastic film canister with lid

Tin candy container with lid (Altoids-style)
Coffee can with lid
Plastic saltshakers or spice jars with lids

Assorted noisemakers (any of the following):
Dried beans (kidney, lentils, pintos, etc.)
Uncooked elbow macaroni
Uncooked rice
Kernels of popcorn
Paper clips
Buttons
Coins
Pebbles

Construction paper, wrapping paper, and/or contact paper

Nontoxic glue stick

Setup:
Fill a container with one or more types of noisemakers and secure the lid, or close up the ends carefully with duct tape, packing tape, or thick rubber bands. Decorate the outside of the container with construction paper or wrapping paper, or use adhesive contact paper for a more durable finish.

Play:
Hand out the assorted homemade shakers and watch (and listen) for the results!

*Safety Alert: Due to choking hazard, these shakers are not safe for infants, toddlers, or children prone to putting objects in their mouths.

315 Homemade Kazoos

Pick a day when your nerves are steady, and set your preschoolers loose on some homemade kazoos.

AGE: **3–5 YRS**

CATEGORY:
PLAY WITH
OTHERS/MUSICAL

NUMBER OF
CHILDREN:
TWO OR THREE

Materials:

Short cardboard tube (5"–6")

Nontoxic markers

Waxed paper

Rubber band

Setup:

If using a paper towel tube, cut tube down to 5 to 6 inches. Decorate with nontoxic markers. Cut a 4-inch square of waxed paper. Place the waxed paper over one end of the tube and secure it with a rubber band. Show your child how to place his mouth over the open end of the kazoo and hum to create a wacky, wavering sound.

Play:

After all the children have their own kazoos, it's time for a Happy Birthday Kazoo Parade, with all the musicians marching together (perhaps with homemade crowns) and humming "Happy Birthday to You" or another familiar song.

316 Comb Kazoo

Cut a small square of waxed paper, wrap it around the front and back side of a clean comb and hum gently on the waxed surface. (Experiment to vary the sound.)

317 Parent-Friendly Drum

This first-rate drum takes only five minutes to make and it produces a sound that doesn't annoy grown-ups!

AGE: 3–5 YRS

CATEGORY:
PLAY WITH
OTHERS/MUSICAL

NUMBER OF
CHILDREN:
TWO OR MORE

Materials:

Empty coffee can

Construction paper or gift wrapping paper

Invisible tape

Scissors (for adult use only)

Large size, heavy-duty balloon (not inflated)

Teaspoon

Setup:

Remove the plastic lid from the coffee can. Cut a rectangle of construction paper (decorated with children's drawings if you like) or gift wrapping paper to fit around the can. Tape it in place. Use scissors to cut off the entire neck of the balloon so that you are left with the large bulb. Use a bit of muscle to stretch this balloon bulb over the empty end of the coffee can. Stretch it securely down over the can so that it creates a resistant surface.

Play:

Use the rounded end of a teaspoon or baby spoon to tap on the rubber surface, or experiment with other safe drumming objects.

318 Drum and Shaker Combo

Put several tablespoons of uncooked rice in the coffee can before you stretch the balloon over the end. Once the balloon bulb is stretched in place, secure with clear, wide packing tape to be double sure the balloon stays in place. Now the drum can double as a shaker!

*SAFETY ALERT: Supervise all balloon play to prevent children less than eight years old from choking on uninflated balloons or balloon pieces.

> **"** *Parents should sing to their children, and they should sing like they mean it, like they love these songs. Most preschool children, if they're given the opportunity, are going to love playing games, singing songs, and dancing around the living room with music—especially if a parent is doing it as well.* **"**
>
> **—John Feierabend, Ph.D.**
> founder and director of the National Center
> of Music and Movement in the
> Early Years at the University of Hartford,
> and author of the *First Steps in Music* series

Preschool Play (age 3 to 5)

Preschool Play (age 3 to 5)

Sing It!

Chances are good that your child's great-great-grandparents sang these classic children's songs and played these familiar clapping and rhyming games. Now it's your turn to warm up the vocal cords and teach these songs to the next generation of singers, clappers, and toe tappers. Included below are the words to some childhood favorites.

319 Old Macdonald

Chorus:
Old Macdonald had a farm
E-I-E-I-O

And on this farm he had some cows
E-I-E-I-O

With a moo-moo here *(mooing sounds)*
And a moo-moo there *(mooing sounds)*
Here a moo *(sound)*
There a moo *(sound)*
Everywhere a moo-moo *(sounds)*

Chorus:
Old Macdonald had a farm
E-I-E-I-O

> **❝** *Every time a child goes through a sequence, it strengthens a brain circuit so that it'll come more easily next time. So, the more you rehearse something, the more you help a child settle disagreements in a positive way with his siblings or with friends, for example, or understand why someone didn't want to play with him right now—all of this is instruction in social and emotional skills. And it all pays off down the line.* **❞**
>
> **—Daniel Goleman, M.D.**
> psychologist and author of
> *Emotional Intelligence* and *Social Intelligence*

Older children can continue to add more verses by adding more animals and sounds:

Pigs *(oink-oink)*

Chickens *(bawk-bawk)*

Sheep *(baa-baa)*

Dogs *(bow-wow)*

Cats *(meow-meow)*

320 The Bear Went Over the Mountain

(Sung to the tune of "For He's a Jolly Good Fellow")

The bear went over the mountain,
The bear went over the mountain,
The bear went over the mountain,
To see what he could see—

To see what he could see,
To see what he could see—

The other side of the mountain,
The other side of the mountain,
The other side of the mountain,
Was all that he could see—

Was all that he could see,
Was all that he could see,
The other side of the mountain,
Was all that he could see!

321 This Old Man

(one)
This old man, he played one,
He played knick-knack on my thumb,
With a knick-knack, paddy-whack,
Give a dog a bone,
This old man came rolling home.

(two)
This old man, he played two,
He played knick-knack on my shoe,
With a knick-knack, paddy-whack,
Give a dog a bone,
This old man came rolling home.

(three)
This old man, he played three,
He played knick-knack on my knee,
With a knick-knack, paddy-whack,
Give a dog a bone,
This old man came rolling home.

(four)
This old man, he played four,
He played knick-knack on my door,
With a knick-knack, paddy-whack,
Give a dog a bone,
This old man came rolling home.

(five)
This old man, he played five,
He played knick-knack on my hive,
With a knick-knack, paddy-whack,
Give a dog a bone,
This old man came rolling home.

(six)
This old man, he played six,
He played knick-knack on the sticks,
With a knick-knack, paddy-whack,
Give a dog a bone,
This old man came rolling home.

(seven)
This old man, he played seven,
He played knick-knack up in heaven,
With a knick-knack, paddy-whack,
Give a dog a bone,
This old man came rolling home.

(eight)
This old man, he played eight,
He played knick-knack on the gate,
With a knick-knack, paddy-whack,
Give a dog a bone,
This old man came rolling home.

(nine)
This old man, he played nine,
He played knick-knack on my spine,
With a knick-knack, paddy-whack,
Give a dog a bone,
This old man came rolling home.

(ten)
This old man, he played ten,
He played knick-knack once again,
With a knick-knack, paddy-whack,
Give a dog a bone,
This old man came rolling home.

322 One, Two, Buckle My Shoe

One, two,
buckle my shoe,

Three, four,
shut the door,

Five, six,
pick up sticks,

Seven, eight,
lay them straight,

Nine, ten,
a big fat hen!

Store-Bought Musical Instruments

You may find some of these music makers at your local toy store or teacher supply store. Two of my favorite online sources for musical instruments for young children who want to experiment with music and have fun are: Hearthsong (www.hearthsong.com) and Groth Music (www.grothmusic.com).

Bells (attached to cloth or leather strap)

Castanets

Child's calypso steel drum

Child's conga

Child's handbells

Cowbell with mallet

Harmonica

Kazoo

Maracas

Recorder (wind instrument)

Slide whistle

Tambourine

Ukulele

Xylophone

323 Hey Diddle Diddle

Hey diddle diddle,
The cat and the fiddle,
The cow jumped over the moon.
The little dog laughed to see such sport,
And the dish ran away with the spoon!

324 If You're Happy ...

If you're happy and you know it,
clap your hands *(clap-clap)*
If you're happy and you know it,
clap your hands *(clap-clap)*
If you're happy and you know it,
and you really want to show it,
If you're happy and you know it,
clap your hands! *(clap-clap)*

If you're happy and you know it,
wave your hands *(wave-wave)*
If you're happy and you know it,
wave your hands! *(wave-wave)*

If you're happy and you know it,
and you really want to show it,
If you're happy and you know it,
wave your hands! *(wave-wave)*

If you're happy and you know it,
stomp your feet *(stomp-stomp)*
If you're happy and you know it,
stomp your feet *(stomp-stomp)*
If you're happy and you know it,
and you really want to show it,
If you're happy and you know it,
stomp your feet! *(stomp-stomp)*

If you're happy and you know it,
shake a leg *(shake-shake)*
If you're happy and you know it,
shake a leg *(shake-shake)*
If you're happy and you know it,
and you really want to show it,
If you're happy and you know it,
shake a leg! *(shake-shake)*

(Add more verses as you like: nod your head, shout hooray, etc.)

325 Miss Mary Mack

Miss Mary Mack, Mack, Mack
(touch knees three times)
All dressed in black, black, black
(touch shoulders three times)
With silver buttons, buttons, buttons
(clap hands three times)
All down her back, back, back
(clap friend's hands, then spin around)

She sent her mother, mother, mother
(touch knees three times)
For fifty cents, cents, cents
(touch shoulders three times)
To see the elephant, elephant, elephant
(clap hands three times)
Jump over the fence, fence, fence
(clap friend's hands, then spin around)

He jumped so high, high, high
(touch knees three times)
He reached the sky, sky, sky
(touch shoulders three times)
And he didn't come back, back, back
(clap hands three times)
'Til the fourth of July, 'ly, 'ly
(clap friend's hands, and spin around)

326 Jack and Jill

Jack and Jill went up the hill
To fetch a pail of water.
Jack fell down and broke his crown,
And Jill came tumbling after!

327 Mary Had a Little Lamb

Mary had a little lamb,
Little lamb, little lamb,
Mary had a little lamb,
Whose fleece was white as snow.

And everywhere that Mary went,
Mary went, Mary went,
Everywhere that Mary went,
The lamb was sure to go.

It followed her to school one day,
School one day, school one day,
It followed her to school one day,
Which was against the rules.

It made the children laugh and play,
Laugh and play, laugh and play,
It made the children laugh and play,
To see a lamb at school.

PARENT TIP

328 Music Concerts

"If you introduce live performance to a child at a very early age, you may create a love that will last a lifetime. Community or high school performances in parks are wonderful for young children. Your child won't be forced to sit in a chair; if she wants to dance, she can, and she might even be able to enjoy an ice-cream cone. An outdoor setting also isn't quite as loud as a concert setting, which is helpful since loud noise can be frightening for a young child."

—Peter from Minnesota

Preschool Play (age 3 to 5)

Sing Your Own Family Songs

Who said you have to be a professional songwriter to create your own song? As an adult, give yourself permission to have fun with music and to invent your own songs. You may be thinking, "I can't write a song," but that isn't so. Simply pick a familiar childhood melody, like "Twinkle, Twinkle, Little Star," and invent your own lyrics. (Create all new words, or sing the same song but change the last word or two in each line.) What to sing about? Preschoolers will be thrilled to hear a song made up on the spot about the child who didn't want to put his winter coat on to go outside (perhaps this is your child!). Or perhaps a song might pop into your mind about the little bear who didn't want to take a bath.

In case your memory needs jogging, here are some familiar childhood songs with melodies that are just waiting for your original lyrics:

"Are You Sleeping?"
"Did You Ever See a Lassie"
"Do Your Ears Hang Low?"
"Happy Birthday"
"Rock-a-Bye Baby"

"She'll Be Coming 'Round the Mountain"
"Shoo Fly"
"The Alphabet Song"
"The Bear Went Over the Mountain"
"This Old Man"

Or, try some of the songs I experimented with below to get inspired. They don't have to make too much sense—preschoolers like to be silly!

329 My Girl/My Boy

It's always fun to personalize a song for your little sweetheart. And you'll be lucky to get through the whole song before you both fall into a fit of giggles while rushing to perform all the actions!

(sung to the tune of "Twinkle, Twinkle, Little Star")

(insert your daughter's or son's name in the appropriate version)
Sophie, Sophie, you're my girl

Stand up, crouch down, jump and twirl
(perform actions)

Dancing, leaping, here we go
(perform actions)

Spinning fast and spinning slow
(perform actions)

Sophie, Sophie, that's my girl

Stand up, crouch down, jump and twirl
(perform actions)

Jackie, Jackie, you're my boy

Use your hands to make some noise
(clap in rhythm)

Clapping, clapping to the beat
(clap in rhythm)

Now try stomping with your feet
(stomp in rhythm)

Jackie, Jackie, that's my boy

Use your hands to make some noise
(clap in rhythm)

330 Rake, Rake, Rake

This one was inspired by all the chores and activities to do around the house. You can make this song and game last as long as you can keep coming up with easy-to-pantomime actions!

(to the tune of "Row, Row, Row Your Boat")

Rake, rake, rake the leaves
(perform action)
Until the sun goes down
Then we all fall in a heap
(drop to the ground, exhausted)
Right here on the ground!

Scrub, scrub, scrub the floor
(perform action)
Until the sun goes down
Then we all fall in a heap
(drop to the ground, exhausted)
Right here on the ground!

Fix, fix, fix the leak
(perform action)
Until the sun goes down
Then we all fall in a heap
(drop to the ground, exhausted)
Right here on the ground!

Plant, plant, plant the seeds
(perform action)
Until the sun goes down
Then we all fall in a heap
(drop to the ground, exhausted)
Right here on the ground!

(and so on, making up the verses that follow as you go along)

Lock, lock, lock the door . . .

Change, change, change the bulb . . .

Dust, dust, dust the shelves . . .

Fold, fold, fold the clothes . . .

Make, make, make the bed . . .

331 Wiggle My Toes!

Here's a song I created one day after playing at the beach.

(to the tune of "I'm a Little Teapot")

Going to the beach gonna wiggle my toes,
(wiggle toes)

Hot sunny day where anything goes,
(spin around in a circle)

Jumpin' in the water, diggin' in the sand,
(jump up, pretend to dig)

Chase the waves, as quick as you can.
(run two steps and back again)

> **"**Many parents emphasize one new friendship skill a month. Maybe this month at playgroups let's emphasize manners. Or this month, let's emphasize greeting each other when you walk in. So kids gradually learn new friendship skills.**"**
>
> **—Michele Borba, Ed.D.**
> former classroom teacher and author of
> *Parents Do Make a Difference* and
> *12 Simple Secrets Real Moms Know*

Preschool Play (age 3 to 5)

UNPLUGGED PLAY

Preschool Play (age 3 to 5)

Games and Activities Around the House

Preschoolers are beginning to enjoy games with loosely structured rules—but rules don't necessarily entail competition. The most successful preschool games have one or two very simple, easy-to-understand objectives or actions. In Camelback Crawl, your preschooler will crawl from the starting line to the finish line with a beanbag on her back; in Hidden Number Hearts, she'll find as many hearts as she can and put them in her basket. These games are just right for preschoolers, since they give them a little taste of playing by the rules, without complicated directions or a focus on competition.

332 Tossers & Talkers

It's never too early to introduce your preschooler to the fine art of sports commentating.

QUICK & EASY

AGE: **3–5 YRS**

CATEGORY: **PLAY WITH OTHERS/INDOOR**

NUMBER OF CHILDREN: **TWO OR MORE**

Materials:
Laundry basket
Rolled-up towel
Beanbags (see page 146 for Homemade Beanbags)

Setup:
Position the laundry basket on the floor and place the rolled-up towel on the floor about 3 to 4 feet behind the basket to mark a tossing line. (Make sure the line is close enough to enable *all* the children to make shots.)

Play:
One child is the designated beanbag tosser and the others are the "talkers" (the official cheerleaders), who sit on the sidelines. The tosser lines up behind the pitching line to toss. When a beanbag lands *inside* the basket, the talkers call out, "Basket!" When the beanbag lands on the floor rather than inside the basket, the talkers are silent. Every child takes repeated turns.

333 Blindfolded Beanbag Toss

If you don't mind a bit more volume, this game takes on a sillier dimension when the tosser is blindfolded. Have him stand about 3 feet away from the basket to toss. If some kids are uncomfortable with wearing a blindfold or with the inevitable laughing fits on the "talker" sidelines; you may want to ask for volunteers or become the chief tosser yourself.

Preschool-Friendly Blindfold Glasses

Some children three to five don't like the feel of a blindfold around their eyes. Create a preschool-friendly blindfold alternative by taping pieces of cardboard (cut to fit) over the lenses of child-size sunglasses. Whenever blindfolds are used in a game, make sure the playing environment is safe, with no sharp corners or edges on furniture, no slippery rugs nearby, and no stairs anywhere near the playing area. And of course provide supervision to ensure everyone's safety!

334 Color Treasure Hunt

This hunt requires no treasure-planting whatsoever—players will be searching for ordinary household items, so it's quite a cinch to set up.

AGE: 3–5 YRS

CATEGORY:
PLAY WITH
OTHERS/INDOOR

NUMBER OF
CHILDREN: TWO
OR MORE

Materials:
4 to 8 index cards or blank
   playing cards
Crayons or nontoxic markers
Pocket-size spiral notebook (1 for each child)
Pencils

Setup:
Color-code the cards on one side with crayons or markers in 4 to 8 shades familiar to the players. No need to go all out with the design; even a scribble will suffice. Shuffle these cards and spread them out facedown on the floor.

Play:
Each player draws a card, announces the color on the card, and begins a treasure hunt. Players look for objects in their designated colors in the first room selected in the house. This game works best if the children search in the same room (with a parent close at hand) and move to an adjacent room together to continue the search. Each time they spot objects matching their color, they make a mark in their notebooks. The players move from room to room, checking every nook and cranny. When they have searched each room, flip through their notebooks and help them add up the points. To add more interest, add the players' numbers together and let them "redeem" points for healthy treats or simple art supplies like erasers or colored pencils of their choice.

335 Camelback Crawl

Crawling isn't just for babies and crabs. Turns out, camels can crawl too! This silly race will have everyone giggling.

AGE: 3–5 YRS

CATEGORY:
PLAY WITH
OTHERS/INDOOR

NUMBER OF
CHILDREN: TWO
OR MORE

Materials:
Beanbags (1 or 2 for each child,
   see page 146 for Homemade
   Beanbags)

Setup:
Create a starting line and finish line.

Play:
The children take turns getting on their hands and knees and crawling from the starting line to the finish line with a beanbag or two on their backs. Only one camel crawls at a time, and the other player(s) stand(s) back at the starting line. If a player drops a beanbag, one of the resting camels rushes to his side, picks it up, and repositions it on the racing camel's back. When the camel reaches the finish line, he grabs his beanbag(s) and runs back to the starting line, where a resting camel is waiting to take his turn.

> **"** If you have a shy child, don't make the mistake of trying to force her to become gregarious and outgoing because you think that's the way happy people are. No. Realize that shyness is, in fact, genetically transmitted, and there are many shy people in this world who are incredibly connected and happy. **"**
>
> **—Edward Hallowell, M.D.**
> psychiatrist and author of *Driven to Distraction*
> and *CrazyBusy*

Preschool Play (age 3 to 5)

336 Beanbag Hats

Place a beanbag on each child's head or shoulder, and he walks or runs from end to end without dropping it.

337 Camelback Crawl for Mom and Dad

Your child will howl with laughter when you play this game, substituting a large pillow for the beanbags.

338 Beanie-Bear

Put on a homemade county fair in your living room with this easy-to-make tossing-board bear.

AGE: 3–5 YRS

CATEGORY:
PLAY WITH
OTHERS/INDOOR

NUMBER OF
CHILDREN:
TWO OR MORE

Materials:

Scissors (for adult use only)
Sheet of poster board
Construction paper
Nontoxic markers
Invisible tape
Socks, newspapers, or beanbags for tossing

Setup:

Round the corners of the poster board (this will serve as the bear's body). Cut a large circle from the construction paper to make a head for the animal. Cut rectangles to represent legs. (Your child may want to draw additional animal details using markers.) Tape the animal target on the wall using invisible tape.

Gather up socks and turn each into a ball; or tightly crumple up sheets of newspapers to create newspaper balls; or make easy beanbags by filling small plastic bags with dried rice or beans and slipping each bag inside a small sock.

Play:

Position each child a few feet away from the target. Take turns aiming and tossing. To fine-tune tossing skills and create more challenge, each child can call out which part of the target they are aiming for. Or you can add spots or circles on the bear to create additional targets. Older children may want to score points for each target hit during the game.

339 Basket Beanie-Bear

Place a cardboard box on the floor a few inches away from the target so that the beanbags bounce into the box after striking the target.

PARENT TIP

340 Would You Like to Try Again?

"When our children were three and five years old, we started a plan called the 'do-over' in our home to help them get along while playing. We would say something like, 'I see you really want that toy to play with, but I'm not comfortable with the way you're asking for it. Would you like a do-over?' ('Would you like to ask again in a better way?') The idea was to give our children an opportunity to rethink things and try it again to come up with a better solution to the problem. In most cases they would respond and say something a little differently or take a different approach. Everybody has those moments when they aren't treating one another well, or communicating well, and this is an immediate plan of action to try again. **"**

—Peggy from Oklahoma

341 Photo Matching

Cutting and pasting, the old-fashioned way! Throw in a matching challenge, and preschoolers will be fully absorbed.

AGE: **3–5 YRS**

CATEGORY:
PLAY WITH OTHERS/INDOOR

NUMBER OF CHILDREN:
TWO OR MORE

Materials:

Scissors (for adult use only)

Magazines with color photos

Nontoxic glue or tape

Large sheets of newsprint paper

Setup:
Cut eight photos from magazines featuring everyday items that preschoolers will recognize (forks, coffee cups, shoes, flowers, etc.). Try to cut the photos so that only this one item is showing. Glue each of these photos on a separate sheet of newsprint or construction paper.

Play:
Give each child four photos and a collection of magazines filled with photos and ads. The children will take their time flipping through the magazines, searching for objects matching the ones they were assigned. When a child finds a match, he cuts it out and pastes it on the paper.

342 Hidden Number Hearts

Hearts provide a sweet twist to this hiding and number-sorting game.

AGE: **3–5 YRS**

CATEGORY:
PLAYING WITH OTHERS/INDOOR

NUMBER OF CHILDREN: **TWO OR THREE**

Materials:

Scissors (for adult use only)

Construction paper

Markers (for adult use only)

Small basket

Setup:
Cut out 12 paper hearts the size of large cookies. Use a marker to write a number on each heart; three of the hearts will have the number 1, three will have the number 2, and so on. Place the hearts in the basket.

Play:
The children take turns hiding and searching. Every child but the first designated hider leaves the room; the hider places the hearts around the room with just a peak of each heart showing. When all the hearts are hidden, call the children back to begin searching for them. They keep searching until all 12 hearts have been found. The hider may enjoy giving clues to signal when the children are "hot" or "cold," to help move things along. When all the hearts are found, everyone places all the hearts on the floor and works together to "match" the hearts according to their numbers. Then, place all the hearts in the basket so that another child may become the hider.

Friendly Reminder from the Kitchen Timer

Preschoolers do well with systems in place to help keep track of turn-taking. Giving up a special toy so a friend can take a turn is a concept that can be difficult for preschool children. Get in the habit of using the kitchen timer, set for a short amount of time (five minutes or so), as a signal that one child's turn is finished and another child gets a turn. This makes children feel secure that they will have their fair share of time with a favorite toy.

Preschool Play (age 3 to 5)

343 | Ping-Pong Plop

Funny sound effects, water, and a homemade Ping-Pong chute—who could ask for anything more? Don't be surprised if the phrase "Ping-Pong plop" becomes a staple around your house.

AGE: 3–5 YRS

CATEGORY:
PLAY WITH
OTHERS/INDOOR

NUMBER OF
CHILDREN:
TWO OR MORE

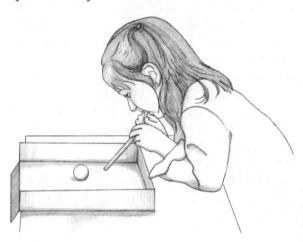

Materials:
Scissors (for adult use only)
Large rectangular cardboard gift box
Tape
Kitchen table or card table
Kitchen chair
Large metal roasting pan
Jumbo drinking straws, cut in half lengthwise
4 Ping-Pong balls

Setup:
Cut one of the shorter flaps off the bottom of the cardboard gift box so you're left with an open-ended "chute." Tape the chute to your kitchen table so that one of the cut ends is aligned with the table's edge. Place a large roasting pan filled with 2 inches of water directly under the edge of the table where the chute ends. Cut the jumbo drinking straws in half so that they are easier to hold.

Play:
One child kneels on a kitchen chair at the starting line of the chute and takes a turn blowing (through a straw) to push the Ping-Pong balls down the length of the chute, aiming for the pan of water below. The other children stand at the opposite end of the table where the water pan is placed and shout "Ping-Pong plop" when the ball hits the water. Some preschoolers will choose to hold a drinking straw an inch behind the Ping-Pong ball and blow the ball along the chute. Others will prefer to simply bend over the ball and blow it along. Give each child repeated tries so that everyone gets to hear their friends shout "Ping-Pong plop!"

"I'm Sorry"

Parents of preschoolers have many small opportunities to begin to teach children to take responsibility for their words and actions, particularly if their child has been unkind to another child. You can say, "When one friend hurts another friend's feelings, he apologizes to his friend to make things better and so they can go on being friends." This lets your child know that it's a fact of life that one friend might make a mistake or hurt another's feelings, but there is something he can do to make amends. Preschoolers like to know that this is how friendship works. This simple friendship rule is likely to be remembered and applied to all sorts of future relationships.

Craft Activities

There is something to be said for making crafts side by side with a friend. For one thing, the *"look what I'm making"* excitement of creating is contagious. For another, preschoolers watch intently to see what their playmate is doing, and very often lots of experimentation and collaboration happens along the way. All this adds up to amazing creative play. Here are a few favorite craft ideas that work very well for two or more children.

344 Sponge Prints

Sponges aren't just for cleanup; they're also a wonderful tool for budding artists.

AGE: 3–5 YRS

CATEGORY:
PLAY WITH
OTHERS/CRAFTS

NUMBER OF
CHILDREN:
TWO OR MORE

Materials:

Scissors (for adult use only)

Several sheets of Sponge Ums (compressed sponge material, available at teacher supply stores) or kitchen sponges (more difficult to cut)

Nontoxic markers

Nontoxic, washable paint

Disposable pie pans

Tablespoon

Plastic spoon

Paper towels or rag

Construction paper

Painter's smock

Setup:

Cut each Sponge Ums sheet in half. The children draw simple shapes (a circle, square, or triangle) on each piece. Parents use scissors to cut out each shape. (For easier setup, you can use store-bought, preshaped sponges.) Pour a small bit of paint in the pie pan. Add 1 to 2 tablespoons of water and stir. (The consistency should be syrupy.) Use paper towels as a sponge blotter between printings.

Play:

Have the children wet the shaped sponges and squeeze out the excess water. Dip one sponge into the paint, coating only the underside. Hold the sponge over the pan to allow excess paint to drip. Place the sponge on the construction paper for about 10 seconds, applying a bit of pressure, then lift the sponge. Repeat this routine, dipping the sponges into various colors. (Applying very little or no pressure to some of the imprints and heavy pressure to others varies the design significantly.)

345 Cookie-Cutter Prints

Purchase an inexpensive assortment of plastic cookie cutters to use for printmaking. Use nontoxic, washable paint and construction paper as described above, using cookie cutters instead of sponges to create a diverse collection of printed outlines. After the prints dry, the children may wish to use nontoxic markers to color in their shapes.

346 Outdoor Handprints

Have a hose or water bucket handy before you begin this outdoor print project. Gather up poster board, paint, disposable pie pans, and paper towels. Fill the bottom of the pans with thin layers of paint. Gently press your child's hand into the paint, let it drip briefly over the pan, then place her painted hand on the poster board and press gently. Use a hose and paper towels to clean off her hand and repeat the same routine with the second hand, creating a pair of handprints. Or get more imaginative and create a collage of various colored handprints on the poster. If you want to get the whole family into it, make a collage with everyone's handprint as an annual printing project—it'll be a wonderful keepsake as you watch your child's hands grow larger and larger.

347 Rainbow Butterfly

Preschoolers love to make crafts that look like something real. These little butterflies look "real enough" and are simple to make.

AGE: 3–5 YRS

CATEGORY: PLAY WITH OTHERS/ CRAFTS

NUMBER OF CHILDREN: TWO OR MORE

Materials:

Recycled vinyl tablecloth or newspapers

Coffee filters (basket style)

Paintbrushes

Nontoxic watercolor paints

Wooden clothespins (with metal hinge)

Pipe cleaners

Setup:
Spread the tablecloth or newspapers on the kitchen table and lay out all the materials.

Play:
Give each child a coffee filter. They'll soak their paintbrushes with watercolors and dab the color on one area of the filter. Repeat with other colors until each color "bleeds" into the next.) Allow the filters to dry completely. Fold or gather the coffee filter accordion style, so that the top and bottom edges can be pinched at the middle to create a butterfly shape. Snap the clothespin in place over the pinched area for the body. Wrap

one or two pipe cleaners around the end of the clothespin (closest to the wire hinge) to create the butterfly's antennae.

★ CLASSIC ★
348 Paper Plate Masks

As long as you have paper plates in the pantry, you are good to go with this tried-and-true preschool craft project.

AGE: 3–5 YRS

CATEGORY: PLAY WITH OTHERS/CRAFTS

NUMBER OF CHILDREN: TWO OR MORE

Materials:

Safety scissors

Paper plates

Single-hole punch

Yarn

Nontoxic, washable markers

Nontoxic glue, tissue paper, cotton balls, stickers (optional)

Setup:
Use scissors to cut out eye holes and small nostrils in the paper plate for air before your child decorates his mask. Punch a hole on either side of the mask near the ears; tie a piece of yarn through each hole that can be knotted at one end (you'll tie the loose ends together behind your child's head to secure the mask in place).

Play:
Your child can use markers to decorate his mask with eyebrows, lips, rosy cheeks, a beard, a mustache, hair, etc. The mask can be jazzed up with any materials you happen to have on hand. Pieces of yarn can be glued on as eyebrows or hair. Colored tissue paper or cotton balls can be used for rosy cheeks or beards. Stickers make good decorations too. (For children who don't enjoy wearing a mask close to their faces, tape a wooden paint stir-stick or Popsicle stick to the bottom of the mask to use as a handle.)

Preschool Play (age 3 to 5)

Outdoor Play

We all know instinctively that children need to run, jump, skip, chase, pedal tricycles, and toss balls in order to build strong bodies. The outdoors provides just the right environment for the boisterous play that every child needs. Some children will find these pleasures in their own backyard, others in a park or neighborhood playground. Sometimes just digging around in the dirt with a stick can fascinate children for a sustained period. Other times, children will enjoy chasing one another around from one end of the yard to the other, free from the spatial boundaries they encounter indoors. Of course, you need to supervise preschoolers when they are outside, with the amount of supervision determined by the age and maturity of your child and his playmate. This section of the book embraces not only the unstructured, freewheeling play that children invent for themselves but also loosely organized games.

Inclusive Cooperative Play

"Just messing around in the backyard with Freddy, Mom" is an accurate description of what two five-year-old boys might want to do outside. Here are some toys and props to set the stage for freewheeling, open-ended play outdoors.

Cardboard box

Dolls and stroller

Dump trucks and cars

Fort

Laundry basket

Plastic bucket

Playground ball, beach ball, child-size soccer ball, tennis balls

Riding toys

Sand and sandbox toys and props

Slide

Small tubs filled with water

Squirt bottles with water

Swings

Wading pool

Wagons

Water sprinkler

> " There is good research evidence from a number of quarters that there is what we call a 'dose-response relationship' between media use by children and being overweight. What we mean by a dose-response relationship is simply that the more hours children watch TV, play videos, or use computers, the more overweight they tend to be. "
>
> **—Michael Rich, M.D.**
> Director of the Center on Media and Child Health at the Children's Hospital–Boston and Assistant Professor of Pediatrics, Harvard Medical School

Preschool Play (age 3 to 5)

There's quite a wide range of abilities and experience when it comes to playing organized games between the ages of three and five. The activities included in this section are preschool-friendly games with easy-to-follow rules or directions, or simple suggestions to jump-start play. Be ready to give a brief demo and extra help to the youngest players in the group so that everyone is engaged in play and having a good time.

Planning a Safe Outdoor Play Area

The National Program for Playground Safety (www.playgroundsafety.org) provides up-to-date information about backyard (residential) and public playground safety. Its site provides valuable info designed to help you:

• Plan your backyard play area

• Select play equipment and protective surfaces

• Prevent outdoor injuries

You'll also find information and recommendations regarding child care play areas and elementary school and public playgrounds.

No Put-downs Allowed!

Preschoolers like to know what is expected and how the world works. They have an appreciation for short and simple rules that help them keep on track with how to behave and how to be a friend. *No put-downs allowed!* is a friendship rule that my children learned in preschool that made sense and was easy for everyone to follow. The children were given a very short description of a "put-down" (insult). Simple examples of put-downs were mentioned, and the children got the idea right away that put-downs hurt feelings. From that point on, the preschoolers were on the lookout for insults during playtime. Whenever anyone said something hurtful to another child, someone in the group was sure to chime in with, "Hey, no put-downs allowed." Very often, this signal was all that was needed to get things moving in a more positive direction.

349 Backyard and Bathtub Bubbles

Perfectly round, iridescent soap bubbles shimmering on a gentle breeze . . . Bubble blowing will always enchant preschoolers, no matter what flying techno-gadget they come up with next.

QUICK & EASY

AGE: 3–5 YRS

CATEGORY: PLAY WITH OTHERS/ OUTDOOR

NUMBER OF CHILDREN: TWO OR MORE

Materials:

Bottle of nontoxic bubble solution (see page 192 for Homemade Bubbles)

Bubble wands

Hula-Hoops, dolls, plastic animals, or chalk

Jump-start:

• **Chasing Bubbles** An adult or older sibling blows bubbles continuously while the preschoolers chase the bubbles and catch them in a large kitchen strainer or toy insect-catching net.

• **Clapping Bubbles** Using a small bubble wand, one child blows bubbles toward a playmate, who tries to pop as many bubbles as possible by clapping his hands together around the bubbles.

• **Bubble Hoops** Hang a Hula-Hoop from a tree at preschooler height. Each child stands several feet away and aims the bubbles into the hoop. If they want added incentive, score points for all the bubbles that the bubble team gets through the hoop (working together).

• **Bubble Buddies** Line up dolls or plastic animals around the porch and challenge the children to blow bubbles to each of the buddies in the row. For an added challenge, number small pieces of paper and tape them in front of each Bubble Buddy; score the number of points indicated on the paper when a bubble pops on a particular pal. (Make this a team game, rather than competition, by adding all the points up together.)

• **Sidewalk Bubbles** Write each child's name in chalk on a sidewalk square. The children use small bubble wands to blow bubbles into their sidewalk squares.

Bubble Play with Everyday Gadgets

You may be surprised at what sort of bubble-makers may be lurking in the corners of your home. Cake pans, a small wading pool, a Frisbee (turned upside down), and other shallow plastic dishes make fantastic sudsy dipping containers. For alternative small bubble wands, try a kitchen funnel (dip the large end in bubbles, blow through the small end); a plastic kitchen baster (remove the bulb, dip large end in bubbles, and blow through small end); a long pipe cleaner twisted into a small wand with handle (blow bubbles or wave it quickly); a pair of old sunglasses or plastic eyeglasses (with lenses removed); a flyswatter (wave it around quickly to make lots of tiny bubbles); or a small kitchen strainer (wave it in the air). But if giant bubbles are more your style, try dipping a plastic embroidery hoop in a large plastic tub full of bubble solution. Or maybe a round (spring-form) cake pan (remove the bottom of the pan to create a ring).

Preschool Play (age 3 to 5)

UNPLUGGED PLAY

Preschool Play (age 3 to 5)

350 Bridge Master

Run under a high bridge, hop over a low bridge, and shimmy under an even lower bridge— all with nothing but a little old jump rope!

AGE: 3–5 YRS

CATEGORY: PLAY WITH OTHERS/ OUTDOOR

NUMBER OF CHILDREN: THREE OR MORE (with adult assistance)

Materials:
Jump rope

Setup:
Find a safe, grassy area for playing. Two adults hold the ropes. One child is selected to be the Bridge Master, who starts the game. Line up all of the players (including the Bridge Master) several feet away.

Play:
The Bridge Master can choose from three different commands: "Under the bridge" means the rope holders raise the rope high enough for the children to run safely under it; "over the bridge" means the rope is held 2 or 3 inches off the ground and the children step over it; "creepy crawl" means the rope is held low to the ground, at a height of about 24 inches, so that the children have to crawl on all fours to get under it.

The two rope-holders pull the rope tightly to begin. The Bridge Master starts the game by shouting "under the bridge," then gets to call out two additional commands. After he's gone through the three commands, another child is appointed as the Bridge Master so that everyone gets a turn.

351 Homemade Bubbles

While store-bought bubble mix is terrific for play (and inexpensive to buy), your child may get a charge out of helping you make homemade bubble solution. Here's an easy recipe that makes good bubbles.

AGE: 4–5 YRS

CATEGORY: PLAY WITH OTHERS/ OUTDOOR

NUMBER OF CHILDREN: TWO (with adult assistance)

Materials:
3 cups water

4 to 6 drops food coloring (optional)

Small plastic container with lid (yogurt or margarine tubs work well)

Large spoon

4 tablespoons light corn syrup

1 cup dishwashing liquid (Dawn brand is especially bubble-icious!)

Play:
Mix the water and food coloring together in the small plastic tub using a large spoon. Add the corn syrup and dish detergent and stir until blended. Store this bubble mixture in the airtight container.

Extend the fun by turning to page 191 for five fantastic Backyard and Bathtub Bubbles jump-start activities.

SAFETY ALERT: Supervise so that very young children do not put bubble solution in their mouths.

352 Drizzle

Running around the backyard in your bathing suit is fabulous fun that can be outgrown pretty quickly. Let your children catch this wave of excitement during the preschool years.

AGE: **3–5 YRS**

CATEGORY:
PLAY WITH OTHERS/ OUTDOOR

NUMBER OF CHILDREN: **TWO OR MORE**

Materials:

Outdoor sprinkler (oscillating)
Large plastic cup
Plastic pitcher
Bathing suits

Setup:
Place sprinkler in the center of the yard and turn it on.

Play:
Each player races back and forth alongside the oscillating sprinkler, trying to fill her cup with water. When the cup is partially filled, the player runs to dump the cup of water into the pitcher.

353 Mini Beach Blanket Toss

This is an easygoing version of a big-kid game (six- to ten-year-olds) that works well for two older preschoolers or a three- to four-year-old child with a grown-up.

AGE: **3–5 YRS**

CATEGORY:
PLAY WITH OTHERS/ OUTDOOR

NUMBER OF CHILDREN: **TWO** (with one adult to assist)

Materials:

Empty king-size pillowcase
Small inflatable beach ball

Setup:
Spread the pillowcase out on the floor. Each child grabs two corners at the ends of the pillowcase and holds on tightly.

Play:
The two children hold their ends of the pillowcase at about waist or chest level and take a few steps backward so the pillowcase is stretched tightly from player to player. A parent helps start the game by placing the beach ball in the center of the pillowcase and counting, 1, 2, 3; on the count of 3, the children lift the pillowcase up in the air and try to toss the ball. (The rhythm can be a little tricky, so if necessary, get a big kid or another grown-up to help you demonstrate.)

★CLASSIC★
354 Shadow Tag

Shadow chasing is a wonderful way to celebrate a bright sunny day.

AGE: **3–5 YRS**

CATEGORY:
PLAY WITH OTHERS/ OUTDOOR

NUMBER OF CHILDREN: **FOUR OR MORE**

Setup:
Designate a safe grassy playing area and show the children the "out-of-bounds area" so you can be sure no one strays out of your sight line.

Play:
One or two children are the designated chasers trying to catch the rest of the children. They all run around the lawn, and the chasers "tag" players by stepping on their shadows. After several minutes of play, the children trade roles. There are no winners or losers in this game, just a lot of running!

Preschool Play (age 3 to 5)

★ CLASSIC ★
355 Follow the Leader

Here's a high-spirited game that encourages kids to move in imaginative, energetic, and silly ways.

AGE: 3–5 YRS

CATEGORY:
PLAY WITH OTHERS/ OUTDOOR

NUMBER OF CHILDREN: TWO OR MORE

Setup:
Select one player as the leader. Line up the other players behind the leader.

Play:
The leader sets off on the lawn or playground, running, skipping, hopping, jumping, waving his arms, shaking his legs, and creating a series of movements that the others must copy as they go along behind. The leader may even circle around an obstacle course on the lawn while the others follow. After several minutes a new leader is selected and the game continues with a new group of followers.

356 Follow the Animal Leader

In this silly version, the leader imitates animal movements and sounds and all the other players follow suit. This version can get rather noisy as the children bark like dogs, roar like lions, and growl like bears.

357 Willy-Nilly

This is the "no-worries" version of volleyball. The children just try to keep the ball in the air as long as they can.

AGE: 3–5 YRS

CATEGORY:
PLAY WITH OTHERS/ OUTDOOR

NUMBER OF CHILDREN: TWO OR MORE

Materials:
6' to 8' of yarn
Large inflated punching ball or beach ball

Setup:
Place a long piece of yarn across the lawn to create a "net" for the game.

Play:
Position one or two children on each side of the net. Toss the ball in the air toward the first player, who swats it toward the other side of the net. When the balls drops to the ground, the child closest to the ball tosses it across the net to another player (or simply swats the ball into the air) to get the ball moving again. Don't worry about how many hits it takes to move the ball across the net to another player. The intent of this game is to have the children swatting the ball up in the air, with each player taking turns to keep the ball airborne as long as possible.

> ❝It's important for parents to recognize the current obesity rate in our country, and realize that children who have physical disabilities are especially susceptible to developing obesity as a secondary disability. I strongly encourage parents to make family fitness and leisure activities a part of the daily routine for the entire family. You can spend fifteen minutes playing a throwing and catching game, using beanbags or a ball, adapted with Velcro for easier catching, or use scarves.❞
>
> **—Kristi Sayers Menear, Ph.D., CAPE**
> Assistant Professor of Human Studies at the University of Alabama at Birmingham

358 Bucket-Head

QUICK & EASY

AGE: 3–5 YRS

CATEGORY:
PLAY WITH
OTHERS/
OUTDOOR

NUMBER OF
CHILDREN: **THREE OR MORE**

At dinner one night, I announced to my family that I hoped someday to write a book with the title Bucket-Head. This got a great laugh from my children, and a lively conversation ensued. I haven't written that book yet, but I decided to create a series of games with this endearing title.

Materials:

5' roll of Velcro with adhesive backing

Scissors (for adult use only)

3 empty plastic whipped-topping containers (8 ounce) or large plastic margarine tubs

3 inexpensive plastic headbands

Small basket

6 small sponge balls or Nerf balls

Permanent marker (for adult use only)

Small basket

Setup:

Cut three sets of 2-foot-long Velcro pieces. (You will be cutting a fuzzy and a scratchy strip of Velcro for each of these hats.) Turn one plastic container upside down. Peel the tape off one of the fuzzy strips of Velcro and position it in the middle of the upside-down container; press firmly. Now peel the tape off one of the scratchy strips of Velcro and stick it to the middle of the headband. Allow the sticky tape to set for 5 minutes, then attach the tub to the headband, using the interlocking Velcro. Repeat this process on the other tubs. Write

each child's name or initials on the tubs in permanent marker.

Play:

Put a Bucket-Head hat on each child's head and place the balls in the basket.

One player ("Bucket-Head") sits on the floor with his hat on, with his back facing the others, holding his head steady and upright. The other children (the tossers) stand 2 to 3 feet away, with the basket. The children take turns aiming a few balls into Bucket-Head's hat. (With Bucket-Head's back toward the tossers, there is less chance of the soft balls being tossed at the face.) Each time a player gets a ball inside the bucket, the players shout, "Bucket-Head!" This signals Bucket-Head to tip his head down so that the ball tumbles onto the floor. All the balls are gathered up and the child sitting as Bucket-Head trades places with one of the other children. Throughout the game, all the children typically wear their Bucket-Head hats, simply because they are fun to wear. The children will probably invent plenty of Bucket-Head activities of their own, so this game expands with imagination and copycat action.

359 Beanbag Runaround

This is a delightful cooperative relay race for preschoolers who work together to "beat the clock."

AGE: **3–5 YRS**

CATEGORY:
PLAY WITH
OTHERS/
OUTDOOR

NUMBER OF
CHILDREN: **THREE**

Materials:
- 3 beanbags
- Cardboard box
- Hula-Hoop
- Kitchen timer

Setup:
Mark a starting line and finish line. Put the beanbags in the box and place it at the starting line. Put the Hula-Hoop on the lawn, a short running distance away. Line all the players up behind the starting line, directly next to the cardboard box.

Play:
Set the kitchen timer for 3 or more minutes, and announce, "Ready, set, go!" The first child in line takes a beanbag from the box, runs to the Hula-Hoop, and dumps the beanbag on the ground inside the hoop. He then runs back to the starting line and taps the next player to signal it's his turn. The relay continues. When everyone has taken a turn dropping a beanbag in the hoop, the game reverses, so that the players retrieve the beanbags from the Hula-Hoop and drop them back in the box. All the while, the clock is ticking, and the children aim to finish before the timer buzzes.

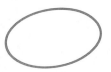

360 Flash In the Pan

This is an obstacle course game for preschoolers featuring a pie pan, ball, and a bit of fast walking to heighten the fun.

AGE: **4–5 YRS**

CATEGORY:
PLAY WITH
OTHERS/
OUTDOOR

NUMBER OF
CHILDREN: **TWO
OR MORE**

Materials:
- Roll of crepe paper
- Small pebbles
- Pie pans
- Playground balls or other bouncy balls

Setup:
Create an obstacle course on the lawn by laying the crepe paper in a trail around the lawn. Use one strand of crepe paper. Anchor it to the ground with small pebbles. (The trail may zigzag back and forth across the yard, around trees, etc.)

Play:
Give each child a pie pan with a ball inside. The first player begins to walk the obstacle course, holding the pan with two hands. Wait 15 to 30 seconds to send the second player on her way through the obstacle course. When each player reaches the end of the crepe paper trail, he or she turns and follows the trail back to the starting point. Since they'll all be at different stages on the trail, the children must maneuver around one another without dropping the balls. When a ball floats off a child's pan, she simply picks it up, puts it back in her pan, and resumes.

361 Beach Ball Soccer

Each child has a ball to kick along the ground, following the crepe paper path. At the end of the path, she turns the ball around and follows the path back to the starting point.

362 Slippery Spoons

"I don't think the spoons are slippery. The balls are the slippery ones," four-year-old Makenzie declared.

AGE: 4–5 YRS

CATEGORY: PLAY WITH OTHERS/ OUTDOOR

NUMBER OF CHILDREN: TWO OR MORE

Materials:

Basket or unbreakable bowl

Ping-Pong balls

Large paper grocery bag

Tablespoons

Setup:

Mark a starting line and finish line on the lawn, with 20 to 30 feet between them. Place the bowl at the starting line and fill it with Ping-Pong balls. Open the paper bag, folding the edge down several times, and stand it up at the finish line.

Play:

Each player is given a tablespoon to start the game. A parent calls out "Ready, set, go!" and each child grabs a ball, places it on her spoon, walks quickly down to the paper bag, and tries to dump the ball into the bag without dropping it. (If a child drops the ball on the way, she simply picks it up, puts it back on the spoon, and keeps heading toward the goal.) The game continues until all the balls are in the paper bag.

363 Slippery Spoons with a Theme

Instead of a ball, substitute an object that ties into the theme of your child's party (a peanut in a shell, a hard-boiled egg, an artist's eraser, a fishing bobber, a Wiffle golf ball, a seashell).

364 Ice-Cream Scoop Relay

Use an ice-cream scooper to carry a Ping-Pong ball, with the children taking turns running to the finish line and back in a relay race. Set a kitchen timer, which the children will try to beat.

365 Beans and Bits

Play this game outdoors using teaspoons and dried kidney beans, navy beans, or uncooked elbow macaroni. Drop a small number of beans or pasta pieces onto each spoon. The object is to get to the finish line with at least one bean or pasta piece still on the spoon to dump into the paper bag.

366 Ice-Cube Toss

Turn a wading pool into a rainbow!

AGE: 3–5 YRS

CATEGORY: PLAY WITH OTHERS/ OUTDOOR

NUMBER OF CHILDREN: TWO OR MORE

Materials:

Food coloring

Small pitcher

Ice-cube trays

Small wading pool

Setup:

Mix a drop or two of food coloring in the pitcher with enough water to fill one ice-cube tray. Fill the first tray, then mix up the rest of your colors to fill the other trays. Place trays in the freezer until frozen solid. Fill the wading pool with water.

Play:

Toss the colored cubes in the water and watch what happens.

367 | **Kitchen Sink Ice-Cube Toss**

To liven up kitchen sink playtime, throw a couple of colored ice cubes into the sink while you are working nearby in the kitchen.

368 | **Colorful End to Bath Time**

Just before bath time, place the colored cubes in an insulated travel mug or soft cooler and take them into the bathroom along with the towels. When bath time is nearly over, toss the colored cubes in the tub. Once the cubes have completely melted, it's time to get out and dry off.

★ CLASSIC ★

369 Sandbox

When the sandbox sits empty, it looks a bit glum, but add a few preschoolers and the place becomes alive with energy, building, and creative play.

QUICK & EASY

AGE: 3–5 YRS

CATEGORY:
PLAY WITH
OTHERS/
OUTDOOR

NUMBER OF
CHILDREN: TWO
OR MORE

Materials:

Sandbox (with lid)

Clean play sand
  (available at toy stores)

Assorted toys for sand play and construction:
  Plastic pitcher

  Wooden clothespins (pretend people)

  Toy cars and trucks

  Cardboard oatmeal tub and orange juice cans
    with both lids removed (tunnels for cars)

  Plastic cups, bowl, and small yogurt tubs
    (molds for building)

  Kitchen strainers and sieve

  Plastic funnel

  Coffee measures

  Water bottle with squirt lid or kitchen baster
    (for adding water)

  Rubber spatulas (ideal for road-building)

  Ice-cream scoopers

  Recycled cake pans and molds

  Kitchen baster

Setup:

Fill the sandbox with clean play sand and assemble sand toys and building gadgets.

Play:

Each child becomes a builder or baker or creator, building roads and bridges, castles and houses, or fancy cakes in his pretend bakery. Experimenting with the sand toys and tools is a big part of the play.

TIP: Remind your child and his playmate about the three simple rules for sand play:

1. No one can ever throw sand, period!

2. You can't knock down anyone else's work.

3. Ask to take a turn with a toy or tool instead of grabbing it away.

SAFETY ALERT: Be sure to make or purchase a sandbox with a tight-fitting lid, and put it away as soon as the children are finished playing, or your cat might mistake your child's sandbox for a giant litter box!

Beach Day

By the time your child is three to five years old, the beach will be one of the most thrilling settings for play in her little world. Whether lakeside or seaside, the sand will become a medium for building and experimenting, and the water an ever-abundant resource for fun and excitement. Preschoolers will find a million ways to play, using their newly developed muscle coordination and manipulation skills to dig, sculpt, and explore!

370 Beachy Bundt Cakes

It's all just pretend of course, but these sand cakes do look very fancy—with well-placed shells for elegant frosting decoration and just the right number of twigs for candles.

AGE: 3–5 YRS

CATEGORY:
PARENT & CHILD/
OUTDOOR
(BEACH)

NUMBER OF
CHILDREN: ONE

Materials:

Shells

Small twigs

Plastic sand shovel and small bucket

Large plastic sherbet or margarine tubs
(or a 9" round cake pan)

Setup:

Walk with your child to collect shells and small twigs found along the beach. Shovel wet sand into the margarine tub (or cake pans) and pat, pat, pat it into the cake pan with the small shovel as you go. Provide a little demo (or on-going help) to quickly flip the cake upside down, and provide a little squeezing pressure to wiggle the cake loose from the pan. Decorate the pretend cake with shells and stones, and add twigs for the candles.

371 Melting Bundt Cakes

Bring a toy sprinkling can along, fill it with water, and once the cake is done, your child may decide to "melt" the cake by slowly sprinkling water over the top. Then pick out the shells and sticks, scoop up the sand and make another fancy creation.

372 Canals and Rivers

The beach is a perfect setting for a child to experiment with nature. He'll be delighted by the way water flows in and out of his handmade canals.

AGE: 3–5 YRS

CATEGORY:
PARENT & CHILD/
OUTDOOR
(BEACH)

NUMBER OF
CHILDREN: ONE

Materials:
Sand shovels

Small twigs or plastic boats

Play:

For a simple preschool waterway, use sand shovels to help your child create a narrow (3 to 4 inches wide) winding trench in the sand. Angle both sides back a bit with the shovel to form a stable riverbank that won't cave in when you add water. Fill the trench with water to create a river, and add homemade "boats" (small twigs) or plastic boats.

SAFETY ALERT: Supervise all preschooler water play carefully.

Preschool Play (age 3 to 5)

Let It Snow!

Brrr! When you're four years old and in the company of newly fallen snow, what's better than making tracks through it, sticking out your tongue to catch falling snowflakes, or packing together a perfectly round snowball with your mittens? Snow play is magical and exciting for preschoolers, and they typically have the physical stamina for long afternoons of trampling through the drifts and bending and moving about in winter gear for hours. There's no doubt that your child will likely discover his own spontaneous, creative ways to play, but here are a few favorites he may be inspired to try.

373 Snow People

One of the most classic snowy pastimes, making a snow person will be fun for the whole family!

QUICK & EASY

AGE: 3–5 YRS

CATEGORY:
**PARENT & CHILD/
OUTDOOR
(SNOW)**

NUMBER OF
CHILDREN: ONE
OR MORE

Materials:

Stones

Large buttons

Dried beans and pasta shapes

Bottle caps

Carrot

Wine cork

Small plastic cup

Small stalk of celery

Licorice

Chunks of apple or orange peel

Hats, scarves, mittens, wigs, etc.

Play:

With a little help, preschoolers can build a snow person or creature using the traditional technique of making a small snowball and rolling it around and around in the snow to make a large round base. Then, in the same manner, create a medium-size ball of snow to stack on top of the large ball. Finally, make a third, small snowball, and place it firmly atop the medium ball for the head. Finish the look using some of the household items from the materials list, like button or bean eyes, a licorice stick or a celery stalk mouth, and a wine cork or a carrot nose. Top his head with a hat, wrap a scarf around his neck, and you've got a new member of the family!

374 Snow Who?

Play around with snow person accessories and features to make different snow characters. Add a funny mustache out of twigs for Snow Grandpa, or a necklace of cranberry "pearls" for Snow Grandma. What can your child use to make a Snow Elf? A Snow Humpty Dumpty?

375 Giant Snow Spider

Your preschooler will delight in making giant designs in the snow with his feet and body. He may get a bit tuckered out, but large-scale designs equals large-scale fun.

QUICK & EASY

AGE: 3–5 YRS

CATEGORY:
**PARENT & CHILD/
OUTDOOR
(SNOW)**

NUMBER OF
CHILDREN: ONE

Play:

Shuffle your feet to create a big, round circle in the center of the lawn (for the spider's body) and then shuffle-

shuffle-shuffle to create one long leg (about 10 to 20 feet) at a time extending out from the body. Your child may need a little demonstration in shuffling technique (how to stomp his feet in a straight line and then turn around and carefully retrace his steps back to the spider's body in the center). Use this same idea to create a giant snow octopus, with wavy arms and legs extending out from the center circle. Or, shuffle your feet to create a giant snow snake that extends from one end of the lawn to the other.

376 Snow Pyramid

Using several different types of containers as molds, create a pyramid from these oddly sized "blocks." Not only will your preschooler be thrilled with filling up the buckets and tubs with snow, but she will also be amazed at the sculpture she's built!

QUICK & EASY

AGE: 3–5 YRS

CATEGORY: **PARENT & CHILD/ OUTDOOR (SNOW)**

NUMBER OF CHILDREN: **ONE OR MORE**

Materials:
 Plastic scoop or large spoon
 Empty plastic tubs and containers

Play:
Use the scoop or spoon to fill the containers with snow. Pack the snow firmly in each container and firmly turn it upside down on the ground to release the snow. Place four of the snow shapes side by side on the ground. Then fill the containers with snow again and stack more snow shapes on top of the first ones to create a snow pyramid together. See what sorts of games develop.

377 Snow Room

Even if there are only a few inches of snow on the ground, you and your child can still create a fort of sorts! Build a few short walls around each other and see what magical things happen inside your room.

QUICK & EASY

AGE: 3–5 YRS

CATEGORY: **PARENT & CHILD/ OUTDOOR (SNOW)**

NUMBER OF CHILDREN: **ONE OR MORE**

Materials:
 Child-size snow shovels

Play:
Using the small shovels, create four walls, each about 6 inches high, packing the snow as you go. Then step over a wall and sit inside the snow room with your child to see what imaginary fun your child might invent inside. Perhaps a bunny lives inside, or maybe little snowflakes come here to sleep.

TIP: You can also purchase plastic Snow Block Makers and fill them with snow to make a wall of snow blocks. Snow Block Makers are available at www.hearthsong.com or www.amazon.com.

378 Snowball Toss

Making snowballs is a fun activity in itself, and great for developing and honing sculpting skills, but you can up the ante by creating a fun tossing game to work on hand–eye coordination too.

QUICK & EASY

AGE: 3–5 YRS

CATEGORY: **PARENT & CHILD/ OUTDOOR (SNOW)**

NUMBER OF CHILDREN: **ONE**

Materials:
 Plastic dishpan or Hula-Hoop

Preschool Play (age 3 to 5)

Play:

Make a stash of snowballs and place them on the ground. Put a plastic dishpan or Hula-Hoop on the ground a few feet away and see if you and your preschooler can hit the target with your snowballs.

379 Snow Pie

Just don't plan on putting this pie in the oven—or you'll end up with snow soup.

AGE: 3–5 YRS

CATEGORY: PARENT & CHILD// OUTDOOR (SNOW)

NUMBER OF CHILDREN: ONE OR MORE

Materials:

Disposable aluminum foil pie pan

Stones

Twigs

Dried beans and pasta shapes

Play:

Help your child pack snow into the pie pan for a decorative dessert. Press stones, twigs, or dried beans and pasta into the surface to give pattern and texture to the "crust." The best part is pretend-eating the pies, Cookie Monster style!

380 Silly Penguin

Here's a penguin-style follow the leader that allows preschoolers to waddle-waddle through the snow.

AGE: 3–5 YRS

CATEGORY: PARENT & CHILD/ OUTDOOR (SNOW)

NUMBER OF CHILDREN: TWO OR MORE

Materials:

A snowy lawn in the backyard or park (with fresh-fallen snow)

Boots, mittens, and snow gear for each child

Plastic play fish or scraps of cardboard in oval or fish shapes (optional)

Setup:

The children create a circle in the snow at one end of the lawn by stomping their feet round and round. This becomes the feeding pond filled with fish for hungry penguins. Create another at the other end of the lawn. Demonstrate how penguins waddle—stand up straight, heels together, and toes pointed out—and walk in little marching steps.

Play:

To start the play, one child is appointed to be the mama penguin and the other child to be the baby. The mama penguin waddles from one fish pond to the other, zigzagging across the frozen Antarctic (snowy lawn), looking for fish. The mama may waddle fast or slow, or even drop to the ground and roll around in the snow, and the baby must copy each action. The mama penguin's turn lasts as long as it takes to visit both fish ponds (from one end of the lawn to the other). The child who played the baby penguin now gets to be the mama, and vice versa.

> 66 There is some very good research about the characteristics of children who make friends easily. One of the things they know how to do is how to break the ice. They offer a greeting. They say their name: 'Hi, I'm Jennifer.' They'll say, 'What's your name? Where do you live?' They invite the other children to participate: 'Do you want to play with me?' And it's not just what they say, it's how they say it. They give the other children a chance to answer the questions and give the message that they're available. And then, once the ice has been broken, this friendly child keeps up the contact by talking about liking them. They say, 'I like you' or 'You're my friend,' and if the child is hurt they may offer comfort or help. 99
>
> **—Betty Farber**
> author of *My Self, My Family, My Friends*

Birthday Play and Large Group Games

What good things can happen when your preschooler plays with a group at a party? He gets to experience the excitement of playing with many children. He meets new friends and plays new games. He gets a little taste of being on a "team," whether he's treasure hunting or playing games. He learns to share and take turns with a large group of children. He learns to give a present to another child and say "Happy Birthday," even if he wants that present for himself. And he gets to eat cake and ice cream!

How Long Should My Party Be?

An hour-and-a-half-long party may be ideal for a group of three-year-olds, whereas a gathering of five-year-olds might play happily for two hours. Either way, be prepared for some momentary situations where you'll need a gentle hand and steady nerves to keep things moving in a positive direction. As you'll see, each theme party has both 90-minute and 120-minute options.

Preschool Play (age 3 to 5)

You Can't Come to My Birthday!

If you've got a preschooler in the family, you've probably heard your child or another child say, "You can't come to my birthday party!" when emotions are in high gear. Among the preschool set, this is often the most serious thing a child can think of, on the spot, to express disapproval, hurt feelings, or perhaps use as leverage to get another child to play a particular game or give up a desirable toy. When you overhear your child shouting this hurtful phrase, you can quietly pull her aside and say, "You hurt Melinda's feelings when you said that. What was going on?" After hearing your child's explanation, you can help her find a way to apologize and perhaps use words to negotiate a fair solution with her playmate.

Arrival Activities

Plan an arrival activity to get the first fifteen minutes of your child's party off to a positive start. For one thing, children arrive at different times, and for another, preschoolers are notorious for needing a little help transitioning to a new situation. Here are a couple of tried-and-true indoor arrival activities with quick-and-easy setups that are worth repeating as birthday party traditions time and time again.

---

381 Make-Your-Own Place Mats

Put the children to work on your table settings. They'll love bringing some of their own flair to a friend's party. And just wait until it's time to put them to use at cake time!

QUICK & EASY

AGE: **3–5 YRS**

CATEGORY:
**BIRTHDAY PARTY/
ARRIVAL ACTIVITIES**

NUMBER OF
CHILDREN: **TWO
OR MORE**

Materials:
Colored construction paper

Nontoxic markers

Crayons

Stickers

Setup:
Before the children arrive, place construction paper and all other supplies on a table indoors.

Play:
Each child decorates her own personalized place mat, to be used at cake time. Help each child write her name or initials on the place mat, and then give the children free range to decorate while all the other guests are arriving. (If you prefer to make these place mats more durable, have precut sheets of clear contact paper available to carefully stick to the front and back of each decorated place mat. Trim the edges so that you have about a half-inch of excess contact paper all the way around.)

---

382 Make-Your-Own Treat Bags

Create a personalized package to hold all the little goodies they'll accumulate at the party.

QUICK & EASY

AGE: **3–5 YRS**

CATEGORY:
**BIRTHDAY PARTY/
ARRIVAL ACTIVITIES**

NUMBER OF
CHILDREN: **TWO
OR MORE**

Materials:
Small white party bags (lunch-bag size)

Nontoxic markers

Crayons

Stickers

Setup:
Place the decoration materials and one bag for each partygoer on the table.

Play:
Help each child write her name or initials on the bag as soon as she sits down at the table, then give the children the freedom to decorate their bags with their own style of scribbles and designs.

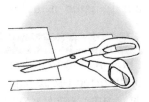

Birthday Party Arts and Crafts

Preschoolers love to make things with their very own hands and also are thrilled when they have something to take home from the party. Here are some birthday crafts that measure up on both counts. The key to making these birthday craft activities is twofold: First, get organized with materials and directions in advance of the party, and second, have at least one adult helper for every three children to keep things cheerfully moving along.

383 Rainbow Row Party Hats

These are quick and easy hats for you to make ahead of time, with the children doing the wild and crazy decorating during the party!

QUICK & EASY

AGE: **3–5 YRS**

CATEGORY: **BIRTHDAY PARTY/ ARTS & CRAFTS**

NUMBER OF CHILDREN: **THREE OR MORE**

Materials:

White paper plates (standard type, with ridged edges)

Scissors (for adult use only)

Stapler (for adult use only)

Rolls of invisible tape (1 for each child)

Single-hole punch

Curling ribbon

Mesh shower pouf (1 for each child)

6 different colors (rolls) of crepe paper streamers

Ziplock bags

Pen or pencil

Setup:

For each plate, cut a slit going from the edge to the center (the radius). Shape the plate into a cone by overlapping

the cut edges and staple in place. For safety, stick a piece of tape over each staple. (Adults do the cutting and stapling to make the basic hats.) Next, use the hole punch to make two holes on opposite sides of the base of the cone. Cut two equal length pieces of ribbon, thread each piece through a hole, and double knot to the hat, leaving ends dangling. Cut a small hole in the point of each hat. Thread the cord of the shower pouf through this hole and tape it to the inside of the hat, so that the pouf is firmly attached to the top of the cone hat. Cut many pieces from each roll of crepe streamer in lengths about 5 inches long. (Each hat requires about 24 to 36 pieces of crepe paper, so cut lots of pieces, and in a large assortment of colors.) Store the streamers, arranged by color, in individual ziplock bags until the party begins.

Play:

Each child is given a hat to decorate. The children tape strips of crepe paper to their hats, twisting and progressing up the hats little by little until they are covered. Finish the hats off by adding a few more pieces of crepe paper to any blank areas in need of coverage. Voilà! The Rainbow Row Party Hats are ready

Preschool Play (age 3 to 5)

to wear. (Use a pen or pencil to write each child's name or initials on the inside of his hat.)

384 Rainbow Row Circle Hats

Cut about 30 to 40 medium-size circles of assorted tissue paper for each hat. (To save time, stack several sheets of paper so that you are cutting a stack of circles with each go.) Use tape to arrange these circles in rows around the hats, overlapping layers of circles one over the other. (To add more texture to the design, fold the paper circles in half, taping one half of the circle to the plate and leaving the other half flapping in the wind.)

Catch Your Child Playing Nicely

Remember that young children want to be appreciated and recognized whenever they do something fair and positive. Take notice when your child is playing nicely, taking turns, and showing care and concern for another child. Make a habit of quietly showing that you are proud of your child's goodness and you believe in his kindness.

Ten Tips for Birthday-Party Play

1. Plan out the games and set up the props in advance of the party.

2. Know your limitations. If it seems unrealistic to manage the group or children completely on your own, line up a helper (another adult or a teenager) before the party begins.

3. Be aware of any food allergies that your guests might have.

4. Put your child's favorite toys away before the party begins to avoid squabbles over toys and sharing.

5. Think of yourself as a camp counselor for the day. Your job is to explain the games, maintain order and safety, and keep the group engaged in positive play.

6. Be on the lookout for the shy child who may need your help in joining in, or who might need an invitation to be your "assistant" for a few of the games as a transition to playing with others.

7. Move in quickly (with fair and firm rules) when you see disruptive behavior.

8. If one of the guests brings an older sibling to the party (uninvited), put this child to "work" by having him help you with the younger children's games and activities.

9. Incorporate guessing games during cake time so that children are eating and playing a quiet game at the same time.

10. In case the weather doesn't cooperate for outdoor play, plan indoor adaptations or alternative games.

385 Homemade Sports Jerseys

These players' jerseys are close enough to the real thing to delight preschoolers at a sports-oriented birthday party.

AGE: 3–5 YRS

CATEGORY:
BIRTHDAY PARTY/
ARTS & CRAFTS

NUMBER OF
CHILDREN: TWO
OR MORE

Materials:

Scissors (for adult use only, pinking shears work best)

Large plain T-shirts of any color

Fabric markers

Setup:
Before the party begins, cut the sleeves off of the T-shirts and turn the crewnecks into V-necks.

Play:
Help each child create a personalized jersey with his last name and a chosen number on the back of the shirt. These jerseys are worn throughout the party, during the games, and also become take-home party favors.

387 Majestic Crowns

These crowns are fun to make, and when the children put them on, the birthday party suddenly turns into a royal court.

QUICK & EASY

AGE: 3–5 YRS

CATEGORY:
BIRTHDAY PARTY/
ARTS & CRAFTS

NUMBER OF
CHILDREN: THREE
OR MORE

Materials:

Brightly colored poster board

Scissors (for adult use only)

Nontoxic markers, crayons, colored pencils

Colored construction paper

Glitter glue

Color dot stickers

Invisible tape

Setup:
Cut 5-inch-wide strips of poster board, each about 24 to 26 inches long (or, long enough to wrap around your child's head) with an extra 2 inches for fastening. With a pencil, create a zigzag pattern along one long edge of the poster board strip. Cut along this line so that your hat has the pointed spikes of a crown. Cut small stars out of colored construction paper.

Preschool Play (age 3 to 5)

PARENT TIP

386 When I Was Four (or Five!)

❝*This is a family birthday tradition we call the 'When I Was Four' booklet; it's a way to celebrate birthdays and special events in your child's life and also have fun with writing. A day or two before your child's birthday, sit down with her and remember all the wonderful things that happened over the last year. You might have to help her out by having a conversation about some of the past year's activities, but you'll still want to focus on what your child thinks are the most important events. Write these down in a special notebook. Some entries will be funny. For instance, she might think that the most important thing that happened during the past year was that she got a new purse, and that's fine. You can add photographs or have your son or daughter draw pictures. Kids enjoy doing this and it can naturally lead into journal writing later.*❞

—Mary from Massachusetts

Play:

The children decorate and embellish the crowns with the stars, glitter glue, markers, crayons, and stickers. Once the creation is complete, tape the children's crowns to fit.

388 Magic Wands for Kings and Queens

A good prop for a birthday party parade around the lawn.

QUICK & EASY

AGE: 3–5 YRS

CATEGORY:
BIRTHDAY PARTY/
ARTS & CRAFTS

NUMBER OF
CHILDREN: THREE
OR MORE

Materials:

Scissors (for adult use only)

Colored construction paper

Utility or X-Acto knife
    (for adult use only)

Foam board

Tape

Curling ribbon or crepe paper streamers

Stickers

Nontoxic markers

Setup:

Before the party begins, cut 3- to 4-inch stars from the construction paper, two for each Magic Wand. Next, use the utility knife to cut wand handles from the foam board, each about 20 inches long and 2 inches wide. Sandwich one end of a foam wand handle between two stars (line up their points), and tape them together. Create long streamers of curling ribbon and/or crepe paper to tape to the wand just below the star.

Play:

Children decorate the wand handle and star with stickers and markers to personalize their Magic Wand.

*SAFETY ALERT: Take care when using a utility or X-Acto knife. These are not for children.

Cranky Playmate or Sleep-Deprived Child?

*H*as your child had enough sleep today? Preschoolers who are sleep deprived often seem irritable, cranky, whiny, uncooperative, hyperactive, or aggressive. You may notice these telltale signs of overtired behavior as they play with others. Take a quick look at how much sleep your child is getting each week and weekend night. Preschoolers need a total of eleven to twelve hours of sleep a day. (This factors in both nap-time sleep and nighttime sleep.) If your preschooler is not getting this much sleep on a regular basis, time to make some changes—you just might see a big improvement in her playtime behavior!

389 Animal Ear Hats

Animal sounds not included—but highly encouraged!

QUICK & EASY

AGE: 3–5 YRS

CATEGORY:
BIRTHDAY PARTY/
ARTS & CRAFTS

NUMBER OF
CHILDREN: THREE
OR MORE

Materials:

Colored poster board or
    large sheets of construction
    paper

Scissors (for adult use only)

Tape

Nontoxic markers, crayons, colored
    pencils

Glitter glue

Odds and ends for decorating (cotton balls, yarn,
    curling ribbon, scraps of furry fabric)

Stapler (for adult use only)

Setup:
Cut 3-inch-wide strips of poster board or heavy construction paper long enough to fit around your child's head (approximately 24 to 26 inches long) plus an extra 2 inches for fastening. Tape the ends of the strip together to create a basic hatband.

Play:
Help children cut animal ears out of construction paper or poster board (rabbit ears that stand up, dog ears that hang down low, etc.). Then children can color and decorate these ears with any of the fuzzy or furry materials listed above. Staple the craft ears to each child's headband, taping over the staples for safety.

> *"Preschool playgroups should be comprised of children representing a range of ages. Children ages three to five greatly benefit by having older children play with them. Research suggests that in certain areas of development, young children make more progress when learning a skill from a competent older child than from an adult."*
>
> **—John Feierabend, Ph.D.**
> founder and director of the National Center of Music and Movement in the Early Years, University of Hartford, author of the *First Steps in Music* series

Learning to Share

Between the ages of three and five, children learn a great deal about getting along with others, but the progress they make comes with lots of missteps. Some days your preschooler may be very capable of playing nicely with playmates. Other days, she will seem out of sorts and will need your help to stay on track.

Part of the problem is that preschoolers aren't sure they *want to* share. Children live in the moment, so from your child's perspective, sharing really means "giving up the toy that I want to play with right now." When you break sharing down into smaller bites, it's a bit easier to sell the idea. You might say, "Let's give the bucket to Billy for a few minutes and wait until it's your turn again." This lets your child know that this sharing business is temporary! (Some parents set a timer for four or five minutes to help orchestrate the turn-taking; see box, page 185.)

You should also realize that waiting passively for the toy to come back will make the minutes seem like hours. So the next step is teaching your child the flexibility to find something else fun to do while Susan has the fire truck. Offer a brief suggestion like, "Why don't you use that shovel to dig a good road over in that corner of the sandbox? Then, when it's your turn with the fire truck again, you'll have a new road to drive it on." Later on, your child may incorporate this into her play on her own.

Learning to share and take turns also involves yet another skill, empathy. When your preschool child begins to see that other children have feelings too, she is able to make a big leap forward in the process of learning to share. Help her along by asking, "How would you feel if Jimmy ate all the cookies and did not share any with you?"

Cake-Time Activities

Grown-ups have a tendency to imagine that "cake time" is an activity in and of itself, with the power to keep children busy for a fair amount of time. In my experience, some of the preschoolers will take a bite or two of cake and quickly get fidgety while the others are still eating. The best idea here is to have a few guessing games going on while the children are eating cake to keep everyone at the table. Following are several games that are ideal for capturing everyone's attention for about ten to fifteen minutes during cake time. These guessing games become instant classics, good for every party, every year.

390 Who Am I?

Plug this activity into cake and ice cream time and it's bound to be a winner. It's a wonderful tradition you'll want to include in every birthday party.

QUICK & EASY

AGE: 3–5 YRS

CATEGORY:
BIRTHDAY PARTY/
CAKE TIME

NUMBER OF
CHILDREN: FOUR
OR MORE

Play:

Pick a person in the group, give one clue about him, and let the children guess who you are describing. Make these clues a bit challenging; for example, "I have an older brother with red hair, who am I?" If the children guess correctly, move on to describe one clue about another child at the party. (If they can't guess after one clue, continue to add more clues to describe the mystery child.) Make a point to describe (and give clues) about each child sitting at the table before cake time is over. To stretch the challenge a bit, you may want to describe the same child twice at some point during this game, using a different clue each time. (Hint: Once you know which children will attend the party, you may wish to write down a few facts about each child to help you ad-lib some clues for this game.)

391 What Kind of Animal Am I?

Play the same simple game, but describe a familiar animal in the zoo, on the farm, or in the natural world. For example, "I sometimes live in the zoo, have a very long neck and tiny ears, what animal am I?" Add more clues until someone guesses the correct animal. Create a bit more challenge as the game progresses.

392 What Food Is It?

In this version, describe a familiar food that the children will recognize, using one clue at a time to describe what it looks like, when it's eaten, whether it's hot or cold. For example, "You drink this from a cup," "It is orange," etc.

393 What Sport Is It?

Give one clue at a time and let the children guess what sport you are describing; for example, "In this game you bounce a large orange ball while you run. What sport is it?"

394 What's My Job?

Select occupations that preschoolers are familiar with, like police officers, cooks, doctors, firefighters, postal workers, teachers, waiters and waitresses, and pose one somewhat challenging clue at a time to describe that person's work. Add additional clues until the children make the correct guess.

395 Cupcake Creations

Instead of just eating a slice of cake at the party, children can create their own fancy cupcakes to eat on-site or take home!

AGE: 3–5 YRS

CATEGORY: BIRTHDAY PARTY/ CAKE TIME

NUMBER OF CHILDREN: FOUR OR MORE

Materials:
- Assorted sprinkles, small pieces of string licorice, tiny pieces of candied fruit, M&M's, etc.
- Assorted edible "letters" (premade) to spell the first initial of each child's name
- Small bowls with teaspoons
- Cupcakes with white frosting (1 for each child)

Setup:
Arrange small bowls of the edible decorations around the table, along with plastic shakers filled with assorted sprinkles.

Play:
Each child decorates his own cupcake using the edible letters, decorations, and ingredients.

396 Cookie Creations

Give each child an extra-large chocolate-chip cookie to decorate, along with a small bowl of thin frosting (confectioner's sugar and milk mixed to a thin, paintlike consistency). The children apply the frosting to the cookies with small pastry brushes and finish off the creations with assorted sprinkles.

397 Ice-Cream Sundae Creations

Each child starts with a scoop of ice cream in a bowl and adds special sundae ingredients of his own choosing to make a colossal treat. In the center of the table, place a variety of plastic shaker jars filled with sprinkles and small bowls filled with butterscotch chips, sliced bananas, M&M's, marshmallows, maraschino cherries, etc.

398 I See Something . . .

Let the children pose the questions and give the answers in this low-key activity.

AGE: 3–5 YRS

CATEGORY: BIRTHDAY PARTY/ CAKE TIME

NUMBER OF CHILDREN: FOUR OR MORE

Play:
Each child takes a turn describing one item he can see from the table. The birthday boy or girl can get the game started by giving the first clue; for example, "I see something really heavy, what is it?" The other children call out their answers. If they are unable to guess, the birthday boy or girl poses another clue: "It's something that gets very, very hot." Let each child take a turn giving a clue for a "mystery item."

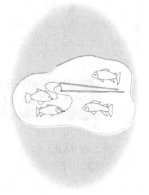

Indoor Party (Group) Games

You just never know about the weather! Here's a diverse assortment of indoor games to have in your hip pocket if your outdoor party suddenly becomes an indoor party. You may recognize some of the classics, like Simon Says and Duck, Duck, Goose!, as flashbacks to your own childhood. Or, try Fish Follies or Bigwig for something totally new. Whether you go old school or new school, or mix and match between the two, the games in this section are ideal to play to help slow down the pace after a round or two of boisterous outdoor games.

Preschool Play (age 3 to 5)

399 Pass the Peanuts (Please)!

I love the image of a group of playful elephants standing in line, passing a peanut from one trunk to another in a graceful, sweeping motion! I've tweaked this idea to create a game for a group of preschoolers who pass pretend peanuts (clothespins) down the line to feed the imaginary elephant at the end.

QUICK & EASY

AGE: 3–5 YRS

CATEGORY:
BIRTHDAY PARTY
(GROUP GAMES)/
INDOOR

NUMBER OF
CHILDREN: SIX
OR MORE

Materials:

2 buckets

6 to 8 wooden clothespins (1-piece, no-hinge style)

Toy elephant (stuffed animal or small plastic elephant)

Small stool or chair

Setup:
Line up all the players at arm's distance from one another. Place one bucket full of clothespins (aka "peanuts") on the ground at the start of the line, and the other empty bucket on the ground at the end of the line. Position the toy elephant on a stool or chair next to the empty bucket.

Play:
Explain to the players that the elephants at the zoo are *very* large and they get *very* hungry, so each child must pass the peanut (clothespin) as fast as he can to feed the hungry elephant at the end! To start the game, the parent announces loudly, "Pass the peanuts, please!" and the child at the start of the line (near the bucket of clothespins) quickly picks up one "peanut" and passes it relay-style to the next child, who passes it along, relay-style. As soon as he passes that first "peanut," the first child grabs another one and passes it along as well, so that "peanuts" are continuously moving down the line. When the very last clothespin ("peanut") is dropped into the bucket at the end of the line, the parent announces, "The animal feeder needs more peanuts, please!" as a signal for the children to pass all of the clothespins back down the line, one by one, and drop them into the animal feeder's bucket. Let the children know that part of the fun of the game is dropping "peanuts" and picking them up "as quick as you can"!

400 Story-Time Stomp

This is a game I include in every preschool party. What kid doesn't love to stomp on cue?

AGE: **3–5 YRS**

CATEGORY: **BIRTHDAY PARTY (GROUP GAMES)/ INDOOR**

NUMBER OF CHILDREN: **FOUR OR MORE**

Materials:
   Children's book with a familiar word repeated throughout

Setup:
Gather the children around in a circle. (Select a place with a little room for moving about, indoors or outdoors.)

Play:
Give the children a quick but inviting introduction about this activity. For example, "I'm going to read a story that might have the word _____ in it. I'm not sure where this word is or exactly how many times I might read it, but it's a special word in this story. Now, here's a special assignment for you: Every time I say this word (_____) you need to jump up and stomp your feet. Then, sit back down so I can continue reading the story!" (You may ask the children one quick time before you start reading, "So what's the magic word that will make you jump up and stomp your feet?") Begin reading the story and pause appropriately each time the magic word is said to allow time for the hoopla that ensues.

Suggested Books for Story-Time Stomp:
Here are a few of my favorite preschool books with a repetitive word or phrase:

Pete's a Pizza by William Steig

Little Gorilla by Ruth Bornstein

Blue Hat, Green Hat by Sandra Boynton

Chicken Soup with Rice by Maurice Sendak

Owl Babies by Martin Waddell, illustrations by Patrick Benson

Down by the Station by Will Hillenbrand

I Went Walking by Sue Williams, illustrations by Julie Vivas

Bark, George by Jules Feiffer

401 Bell-Ringing Story-Time Stomp

Play this same game but give a small cowbell to the birthday child (or rotate the bell among all the children). Each time the magic word is mentioned, the child rings the bell and everyone jumps up and stomps their feet or runs to tag a distant tree in the backyard. Afterward, all the children return, settle back into the circle, and the story resumes.

402 Story-Time Runaround

For a slightly more boisterous version of this game, go outside, gather the children around in a circle on the lawn, and challenge them to run to the porch, touch it, and run back to their place in the circle every time you read the magic word in the story.

403 Long Lookers

In some circles this game is known as Memory . . . but little ones need an extra bit of time to look at the items on the tray, so I call this preschool version "long lookers."

AGE: **3–5 YRS**

CATEGORY: **BIRTHDAY PARTY (GROUP GAMES)/ INDOOR**

NUMBER OF CHILDREN: **FOUR OR MORE**

Materials:
   Assortment of 12 to 14 small, familiar objects (ball, spoon, pencil, keys, etc.)
   Cookie sheets
   Dish towels

Preschool Play (age 3 to 5)

Setup:

Before the party, place six familiar objects on each cookie sheet and cover each cookie sheet with a dish towel to keep the objects hidden. If your party has a theme, you may wish to choose objects relating to the theme.

Play:

Gather all the children around the table; place the first cookie sheet in the middle of the table and remove the towel. Ask the children to look at all the objects for about one minute. Put the towel back on the cookie sheet and ask the children to take turns telling you one item they saw on the tray. (If they can't get all the items, give a quick, 3-second peek at the items and put the towel back on.)

404 Long Lookers and a Thief

Select one child to be the *thief;* the others will be the *lookers.* Have all the children look carefully at the objects on the cookie sheet. The lookers leave the room while the thief stays behind to steal one item from the cookie sheet and put it inside a shoe box. Once the item is in the box, call all the children back to the table and ask the group to identify what is missing. (Give clues about the missing object if a gentle nudge is needed.) Once they've identified the missing object, assign a new thief. If the children guess too quickly and easily, allow the thief to steal two or three items to increase the challenge. (Three-year-olds will probably be able to identify only one missing item at a time.) Add new items to the mix as needed to keep this game interesting.

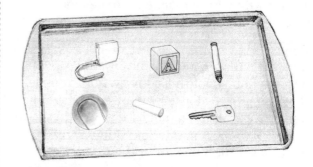

When Your Preschooler Is Shy

Every child comes into the world with her own distinct temperament. You may see clues about your child's personality in your everyday routines together, and you are *sure* to see her temperament in action when she plays with others. Some preschoolers jump right into playing with new children, while others warm up to new playmates at a slower pace. If your child is a bit on the shy side, give her the gift of understanding and support to allow her to ease into these new play scenarios at her own pace. Don't force her to join in immediately or make comments to others about how "shy" she is. (Your child might interpret your remarks as a sign of disappointment.) Instead, take a longer view of playtime, giving your child the freedom to hang back and observe if that feels just right in the moment. Or perhaps she'll feel more confident playing side by side (but on her own) with the others as a way to get familiar with these new playmates and how they play. As time goes by and a comfort level develops, even a very shy child eventually wants to join in the fun and begins to forge new friendships.

405 Picture Clue Treasure Hunt

A visual treasure hunt will get everyone excited and involved.

AGE: 3–5 YRS

CATEGORY: BIRTHDAY PARTY (GROUP GAMES)/ INDOOR

NUMBER OF CHILDREN: **FOUR OR MORE**

Materials:

Polaroid or digital camera, or traditional camera and film

Envelope

Treasure box (cardboard box, decorated)

Prizes or treat bags for all

Tape

Setup:

If you've got either a Polaroid camera or a digital camera and access to a printer, you'll be able to set up the treasure hunt the day of, or the day before, the party; if you're working with a traditional camera, you'll need to allow time to develop your film.

Select 10 to 12 spots in the house (or in the yard) to use as the photo clues in your treasure hunt. The clues should be recognizable places like the front door, the dishwasher, the hall closet, the kitchen table, etc. Take one photograph of each of these spots. Select the order you want the treasure hunt to move in, then put the starting clue in a plain white envelope, seal it, and set it aside. Fill the treasure box with the prizes or treats and place it in the spot you've selected as the treasure hunt's ending point. Tape the second clue (not in an envelope) to the first spot in the hunt. (If, for example, the starting place for the hunt is the front door, you'll hold the photo of the front door aside and you'll tape the second clue—a photo of a rubber boot in the hallway—to the front door.) Repeat this same process until all the clues but the first have been taped up. The very last clue should lead the children to the place where the treasure box is hidden.

Play:

Gather the children together and open the envelope holding the very first photo clue. Follow along with them as they move from spot to spot. As you approach each clue, designate the child who will get to hold the photo. The very last clue leads the children to the treasure chest, which you've filled with treats or prizes for everyone.

★ CLASSIC ★

406 Simon Says

"It's hard to take yourself seriously when you're wearing a donkey hat, hopping on one foot, and singing 'Yankee Doodle Dandy,'" a straitlaced dad once told me.

QUICK & EASY

AGE: 3–5 YRS

CATEGORY: BIRTHDAY PARTY (GROUP GAMES)/ INDOOR

NUMBER OF CHILDREN: **FOUR OR MORE**

Setup:

One adult or child is selected to play the role of Simon (the leader). All the other players line up facing Simon, standing a short distance away.

Play:

Simon gives commands to the group—stomp your feet, wave your hands, hop like a rabbit, skip around the room! When Simon starts a command with the words "Simon says," the children must follow Simon's orders. When he issues a command not prefaced by "Simon says," the children should not follow his orders. In this preschool-friendly (noncompetitive) version of the game, no one is "out" when they mess up.

407 Simon Says Wiggle-Waggle

This quiet version of the Simon Says game uses only thumbs and fingers. Commands for this game include: Simon Says thumbs up; Simon

Says thumbs down; Simon Says suck your thumb; Simon Says wiggle your pinky; Simon Says wiggle-waggle (put your hands together, interlock your fingers, wiggle both thumbs in a circular motion). But remember not to do any of these things unless "Simon Says"!

Preschoolers Develop Empathy by Playing with Others

When children three to five play together, they begin to see what makes other children happy, sad, frustrated, or mad. Preschoolers also have the language skills to express the empathy they're beginning to feel by asking, "Why are you crying?" or "Do you want to take a turn with the wagon now?" You can help your child show empathy to a playmate by posing a well-placed comment as they play—"Julia looks unhappy because all the zoo animals are being used by the other children. Is there anything you can do to make her feel better?" The beauty of a question like this is that each child will come up with something different. One child might offer a toy to a sad playmate. Another child might suggest a new game for the two children to play together that doesn't rely on zoo animals at all. If your child needs a little extra help in the empathy department, role-play a few typical preschool play scenarios before the playmate arrives. This will help your child come up with possible ways to settle disputes.

408 | Fish Follies

Years ago, children would go "fishing" for prizes at their school fairs. You can create your own version of this beloved game with a few simple props.

AGE: 3–5 YRS

CATEGORY: BIRTHDAY PARTY (GROUP GAMES)/ INDOOR

NUMBER OF CHILDREN: FOUR OR MORE

Materials:

Markers (for adult use only)

Construction paper

Scissors (for adult use only)

Metal paper clips

String or yarn

10" to 12" dowel

Invisible tape

Small horseshoe magnet or kitchen magnet

Kitchen strainer

Small bucket

Setup:

Draw 10 to 20 small fish (about the size of lemons) on the construction paper. Cut out the fish with scissors. Tape a paper clip to the mouth of each fish, with about half of the metal clip extending out from the mouth. On the underside of each fish, write a preschooler-friendly command like, "Hop on one foot and sing the first part of 'Old MacDonald,'" or "Find two green things in the room." Next, create a fishing rod by looping one end of a 12- to 14-inch piece of string to the dowel; tie off the string, knot it, and secure it to the dowel with a good bit of invisible tape. Tie the small horseshoe magnet to the other end of your fishing line.

Create a "pond" on the floor or in the backyard by placing a long strand of yarn in a large circle. Distribute the fish (message-side down) throughout the pond, allowing at least a few inches between each fish so that each child is likely to catch only one fish at a time.

Play:

Spread all the children out around the edge of the pond. Select one child to catch the first fish (perhaps the birthday child) while the others stand back and watch. Give the child the fishing rod, and as he dangles it over the fish, the magnet should catch on one of the paper clips. When a fish is caught, scoop it into the net (the strainer), carefully remove the fish from the magnet, and read the command. Drop the fish into the bucket while the child acts out the command.

409 Fish Follies Scavenger Hunt

Create a scavenger hunt for a small group of partygoers. Instead of commands, write clues on the fish; each clue leads to a treasure chest (a shoe box) containing small treats for the group. When a fish is caught, the whole group goes off in search of the treasure. Treats might include individual bags of Goldfish crackers, small bags of candy "worms," chocolate malt balls ("bait balls"), or lace licorice (fishing line).

410 Special Delivery

This is a cooperative game all about finding and trading hearts.

AGE: 3–5 YRS

CATEGORY: BIRTHDAY PARTY (GROUP GAMES)/ INDOOR

NUMBER OF CHILDREN: FOUR OR MORE

Materials:

Scissors (for adult use only)

Colored construction paper

Markers (for adult use only)

Paper lunch bags

Decorative stickers and stars (with adhesive on back)

Setup:

Cut four paper hearts for each child attending the party. Write the children's names on each of the four hearts and hide them around one room with a peek of each heart showing. Create a mailbag for each child by writing his name on the outside of a lunch bag and decorating it with stickers and stars.

Play:

Give each child their personalized mailbag and ask the children to search around the designated room or outdoor space to find four of the hidden hearts, without worrying about what's written on them. Let the children know that if one finishes earlier than the others, he should help his friends find some of their hearts. (Preschoolers typically love to help out after their search has been successful, so everyone should have four hearts in their mailbag fairly quickly.)

Once the hearts have all been found, the children sit in a circle. Now you'll help each child "read" the names on the hearts inside his bag and hand deliver them to the proper person.

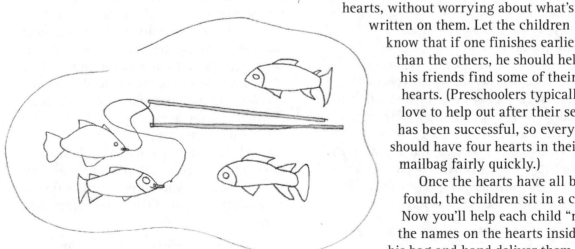

Preschool Play (age 3 to 5)

411 Ice-Cream Scoops

Hide cutout circles in various colors to resemble scoops of ice cream (or other items related to the theme of your child's party).

412 I've Been Working on the Railroad

Using the construction paper, cut four large *T*s (for the word *train*) for each child attending the party. (Or if you have the time, draw one train car as a template and trace it to cut four paper train cars for each child.) Hide these colored letters or shapes as directed in the first game, but give this game a train twist: Sing one line from a railroad song, such as, "I've Been Working on the Railroad, Jason," mentioning the searcher's name, and varying your volume as a clue that the child is "hot" or close. When the children are nowhere near the hidden letters sing this song very quietly as a signal that the searchers are "cold" or far away.

PARENT TIP

413 Talk About It

❝I noticed my daughter was always listening to what I was saying when I talked to my friends about her, even though she pretended she was playing. We had problems with her sharing her toys with others. So one day, I told my friends that my daughter was good about sharing her toys. When she heard this, she started sharing with the other children. This is a great way to inspire positive behavior in your children. Let them overhear you speaking positively about them. You get great results!**❞**

—Helen from New York

414 Farmyard Special Delivery

Cut oval shapes from construction paper to represent duck or chicken eggs. Hide the eggs throughout the room or yard, with a peek of each egg in plain sight. Make this game more fun by quacking or clucking (and calling out a searcher's name) when a particular child is getting close to one of the hidden eggs.

★CLASSIC★

415 Duck, Duck, Goose!

Three simple words. No props. This true classic needs no introduction.

AGE: 3–5 YRS

CATEGORY: BIRTHDAY PARTY (GROUP GAMES)/ INDOOR

NUMBER OF CHILDREN: FOUR OR MORE

Setup:
Select one player to start the game (the leader); the others sit in a circle on the floor with their legs crossed.

Play:
The leader walks around the outside of the circle saying "Duck" as she lightly taps each player on the head. Eventually, she taps someone, calls out "Goose!" and begins to run. The "goose" must jump up and chase the leader around the circle, hoping to tag her before she sits down in his empty spot. If the goose does not tag the leader before she sits, the goose becomes the new leader. If by chance the goose tags the leader before she sits down, then the leader remains the leader for another round of play. Encourage the children to pick different geese as they play so that everyone gets a turn as the goose. Emphasize the fun of the chase rather than winning.

NOTE: When you have a larger group, take this game outside!

Preschool Play (age 3 to 5)

★CLASSIC★

416 Huckle Buckle Beanstalk

Don't fret over the fact that most preschoolers accidentally shout out where the seashell is hiding—it's just a part of the preschool version of Huckle Buckle Beanstalk.

AGE: 3–5 YRS

CATEGORY: BIRTHDAY PARTY (GROUP GAMES)/ INDOOR

NUMBER OF CHILDREN: FOUR OR MORE

Materials:
Thimble, small seashell, or stone

Setup:
While the children are out of the room, "hide" the thimble (in plain view) somewhere in the room.

Play:
The players search around the room for the thimble. When someone spots it, he tries not to point to it or touch it. Instead, he simply runs to a designated "home base" in the room (a chair or sofa), and shouts, "Huckle Buckle Beanstalk!" as a signal that he has spotted it. (This helps the others narrow their search by looking in the area where the child was last standing.) The game continues until everyone has spotted the thimble and shouted, "Huckle Buckle Beanstalk."

417 Hot Buttered Beans

One child hides the thimble (in full view) while the rest of the children are in another room. Once it's hidden, he calls out, "Hot buttered beans! Please come to supper." As the players start looking for the thimble, the hider lets the children know if they are hot or cold (close or far from the thimble). When a child discovers the thimble, he stops in his tracks, plops down on the floor, and says, "Hot Buttered Beans." This continues until every child has spotted the thimble. The child who first discovered it gets to hide it next.

★CLASSIC★

418 Drop the Handkerchief

Whisper children's names into the hankie-holder's ear to make sure everyone gets to drop the hankie.

AGE: 3–5 YRS

CATEGORY: BIRTHDAY PARTY (GROUP GAMES)/ INDOOR

NUMBER OF CHILDREN: FOUR OR MORE

Materials:
Bandana or handkerchief

Setup:
Select one child to carry the bandana.

Play:
All the children but one stand in a circle in a large, open room or outdoors on a safe grassy area. One child stands alone along the outside of the circle, carrying the bandana. He begins to sing this classic ditty:

A tisket, a tasket, a green and yellow basket.

I wrote a letter to my love

And on the way I dropped it.

I dropped it, I dropped it,

And on the way I dropped it.

A little child picked it up

And put it in his pocket!

At some point while singing this song, the singer quietly drops the bandana behind one of the other children; when that child turns and sees the bandana behind him, he jumps up and chases the other player around the circle, trying to tag him before he sits down in the empty spot in the circle. If the chaser is unable to tag the player before he sits down, the chaser picks up the bandana and begins another round. Everyone gets one turn to be the chaser.

419 Skip to My Lou

This classic game is similar to Drop the Handkerchief but does not include a chase between two children. One child is selected to be the "skipper," and skips around the outside of the circle, carrying a bandana or beanbag while the entire group sings "Skip to My Lou":

Lou, Lou, skip to my Lou

Lou, Lou, skip to my Lou

Lou, Lou, skip to my Lou

Skip to my Lou, my darling.

At the moment the group sings the very last word, the skipper drops the beanbag behind the nearest child and continues to skip one additional time around the circle. When the seated child notices the dropped beanbag (or the others shout out his name), he jumps up, grabs the beanbag, and begins to skip around the circle. The original skipper circles around to the empty spot and sits down, and the entire group sings again as the new skipper takes a turn. The game continues until everyone has had a chance to be the skipper.

420 Pinky Puzzle

At preschooler birthday parties, pink never goes out of style!

AGE: 3–5 YRS

CATEGORY: BIRTHDAY PARTY (GROUP GAMES)/ INDOOR

NUMBER OF CHILDREN: FOUR OR MORE

Materials:

Nontoxic marker

2 sheets of pink construction paper

Scissors (for adult use only)

Construction paper in various other colors

36 or more white business envelopes (self-adhesive)

Basket

Setup:

Use a marker to draw a grid with nine equally spaced squares (three squares across and three squares down) on one piece of pink paper. (Set this pink sheet aside to use as your Pinky Puzzle sample when the game begins.) Using the second piece of pink paper, draw the same grid. Cut *these* squares out with scissors and seal each inside an envelope. Drop these (nine) envelopes in the basket.

Cut additional squares from at least three different-colored sheets of paper, sealing each square in its own envelope. *(Note: the bigger the party, the more squares you should cut.)* Drop these envelopes in the basket and stir them all around. Before the children arrive for the party, hide all of these envelopes around one special room (or outdoors) with a piece of each envelope showing. (Pick a hiding place you'll be able to designate as "off-limits" to the children until you are ready for the game to begin.)

Play:

Place the *uncut* Pinky Puzzle in the center of a table, safely out of the way of traffic. (This sample puzzle will show the children what the finished Pinky Puzzle will look like when all nine pieces have been assembled.) Call out "Ready, set, go!" as a signal for the children to begin searching around the room for envelopes. When an envelope is found, the finder opens it (possibly with help from an adult). If the square inside is pink, the child places it on the table. When another color square is found, it gets tossed in the basket, or more likely thrown on the floor! Every pink piece found is added to the puzzle. When the last pink puzzle piece is in place, shout out, "Pinky Puzzle!"

421 Peanut Party-Line

Faster, faster, peanut passer!

Materials:

Peanuts in the shell
  (or wooden clothespins)
2 large bowls
Small basket or bowl
  (1 for each child)
Kitchen timer

AGE: 3–5 YRS

CATEGORY:
BIRTHDAY PARTY
(GROUP GAMES)/
INDOOR

NUMBER OF
CHILDREN: FOUR
OR MORE

Setup:

Pour the peanuts into one of the large bowls.
The children sit in a circle on the floor. Place the
bowl of peanuts next to the birthday child, who
as the first Master Passer will start the game.
Place the other large bowl next to the child on
his left. (This bowl will be the final resting place
for the peanuts.) Give all the other children a
small bowl to place on their laps.

Play:

Call out "Ready, set, go!" and start the kitchen
timer (set at 1 or 2 minutes, depending on the
number of kids playing and their age/attention
span). The birthday child grabs one peanut as
quickly as he can and drops it into the bowl of
the child on his right. The second child scoops
up the peanut and passes it into the bowl of the
child to his right. The peanut moves quickly
around the circle in this way, and when it
reaches the last child, he calls out, "Peanut
Party!" and drops the traveling peanut in
the large empty bowl. (It helps if you call out
"Peanut Party" too.) The words *Peanut Party*
are the birthday child's signal to grab another
peanut and begin passing it around the circle
as quickly as he can. The goal is to get as many
peanuts as possible into the empty bowl before
the buzzer sounds. Play additional rounds until
every child has gotten to be the Master Passer.

422 Musical Peanut Passers

Turn this into a musical game by using
a stereo rather than a kitchen timer. Place
the empty bowl in the center of the circle.
When the music stops, the child holding
the peanut places it in the empty bowl.
Turn the music off and on frequently so
that all the children get a chance to end up
with the peanut. Each time the music starts
up again, designate another child as the
Master Passer.

SAFETY ALERT: Find out in advance if any
child has a peanut allergy; if so, use wooden
clothespins instead of peanuts.

Three Books About Friendship

All children want to have friends,
and the preschool years are a good
time to learn about what it means to
be a friend and have a friend. Here
are three of my favorite books about
friendship for children three to five
years old:

Will I Have a Friend? by Miriam
Cohen, illustrations by Lillian Hoban.
A little boy who is about to go to
nursery school for the first time wonders
if he will meet a friend.

Frog and Toad Are Friends by Arnold
Lobel. A warm and funny story about
two best friends.

That Toad Is Mine! by Barbara Shook
Hazen, illustrations by Jane Manning.
Two best friends encounter a bit of
trouble with sharing.

Preschool Play (age 3 to 5)

★CLASSIC★

423 The Farmer in the Dell

I've revised the traditional Farmer in the Dell to shift the focus from the farmer and his wife to an assortment of barnyard animals.

QUICK & EASY

AGE: **3–5 YRS**

CATEGORY: **BIRTHDAY PARTY (GROUP GAMES)/ INDOOR**

NUMBER OF CHILDREN: **FOUR OR MORE**

Setup:

One child is selected to be the farmer and stands in the middle of the room. The rest of the children, the farm animals, form a circle around him. (The farmer will eventually designate each child as a particular farm animal—a pig, a cow, a chicken, a rooster, a duck, a goose, a horse, a goat, a donkey, a cat, or a dog.)

Play:

The children hold hands and begin moving around the farmer in a clockwise direction, while the entire group sings the opening chorus to "The Farmer in the Dell":

The farmer in the dell,

The farmer in the dell,

Hi-ho, the dairy-o,

The farmer in the dell.

At the end of the chorus, the farmer points to or calls out the name of one child in the circle, and shouts the name of any farm animal of his choice *(Cow!),* and exchanges places with the "cow." The group then sings the second verse, inserting the name of the animal:

The farmer takes a *(cow),*

The farmer takes a _____,

Hi-ho the dairy-o,

The farmer takes a _____.

Next, the cow calls out the name of another child (or points to another child) and shouts out a new farm animal *(Chicken!);* and the song, now featuring the new animal, goes on. All the while the circle continues to move. When the last child is designated as an animal (everyone should have had a turn), the children all sing a slightly different verse to end the round:

The *(animal's name)* stands alone,

The _____ stands alone,

Hi-ho the dairy-o,

The _____ stands alone.

The last child selected has the added bonus of becoming the farmer (first child in the middle), and the game starts all over again!

424 Traditional Farmer in the Dell

This game is played with one child selected to be the farmer and a large group of children holding hands to form a circle around the farmer. The circle moves clockwise around the farmer as the children sing and play the game. In this version, the farmer selects a wife to start the game, and then the wife selects a child, and so on, and each time a person is selected, he or she moves inside the circle with the farmer. Here are the verses for the traditional version of the game:

The farmer takes a wife *(or a husband)* . . .

The wife takes a child . . .

The child takes a nurse . . .

The nurse takes a dog . . .

The dog takes a cat . . .

The cat takes a rat . . .

And the last child remaining outside the circle is chosen to come into the circle with the following verse:

The rat takes the cheese,

The rat takes the cheese,

Hi-ho the dairy-o,

The rat takes the cheese!

At the conclusion of the last verse, the children clap, the "cheese" becomes the next farmer, and the others form a circle and begin the game all over again.

★ CLASSIC ★

425 Here We Go 'Round

Even daily chores become funny when there's singing involved.

QUICK & EASY

Setup:
Players form a circle and hold hands.

Play:
The circle moves clockwise as the children sing this chorus:

AGE: 3–5 YRS
CATEGORY:
BIRTHDAY PARTY
(GROUP GAMES)/
INDOOR
NUMBER OF
CHILDREN: FOUR
OR MORE

Here we go 'round the mulberry bush,

The mulberry bush, the mulberry bush,

Here we go 'round the mulberry bush,

So early in the morning.

After the initial verse, the song is altered to include a chore, with a parent typically suggesting the chores to keep the game moving along. For example, the parent sings, "This is the way we wash our hands," and the group sings a complete verse to match. The children

pantomime each activity, using their hands and bodies. Here's how the verse goes:

This is the way we wash our hands *(pretend to wash hands)*

Wash our hands, wash our hands

This is the way we wash our hands

So early in the morning.

Other fun chores to pantomime are combing hair, brushing teeth, sweeping the floor, or ironing clothes. When everyone is tired from doing all those chores, the game ends with the following verse:

This is the way we go to bed,

Go to bed, go to bed,

This is the way we go to bed

When all our chores are done! *(All the children fall to the floor and pretend to go to sleep)*

For a more spontaneous version, let the children take turns shouting out a chore or activity of their choice.

Use Your Words!

The teachers at my children's Montessori school taught all the preschoolers that words can be very powerful. The teachers explained that whenever something was going on that made you mad (like another child grabbing your toy), your words were the most powerful way to fix the problem. These simple instructions from a teacher—"Use your words, not your hands"—offered a gentle, appropriate reminder to speak up instead of pushing or hitting.

Preschool Play (age 3 to 5)

Preschool Play (age 3 to 5)

426 Bigwig

This game was inspired by the elaborate wigs worn by the judges and barristers of England. (Have a large mirror on hand so everyone can admire their bigwigs.)

AGE: 3–5 YRS

CATEGORY: BIRTHDAY PARTY (GROUP GAMES)/ INDOOR

NUMBER OF CHILDREN: FOUR OR MORE

Materials:

Large paper grocery bags (1 for each child)
Crayons
Nontoxic markers
Duct tape
Jump rope

Setup:

Each child selects a color for his "bigwig" and scribbles on his bag in his color of choice. Roll the top edge of each bag over several times. Position the bags on the children's heads and use lengths of tape around the cuffs to tighten in place. (The end result should look somewhat like a large, floppy chef's hat.)

Play:

Once all the children have their bigwigs on, two adults or taller children hold up the jump rope, the "limbo line" for this game. Instead of bending backward, the children will eventually bend forward at the waist to walk under the rope.

At first, the rope is held high enough for all the children to walk underneath without bending. With every round, it is lowered until it eventually becomes so low that the children must crawl on all fours to get under the rope—all without losing their bigwigs. (If a child does lose her bigwig, reposition it on her head and let her have another turn.)

427 Bigwig Hoopla

Start out using a Hula-Hoop as your limbo line. Hold the hoop vertically with one edge on the floor, and have the children step through it. Over the course of the game, raise it higher and higher until, at last, you wave it high up in the air and call out "It's time for bigwig crawl!" Then hold the hoop horizontally for the children to crawl under it while trying to keep their bigwigs on.

*SAFETY ALERT: Supervise this and other games involving jump ropes.

428 Bunny Hop

Time to do the Bunny Hop!

Play:

Sing "The Bunny Hop Song" below to the tune of "If You're Happy and You Know It Clap Your Hands!" while the children do the hopping and other actions listed below.

AGE: 3–5 YRS

CATEGORY: BIRTHDAY PARTY (GROUP GAMES)/ INDOOR

NUMBER OF CHILDREN: THREE OR MORE

The Bunny Hop Song

If you feel like a bunny go hop-hop
(hop twice)
If you feel like a bunny go hop-hop
(repeat action)
If you feel like a bunny, and you think it's rather funny,
If you feel like a bunny go hop-hop
(repeat action)

If your ears are kind of droopy go flap-flap
(child places hands by his ears and flaps them up and down)
If your ears are kind of droopy go flap-flap
(repeat action)
If your ears are kind of droopy and you're feeling rather loopy,
If your ears are kind of droopy go flap-flap
(repeat action)

If your nose is feeling stuffy shake your head
(shake head from side to side)
If your nose is feeling stuffy shake your head
(repeat action)
If your nose is feeling stuffy and your fur is rather fluffy,
If your nose is feeling stuffy shake your head
(repeat action)

If you like to chase you tail, turn around
(turn around in a circle)
If you like to chase your tail, turn around
(repeat action)
If your tail likes to wiggle and it makes your Mommy giggle,
If you like to chase your tail turn around
(repeat action)

If your feet are getting sleepy, touch your toes
(bend over and touch toes)
If your feet are getting sleepy, touch your toes
(repeat action)
If your toes like to wiggle and it makes your Mommy giggle,
If your feet are getting sleepy, touch your toes
(repeat action)

Final Verse:
If you feel like a bunny go hop-hop
(child hops twice)
If you feel like a bunny go hop-hop
(repeat action)

If you feel like a bunny, and your Mommy calls you honey,
If you feel like a bunny go hop-hop
(repeat action)

For complete lyrics to "If You're Happy and You Know It, Clap Your Hands," see page 178.

Read All About It: Animals, Animals Everywhere

There are so many wonderful picture books about animals that it's really difficult to select just a few. There are silly books about barnyard animals, zoo animals, and every other kind of animal in between. Here are a few of my favorites for preschoolers:

The Runaway Bunny by Margaret Wise Brown

Harry the Dirty Dog by Gene Zion, illustrations by Margaret Bloy Graham

One Gorilla: A Counting Book by Atsuko Morozumi

Olivia and *Olivia Saves the Circus* by Ian Falconer

Cock-a-Doodle-Moo! by Bernard Most

The Cow That Went Oink by Bernard Most

Is Your Mama a Llama? by Deborah Guarino, illustrations by Steven Kellogg

May I Bring a Friend? by Beatrice Schenk de Regniers, illustrations by Beni Montresor

Preschool Play (age 3 to 5)

Outdoor Party (Group) Games

Sometimes the excitement level at group gatherings gets so high that there's no sense in trying to corral it. So if the idea of entertaining four or more high-energy preschoolers in your home for two hours seems overwhelming, relax. Just take a deep breath, and take it outside! Whether you have a yard or make your way to a park, your preschool party guests will be entertained in ways no prepackaged birthday party or hired performer can provide. Some of these outdoor games are peaceful and slow-paced (Melting Monsters and Sandbox Animal Hunt). Other games are energetic and loud (Chef Hat Relay, Kazoo Birthday Parade, Tug-of-War). Mix and match them to set a pace that seems just right for the group; steady your nerves and enjoy the ride!

★ CLASSIC ★
429 Tug-of-War

If we tug really hard and work together, maybe we can be just as strong as Mom and Dad!

QUICK & EASY

AGE: 3–5 YRS

CATEGORY: BIRTHDAY PARTY (GROUP GAMES)/OUTDOOR

NUMBER OF CHILDREN: FOUR OR MORE PLUS DAD AND MOM OR OLDER SIBLINGS

Materials:

Roll of 2"-wide painter's tape (or masking tape)

4 or more bedsheets, tied together from end to end

10 to 12 thick rubber bands

Bandana

Setup:
Create a center line on the lawn by placing a 6-foot-long strip of tape on the grass. (The easiest way to do this is to roll out the tape, sticky-side down, in 12-inch sections, pressing it down with your feet as you go to secure it.) Next, tie two bedsheets together end to end to create a long "rope" that won't chafe the preschoolers' hands. Roll the "rope" tightly and position thick rubber bands along its length to keep the material compact. Tie a bandana around the middle of the "rope" and place this middle spot over the center line on the ground.

Play:
Line up all the preschoolers at one end of the rope and position Dad or Mom or a couple of older siblings at the other end of the rope. Call out "Ready, set, go!" and all the tuggers begin tugging. The first round of the game ends when one team is successful in pulling the players on the opposing team over the center line. (Hint: Preschoolers love to win two out of three rounds of this game!)

430 Zoo Animal Tug-of-War

In this version of the game, it's the animals on one side of the rope, tugging against Mom and Dad (or older siblings and a grown-up or two) on the other. Each child calls out a favorite zoo or circus animal before the game begins, and he pretends to be this animal—complete with corresponding animal sounds—as the children tug with all their ferocious might.

431 Melting Monsters

Preschoolers like to chatter about "monsters" during their pretend play. Well, here is a game that makes the monsters disappear!

QUICK & EASY

AGE: 3–5 YRS

CATEGORY: BIRTHDAY PARTY (GROUP GAMES)/ OUTDOOR

NUMBER OF CHILDREN: FOUR OR MORE

Materials:

Large sheets of drawing paper

Nontoxic, washable markers

Masking tape

Spray bottle filled with water

Setup:

Prepare a safe drawing space outdoors.

Play:

Give each child a sheet of paper on which to draw scary monsters. After all the drawings are done, tape them to a vertical outdoor surface. Give each child a small spray bottle filled with water to spray away their monster; they'll get a kick out of watching the monsters "melt." (Be prepared with lots of paper, because children will typically want to do this again and again.)

432 Many, Many Melting Monsters

Turn this into a group painting of monsters by having all the artists scribble on one long sheet of butcher paper.

Everyone Loves a Second Chance

Preschoolers gain confidence (and the fun factor increases) when they are allowed to play a party game a second time. So remember to offer a "trial run" or simply repeat the games as long as the children are excited to play.

433 Rainbow Run

Run, run, run for the rainbow!

AGE: 3–5 YRS

CATEGORY: BIRTHDAY PARTY (GROUP GAMES)/OUTDOOR

NUMBER OF CHILDREN: FOUR OR MORE

Materials:

Yellow, orange, red, blue, purple, and green crepe paper streamers

Stones or pebbles

Setup:

Cut approximately 5-inch-long pieces from each colored paper streamer roll. Position each streamer in a different spot on the lawn, using the pebbles to hold them in place.

Play:

Gather the children in a circle and tell them to take notice of where you've placed the streamers. Call out a first color, such as purple, and, "Ready, set, go!" and the children all run to the purple streamer. As the last child reaches the streamer, quickly announce the next color. To make things more interesting, you can call out a color you don't have a streamer for. If the children run when the imposter color is called, they must run back to the last streamer before you call out the next command. Once they've gotten the hang of the game, let the children take turns calling the colors.

Preschool Play (age 3 to 5)

Preschool Play (age 3 to 5)

434 Mother May I?

In this topsy-turvy game, "Mothers" say things like, "Hop around three times while quacking like a duck!"

QUICK & EASY

AGE: 3–5 YRS

CATEGORY:
BIRTHDAY PARTY
(GROUP GAMES)/
OUTDOOR

NUMBER OF
CHILDREN: FOUR
OR MORE (plus
a parent or older
sibling)

Materials:

Roll of 2"-wide painter's tape

Setup:

Mark a starting and finish line on the lawn by laying a 6-foot-long strip of tape along the ground. (Roll out the tape, sticky-side down, in 12-inch sections, pressing it down with your feet as you go.) Select one adult (or child) to play the part of "Mother."

Tip: If the lawn is wet, and your tape lines aren't sticking, see "Start and Finish" box, page 348.

Play:

Mother stands at the finish line facing the other children at the starting line. Mother gives an instruction to the group, for example: "Take three giant steps." All the children must answer back, "Mother may I?" In return, Mother answers, "Yes, you may." The children then take three giant steps toward the finish line. The first player to get to the finish line becomes the new Mother, and another round of play begins.

435 Sandbox Animal Hunt

Sometimes circus animals like to hide in the sand; let's dig them out and set them free!

QUICK & EASY

AGE: 3–5 YRS

CATEGORY:
BIRTHDAY PARTY
(GROUP GAMES)/
OUTDOOR

NUMBER OF
CHILDREN: FOUR
OR MORE

Materials:

Construction paper

Marker or pen

Circus or zoo animal stickers (or small animal photos)

Large plastic tub

Clean play sand

Assorted small plastic circus or zoo animals

Setup:

On construction paper, list each animal you're using for this game, alongside a matching sticker. Fill the tub with sand and bury each animal before the children arrive.

Play:

Place the list of hidden animals next to the tub filled with sand. Each child takes a turn digging around in the sand to find two animals. The game is over when all the animals have been found. (If a child grabs more than two animals as she's digging about, no problem—bury them back deep in the sand for another child.)

> 66 *With a preschooler, start drawing the distinction between a disciplinary time-out and a break to go settle yourself down. If a child starts getting too wound up, this is the age where you may start teaching, 'You're starting to get wound up, honey. Go in the other room and take a time-out.' As preschoolers, what they're really learning is that there is a difference between this type of settling down and getting chased off to their room for being naughty.* 99

> **—Peter Williamson, Ph.D.**
> psychologist and author of *Good Kids, Bad Behavior*

★ CLASSIC ★

436 Red Light, Green Light

I've tweaked this classic just a bit for preschoolers, making it noncompetitive but just as fun.

AGE: **3–5 YRS**

CATEGORY: **BIRTHDAY PARTY (GROUP GAMES)/ OUTDOOR**

NUMBER OF CHILDREN: **FOUR OR MORE**

Materials:

Roll of 2"-wide painter's tape

Kitchen timer

Setup:

Mark a starting and finish line on the lawn by laying a 6-foot-long strip of tape along the ground. Roll out the tape, sticky side down, in 12-inch sections, pressing it down with your feet as you go. Select one adult to act as the "Traffic Light."

Tip: If the lawn is wet, and your tape line isn't sticking, see "Start and Finish" box, page 348.

Play:

The children spread out along the starting line, and the Traffic Light stands at the finish line. The Traffic Light calls out, "When I say 'Red light' it means *stop,* and when I say 'Green light' it means *go.*" Then she sets the kitchen timer for 5 minutes. When she calls out, "Green light!," the children all rush toward the finish line; she calls out "Red light!" and the children stop in their tracks. She continues to alternate her commands to keep the children starting and stopping as they run toward the finish line. When they reach the finish, they turn and head back to the starting line, continuing to listen to the Traffic Light's commands until the timer buzzes. (Since the children cycle back and forth from the starting line to the finish line, there are no winners or losers.)

437 Bandana Float

Dance up a storm while the bandana is floating in the air. Freeze as soon as it touches the ground.

AGE: **3–5 YRS**

CATEGORY: **BIRTHDAY PARTY (GROUP GAMES)/ OUTDOOR**

NUMBER OF CHILDREN: **FOUR OR MORE**

Materials:

4 to 8 bandanas, silk scarves, or loosely crumpled pieces of crepe paper streamers

Medium unbreakable bowl or basket

Tennis racket (for adult use only)

Setup:

Stand in the middle of your lawn with a bowl or basket of bandanas at your side and the tennis racket in your hand. Gather the children on the lawn a short distance away.

Play:

Grip the tennis racket in front of you with both hands, with the oval head of the racket facing up. Wad up one bandana and place it on the strings of the racket. Launch the bandana up in the air as high as possible, by simply (and quickly) lifting your hands (and the racket) several feet higher. The launch of the bandana is the cue for all the children to start dancing around energetically. They continue to dance with spirit and drama while the bandana is floating down, but must freeze (or sit down) as soon as it reaches the ground. Grab one bandana after another to launch into the air for more rounds of dancing. (Appoint another adult or older sibling to retrieve the bandanas on the ground and toss them back into the bandana basket for a continuous supply of bandanas.)

438 Bandana Choo-Choo

The children all imitate the sounds of a train while the bandana is floating down (making a

Preschool Play (age 3 to 5)

Preschool Play (age 3 to 5)

chugging "choo-choo" or a cheery "toot-toot" sound); all sound stops as soon as the bandana reaches the ground.

439 Barnyard Bandana

This time, the children all make various farm animal sounds while the bandana is floating down. Assign each child (or pair of children) a particular animal sound so that the effect is an orchestra of barnyard sounds.

440 Chef Hat Relay

Real grown-up chef hats are just the prop to make this game come alive.

QUICK & EASY

AGE: **3–5 YRS**

CATEGORY: **BIRTHDAY PARTY (GROUP GAMES)/ OUTDOOR**

NUMBER OF CHILDREN: **SIX OR MORE**

Materials:

Disposable paper chef hats (1 for each child, available at paper or party supply stores)

Permanent markers of various colors (for adult use only)

Roll of 2"-wide painter's or masking tape

Cooking pans or unbreakable mixing bowls (1 for each child)

Kitchen timer

Setup:
Before the party begins, use the permanent markers to write the name of each child on a chef hat. Draw a unique but simple design or shape (star, flower, etc.) next to each child's name in a different color so that each hat is distinctive and easily identifiable. Mark a starting line and finish line for the relay by laying down a 6-foot-long strip of painter's tape, sticky-side down. (Use your feet to stamp this tape down so it sticks to the grass.) Place all the pans or mixing bowls in a row along the finish line. Toss one chef hat in each.

Tip: If the lawn is wet, and your tape lines aren't sticking, see "Start and Finish" box, page 348.

Play:
Line up all the children behind the starting line. Set the timer for 2 to 3 minutes (or enough time for all the children to run the relay before the timer buzzes!). On your "Go," the first child runs to the finish line and looks for her hat in the various pans or mixing bowls. When she finds it, she puts it on her head, runs back to the starting line, and tags the next player in line. Each child continues this routine until all the players are in line with their hats on. (Some children may prefer to carry their hat back to the starting line rather than wearing it.) All the players must get back to the starting line with their hats before the kitchen timer rings.

441 White Smock Relay

This variation requires two adult-size white short-sleeve button-down shirts (artist's smocks), or two old long-sleeve dress shirts with the sleeves cut off. To start the game, place one smock in a laundry basket at the finish line and put the other smock on the birthday child, who stands at the head of the line. Don't bother buttoning the shirt. If possible, have one adult at the starting line and one at the finish to help slip the shirts on and off as needed. The birthday child runs to the finish line, swaps his smock for the one in the basket, and runs back to the starting line. He gives the smock to the second child in line, who repeats the same smock-swapping-and-running scenario. Each child must run the relay before the kitchen timer sounds.

442 Fishing Tackle Relay

Place a small, empty tackle box at the finish line and collect all the children at the starting line. Start the kitchen timer, and on your "Go," the first child runs to the finish line, grabs the tackle box, and brings it to the second child in line. The second player runs to the finish line, drops off the tackle box, and runs back to tag the next player in line. So it continues, with each child carrying the tackle box in one direction. In the excitement, some children will carry the box back and forth from one line to the other, which only adds to the fun. Anything goes in this game, with the main object being for each player to take a turn before the kitchen timer sounds. Be sure to let the team have several tries if they need it!

443 Train Ticket Relay

Use full sheets of construction paper to make a giant train ticket (good for one ride) for each child at the party. Write each child's name on one ticket in bold letters and add a colored star or flower so their ticket is easy to identify. Place all the tickets in the laundry basket, faceup, at the finish line. Line up all the children at the starting line. Set the kitchen timer, and on your "Go," the first child runs to the basket, pulls out his train ticket, and runs back to tag the next player. The goal is for everyone to run the relay before the kitchen timer sounds.

444 Loop-Fruits

A Hula-Hoop makes a nice big target for flying plastic fruit.

Materials:
Hula-Hoop
Rope
Fake fruit (plastic apples, etc.)

Setup:
Use rope to hang the Hula-Hoop from a tree so that it is approximately 2 feet off the ground. Mark a free-throw line a short distance away from the hanging loop.

Play:
Line up the children behind the free-throw line. Each child takes three or more turns tossing fake fruit through the loop. (We're aiming for group success here, so let the children stand as close to the hoop as necessary.)

AGE: **3–5 YRS**

CATEGORY: **BIRTHDAY PARTY (GROUP GAMES)/ OUTDOOR**

NUMBER OF CHILDREN: **FOUR OR MORE**

445 Loop Toss

Substitute a beach ball, playground ball, Wiffle ball, plastic toy animal, or other tossing object to match the theme of your child's party.

Preschool Play (age 3 to 5)

66 *The best way to deal with a preschooler who is whining? You've got to let your child know, number one, that it doesn't work. So you say, 'My ears don't listen to the whining.' Then you tell them, 'Please calm down. Ask me again in a polite voice and we'll talk about it.' If your child does calm down, and says in a polite voice 'I want that cookie,' but you still don't plan on giving him one right before dinner, you say, 'I know you really want a cookie now, and I'll tell you what: You can have a cookie after dinner.' You can take a cookie out, put it in a little plastic bag, put it out on the counter so he can see it and let him know, 'This is your cookie, and as soon as we're done with dinner, you can have it.'* 99

—Sal Severe, Ph.D.
school psychologist and author of *How to Behave So Your Children Will, Too!*

446 Musical Scoop-Ball

Scoop-a-dee-doo-dah, scoop-a-dee-day, my-oh-my what a wonderful day . . .

QUICK & EASY

AGE: 3–5 YRS

CATEGORY: BIRTHDAY PARTY (GROUP GAMES)/ OUTDOOR

NUMBER OF CHILDREN: FOUR OR MORE

Materials:
- Laundry basket
- 30 newspaper balls (scrunched-up newspaper pages)
- Large plastic pet food scoops (1 for each child)
- Music

Setup:
Place the laundry basket in the center of the lawn and scatter all the newspaper balls around the lawn. Give each child his own scoop.

Play:
When you start the music (or set the kitchen timer), the children dash around the lawn, scooping up the balls and bringing them back to the laundry basket as quickly as they can. When the music stops, count the balls to see how many have been gathered.

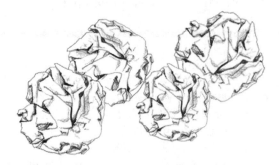

447 Scoop-Ball Pass

Position the children in a large circle, holding their scoops with both hands. Place the box full of newspaper balls in front of the birthday child.

Place a second, empty box in front of the child to her left. When the music starts, the birthday child scoops one or more balls into her scoop and drops them into the scoop of the player to her right, who drops them into the scoop of the child to *her* right; the balls are passed clockwise around the circle in this way. Meanwhile, the birthday child is continuously scooping up and passing more balls. The child at the end of the circle (to the left of the birthday child) dumps the balls into the empty cardboard box. When the music stops, it's time to count the balls in the cardboard box.

448 Small Musical Scoop

For a more challenging version of this game, use plastic ice-cream scoops and have the children scoop up very small, tightly squeezed paper balls, or use Ping-Pong balls instead.

> **❝** *Bossy children are so delightful during the preschool years in pretend play. These bossy little girls come up and say, 'You be the baby and you be the dad, and here comes the ambulance. Wa-wa-wa-wa! Now go over there. Get the dog. We gotta get out of here.' The next thing you know, she just incorporates that shy child in, tells the child what to say, what to do, and the child never just has to stand there. The bossies are able to bring those shy children into the play, and the shy child really doesn't have to do much, except be present at first, until they can reduce their anxiety of being there.* **❞**
>
> **—Becky Bailey, Ph.D.**
> developmental psychologist, specialist in early childhood education, author of *I Love You Rituals*

Preschool Play (age 3 to 5)

449 Musical Hoops

In this alternative to musical chairs, everyone is a winner.

QUICK & EASY

AGE: 3–5 YRS

CATEGORY: BIRTHDAY PARTY (GROUP GAMES)/ OUTDOOR

NUMBER OF CHILDREN: **FOUR OR MORE**

Materials:
   4 Hula-Hoops
   Music

Setup:
Place all four hoops in a large square formation on a safe, grassy area, allowing 5 feet of space between each hoop. Position the children evenly around the outside edge of the hoops.

Play:
When you start the music, the children begin to walk clockwise around the square. When you stop the music, each child must find a Hula-Hoop in which to stand. (The children typically scramble to the closest hoop.) After the children have settled into a hoop, they step back outside the square and you remove one hoop. Start the music again. Continue in this way, removing one hoop at a time. The game ends when all the children are standing inside the one remaining hoop.

450 Musical Island

Get out of the water and run for the islands as fast as you can when the music stops.

QUICK & EASY

AGE: 3–5 YRS

CATEGORY: BIRTHDAY PARTY (GROUP GAMES)/ OUTDOOR

NUMBER OF CHILDREN: **FOUR OR MORE**

Materials:
   2 or more Hula-Hoops
   Music

Setup:
Place the Hula-Hoops (islands) on the lawn, one at each end of the yard, about 30 feet away from one another. Disperse the children evenly among the hoops.

Play:
Explain that the lawn is the water and the hoops are the islands. While the music plays, the children are to run from one island to the other. When the music stops, each child is to scramble to the closest island. (Stop the music when the children are at the halfway point, and there will be a mad scramble to decide which island is closest.) Once all the children are safely on an island, start the music again.

451 The 5-Minute Rule

❝ *The five-minute rule evolved to help me and my kids deal with 'sharing' problems. When one child wants to play with a toy or game that another child is playing with, they say, 'five-minute rule,' and this means that you have to give up that toy to the other child in five minutes. Sometimes Mommy has to set the timer for five minutes so everyone knows how much time has passed. Any child can invoke the five-minute rule. For a favorite toy, this means a lot of back-and-forth after five minutes. The five-minute rule cuts down on one child grabbing a toy from another one. It teaches delayed gratification because the child has to wait for the toy that he wants. It also helps with one child refusing to let another one play with a toy. One thing that is really great about this rule is whenever a child comes to me about a sibling not sharing, I say 'We have the five-minute rule in our house,' and I set the timer. This cuts down on how much I have to referee.* ❞

—Candace from Texas

> *"When we give children the gift of nature— I'm talking about dirty hands and wet feet types of experiences—we give them a gift that will last for the rest of their lives. When they are forty, when they are fifty, even if they've been out of nature for a while, they can always come back to it."*
>
> **—Richard Louv**
> author of *Last Child in the Woods: Saving Our Children from Nature-Deficit Disorder*

their kazoos. Add other familiar songs, such as "Old MacDonald," "Twinkle, Twinkle," "Bingo," etc., to stretch out this game.

452 Kazoo Birthday Parade

A kazoo parade has just the right amount of pomp and circumstance for a preschool birthday party.

QUICK & EASY

AGE: **3–5 YRS**

CATEGORY: **BIRTHDAY PARTY (GROUP GAMES)/ OUTDOOR**

NUMBER OF CHILDREN: **FOUR OR MORE**

Materials:
Store-bought kazoos (1 for each child)
Marker or pen
Color dot stickers (available at office supply stores)
Party hats or crowns

Setup:
Write each child's initials on a kazoo, also putting a different color dot sticker on each instrument.

Play:
Line up the children with party hats on and kazoos in hand, with the birthday child at the head of the line. The children march around the lawn humming "Happy Birthday to You" into

453 Dolphin Tag

A friendly, noncompetitive way to run off a bit of energy in the backyard.

QUICK & EASY

AGE: **3–5 YRS**

CATEGORY: **BIRTHDAY PARTY (GROUP GAMES)/ OUTDOOR**

NUMBER OF CHILDREN: **SIX OR MORE**

Setup:
Select a flat, grassy place to play, marking the out-of-bounds areas. Elect two players as the dolphins to start the game.

Play:
The dolphins stand in the center of the playing area. When they announce "We need more dolphins," it is a signal for the chase to begin. The two dolphins try to tag each of the other players. When a player is tagged, he becomes a dolphin too and turns from a chasee to a chaser. The game ends when everyone has been turned into a dolphin. Then, announce that you're turning them all back into children and select two new dolphins so the chase can start all over again.

454 | Hop-Along (Cassidy)

Preschoolers like to hop—there are no two ways about it! The extra challenge of a playground ball between the knees will make this a party favorite.

Materials:
- Roll of 2"-wide painter's tape (or masking tape)
- Playground ball (or soft, medium-size ball with a little "give," 1 for each child)

Setup:
Mark a starting and finish line on the lawn by laying a 6-foot-long strip of tape along the ground. Roll out the tape, sticky side down, in 12-inch sections, pressing it down with your feet as you go.

Play:
Have the children line up. Give each child a soft playground ball to put between his knees. Let him practice hopping with it in place. When you announce "Ready, set, go!" all the children hop down the lawn, trying not to let their balls go. When a child drops his ball, he simply places it back between his knees and keeps on hopping. Allow all the children ample time to hop down to the finish line and back one or more times. When everyone is tired, call for a rest. ("Looks like we're tiring out those balls! Time to give them a rest.")

455 | Bean Hopper

The kids really like wearing the paper hats needed for this game—and it's a terrific photo op thrown in for good measure!

Materials:
- Scissors (for adult use only)
- Velcro with sticky-back adhesive (available at discount or hardware stores)
- Heavy-duty paper or plastic plates (1 for each child)
- Plastic headband (1 for each child)
- Roll of 2"-wide painter's tape (or masking tape)
- Large cardboard boxes or plastic storage tubs
- Dried navy beans or kidney beans

Setup:
Cut four 1-inch-long sets of Velcro pieces (four fuzzy pieces and four scratchy pieces). Turn each paper plate upside down. Peel the tape off one of the fuzzy strips of Velcro and position it in the middle of the upside-down plate; press firmly. Now peel the tape off one of the scratchy strips of Velcro and position it in the middle of the headband, pressing firmly. Allow the sticky tape to set for 5 minutes. Attach the paper plate onto the headband.

Mark a starting and finish line on the lawn by laying a 6-foot-long strip of tape along the ground. Roll out the tape, sticky-side down, in 12-inch sections, pressing it down with your feet as you go.

Tip: If the lawn is wet, and your tape line isn't sticking, see "Start and Finish" box, page 348.

Play:
Line up all the children with their Bean Hoppers on their heads. Sprinkle a handful of dried

beans onto each child's plate. Once everyone has been served, the children try to get to the finish line without spilling the beans. When they reach the box, they carefully bend over and spill the beans into the box. (You might need to do a little demo for them first.)

Time-out for Misbehavior

Time-out is a tried-and-true way of dealing with typical preschool misbehavior in a playgroup. It works for several reasons. First, removing a child who has grabbed or pushed another child stops the destructive action in its tracks. It creates a brief break in the play, giving everyone an opportunity to regroup. Second, it sets up a simple system that all the preschool playmates understand: *"There are rules I have to follow when I play. If I don't follow the rules, I don't get to play."*

❝It's important to always tell your kids the rules ahead of time when they're going to get together with other playmates. You want to emphasize the positive: 'I want you to be his good friend. A good friend takes turns; a good friend shares; a good friend uses polite language.' Then, while the playdate is going on, all the parents involved need to provide ample reinforcement when the children do the right thing. If there is an altercation, you simply separate the children for a moment and say, 'Listen, you don't hit. You need to be a good friend.' If it becomes a constant thing with one child, which it often does, then that child needs to learn that if he pushes, hits, kicks, does any of these infractions, then he's going to be isolated from the other kids for a minute or two. If you apply that consistently and, again, encourage them when they are doing the right thing, you'll see pretty dramatic changes for most kids.❞

—Sal Severe, Ph.D.
school psychologist and author of *How to Behave So Your Children Will, Too!*

Ten Terrific Theme Parties

Many parents say they would prefer to host an at-home birthday party than to pack the kids off to a family restaurant or commercial birthday party venue, but they lack the confidence to create an action-packed party the children will truly enjoy. With this concern in mind, I've created ten theme parties with complete party plans that have proven to be fun for preschoolers.

You'll notice at first glance that these parties seem to include a lot of activities, but I've learned from experience that you often need more games than you'd think to fill a party that is an hour and a half or two hours long. You also need a mix of high-energy games and quieter games to keep things moving and also allow time for kids to catch their breath. If you plan for lots of games, you can always drop a few as you go. On the day of the birthday party, use your instincts and observations to tailor the party to your particular children and circumstances. Using games from both the *Birthday Party* and the *Playing with Others* sections, here are some no-fail play plans for your next themed preschool birthday party.

Preschool Play (age 3 to 5)

456 Chef Party

90-Minute Party:
Arrival Activity: Make Chef Party Place Mats (add a food or cooking theme for decorations and stickers), page 204

Slippery Spoons, page 197

Story-Time Stomp, page 213

Cake-Time Activity: Cupcake Creations, page 211

Chef Hat Relay, page 230

Additional Activities for a 120-Minute Party:
Long Lookers, page 213

Loop-Fruits, page 231

Backup Games:
Picture Clue Treasure Hunt, page 215

Tug-of-War, page 226

457 Artist Party

90-Minute Party:
Arrival Activity: Make Artist Party Treat Bags, page 204

Rainbow Run, page 227

White Smock Relay, page 230

Cake-Time Activity: Who Am I?, page 210

Rainbow Row Party Hats, page 205

Additional Activities for a 120-Minute Party:
Melting Birthday Cakes, page 199

Long Lookers, page 213

Backup Games:
Story-Time Stomp, page 213

Tug-of-War, page 226

458 Sports Party

90-Minute Party:
Arrival Activity: Make Homemade Sports Jerseys, page 207

Loop-Toss, page 231

Long Lookers, page 213

Cake-Time Activity: What Sport Is It?, page 210

Picture Clue Treasure Hunt, page 215

Additional Activities for a 120-Minute Party:
Special Delivery, page 217

Scoop-Ball Pass, page 232

Backup Games:
Story-Time Runaround, page 213

Tug-of-War, page 226

459 Circus Party

90-Minute Party:
Arrival Activity: Make Circus Party Treat Bags, page 204

Slippery Spoons with a Theme (peanuts), page 197

Sandbox Animal Hunt, page 228

Cake-Time Activity: Who Am I?, page 210

Peanut Party-Line, page 221

Additional Activities for a 120-Minute Party:
Pass the Peanuts (Please)!, page 212

Story-Time Stomp (animal-themes book), page 213

Backup Games:
Kazoo Birthday Parade, page 234

Loop Toss (substitute a plastic circus toy as the tossing object), page 231

460 Beach Party

90-Minute Party:
Arrival Activity: Make Beach Party Place Mats (have a few seashells to trace), page 204

Beach Ball Loop Toss, page 231

Musical Island, page 233

Cake-Time Activity: I See Something . . . page 211

Long Lookers, page 213

Additional Activities for a 120-Minute Party:
Story-Time Runaround, page 213

Seashell on a Spoon Relay, page 197

Backup Games:
Pinky Puzzle, page 220

Tug-of-War, page 226

461 Fishing Party

90-Minute Party:
Arrival Activity: Make Fishing Party Treat Bags (with fishing-related stickers and decorations), page 204

Fish Follies Scavenger Hunt, page 217

Story-Time Stomp, page 213

Cake-Time Activity: Who Am I?, page 210

Dolphin Tag, page 234

Additional Activities for a 120-Minute Party
Long Lookers, page 213

Fish Follies, page 216

Backup Games:
Bobber on a Spoon Relay, page 197

Fishing Tackle Relay, page 230

462 Ice-Cream Shop Party

90-Minute Party:
Arrival Activity: Make Ice-Cream Party Place Mats (children trace jar lids and color them in with crayons to resemble scoops of various flavored ice cream), page 204

Ice-Cream Scoop Relay, page 197

Special Delivery, page 217

Cake-Time Activity: Substitute ice cream for cake and see Ice-Cream Sundae Creations, page 211

Small Musical Scoop, page 232

Additional Activities for a 120-Minute Party:
Long Lookers, page 213

Story-Time Runaround, page 213

Backup Games:
Picture Clue Treasure Hunt, page 215

Loop Toss, page 231

> **"**You set up a playdate and give the preschoolers a place where it's safe for them to play. They're in a room where they can be comfortable. Then you get out of the way. They will sometimes play together, they will sometimes play apart. What they like to know is that there is some adult in the house within earshot who's sort of looking over their play, but you don't have to be in there every second. **"**
>
> **—Michael Thompson, Ph.D.**
> clinical psychologist and
> coauthor of *Best Friends, Worst Enemies*

463 Zoo Party

90-Minute Party:
Arrival Activity: Make Farm Party Treat Bags (using animal stickers and animal stamps with ink pads), page 204

Peanut on a Spoon Relay, page 197

Zoo Animal Tug-of-War, page 226

Cake-Time Activity: What Kind of Animal Am I?, page 210

Picture Clue Treasure Hunt, page 215

Additional Activities for a 120-Minute Party:
Sandbox Animal Hunt, page 228

Musical Peanut Passers, page 221

Backup Games:
Bean Hopper, page 235

Story-Time Stomp, page 213

464 Train Party

90-Minute Party:
Arrival Activity: Make Train Party Place Mats (children trace jar lids for wheels, and draw a train car and add their name to the placemat), page 204

Train Ticket Relay, page 231

Story-Time Stomp, page 213

Cake-Time Activity: I See Something . . ., page 213

Picture Clue (Railroad) Treasure Hunt (Hide each photo clue inside a toy railroad car hidden about the house or yard), page 215

Additional Activities for a 120-Minute Party:
Bandana Choo-Choo, page 229

Special Delivery, "I've Been Working on the Railroad" version, page 218

Preschool Play (age 3 to 5)

465 Farm Party

Part III:
Grade School Play
(age 6 to 10)

Children six to ten years old are sophisticated players. They create elaborate hideouts and build impressive forts. They learn to read and write and can solve mysteries, play word games, invent outlandish tall tales, and create treasure maps. They are capable of a tremendous range of physical play (chasing, throwing, catching, dribbling, twirling, and bike riding). They can follow rules and remember directions; they can also make up their own rules as they play. All these possibilities add up to nonstop fun, but beyond all this excitement, there is a complex world of learning and growing going on. Here is a glimpse of how six- to ten-year-olds develop through play.

Physical Development

Children develop and refine large muscles, coordination, strength, stamina, and balance when they run, climb, kick a ball, ride a bike, walk a plank, do somersaults and cartwheels, jump rope, and chase. They strengthen hand–eye coordination when they bounce, catch, and swat a ball, and by doing arts and crafts and building and construction play. Through active play, they learn to challenge themselves and set goals, they discover their interests and talents, and, last but not least, they form fitness habits that will last a lifetime.

Intellectual Development

As they play, gradeschoolers are expanding their minds. They sharpen their memory and practice the application of logic. They learn to brainstorm, hypothesize, and problem solve. They discover math concepts such as patterns and sequencing. They learn about the complexities of science and nature. They expand and refine their use of language and improve their reading skills. They find ways to express their own unique thoughts and ideas through music, dance, poems, stories, drawings, paintings, and crafts.

A Wee Bit of Help

In general, children six to ten are capable and competent solo players, but they still benefit from well-placed, grown-up help from time to time. Try setting up any props and toys the first time a game is played so that your child sees and experiences the game as it's intended. Give a short demo to show how to use a new tool, art material, or building supply for creative projects. Some old classics (like Jacks or Clapping Call-Ball) may even require you to dust off your own playing skills. And, when it comes to creative and imaginative activities (involving drawing or storytelling, for example), it helps to be a clever brainstorming mentor so your child becomes comfortable with the creative process of thinking up her own ideas (and so she'll see that the sky's the limit). When she asks, "What can I write?," respond with a few questions rather than an answer. If she's stumped about how to begin her story about Charlie the neighborhood cat, you might ask, "Well, what sort of hat could you imagine Charlie wearing if he decided to wear a hat? Where would he go once he had that hat on? How might he travel if he weren't walking on his own four feet?" When it comes to solo play it's best to think of yourself as a play mentor, rather than a micromanager, so your child can take over and direct the play.

Social and Emotional Development

As children six to ten play, they learn to read facial expressions and body language. When they navigate through group play, they begin to cooperate, share, negotiate, and take turns. On a deeper level, they learn values like empathy, fairness, loyalty, and trust. They even learn from their negative play experiences, figuring out how to rebound from rejection, develop patience, manage their emotions, and control their behavior. They also make the brilliant discovery that playing is a good way to find a friend.

Safe Grade School Play

As your child grows, she'll become increasingly involved in keeping herself safe as she plays. She understands a bit more about the dangers of traffic and strangers. For the most part, children at this age tend to like the security of having rules in place, which can be used to your advantage. While you won't be able to prevent every sprained ankle, you can work to sidestep serious injuries and danger. Here are some safety ideas to keep in mind for the six- to ten-year-old child:

• Set up firm rules about where your child is and isn't allowed to play.

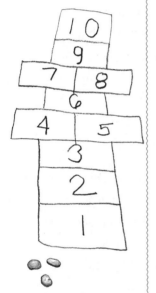

- Set up a rule that your child must ask for permission before he can leave your yard.

- Make your home a kid-friendly environment. (Healthy snacks are a big plus!) Provide supervision, maintain a cheerful attitude, and step in when safety issues like violent or dangerous play arise.

- Set up a helmet or helmet and knee pads rule for bicycling, using in-line skates, and skateboarding.

- Absolutely, positively, keep matches and lighters out of reach, and set up clear rules forbidding play with matches or fire.

- Supervise your child on swing sets, slides, and jungle gyms.

- Clearly convey safety rules and the need for supervision to all of your child care providers or teenage babysitters.

- Check the National Program for Playground Safety website (www.playgroundsafety.com) to receive up-to-date information about backyard (residential) and public playground safety.

The Well-Stocked Grade School Toy Cupboard

If you stock it, they will play! See page 372 for a list of my favorite toys and games to inspire lively, freewheeling play for six- to ten-year-olds. Also embedded in that list are all of the toys and miscellaneous household items needed for every single game or activity in the pages of this section.

Cranky Companion or Sleep-Deprived Child?

Did you know that children six to ten years old need nine to eleven hours of sleep each night in order to be at their best? Recent studies show that many children are not getting enough sleep, and it often shows up in their behavior with friends and family. A sleep-deprived child may get frustrated or hyperactive and have meltdowns more easily as she plays. She may be more aggressive with playmates, have trouble following rules, or lack the energy to engage in physical play. Take a quick look at how much sleep your child is getting each and every night. If your child is not getting between nine to eleven hours of sleep on a regular basis, time to make some changes—you might just see a big improvement in playtime behavior!

Solo Play

What good things can happen when your six- to ten-year-old child plays alone? He builds muscles, strength, and stamina through physical play. As he runs around outside, he burns off the nervous energy he's accumulated by sitting in school all day. He winds down from an active, busy day with quiet play. He invents and creates and figures out how things work. He watches intently and predicts what might happen next. He gets big ideas and discovers which ones work and which ones flop. He begins to see the steps it takes to turn an idea into action. And, let's not forget, he learns to entertain himself, without electronic toys and without Mom or Dad.

Kitchen Table Play

Although children six to ten years old are much more independent than preschoolers, they still enjoy the comfort of playing alongside Mom or Dad. With these solo play kitchen activities, I've also included some terrific thinking and guessing games that your child can either play alone (with pencil and paper to jot down guesses) or with you, as you prepare dinner nearby.

> **"**Be sure not to overschedule and overcontrol and overmanage all your child's free time, because those down moments, when kids just get together on their own and do what they want, are the most joyous. Some parents get into being overachievers and wanting their child to master the violin and be the best soccer player and also learn ballet. That's well and good, but you want to be sure not to squelch all the time for play.**"**
>
> **—Daniel Goleman, M.D.**
> psychologist and author of *Emotional Intelligence* and *Social Intelligence*

466 Ten-in-Sixty

Guess ten names in sixty seconds in this quick-moving game.

AGE: 6–10 YRS

CATEGORY: SOLO PLAY/ KITCHEN TABLE

NUMBER OF CHILDREN: ONE OR MORE

Materials:

Scissors

Paper

Pencil

Unbreakable bowl

Baby name book

Kitchen timer or 1-minute egg timer

Setup:

Your child selects any 20 letters from the alphabet. She cuts 20 small pieces of paper, and writes one of these letters on each piece; she then folds the pieces of paper in half, places them in a bowl, and mixes them around. She can skim through the baby name book to familiarize herself with names (and spellings) beginning with each of those 20 letters before the guessing begins.

Play:

Your child sets the timer for 60 seconds (or longer if needed). She draws a letter from the bowl and, without consulting the names book, quickly begins writing down names starting with this letter. When the buzzer sounds, she scores herself one point for each name on the list. She continues drawing letters from the bowl, setting the timer and writing down as many names as possible. She can set a goal of jotting down 100 or 200 total names before dinnertime. (To increase the challenge, she can then use the baby name book to check the spelling of each name on her list. Points are scored only for those names spelled correctly in this version of the game.)

467 Ten-in-Thirty

This version of the game is played by one child and one grown-up, and typically less time is needed, since you are not writing down each name, but calling it out. The child selects a letter from the bowl and Mom or Dad calls out as many names as possible (before the buzzer sounds) that begin with the selected letter. During the next round of play, the child selects a letter for herself, and she must call out as many names as possible before the buzzer sounds. Play for fun, or if you prefer, keep score, with one point scored for each name.

468 Puzzler Mix-up

Making the puzzles is part of the fun, but scrambling through the pieces to put three puzzles together simultaneously adds challenge!

AGE: 6–10 YRS

CATEGORY: SOLO PLAY/ KITCHEN TABLE

NUMBER OF CHILDREN: ONE

Materials:

3 interesting full-page color photos from a magazine

Nontoxic white glue

Poster board

Scissors

Large plastic bag

Kitchen timer

Setup:

Your child selects three full-page color photos from a magazine. (Photos with distinct colors featuring children, animals, or objects of interest are best.) He glues each of the three photos to a piece of cardboard or poster board, then cuts each photo into 12 or more puzzle pieces. The pieces of all three puzzles are tossed into the bag and shaken up.

Play:

Your child sets the kitchen timer for 5 to 8 minutes (adjusting the time as needed to create just the right challenge). With all the jumbled puzzle pieces spread out on the kitchen table, he begins piecing together all three puzzles, trying to complete the task before the buzzer sounds. (If he wishes to keep score, he can count out the number of loose puzzle pieces left on the table after the buzzer has sounded, scoring one point for each remaining piece on the table, with "0" being the top score.)

469 Blind Sketching

No peeking at the drawings. There'll be lots of guesses from the peanut gallery when they're done.

AGE: 6–10 YRS

CATEGORY:
SOLO PLAY/
KITCHEN TABLE

NUMBER OF
CHILDREN: ONE
OR MORE

Materials:

Pencils, markers, or crayons

Newsprint or drawing paper

Bandana

Setup:

Your child makes a list of 10 things that she is able to draw with some measure of accuracy (a building, tree, pet, hand, face, leaf, flower, bicycle, frying pan, or coffee cup, for example).

Play:

After placing some pieces of newsprint paper on the table in front of her, your child ties the bandana around her head, blindfolding herself so that she cannot see the paper. On each piece of paper, she draws a picture of one of the items on her list, developing her collection of mystery drawings. After dinner, she holds up each drawing to see if any family member can guess what the items are supposed to be. (She gets to choose to reveal her list of items or not.)

470 Alphabet Garden

A is for apples, B is for beans. There's an alphabet in your garden that's ripe for the picking.

AGE: 6–10 YRS

CATEGORY:
SOLO PLAY/
KITCHEN TABLE

NUMBER OF
CHILDREN: ONE

Materials:

Garden seed catalog

Large sheet of poster board

Pencils or markers

Setup:

To create the Alphabet Garden chart, your child prints one letter of the alphabet (from *A* to *Z*) along the left edge of the poster board, placing only one letter per line.

Play:

Paging through the catalog, your child finds vegetables and edibles starting with every letter of the alphabet; when he finds a plant, he writes its name on the appropriate alphabet line. (He might need help with some of the more difficult words.) At the end of the game, tally up the total foods for every letter.

Growing Veggies

Kids get a big kick out of harvesting their own veggies. If your family lives in a city, you can still plant on a patio. The following are well suited to container gardening: tomatoes, leaf lettuce, peppers, eggplant, squash, green onions, green beans, radishes, parsley, and cucumbers. Check seed catalogs for varieties best suited to your climate and growing conditions.

471 | Dog Diaries

Write a story about what you think the little brown dog next door does when he thinks no one is watching.

AGE: 6–10 YRS

CATEGORY:
SOLO PLAY/
KITCHEN TABLE

NUMBER OF
CHILDREN: ONE
OR MORE

Materials:

Notebook or small journal

Pencils

Colored pencils or markers

Photos (optional)

Setup:

Ask your child to imagine what a particular neighborhood dog (or family dog) might do if traveling about the neighborhood freely. Brainstorm about favorite discoveries in the neighborhood, foods, games to play, and other animal friends.

Play:

Your child starts the Dog Diaries by writing down the names of all the dogs in the neighborhood, or by inventing a group of imaginary dogs of various shapes and sizes. Next, he writes a short description of each dog. They might have distinctive or funny haircuts, hats, and accessories. After the characters have been created, pick one or two dogs and write about their imaginary adventures for the day. Where did they travel? What did they see? What treats did they find to eat? What kind of mischief did they get into? If you and your child sit down once a week to create a new chapter, this diary can keep going for quite some time.

472 | Cat Chronicles

No need to offend the cat lovers in the group! Kids can create lively tales with their favorite felines as the main characters.

❝ *Daydreaming time is so important for kids, to use their imaginations, create, dream, think, figure things out.* **❞**

—Deb Kratz

LICSW parenting educator and coauthor of
The Field Guide to Parenting

473 | Beyond the Happy Ending

But what happens after the prince and the princess get married? Let your child take over where the fairy tale ends.

AGE: 6–10 YRS

CATEGORY:
SOLO PLAY/
KITCHEN TABLE

NUMBER OF
CHILDREN: ONE
OR MORE

Materials:

Classic fairy-tale books

Journal or notebook

Pencil

Eraser

Play:

Your child selects a well-known fairy tale, like *Cinderella* or *Goldilocks and the Three Bears,* and uses her imagination to extend the story with new details and characters that might take place *after* the classic ending to the story. (Older children with good writing skills and vocabulary can write their new story ending in a journal. Younger children can simply tell their story and perhaps draw a picture that tells something about their new ending.) This might extend over the course of several days or weeks, with your child brainstorming and adding more to the story on an ongoing basis. (It's great for long car, plane, and train trips as well.) Since revisions are a part of the writing process, the eraser is a handy tool for this activity.

474 Tall Tales

Turn writing and brainstorming into a fun game that makes it easy to come up with story ideas.

AGE: 6–10 YRS

CATEGORY: SOLO PLAY/ KITCHEN TABLE

NUMBER OF CHILDREN: ONE OR MORE

Materials:

Paper

Scissors

Pencil

2 large yogurt or cottage cheese containers with lids

Setup:

Cut 20 small pieces of paper. Select 10 letters of the alphabet that can be readily associated with boys' and girls' names; write each letter on a piece of paper. Fold these papers in half and toss them into one of the plastic containers, stirring them around. Think of 10 animals or creatures (real or imaginary) and write the name of each on a piece of paper. Fold these papers in half, toss them in the second plastic container, and mix them around.

Play:

Select a slip of paper from each container. Invent a name for the animal, starting with the chosen letter, and write an action-packed, silly, or unbelievable story about what your character did or discovered today. Some children may need idea starters—What happened with Martha the Goat on the playground today? Where did she go on vacation? What happened when she went to the grocery store? Older children can write the stories down on paper and read them to the family at dinner. Younger children may wish to tell their story as they invent it.

475 Rhymin' Simon

There may be a future songwriter or poet in your midst. All he needs is a little nudge to get the talent flowing.

AGE: 6–10 YRS

CATEGORY: SOLO PLAY/ KITCHEN TABLE

NUMBER OF CHILDREN: ONE OR MORE

Materials:

A book with classic poems and counting rhymes

Journal (or paper)

Pencils

Setup:

Select one classic poem or counting rhyme to use as a template.

Play:

Your child keeps the first line of the rhyme, but continues the game by adding his own original rhymes thereafter to invent a new poem with new characters and action. To get started, here are the first lines from several nursery rhymes:

• Hickory, dickory, dock

• Baa, baa, black sheep, have you any wool?

• Two little blackbirds sitting on a hill

• Higglety pigglety pop!

• One, two, three, . . . *(add your own next line)* . . . Four, five, six, . . . *(add another line)*

"*If a child is bored, that means that they're having some time to sit and think, 'What can I do next,' and that's a valuable skill.* **"**

—Maureen O'Brien, Ph.D.

child development specialist and author of *Watch Me Grow: I'm One-Two-Three*

> *"Chess has very simple rules. Any adult can learn in under an hour with no problem. One famous book is* Bobby Fisher Teaches Chess. *That's a classic. It will guide a parent into learning how to play the game, and from there they'll have some competence in how to teach their children to play."*
>
> **—Maurice Ashley**
> international chess grand master and author of
> *Chess for Success: Using an Old Game to Build New Strengths in Children and Teens*

476 Draw Me a Story

Sometimes the pictures come first when bringing a story to life.

AGE: 6–10 YRS

CATEGORY: **SOLO PLAY/ KITCHEN TABLE**

NUMBER OF CHILDREN: **ONE OR MORE**

Materials:
  Artist sketchbook or journal
  Pencil and kneaded eraser
  Assorted fine-tipped color markers

Jump-start:
Most children respond to the idea of creating one main character (a fantasy creature, futuristic insect, person, or animal) to start their story. From this simple beginning, your child can go on to imagine what the character looks like, what he wears, where he lives, who his friends are, and what exciting event has just happened in his life. From these drawings and sketches and jotted-down details, a story tends to follow. If she doesn't like what she's drawn or written, she can use the eraser freely, or add and delete pages using scissors and tape.

477 Comic Strip

Who says that comics have to be saved for Sundays?

AGE: 6–10 YRS

CATEGORY: **SOLO PLAY/ KITCHEN TABLE**

NUMBER OF CHILDREN: **ONE OR MORE**

Materials:
  Artist sketchbook
  Pencil and kneaded eraser
  Assorted fine-tipped color markers

Jump-start:
Challenge your child to create her own comic strip. The characters she invents might be from her own life or far-out fantasy creatures with their own language. Have her write a few notes to herself to create a life for her main character (how old is he, where does he live, who are his friends, what is his special talent, what does he like to eat). Sketching out a drawing will help capture the character's extraordinary features. Have that drawing lead to the action and conversations that follow, frame by frame.

> *"When parents decide to limit their child's video games and screen time, yeah, the kids will scream, and then the next thing you know, they'll be outside playing. It happens at my house all the time. The 'Oh, woe is me' lasts a minute or two, and then the next thing you know, they're engaged in something much better for them. So I'm willing to take that heat."*
>
> **—Edward Hallowell, M.D.**
> psychiatrist and author of
> *Delivered from Distraction* and *CrazyBusy*

Grade School Play (age 6 to 10)

UNPLUGGED
PLAY

Indoor Play

Children like to be in charge of their own play. But there will be days when even the most self-directed child says, "Mom, I'm bored." Here are some ideas to jump-start traditional independent play, as well as some lively games that can be played using everyday household materials. As time goes by, these games may become like familiar old friends—comforting, go-to escapes at the end of a long school day. Perhaps your child is taken by Jacks, which challenges her to improve or refine her skills each time she plays. Or the classic paper Fortune Teller that adds a little magic to an afternoon. Or Construction Play for problem solving. In many of these games, your role as a parent is to nudge the play at the start and let your child take it from there.

478 Car and Ramps

Here are some creative challenges to help encourage miniature-car play.

QUICK & EASY

AGE: 6–10 YRS

CATEGORY: SOLO PLAY/ INDOOR

NUMBER OF CHILDREN: ONE OR MORE

Materials:
Cardboard or foam board
Hardcover books
Miniature cars and trucks
Shallow bowl filled with water
Hula-Hoop

Jump-start:

• *No Flip* Using cardboard and stacked books, your child makes the highest ramp for the cars to race down without having them flip over.

• *Bounce* He creates a ramp for the cars, then places a shallow bowl of water near the end of the ramp, and sees how many cars he can "bounce" into the pan.

• *Hula* He places a small Hula-Hoop near the end of the ramp and sees how many cars he can get to land inside without "bounce-out."

*SAFETY ALERT: To prevent injury, make sure no one stands by the end of the ramp.

> **"**Research shows us very clearly that electronic playmates do not evoke the same brain response that being with a real human does, and that a child's future success is going to be very much determined by the way he or she is able to relate to other people and work in a group and negotiate. **"**
>
> **—Jane M. Healy, Ph.D.**
> educational psychologist and author of
> *Your Child's Growing Mind* and *Failure to Connect: How Computers Affect Our Children's Minds*

479 Construction Play

The six- to ten-year-old crowd are sophisticated thinkers and problem solvers, ready for hours of open-ended construction toy play.

AGE: **6–10 YRS**

CATEGORY: **SOLO PLAY/ INDOOR**

NUMBER OF CHILDREN: **ONE OR MORE**

Materials:

LEGOs (or other interlocking building blocks)

Jump-start:

LEGOs can be turned into airplanes, cars, tanks, rockets, robots, monsters, houses, and much more. How many different vehicles can your child make? Have your child build a replica of your house (and neighboring homes), garage, deck. How many buildings can your child make in 20 minutes?

480 Tinkertoys

These plastic wheels, spokes, and connectors come with a design guide to help children get ideas on how to get started and what to make. Follow the directions in the box to create amazing structures. Use your own imagination to invent another way of building each of these structures. Build a crazy "contraption." Challenge your child to build another one exactly like it. Create prehistoric creatures or extraterrestrial beings.

*SAFETY ALERT: This set contains small parts that cause a safety hazard for small children.

481 Bonz

These plastic pieces can be used to build real and imagined "creatures." Challenge your child to create an insect that can fly, a dinosaur, or her favorite monster. Or she can make her favorite animal in the zoo.

482 Balloon Breeze Obstacle Course

A little finesse goes a long way in getting around this indoor obstacle course with a balloon bouncing on a paper plate.

AGE: **6–10 YRS**

CATEGORY: **SOLO PLAY/ INDOOR**

NUMBER OF CHILDREN: **ONE OR MORE**

Materials:

Large oval balloons*

Large, sturdy paper plate (oval plate works best)

Setup:

Blow up one or two balloons. Create and mark off a simple obstacle course indoors, using chairs, cardboard boxes, and pillows as the obstacles.

Play:

Your child holds the paper plate with two hands and uses it to bounce the balloon in the air continuously as she weaves around, over, and under the obstacles. To add more challenge, set the kitchen timer for a short amount of time. As your child gets the hang of this game, she can bounce the balloon higher and higher.

483 Balloon Putt

Turn this game into a miniature golf–like obstacle course, using a balloon and a flyswatter to putt the balloon from place to place. Set the timer and see how many times your child can get around the course before it buzzes.

TIP: If you don't have a flyswatter, you can make a simple alternative by attaching a 10"-by-10" piece of cardboard to a painter's wooden stir stick. Overlap the stir stick with one edge of the cardboard, and use duct tape to secure it in place to create a handle.

Safety Alert: Supervise all balloon play to prevent children less than eight years old from choking on uninflated balloons or balloon pieces.

484 Button Bowl

I bet I can do it with my eyes closed!

Materials:
- 5 or more unbreakable bowls or cooking pans
- Scissors
- Black construction paper
- Invisible tape
- Sunglasses
- Plastic coffee cup with handle
- Assorted buttons
- Kitchen timer

AGE: 6–10 YRS

CATEGORY: SOLO PLAY/INDOOR

NUMBER OF CHILDREN: ONE OR MORE

Setup:
Mark a pitching line across the floor. Position the bowls in a vertical line in incremental distances from the pitching line, starting about 4 feet away. Assign each of these bowls a score, starting with one point for the closest bowl, two points for the next, and so on. Next, make a simple "blindfold" by cutting two ovals from the construction paper and taping them to the lenses of the sunglasses. Fill the plastic cup with buttons.

Play:
Your child sets the kitchen timer for one to two minutes and gets in position behind the pitching line. She grabs the button cup with one hand and puts the blindfold glasses on. Then she pitches the buttons toward the bowls until the buzzer sounds. When the buzzer sounds, she'll add up all the points scored by figuring out how many buttons landed in each bowl and doing some simple math.

485 Button Bowl Scatter

For an easier version of this game, omit the blindfold and simply scatter pie pans or cake pans across the floor at varying distances from the pitching line. Assign points to each pie pan.

Safety Alert: Due to choking hazard, play this game clear of young children or pets. Clean up all buttons after playing.

486 Bouncing Bazooka Bull's-Eye

The bouncing balls have a mind of their own, so scoring in this game presents a real challenge!

Materials:
- Laundry basket
- Large unbreakable mixing bowl
- Yardstick
- Ping-Pong balls, tennis balls, or small rubber balls

AGE: 6–10 YRS

CATEGORY: SOLO PLAY/INDOOR

NUMBER OF CHILDREN: ONE OR MORE (a good practice game for one, and a competitive game for two)

Setup:
This game should be played against a wall clear of furniture. Position the laundry basket snugly up against the wall. Place the large mixing bowl on the floor, 3 feet in front of the laundry basket. Use the yardstick to create a pitching line 6 to 8 feet away from the wall.

Play:
Your child stands behind the pitching line and tosses the Ping-Pong ball against any area of the wall, trying to get the ball to land either inside the basket or inside the bowl for a bull's-eye. Each ball must bounce against the wall before dropping inside the basket or bowl in order to score a point. Score 5 points for each ball in the basket and 10 points for each ball in the bowl. If a ball bounces inside the bowl and bounces out again, score 7 points.

487 Jacks

A first-rate traditional game that works well as practice-play for one player.

AGE: 6–10 YRS

CATEGORY: SOLO PLAY/ INDOOR

NUMBER OF CHILDREN: ONE OR MORE

Materials:
Set of plastic or metal jacks
Small rubber ball

Setup:
Find a smooth floor on which to play.

Play:
There are five traditional ways to play the game of jacks, each with its own distinct level of difficulty. Each version of the game begins with the player tossing the jacks on the floor so that they scatter in one small area.

- **Basic Jacks** The player tosses the ball in the air, picks up one jack, and catches the ball after one bounce. Tossing the ball again, he picks up one more jack (keeping the first jack in his hand) and catches the ball after one bounce. He continues picking up one jack at a time in this way until all the jacks have been collected in his hand.

- **Onsies, Twosies, Threesies** After the first round, the player scatters the jacks on the floor again, and this time, picks up two jacks at a time, still catching the ball after one bounce. He scatters the jacks again and picks up three at a time. The player continues by picking up four at a time, five at a time, and so on until the final round of play when he scoops up all ten jacks at a time. (If the player falls short of his goal on any particular round, he tries to scoop up the remaining jacks in one try.)

- **Eggs in the Basket** Player tosses the ball, picks up one jack (or more) at a time, and quickly moves the jack(s) to his free hand before catching the ball.

- **Crack the Eggs** This version adds one extra step to Eggs in the Basket. The player must tap each jack on the ground with the scooping hand (pretending to crack an egg) before moving the jack(s) to the free hand.

- **Double Bounce** To ease up the challenge a bit, the player takes on any of the jack variations, allowing the ball to bounce twice before catching it.

488 Jacks for Two

Any of the traditional jacks games above can be played with two or more players. In this scenario, one player starts the game and continues to take turns tossing the ball and scooping up jacks as long as he catches the ball on one bounce and scoops up the predetermined number of jacks. When he doesn't catch the ball on one bounce or grab the correct number of jacks, his turn is over and the second player takes a turn. The game can simply be played for fun or the player who finishes the entire round of play first wins.

★CLASSIC★

489 Paper Airplane

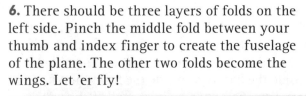

Every child should know how to make old-fashioned paper airplanes. Here's a basic design to get you started.

QUICK & EASY

AGE: 6–10 YRS

CATEGORY: SOLO PLAY/ INDOOR

NUMBER OF CHILDREN: ONE OR MORE

NOTE: Fold your plane on a hard surface, such as a table, and press very firmly when making each crease.

Materials:
Copy or computer paper (8½" by 11")

Create:
1. Fold the paper in half lengthwise, make a crease, and unfold it.

2. Holding the paper vertically, fold each top corner in to the center crease, creating two equal-sized triangle flaps.

3. Fold the right diagonal edge of the plane in to line up with the center crease. Then fold the left diagonal edge in to line up with the same center crease.

4. Flip the plane over and fold the new right diagonal edge in to line up with the center crease. Then fold the new left diagonal edge in to line up with the center crease. This creates a sturdy nose for your plane.

5. Flip the plane over, and fold the left edge of the plane over to meet the right (using the original crease from step 1).

6. There should be three layers of folds on the left side. Pinch the middle fold between your thumb and index finger to create the fuselage of the plane. The other two folds become the wings. Let 'er fly!

490 Flying High

To create a slightly different plane (and different flying capabilities), vary the width of the crease in step 4 above, so that the fuselage—where you hold the plane—is narrow, medium, or extremely wide.

TIP: Attach a paper clip to the tip of the airplane to add weight and speed. See how its flight path differs. Make one with and one without, and compare the arc and speed!

PARENT TIP

491 Library Night

❝*Reading is very important in our household. To eliminate boredom with books that have already been read, we've come up with 'Mom & Dad's Library Night.' Once a month, we bring out the children's books we've picked up in the weeks prior at yard sales and thrift stores. We set up a 'library' on the kitchen table and distribute handmade library cards (index cards) to our kids so they can 'check out' a couple of books. Then we put the latest collection in a cardboard box with the spines facing out, and let the children select books. When they've grown tired of these books, we donate them back to our local thrift store and search for more used books for next month.*❞

—Colleen from Indiana

492 Fortune-Teller

What fortune and fun does that piece of paper hold in its magical folds? Children today still find these fun to make and entertaining to play with.

AGE: **6–10 YRS**

CATEGORY: **SOLO PLAY/ INDOOR**

NUMBER OF CHILDREN: **ONE OR MORE**

Materials:

Typing paper or computer paper

Pen

Scissors

Create:

1. Cut an 8½"-by-8½" square from a sheet of typing paper and lay it flat on the table.

2. Fold one corner to the opposite corner, making a diagonal crease. Open the paper, and fold it diagonally in the other direction. Make a crease, and open the paper.

3. Fold each of the four corners into the center.

4. Flip the paper over, and fold the new corners into the center.

5. Write a number from one to eight in each of the small triangles on this side of the paper, as shown.

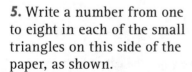

6. Open each of the numbered flaps and write eight different messages inside (see Tip, this page). Close the flaps.

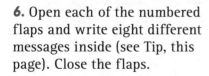

7. Flip the folded paper over and write the name of a different color on each of the four squares.

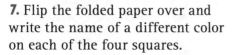

8. Fold the fortune-teller in half so that the four colors are facing out.

9. Position the thumb and index finger of each hand underneath the flaps, finessing the folds a bit so that the fingers are in each of the four points.

Play:

Your child holds her fortune-teller with the color flaps showing. She asks her friend to pick a color. If the color is blue, your child flaps her fingers back and forth one time for each letter in the word: *b-l-u-e* (four times). Then she asks her friend to select one of the numbers on the four flaps that are showing. She moves her fingers back and forth as she counts out the number. At last her friend selects one of the numbers showing, and that flap is lifted to reveal her fortune.

TIP: Tired of those worn-out fortune-teller messages of yesteryear, like "You will marry someone rich" or "You will become a movie star"? Here are some themes to spark imaginative, kid-friendly messages:

- Surprises or discoveries you will make
- Wacky jobs you might have as an adult
- Fabulous adventures and travels
- Silly outfits you will wear
- Sports you will master
- Outrageous outer-space beings you will encounter
- Type of vehicle you will drive
- Wild and wacky gizmos you will invent
- Incredible edibles you will cook up
- Silly or fantastic type of dwelling you will live in

Arts and Crafts

Children love to draw and paint and create. Behind the scenes, life skills are being developed in subtle ways. Your child learns to improvise, problem solve, and tolerate frustration when things go awry. She also sees that sometimes a mistake is a new beginning, and the end product is something more spectacular than originally planned. She learns patience and perseverance. She may also discover that she can escape the busy pace of life when she paints, draws, or creates, and this is a lesson to carry forward over many years to come. Here are some open-ended art ideas with room for individual creativity and experimentation.

★ CLASSIC ★

493 Drawing

Call it doodling, sketching, or designing; every child needs paper to draw on.

QUICK & EASY

AGE: 6–10 YRS

CATEGORY:
SOLO PLAY/
ARTS & CRAFTS

NUMBER OF
CHILDREN: ONE
OR MORE

Materials:

24 felt-tip fine-point color markers (available at art supply stores)

Multipurpose paper (for practice drawing)

Drawing paper or sketch pad

Cardboard blotter

Create:

All that you really need to get started is paper and markers or pencils and a good, flat, hard surface for drawing, like the kitchen table. Some children will be satisfied making abstract designs with shapes and colors that spontaneously come to life. Others will ask, "What should I draw?" and need a bit of brainstorming help to settle on an object or person of interest to represent through their drawing. Some like to chat or listen to music while they doodle or draw. Others become engrossed in an imaginative process that is surrounded by silence.

494 Pencil Drawing

Children six to ten will appreciate the wide assortment of real artist's pencils that are available at art supply stores. (As these pencils are inexpensive and last a long time, you may want to purchase several different types.) Every artist also needs a real artist's eraser, a kneaded eraser that erases without leaving behind any pink traces.

495 Chalk Pastels

For a different drawing experience, use colored chalk with colored construction paper, sketch paper, poster board, or mat board, which has a rough texture that can create distinctive drawings.

> ❝Every human being has the capacity to create—not only the capacity, but the need to create. To create is part of inner growth. ❞
>
> —**Michele Cassou**
> artist and author of *Kids Play: Igniting Children's Creativity* and *The Magic of Spontaneous Expression*

496 Design a Castle

The sky is the limit to all the brainstorming that can take place when your child designs his castle.

AGE: 6–10 YRS

CATEGORY: SOLO PLAY/ ARTS & CRAFTS

NUMBER OF CHILDREN: ONE OR MORE

Materials:
- Drawing paper
- Pencil
- Kneaded eraser

Jump-start:
If you asked your child to draw a realistic picture of the outside of a castle, with all its turrets and steeples, he might be stumped. But if you ask him to design the inside of a thirty-room castle, now that's another matter. The interior rooms can be drawn as squares and rectangles, with bold lines to show the placement of doors and windows. Secret passageways, leading to underground rooms that no one knows about, can be added. On separate sheets of paper, elaborate inventions can be designed for cooking and cleanup in the kitchen. Ingenious communication devices might be invented and illustrated, to alert the lord and lady when an intruder arrives. In fact he may save all these floor plan designs and pages of inventions in a Design Notebook and add to it when a new idea strikes.

Once your child has tackled the castle design, see the variations below for some other design challenges to try.

497 Space Station

Design the interior of a spaceship, rocket, time-travel machine, or futuristic car.

498 The High Seas

Design the inside of a pirate ship, a sailboat that travels around the world, a futuristic submarine.

499 Animal House

Design a barn or zoo that would have inventions that all sorts of animals might request if they could talk.

500 Plan for the Future

Create the floor plans of houses you might live in 10 years, 20 years, and then 50 years from now.

501 One Giant Floor Drawing

Here's a BIG idea that is sure to get your child's attention!

AGE: 6–10 YRS

CATEGORY: SOLO PLAY/ ARTS & CRAFTS

NUMBER OF CHILDREN: ONE OR MORE

Materials:
- Roll of butcher paper
- Invisible tape
- Crayons or washable markers

Setup:
Cover the entire kitchen floor (or one large area of the floor) with long strips of butcher paper on a day when foot traffic in the kitchen can be restricted for a few hours. Use invisible tape to adhere the paper to the floor and tape the seams together so you have one giant, super-duper sheet of drawing paper. (Set up some rules about keeping crayon marks off the cupboards, baseboards, and floor, and decide in advance if this drawing will be saved afterward or sent to the recycling bin.)

Create:
Give your child a pack of crayons or washable markers and let him have the pleasure of making a huge drawing of his own choosing. Some children may decide to make one continuous drawing or design, others may create a make-believe village with roads for

toy cars, and others may write stories, songs, or poems. This is a fun way to give your child's creativity a big space to blossom, and it might also appeal to a child who has previously been reluctant to draw or make art.

Art Portfolios

My family has a collection of my grandmother's pastel drawings and oil paintings dating back to 1915, when she was sixteen years old. She's no longer with us, but we still get pleasure from the paintings she created so many years ago. We also have my mother's artwork and many of the pen-and-ink drawings, paintings, and sculptures that I created. So when my children were young, I knew that it was important to me to find a safe place to store their creations. I purchased large professional artist's portfolios, one for each child. Storing your child's artwork may be low on your to-do list right now, but trust me, you'll thank me later. An artist's portfolio is always a good choice, but you can also use a large recycled suitcase or a plastic storage container on wheels.

★ CLASSIC ★

502 Painting

There's no rule that says painting is always about representing real objects. Sometimes painting is all about color, shapes, and imagination.

AGE: 6–10 YRS

CATEGORY: SOLO PLAY/ ARTS & CRAFTS

NUMBER OF CHILDREN: ONE OR MORE

Materials:

Vinyl tablecloth or newspapers

Tempera paints or washable paints

Assorted paintbrushes

Several plastic containers

Paper

Disposable foil muffin tin or paper plate

Recycled men's dress shirt (artist's smock)

Setup:

Put a vinyl tablecloth or newspapers on the kitchen table to protect against spills and leaks, and assemble all your paints, brushes, water containers, and paper. Put a dab of each color in separate sections of the disposable muffin tin.

Jump-start:

- **Paint Story** Have your child illustrate a character or events in a favorite book, story, or fairy tale.

- **My Hero** Have your child paint a fantasy character or action hero of her own invention.

- **Window Mixer** Have him pick three colors (and mix them to create more colors) and paint something he sees out the window.

- **Paint Time Travel** Have her paint a picture of what she looks like now or of what she looked like when she was a baby or a toddler.

- **Six-Four** Encourage your child to make a design that fills the entire paper, using six colors and four different shapes.

- **Paint-A-Day** Have her paint a picture of something funny that happened this week.

Honor Your Child's Artwork

- Designate one large frame (with glass and wire for hanging) for each child in the family. When your child creates a new drawing, pastel, or painting, slip it inside the frame and hang it on the wall. Continue to rotate your child's latest paintings into the frame as new work is created.

- Use both sides of your child's bedroom door as "art gallery space" on which to hang drawings and paintings.

- Tape a featured artwork of the week to the inside of your front door.

- Have a few of your child's special paintings or drawings matted and hung permanently at home.

- Save your child's artwork in a safe place and have a family art show once or twice a year. Display all of the artwork in one or two rooms of your home. Have a little family party to celebrate the "opening." (See Friday Evening Art Show, page 128)

- Send artwork to relatives and friends, who live far away.

- Create greeting cards and note cards from your child's drawings.

503 Fingerprint Collage

Who says you need paint-brushes to paint? Getting your hands dirty is part of the fun.

AGE: 6–10 YRS

CATEGORY: SOLO PLAY/ ARTS & CRAFTS

NUMBER OF CHILDREN: ONE OR MORE

Materials:

Washable paints

Disposable plastic plate (or hefty paper plate)

Construction paper (or heavy, textured paper)

Paper towels and water for cleanup

Create:

The artist squirts a small amount of each color in different sections of the plastic plate. She dips a finger in one color at a time, pressing it on the paper to create a multicolor collage of fingerprints. The prints can be clustered into shapes or spread out at random.

504 Fingerprint Greeting Cards

The artist uses her pinky to create borders or designs on colored paper. She can cluster her fingerprints in the shape of flowers, wreaths, packages, and bows. The designs can then be fine-tuned or embellished using fine-tipped markers.

505 Sponge Print Collage

The artist cuts small squares from a sponge and dips these squares in nontoxic washable tempera paint to create a collage. (The sponges should be slightly dampened with water beforehand.) The artist can make random designs, using overlaid colors, or draw an object like a tree and make it come alive by pressing dabs of colors on top. To avoid dripping, let the design dry thoroughly before moving or hanging the paper.

Grade School Play (age 6 to 10)

UNPLUGGED PLAY

506 | Glitter-Glue Prints

Create sponge shapes (or letters), dip the sponge in glue, make an imprint on paper, and sprinkle glitter on top to make a sparkling design.

AGE: 6–10 YRS

CATEGORY: SOLO PLAY/ ARTS & CRAFTS

NUMBER OF CHILDREN: ONE OR MORE

Materials:

Newspaper

Felt-tipped marker

Sponge Ums (compressed sheets of sponge material available at teacher supply stores)

Scissors

Nontoxic white glue

Disposable plastic plates or pie plates

Several different colors of glitter

Poster board or construction paper

Bowl of water

Setup:

Spread the newspaper all over the table or floor before beginning this project to help contain the mess. Your child uses the felt-tipped marker to draw a shape or letter of the alphabet on a small section of a Sponge Um sheet, and then cuts out the shape with scissors. She continues drawing shapes and letters on the Sponge Ums and cutting them out so that she creates a collection of sponge-shapes. Next, she pours a small amount of white glue into the plastic plate and arranges the glitter and poster board or paper on the table.

Create:

First, your child should wet each sponge with water and wring out the excess. Next, she dips a sponge in the glue and places it on the poster board, pressing lightly for a few seconds to make an imprint. (The sponges should be placed on another plastic plate when not in use.) After the glue is in place, she selects one color of glitter and shakes it over the imprint. To remove the excess glitter, she tips the poster board on its side. This process is repeated with other sponges and glitter colors to create an interesting mix of shapes, colors, and texture.

SAFETY ALERT: Keep glitter and glue clear of younger brothers or sisters.

Fishing Tackle Art Box

Every creative child needs to store and organize her art supplies in one handy place. The fishing tackle art box is a perfect container for storing brushes, pencils, erasers, scissors, hole punch, paints, bags of beads, and rolls of string. Whether you recycle a real fishing tackle box or purchase a plastic art box with compartments, you've got a good start on keeping all your child's art supplies in one place. For larger art supplies like tablets of paper, boxes of felt-tip markers and crayons, and bottles of glue, a large plastic storage tub is a good choice. (If space is limited in your home or apartment, purchase a large plastic storage container with wheels that can slide under your child's bed.) Organizing your child's art and craft supplies will enable your child to easily initiate art projects on her own and also sends a clear message that being creative and making art is something valuable and honored.

507 Tattered and Torn Mosaic

Tear a picture or some colored construction paper to bits, and put it together to create something entirely new.

AGE: 6–10 YRS

CATEGORY:
SOLO PLAY/
ARTS & CRAFTS

NUMBER OF
CHILDREN: ONE
OR MORE

Materials:

Nontoxic white glue

Small plastic yogurt container or margarine tub

Construction paper

Small paintbrush

Setup:

The mosaic artist pours a small amount of glue in the plastic container and adds a few drops of water to thin the glue slightly.

Create:

Your child tears construction paper into small, random shapes, then arranges the pieces into piles by color. He then sketches a simple object, shape, or design on a sheet of construction paper in colored pencil. Working piecemeal, he paints a little glue onto one area at a time, filling it in by sticking on small pieces of paper to create the mosaic.

508 Tattered and Torn Yarn Mosaic

Your child makes a pencil outline on the paper. He squeezes a trail of glue all over the outline and covers it with a piece of yarn; now he fills it in with the pieces of paper to make a spiced-up paper mosaic design.

509 Tattered and Torn Magazine Mosaic

First your child flips through magazines, looking for photos in vibrant colors, tearing out the photos, and arranging them in small piles according to color. After writing a silly message or drawing a design on a piece of construction paper, he glues on the photo scraps to create a shiny mosaic.

510 Homemade Doll Clothing

Your six- to ten-year-old girl may say she has "outgrown" playing with dolls, but throwing in an element of fashion design just might change her mind.

AGE: 6–10 YRS

CATEGORY:
SOLO PLAY/
ARTS & CRAFTS

NUMBER OF
CHILDREN: ONE
OR MORE

Materials:

Baby dolls, fashion dolls, and every type of doll in between

Small pieces of fabric (cotton, polyester, woven fabric, thin terry cloth, felt, ribbon)

Needle

Thread

Scissors

Small, thin piece of white chalk

Create:

It's easier than you think for the two of you to create simple, hand-stitched clothing for your child's doll. Your child will learn very basic hand-stitching skills and use her imagination to create unique clothes. Keep a creative and relaxed attitude in place. These doll fashions don't need to be perfect or resemble designer clothing to be a big hit. Cut a simple pattern for a sweater or tunic from a scrap of fabric. Use needle and thread to sew the pattern pieces together. Add small pieces of ribbon or small buttons to decorate the outfit.

SAFETY ALERT: Athough the occasional pinprick is hard to avoid when sewing, remind your child to be careful with needles. Pick up needles or pins immediately after a spill, and always store them in a safe place.

511 International Flare

Go to the library and gather up books about the doll's country of origin and cultural customs. Learn about and make doll clothing that suits this culture. Find out about childhood fairy tales and games played in the doll's homeland. Sample (or cook) traditional foods eaten in the doll's birthplace.

512 Make Your Own Paper Dolls

Introduce your daughter to the idea of making her own paper dolls and clothes. Dolls can be outlined freehand on a sheet of cardboard or poster board, and markers can be used to color the face, hair, and other features. (For a more picture-perfect doll, you can cut photos of fashion models, male and female, from fashion catalogs.) Use copy paper to trace over the doll and create dresses and outfits, always remembering to leave two large paper tabs at the top to bend and hold the outfit in place on the doll's shoulders. Embellish these designer outfits by gluing on glitter and scraps of ribbon and other paper.

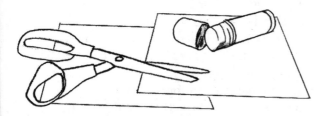

513 Front Door Artwork

PARENT TIP

"Our front door is a giant venue for seasonal decorations, and our six-year-old just happens to love making them. We keep construction paper, scissors, and tape on hand at all times, so that whatever the season, his little hands are busy, and our front door is never bare. Two little tips: keep a vacuum cleaner handy and be sure to have plenty of extra tape so that whatever you put on the door will stay up!"

—Ella from Virginia

514 Flower Petal Spiral

Quite an impressive collage comes to life from recycled magazines.

Materials:
- Pencil
- Sheet of colored construction paper
- Scissors
- Flower and shrub (or garden seed) catalogs with lots of photos of colorful flower blossoms
- Nontoxic white glue

AGE: 6–10 YRS

CATEGORY: SOLO PLAY/ ARTS & CRAFTS

NUMBER OF CHILDREN: ONE

Setup:
Using a pencil, help your child draw the spiral template to begin this design. Draw a circle about the size of a quarter in the center of the construction paper, spiraling out to create a snail-like circular design until you've filled up nearly the entire page. Don't worry about drawing perfect circles; you can use a pretty free-form oval shape.

Create:

Your child cuts small pieces of flower photos from the catalogs and arranges them in color-coded piles on the table. (Lots of photos in lots of different colors are needed to fill this design.) Your child begins cutting pieces to fit the spiral and gluing them to the page in whatever design strikes her fancy. Some children may want a random, colorful design; others will use all the white flowers in a cluster in the center, for example, then cut various small pink squares to create the next progression of color. There is absolutely no right way to do this flower spiral.

515 Paper Mosaic Spiral

Beginning with the same snail-like pencil drawing, your child cuts small squares from various colors of construction paper and uses them to fill in the spiral. Arrange the colors in a recurring pattern or leave it to fate.

Art Supplies!

A well-stocked art supply store should have a complete line of art supplies just right for children. I am always amazed at what I can find to keep children busy creating, without breaking the bank. Here are a few of the things you might find there:

Acrylic paints

Art bins and tackle boxes

Artist's easel

Artist's portfolio

Beads and string

Blank journals

Cardboard boxes

Chalk

Chenille craft stems (aka pipe cleaners)

Child-safe scissors

Colored pencils

Craft dough cutters

Craft sticks (aka Popsicle sticks)

Crayons

Crepe paper or streamers

Drawing boards

Drawing pencils

Eyedroppers

Face paint

Fine-tip pens (assorted colors in a set)

Finger paints

Giant foam board (40" by 60")

Glitter (and glitter glue)

Ink pad and stamps

Modeling clay

Nontoxic glue

Oil pastels (crayons)

Paintbrushes and rollers

Paper of every size and texture

Play dough

Poster board

Precut mat boards (to frame drawings)

Printing supplies (sponges, paints, and paper)

Rolls of butcher paper

Single-hole punch

Spill-proof paint containers

Tempera paints

Washable paints (nontoxic)

NOTE: *If your local store has mainly adult supplies, children's art supplies can also be purchased from online art supplies vendors such as www.teachingsupplystore.com (click on Arts & Crafts) and www.artistcraftsman.com (click on Children's Art Supplies).*

Grade School Play (age 6 to 10)

516 Homemade Greeting Cards

A homemade greeting card expresses so much more than the message it contains.

QUICK & EASY

AGE: **6–10 YRS**

CATEGORY:
SOLO PLAY/
ARTS & CRAFTS

NUMBER OF
CHILDREN: **ONE
OR MORE**

Materials:
Construction paper
Nontoxic white glue
Glitter
Markers, crayons, colored pencils
Scraps of brightly colored fabric, yarn, and ribbon
Scissors
Envelopes

Create:
Your child folds each sheet of paper in half (widthwise) or quarters to make a large or medium-size greeting card and decorates each card with a unique design. Fabric or paper cutouts and shapes can be glued to the front.

517 Pop-Up Greeting Cards

This three-dimensional pop-up card looks pretty wiggly and animated, and kids love the element of surprise.

AGE: **6–10 YRS**

CATEGORY:
SOLO PLAY/
ARTS & CRAFTS

NUMBER OF
CHILDREN: **ONE
OR MORE**

Materials:
Construction paper
Scissors
Colored pencils, markers, or crayons
Glitter
Nontoxic white glue
Clear tape
Envelopes

Create:
Your child folds a piece of construction paper in half or quarters to make a greeting card (see above), using colored pencils, markers, or crayons to decorate the front of the card. She decides what she wants the "pop-up" shape to be and outlines it in pencil on another sheet of construction paper. (Ideas might include a heart, birthday cake, present, the words "I Love You" or "Celebrate," etc.) She cuts out the image, following her outline, then cuts four ½"-by-5" construction paper strips. Next, she folds each strip accordion-style (folding the end of a strip over ½ inch, then under ½ inch, over and under, to create a series of folds). To support the pop-up shape, she attaches one end of each accordion strip to the back of the pop-up shape with small pieces of clear tape; the other end of the accordion strip is taped to the inside of the card. She can test out the mechanism by pressing the pop-up image down to make sure it pops up when released. (The length of the paper strips may need to be adjusted, depending on the size of the pop-up shape. If the strips are too long, the pop-up shape may droop; too short, and it may not "pop" enough.)

Outdoor Play

It's crucial to get your child outside during these years. As he gets older, homework, time spent at school, trips to the movies, and other indoor activities will increasingly pull at his time. The outdoors is where he gets to experience the joy of movement and soak up all those great smells, sights, and sounds that will nurture his body and his imagination for years to come. Being comfortable doing stuff outdoors is a marvelous gift to carry into adulthood. Think sports, camping, hiking, exploring, or even fixing things or painting on a sunny day—these are the experiences that outdoor play leads to.

Free Time for Daydreaming

Don't be fooled into thinking that nothing much is going on when you glance out the window and see your son swinging happily on the swing set. He may be dreaming up all sorts of good ideas—creating new lyrics for a popular song, inventing his own story about a fantasy character, or wondering about shapes in the clouds overhead. All this thinking, wondering, inventing, and creating are powerful parts of play. Children need time for unstructured play and daydreaming in their daily routine. Here are some outdoor play activities that provide opportunities to dream, invent, and create:

- Set up a tent and have a "campout" for a few hours.
- Build a fort, hideout, or lean-to with cardboard boxes.
- Draw designs (or a maze) on the sidewalk with chalk.
- Create roadways and a village in the sandbox.
- Skip stones across a pond or a lake.
- Have a spontaneous nature scavenger hunt outside.
- Use binoculars to watch birds and squirrels in the trees.
- Write letters and words in the sand at the beach.
- Sketch or draw in a peaceful place outside.
- Invent a fantasy team of your favorite baseball players.
- Gaze at the stars from the deck or backyard.
- Invent an obstacle course or a miniature-golf course.
- Look for a four-leaf clover.
- Chase fireflies on a summer evening.

Let's Play Ball!

Here are some captivating outdoor ball games and drills for one. These games help develop tossing, dribbling, and kicking skills, strengthen hand–eye coordination, speed, and agility, and foster perseverance along the way! What's more, these active outdoor play ideas may inspire opportunities for reflective daydreaming too. As your child plays in the yard, he may be imagining walking up to bat in a major league baseball game or kicking the game-winning goal in the soccer championship. (As an added bonus, all of these ball games can be easily adapted for two or more players.)

★CLASSIC★

518 Seven Up

Soft-drinks not included!

Materials:

Sidewalk chalk

Tennis ball or small rubber ball

QUICK & EASY

AGE: 6–10 YRS

CATEGORY:
SOLO PLAY/
OUTDOOR

NUMBER OF
CHILDREN: **ONE
OR MORE**

Setup:

The player will need a windowless outside wall (a garage door tends to be a good choice) against which to bounce the ball. He uses the chalk to draw a line on the pavement 5 feet or more away from the building.

Play:

This game has a predetermined series of different actions the player performs while bouncing and catching the ball, starting with "onesies" and ending with "sevensies." Here are the motions for each of the seven rounds of play:

- **Onesies** Bounce the ball against the wall one time and catch it.

- **Twosies** Bounce the ball hard on the pavement so it flies high in the air, twirl around once, catch the ball. Repeat this action a second time.

- **Threesies** Bounce the ball against the wall, clap once, and catch it before it bounces. Bounce it again, clapping twice, and catch it before the bounce. Bounce the ball one more time, clap three times quickly, and catch it before it bounces.

- **Foursies** Bounce the ball against the wall, clap once in front of your face, then quickly clap once behind your head, and catch the ball. Repeat this action four times.

- **Fivesies** Bounce the ball against the wall, slap your hands on your thighs, cross your hands over your chest, clap once, and catch the ball. Repeat this action five times.

- **Sixies** Throw the ball in the air, lift up your right knee and wrap your arms around it so you can clap underneath, lift your left knee up and clap underneath it, and catch the ball. Repeat this three times (you should have clapped six times).

- **Sevensies** Throw the ball up in the air under one leg and catch it. Repeat this seven times.

519 Soccer Dribble and Score

Dribble, turn, tap, kick—quick, quick, quick!

QUICK & EASY

AGE: 6–10 YRS

CATEGORY: **SOLO PLAY/ OUTDOOR**

NUMBER OF CHILDREN: **ONE OR MORE**

Materials:

4 plastic sports cones (or 4 shoes to use as obstacles)

Backyard soccer net (or 2 shoes positioned approximately 8' to 10' apart as goalposts)

Stopwatch or kitchen timer

Soccer ball

Setup:

The player sets up the cones in a straight line, each 6 to 10 feet apart, at one end of the lawn. She sets up the soccer net at the opposite end of the lawn. (The cones are positioned to create a straight line leading toward the goal.)

Play:

Player sets the stopwatch for 3 to 10 minutes. (Or the player simply does five repetitions of the drill, times herself, and does it again with the challenge to quicken the pace.) She places the soccer ball on the ground in the middle of the lawn and uses her feet to dribble the ball around each cone in the line. When she reaches the last cone, she dribbles around it and heads back toward the first cone, dribbling around each cone as she goes. When she gets back to her starting position, she dribbles so that she's clear of the cones and takes a shot at the goal. She then retrieves the ball, quickly dribbles back to the line of cones, and starts it all over again. She tries to complete as many runs and score as many goals as possible before the timer sounds.

520 Double-Dribble

Your child plays the game at left, adding any of the three dribbling challenges below (listed in order from least to most difficult.)

- Player uses the inside of her right foot to make two touches (taps to the ball) as she dribbles around the first cone, then switches to the inside of her left foot as she goes around the next cone. She continues alternating from one foot to the other.

- Player uses the inside of her right foot to make two touches as she dribbles around the first cone. She switches to the outside of her right foot as she dribbles around the next cone, continuing in this way and switching to the left foot on the next run.

- Player uses the outside of her right foot to make two touches as she dribbles around the first cone, then she uses the outside of the left foot, making two touches to dribble around the second cone, and so on, around each cone.

> **"** Mastery is this wonderful, exciting feeling: I'm better at it today than I was last week. It doesn't mean I'm the best in the world; it doesn't mean I won the Nobel Prize; it means simply: I'm getting better. I can do it better now than I could before—that is the root of motivation and self-esteem, and it's really magical. **"**
>
> **—Edward Hallowell, M.D.**
> psychiatrist and author of
> *Driven to Distraction* and *CrazyBusy*

Grade School Play (age 6 to 10)

521 Basketball Challenge

Use an adjustable basketball hoop and see what kind of unique shot styles your child develops.

AGE: 6–10 YRS

CATEGORY:
SOLO PLAY/
OUTDOOR

NUMBER OF
CHILDREN: ONE
OR MORE

Materials:

Sidewalk chalk

Basketball or playground ball

Adjustable basketball hoop

Sports cones

Setup:
Use the chalk to create a foul shot line on the pavement.

Jump-start:
Your child can set up a series of solo challenges for herself:

- **Foul Shots** Take 20 foul shots (from a standing position, about 6 feet away) and score one point for every one that goes in.

- **Bank Shots** Take 20 bank shots (a shot in which the ball touches the backboard before landing in the basket) or layups (where you dribble up to the basket and take the shot from up close), scoring one point for every shot that goes in.

- **Dribble Drill** Set up sports cones in a straight line down the center of the pavement. Dribble the ball, circling around each cone in the line as many times as possible without stopping or dropping the ball. Repeat the drill, using your other hand.

- **Trick Shots** Create your own dribbling and shooting challenges and trick shots and use a small notepad to record how many shots or successful challenges were achieved each day. Set new challenges to beat your previous record.

522 A Few Dollars Well Spent

PARENT TIP

❝We bought our daughter a stopwatch from the sports store and she uses it to time herself during all sorts of games she plays outdoors. She has always enjoyed running and playing, but this simple tool has created hours of fun setting up challenges and playing ball games in our backyard.❞

—Larry from Colorado

523 Clapping Call-Ball

A simple challenge with clapping, throwing, and catching, and the thrill of bouncing the ball higher and higher.

AGE: 6–10 YRS

CATEGORY:
SOLO PLAY/
OUTDOOR

NUMBER OF
CHILDREN: ONE
OR MORE

Materials:

Tennis ball or small rubber ball

Play:
This should be played in a safe, grassy playing area free of obstacles. Your child tosses the ball in the air, calls out "one," and claps once before catching the ball. She tosses the ball a bit higher in the air, calls out "two," and claps twice before catching the ball. She continues tossing the ball and increasing the number of claps on each round of play, catching the ball after zero or one bounce.

524 Bouncing Call-Ball

Your child will need a bouncy rubber ball and access to a blacktop court. (A playground ball with lots of air works well, or for more challenge, she can use a smaller ball with lots of bounce.) She gives the ball a hard bounce on the pavement and sees how many times she can clap, attempting to catch it before it bounces on the pavement a second time. (The higher she can bounce the ball, the more claps she'll be able to fit in.)

SAFETY ALERT: Play this game in an area free from obstacles, and teach your child how to throw the ball in the air a slight distance from her standing position in order to avoid her face or eyes.

525 A Real Scavenger

Nature holds a lot of buried and unburied treasures—find them!

AGE: 6–10 YRS

CATEGORY: **SOLO PLAY/ OUTDOOR**

NUMBER OF CHILDREN: **ONE OR MORE**

Materials:
Paper
Pencil
Paper grocery bags
Jars with holes in the lids

Setup:
Make a list of items that can be found in nature: colorful stones, acorns, nuts, pinecones, pine needles, brilliant leaves, bark, bugs (take the jars with holes in the lids along for collecting), seed pods, flowers, worms, snails, twigs with interesting bumps and shapes, cattails, reeds, four-leaf clovers. Have your child collect her finds in jars and paper bags, checking off items on her list (and adding some more, no doubt) as she explores.

Play:
Create a simple scavenger hunt for your child to have an outdoor adventure in your own backyard, neighborhood park, or playground.

SAFETY ALERT: Supervise your child while she explores and teach her to identify anthills, hornet and wasp nests, poison ivy, poison oak, and snakes so she feels safe and confident exploring nature.

526 Point It Out

Create a list of nature's treasures for your child to spot without collecting. In this case, you might include items you have spotted such as spiderwebs, anthills, rotting tree stumps, or patches of clover.

527 Wiffle Golf Hole in One

Who needs a golf course when you've got a backyard and a Hula-Hoop?

AGE: 6–10 YRS

CATEGORY: **SOLO PLAY/ OUTDOOR**

NUMBER OF CHILDREN: **ONE OR MORE**

Materials:
Large Hula-Hoop
Golf tee
Bucket of Wiffle golf balls
Child-size plastic golf club

Setup:
Place the Hula-Hoop at one end of the lawn and designate a shooting line at the other end by pressing a golf tee into the ground. (Place the Hula-Hoop close enough to the golf tee for your child to send balls into the hoop and experience the joy of succeeding with a bit of challenge thrown in for good measure.)

Play:
Place a Wiffle ball on the tee. Your child will use the club to try to send the ball into the large hoop at the other end of the lawn to score a "hole in one." She keeps going until every ball in the bucket has been played and counts a point for every ball that lands inside the hoop.

528 Frisbee Toss Hole in One

This version of the game requires two Hula-Hoops and one Frisbee. Player places the hoops on the ground at opposite ends of the lawn. She stands inside one of the hoops, facing the hoop at the opposite end, and tosses the Frisbee toward the hoop, aiming to land it inside. She retrieves the Frisbee and goes to stand inside whichever hoop is closest and continues, scoring one point for every goal.

529 Stoop-Ball

Playing Stoop-Ball alone is an excellent skill builder for tossing, catching, hand–eye coordination, and anticipating the ball's direction and timing.

AGE: 6–10 YRS

CATEGORY: SOLO PLAY/ OUTDOOR

NUMBER OF CHILDREN: ONE OR MORE

Materials:
Tennis ball or small rubber ball
Timer

Setup:
The player finds a stoop (outdoor steps) not too close to a road.

Play:
The player stands 4 feet or more away from the stoop and tosses the ball toward the steps, aiming to catch it as it bounces off one of the steps. Points are scored based on which part of the stoop the ball hits.

• If the ball hits in between two steps, score one point.

• If the ball bounces directly off the edge of a step, score 10 points.

• If the ball misses the stoop or player doesn't catch it after one bounce, deduct one point.

The overall goal is for the player to score 100 points in a specific amount of time. To begin, set a kitchen timer or watch for 10 minutes and see if 100 points can be scored in this time. Adjust the timer to create a manageable challenge, given players' abilities and attention spans.

530 Jump Rope

Children love to get really good at jumping rope on their own so they can wow their friends on the playground with their smooth moves.

AGE: 6–10 YRS

CATEGORY: SOLO PLAY/ OUTDOOR

NUMBER OF CHILDREN: ONE OR MORE

Materials:
Jump rope
Sidewalk or other paved playing surface

Jump-start:
After your child has gotten comfortable with the rhythm of using a jump rope, here are some challenges she can set for herself to make things more interesting:

• *Left-Right* Skip on one foot, alternating feet with every skip.

• *Long Hopper* Skip on one foot for as long as you can, then switch to the other.

• *Hopper Time* Set the kitchen timer and count how many times you can jump in 3 minutes, 4 minutes, or 5 minutes.

*SAFETY ALERT: Make sure your child wears athletic shoes. Sandals, flip-flops, or shoes with buckles can catch on the rope and increase the risk of injury.

531 Beanbag Target Toss

A perfect after-school game for a child who needs to burn off a little steam after sitting at a desk all day.

AGE: 6–10 YRS

CATEGORY:
SOLO PLAY/
OUTDOOR

NUMBER OF
CHILDREN: ONE
OR MORE

Materials:
 Sidewalk chalk
 Stopwatch or kitchen timer
 Beanbags

Setup:
Your child draws a large chalk circle on the sidewalk or pavement, then draws straight lines inside the circle to create four, six, or eight slices of the pie. He assigns a specific number of points to each slice, then uses the chalk to draw a pitching line several feet away.

Play:
Your child stands behind the pitching line and sets the kitchen timer for 5 minutes or more, then begins pitching beanbags into the pie slices, scoring points accordingly. (No points are scored when the beanbag lands on a dividing line or outside the circle.) He tries to score 50 points before the buzzer sounds.

532 Double Challenge

Create a second pitching line several feet behind the original one with the option of scoring double points by throwing from the farthest line. Move back and forth between the two to vary the level of challenge.

533 Bull's-Eye

Your child adds a smaller circle (bull's-eye) in the center of the pie. He scores 10 or more points for a bull's-eye.

Challenge!

Your child may see another child playing a game and think, "I wonder if I could do that." The desire to challenge oneself is a driving force for many solo games for boys and girls all around the world. While organized sports may have a place in your child's routine, your child gains a unique sense of independence by simply going outside with a ball and "messing around on her own" to see what she can do.

534 Giant Ring Toss

The giant rings and random assortment of targets bring a little bit of Alice in Wonderland *to this game.*

AGE: 6–10 YRS

CATEGORY:
SOLO PLAY/
OUTDOOR

NUMBER OF
CHILDREN: ONE
OR MORE

Materials:
 Hula-Hoops
 Several unbreakable items
  for use as targets:
  Kitchen stool
  Small plastic cooler
  Large empty flowerpots (turned upside down)
  Construction paper
  Markers

Setup:
Your child positions the targets strategically around the lawn, deciding how many points each target is worth and writing down her scoring system on a piece of construction paper. She creates a starting line at a spot of her choice.

Play:

Your child tosses the Hula-Hoops over the targets, going to retrieve them when she's exhausted her supply. She keeps track of her score on her own. For an additional challenge, she may enjoy using a stopwatch to challenge herself to score a set number of points in a given time period (say, 3 to 5 minutes). This approach includes a bit more running back and forth retrieving Hula-Hoops, which is a fun way to add more movement and speed to the game.

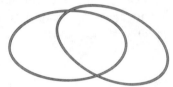

535 | Giant Steps Ring Toss

Use only one target for this variation but take one giant step back after each toss. For added interest, your child may enjoy scoring one point if she gets the ring on the target in the first toss, two points for the next toss (a giant step farther away), three points if she gets the ring on the target on the third giant step back. (After three or four giant steps back, she moves again to the starting line, and begins the tossing progression again.)

536 | Batty-Bird 100

This is a great game for a child who likes to test his focus; there's also some multitasking involved.

QUICK & EASY

AGE: 6–10 YRS

CATEGORY:
SOLO PLAY/
OUTDOOR

NUMBER OF
CHILDREN: ONE
OR MORE

Materials:

Badminton racket

Birdie (officially called a shuttlecock)

Play:

This game should be played on a flat lawn. The player holds the racquet so that the netting is parallel to the ground and uses it to tap the birdie continuously, sending it about a foot up into the air each time. The player tries to get to 50 continuous taps; if the birdie slips off the racket, he must start all over again. When the player gets to 51 taps, the difficulty of the game increases, and the birdie gets tapped higher into the air, about 3 feet above the racket. When the player reaches 75 taps, he increases the power of his taps again, sending the birdie even higher into the air (8 to 10 feet). The aim is to get to 100 taps. (At the third level, catching the birdie is likely to involve some running around the lawn.)

PARENT TIP

537 | Toys Take a Vacation

I realized one day that most of the toys my children had were not being played with on a regular basis. After many years of putting their toys away for them, I came up with the idea of 'vacation for toys.' It works like this: The children choose which toys will go in a box that eventually goes on vacation (storage). At first they were resistant, but finally they realized that everyone needs a vacation, even toys! After about six months, the toys come back from vacation and the kids are excited to have their old toys again. Now they enjoy sending their toys on vacation, and I enjoy having a room with less clutter and mess to clean up!

—Wanda from Alaska

Play Ideas for Parent and Child

Say "yes" to "Mom/Dad, will you play with me?" whenever possible. Time with your child is all about doing—moving, thinking, guessing, and creating. Children six to ten are keen observers who pick up nuances of skill, strategy, and technique. So, without much fanfare (and perhaps few words), your child is absorbing, learning, and expanding because he is playing with you. And play can also bring out amazing questions or comments from your six- to ten-year-old that lets you know what he's thinking, what he's imagining, or even what he's concerned about. Here are some games to play and crafts to make on those happy days when you say "yes" to playing together.

Indoor Play

Parents are terrific at multitasking, so guessing and word games can easily be played together while you are chopping veggies or stirring the stew. (Or, play in the car when you're driving across town.)

Kitchen Table Play

Although children six to ten years old are much more independent than pre-schoolers, they still enjoy the comfort of playing alongside Mom or Dad. With these kitchen activities, I've also included some thinking and guessing games that your child can either play with you, as you work nearby, or alone (with pencil and paper to jot down guesses).

Kitchen-Table Play Classics

Cat's Cradle string game	LEGOs	Rush Hour
Dominoes	Models (planes, boats, cars)	Solitaire
Etch A Sketch	Pick-up Sticks	Squeezed Out*
Jacks	Puzzles	Yo-yo

*Squeezed Out and other classic games are available from Back to Basics Toys, www.backtobasicstoys.com.

538 Class Count

Test your child's observation skills with this fun way to get her talking about school.

AGE: 6–10 YRS

CATEGORY: **PARENT & CHILD/ INDOOR**

NUMBER OF CHILDREN: **ONE OR MORE**

Materials:
Paper
Pencil

Play:
Challenge your child to write down or call out the name of every child in her class, giving one detail about what each classmate likes to do, play, wear, eat, say, etc.

539 Lost and Found

Quick searching skills and nimble fingers win out in this kitchen table game.

AGE: 6–10 YRS

CATEGORY: **PARENT & CHILD/ INDOOR**

NUMBER OF CHILDREN: **ONE OR MORE**

Materials:
Paper
Pencil
Magazines with lots of photos
Kitchen timer

Setup:
Suggest 10 to 20 items that might be found in the pages of a magazine, and have your child make a list of these items. Some items should be quite common and others more challenging. Common examples might include a dog, cat, dinner plate, fruit, vegetable, shoe, baby, pair of eyeglasses, bottle, jewelry. Challenging items might include a red car, a barbecue grill, yellow flowers, a boat, a hammer, a boot, a lawn chair, an airplane, a fence, or a motorcycle.

Play:
Set the kitchen timer for 10 to 15 minutes. Your child begins searching through the magazines for each item on the list. When an item is found, he tears the page from the magazine and/or checks it off the list. Once the timer sounds, add up the number of items found in the magazine.

540 What's Cooking?

Can Mom or Dad discover the mystery recipe?

AGE: 6–10 YRS

CATEGORY: **PARENT & CHILD/ INDOOR**

NUMBER OF CHILDREN: **ONE OR MORE**

Materials:
A basic cookbook or familiar ethnic or regional cookbook
Large rubber bands

Setup:
The two sections of the cookbook to be used for this game are Main Dishes and Desserts. Use the rubber bands to parcel off the unneeded sections of the cookbook to make it easier to navigate the two sections used to play.

Play:
Your child selects one familiar recipe from the Main Dishes or Desserts section of the cookbook. He announces the category (either main dish or dessert) and then reads any one ingredient in the recipe to get the guessing game started. For example, if the selected recipe is beef stew, he would reveal that the category is a "main dish" and perhaps give the first clue ingredient as "celery." You can then either take a wild guess on that first clue or simply say, "More clues, please." Your child continues offering ingredients as clues until you make a correct guess or give up and ask for the correct answer.

Note: Younger children may need to spell some of the difficult ingredients given as clues, which makes this game a terrific way to learn spelling, vocabulary, and pronunciation.

541 Window Wager

It all started with a piece of paper, a pencil, and a wager....

AGE: 6–10 YRS

CATEGORY: PARENT & CHILD/ INDOOR

NUMBER OF CHILDREN: ONE OR MORE

Materials:
Pencils
Paper
Notepad

Play:
The game begins with a question like, "How many windows are in our home?" (Other items you might place wagers on are doorknobs, lightbulbs, framed photos or paintings, and shoes.) Each player quickly writes down a guess on a piece of paper and folds it in half without the other player seeing it. Give your child a notepad and pencil and let her be the Auditor who sets out to discover whose guess comes closest.

542 Dictionary Detective

A fun challenge that has the added benefit of putting the dictionary into frequent circulation.

AGE: 6–10 YRS

CATEGORY: PARENT & CHILD/ INDOOR

NUMBER OF CHILDREN: ONE OR MORE

Materials:
Children's dictionary

Play:
Your child flips the dictionary open to any page, selects a word of her choice, and, without saying the word, reads the definition out loud. You (or another player) must try to guess the mystery word described after hearing the definition.

543 Spelling Bee

In this variation, you select a page in the dictionary and find one word on that page that your child must try to spell. Or pass the dictionary to your child and let your child select challenging words for *you* to spell correctly.

NOTE: This game is best suited to children with reasonably good reading and spelling skills.

544 I'm Thinking of a Food . . .

Try to stump Mom or Dad by offering a series of clues about a mystery food.

AGE: 6–10 YRS

CATEGORY: PARENT & CHILD/ INDOOR

NUMBER OF CHILDREN: ONE OR MORE

Materials:
Garden seed catalog (color)

Play:
Your child starts the game by thinking of a specific food found in a seed catalog, such as a pineapple, and offering a series of clues about this food that follow the specific order listed below (the clues progress from least revealing to most revealing):

1. Any one letter found in the name of the mystery food

2. The color of the food

3. The shape of the food

4. The texture of the food

5. The category of the food (fruit, vegetable, meat, or grain)

NOTE: It's best to pick a single item of food rather than a recipe.

Reading Aloud

Even though they can read on their own, children still get tremendous pleasure and comfort from listening as you read to them. And reading aloud to the six- to ten-year-old crowd often happens to be the one kind of play that a busy, tired parent can manage at the end of a long day! Here are a few of my favorite books for children six to ten years old. Please keep in mind that some of these books may be too "old" for your particular child, while others may seem too "young." There's a wide range of individual preferences and interests within this age group, so use what you know about your child to select a book that is just right.

Picture Books

Amelia Bedelia by Peggy Parish, illustrations by Fritz Siebel

Arthur series by Marc Brown

Babar by Jean De Brunhoff

A Birthday for Frances by Russell Hoban, illustrations by Lillian Hoban

The Cat in the Hat by Dr. Seuss

Chester's Way by Kevin Henkes

Cloudy with a Chance of Meatballs by Judi Barrett, illustrations by Ron Barrett

Doctor DeSoto by William Steig

Double Trouble in Walla Walla by Andrew Clements, illustrations by Salvatore Murdocca

Eloise by Kay Thompson, illustrations by Hilary Knight

Green Eggs and Ham by Dr. Seuss

Henry and Mudge and the Great Grandpas by Cynthia Rylant, illustrations by Sucie Stevenson

Little Bear by Else Holmelund Minarik, illustrations by Maurice Sendak

Martha Speaks by Susan Meddaugh

Miss Nelson Is Missing!, Miss Nelson Is Back, and *Miss Nelson Has a Field Day* by Harry Allard

Nate the Great by Marjorie Weinman Sharmat, illustrations by Marc Simont

Once There was a Bull . . . (Frog) by Rick Walton

One Fish, Two Fish, Red Fish, Blue Fish by Dr. Seuss

Peter's Chair by Ezra Jack Keats

Terrific by Jon Agee

The Polar Express by Chris Van Allsburg

The Stinky Cheese Man and Other Fairly Stupid Tales by Jon Scieszka, illustrations by Lane Smith

Traction Man Is Here by Mini Grey

Chapter Books

The Adventures of Captain Underpants by Dav Pilkey

> **❝**One thing I encourage parents to do is turn off the car radio, turn off the headsets and computer games, and just talk. Tell stories, talk about the events of the day, have 'what if' conversations. What if you were walking down the street and saw a bag full of money, what would be the best thing to do?**❞**
>
> **—Mary Pipher, Ph.D.**
> psychotherapist and author of *Reviving Ophelia* and *The Shelter of Each Other*

All-of-a-Kind Family by Sydney Taylor, illustrations by Helen John

American Girl Collection (series)

Babe, the Gallant Pig by Dick King Smith

A Bear Called Paddington by Michael Bond, illustrations by Peggy Fortnum

The Best Christmas Pageant Ever by Barbara Robinson

Charlie and the Chocolate Factory by Roald Dahl, illustrations by Quentin Blake

Charlotte's Web by E. B. White, illustrations by Garth Williams

The Cricket in Times Square by George Selden, illustrations by Garth Williams

Frog and Toad Are Friends (and others in the series) by Arnold Lobel

Harriet the Spy by Louise Fitzhugh

Harry Potter and the Sorcerer's Stone by J. K. Rowling

> **❝**I would set firm limits on screen time. That means a limited number of hours per week and choice of programs to be determined with the parent. For school-age kids, homework is more important, play is more important, activities are more important; and the television needs to be secondary to all those things.**❞**
>
> **—Jane Healy, Ph.D.**
> author of *Your Child's Growing Mind*

James and the Giant Peach by Roald Dahl, illustrations by Lane Smith

Little House on the Prairie by Laura Ingalls Wilder, illustrations by Garth Williams

Miracle at the Plate (and other sports classics) by Matt Christopher

The Mouse and the Motorcycle by Beverly Cleary

Mr. Popper's Penguins by Richard Atwater

Mrs. Piggle-Wiggle by Betty MacDonald, illustrations by Hilary Knight

Ramona Forever by Beverly Cleary, illustrations by Tracy Dockray

Ramona Quimby, Age 8 by Beverly Cleary, illustrations by Tracy Dockray

Ramona the Pest by Beverly Cleary, illustrations by Tracy Dockray

Sarah Plain and Tall by Patricia MacLachlan

The Secret Garden by Frances Hodgson Burnett

Stuart Little by E. B. White

Reference Books (valuable resources for ad-lib games):

Merriam-Webster Children's Dictionary

National Geographic World Atlas for Young Explorers

Scholastic Encyclopedia of Animals

Scholastic Rhyming Dictionary

> **❝**When you interact with your child, there's the emotional part of that interaction that is also helping your child to modulate moods and attention. It takes a person to help a child regulate, not a computer.**❞**
>
> **—Marilyn Benoit, M.D.**
> Clinical Associate Professor of Psychiatry at Georgetown University Medical Center; past president, American Academy of Child and Adolescent Psychiatry

Grade School Play (age 6 to 10)

UNPLUGGED
PLAY

545 First Story in Cursive

One of my favorite pieces of art is a large, framed story, complete with illustrations, that my son made when he was just beginning to "write cursive." This drawing captures one frozen moment of time when my son had mastered the "writing" of these cursive letters but was not yet sure how the letters all fit together to form words. Nonetheless, he enthusiastically wrote seventy cursive letters and connected them all together, with a period at the end, to tell his story. This masterpiece makes me smile every time I see it hanging in our hallway!

AGE: 6–10 YRS

CATEGORY:
PARENT & CHILD/
INDOOR

NUMBER OF
CHILDREN: ONE
OR MORE

Materials:
Markers with a medium or fine writing tip

Poster board or large paper

Writing tablet or chart showing how to write cursive letters

Setup:
Help your child practice writing cursive letters.

Play:
Ask your child to draw a picture along the top or bottom half of the poster board. Then encourage him to tell the story of his picture

in cursive on the other half of the poster board. Let him know that this project is about expressing an idea and telling a story rather than about perfect penmanship.

546 Cursive Story with a Theme

For older children with better writing skills, pick a theme, an idea, or a fantasy that they are excited about, and ask them to create and illustrate their very own story on this theme.

547 Going on a Picnic

This game is terrific to play on long car trips or to pass the time while waiting in the doctor's office.

AGE: 6–10 YRS

CATEGORY:
PARENT & CHILD/
INDOOR

NUMBER OF
CHILDREN: ONE
OR MORE

Setup:
Select one player to begin the game.

Play:
One child begins by saying, "I'm going on a picnic and I'm bringing _____ " (*insert the name of a picnic item that begins with the letter A*). The second player repeats this statement the same way and then adds on: "I'm also bringing _____ " (*insert item beginning with the letter B*). As the game moves on through the letters of the alphabet, each child must remember all the items previously mentioned. When a child stumbles and cannot remember an item in the list, she starts the game over, beginning with the letter A. (If you prefer to keep score, mark a point each time a player gets through the entire list of items correctly and adds one new item with the next letter of the alphabet. The child with the most points wins.) Keep in mind that there are plenty of nonfood items to bring to a picnic!

548 I Spy

A quick eye and a quick mouth are all you need to play this game.

AGE: 6–10 YRS

CATEGORY: PARENT & CHILD/ INDOOR

NUMBER OF CHILDREN: ONE OR MORE

Play:
One player is elected as the spy. The spy fixes on a particular object within his field of vision, either indoors or out. The spy says, "I spy with my little eye, something that begins with the letter ___." The other players look around the room and call out guesses as fast as they can: "Is it a banana?" "A bowl?" "A bottle?" The spy answers no, not giving away any other hints, until someone guesses correctly. The person who guesses the correct object becomes the next spy.

549 Concentration

This game tests both observation and memory; it's always been a favorite in my family.

AGE: 6–10 YRS

CATEGORY: PARENT & CHILD/ INDOOR

NUMBER OF CHILDREN: ONE OR MORE

Materials:
Deck of playing cards with matching pairs (a standard deck, Go Fish deck, or Animal Rummy deck)

Setup:
Shuffle the deck of cards and lay them out (no piles) on the floor or table, facedown in a rectangular configuration.

Play:
Players must try to remember the position of each card they see turned over. The first player turns over any two cards in the rectangle, looking to match the numbers, face cards (jack, queen, king), or animals. If the cards match, he removes these two cards (putting them in his "pile") and turns over two more cards, looking for another match. If the cards do not match, they are returned to their original facedown positions and the next person takes a turn. At first, he'll be turning cards over at random, but soon he'll have built up enough of a memory bank to make matches by going back to cards he's seen turned over. The game continues until all the matches have been made. Each player counts the cards in his pile, and the player with the most cards wins.

550 What Would You Invent?

Here's a way to tap into your child's creative thinking abilities.

AGE: 6–10 YRS

CATEGORY: PARENT & CHILD/ INDOOR

NUMBER OF CHILDREN: ONE OR MORE

Materials:
Pencil

Paper

Setup:
Help your child practice writing cursive letters.

Play:

Create a list of real-life places and ask, "What gadget would you invent to make things easier or better in/on *(insert the name of the place)*?" For example: What gadget would you invent to make a barn better for cows? This simple question starts some marvelous ideas flowing with many twists and turns. Other familiar places might include:

- The kitchen
- The school cafeteria
- The soccer or baseball field
- The train or subway station
- The highway
- An airplane
- A car or truck
- A farm
- The garage
- The doctor's office
- An office
- A restaurant
- The post office
- The grocery store
- The ocean

Note: If your child likes the idea of being an inventor, here's a good book to enjoy together: *So You Want to Be an Inventor* by Judith St. George, illustrations by David Small.

★ CLASSIC ★

551 Tic-Tac-Toe

It's hard to imagine a world without tic-tac-toe. It seems like this game has been around since the dawn of time. . . .

QUICK & EASY

AGE: 6–10 YRS

CATEGORY:
PARENT & CHILD/
INDOOR

NUMBER OF
CHILDREN: ONE
OR MORE

Materials:
Paper
Pencil

Setup:
Draw a simple grid with two vertical lines and two horizontal lines intersecting them. (Leave an inch between each of these lines to allow player to fit *X*s and *O*s in the squares created by the grid.)

Play:
One player chooses *X* as his mark and the other chooses *O*. Toss a coin to see which player goes first. The first player then puts his mark in one of the squares on the grid. (The middle square is the best bet for the first mark!) The second player puts one mark down. Each player continues filling in his *X* or *O* with the goal of getting three marks in a row, horizontally, vertically, or diagonally. If neither player is successful getting three marks in a row, the round is considered a "draw" and a new game begins.

★ CLASSIC ★

552 Invisible Words

No pencil and paper needed for this writing game!

AGE: 6–10 YRS

CATEGORY: PARENT & CHILD/ INDOOR

NUMBER OF CHILDREN: ONE OR MORE

Play:
Using your finger, outline one letter at a time on your child's back to create an invisible word. When you are finished, your child takes a guess. If the guess is correct, he trades places and writes a word on your back. (If he guesses incorrectly, write the word again and let him take another guess.)

553 Picture Perfect

Rather than writing, try outlining a simple shape—the sun, a tree, a rocket ship—on your child's back and let the guessing game begin!

554 Desert Island

The desert-island question often leads to lively debate, with everyone adamantly defending their tastes.

AGE: 6–10 YRS

CATEGORY: PARENT & CHILD/ INDOOR

NUMBER OF CHILDREN: ONE OR MORE

Materials:
Small notepad
Pencil

Play:
"If you were stranded on a desert island, what ten items would you really want to take with you?" You pose the questions, and your child writes his list on a piece of paper. See if you can guess what's on his list. Mix it up for the second round of play, with your child posing the question while you write down your most favorite can't-do-without-it things, and see if your child can use what he knows about you to guess what's on your list.

555 Ten Foods

"What ten *foods* would you take with you on a desert island?"

556 Family Favorites

Pick a category of foods, such as dessert, ice-cream flavors, breakfast foods, restaurant dishes, or "dishes Dad makes." Each player writes down his five or ten favorite items and the rest of the family guesses what favorite foods each person has on his list.

PARENT TIP

557 House Rules

❝My six-year-old knows that we have 'house rules' concerning playing. Most of these rules involve safety or playing fair. We simply mention a 'house rule' on an as-needed basis when we see him doing something unsafe or when he pushes to do something that he knows is off-limits. What we've noticed is that he often passes these house rules along to the other kids when they come over to play. Recently I overheard him say, 'My dad says we can't leave the backyard, that's one of our house rules,' when a playmate suggested they go down to the schoolyard to play. It's an easy way to talk about what's okay and what is not okay, and also it gives him a way to save face if a friend suggests something he knows is not allowed in our family.❞

—Michael from Ohio

Grade School Play (age 6 to 10)

558 Did You Know?

This splendid storytelling game encourages kids and parents to weave the most outlandish tall tales.

AGE: 6–10 YRS

CATEGORY: PARENT & CHILD/ INDOOR

NUMBER OF CHILDREN: ONE OR MORE

Play:

Find an object in the room and tell a spontaneous tall tale about it. The more outlandish, the better—"Did you know that that purple car outside was once driven by a chimpanzee who was in a rush to get to his doctor's appointment? He hit his big toe with a hammer when he was building a special slide for his friend the giraffe. His toe swelled up like a balloon, and he couldn't fit his foot into his shoe, so he had to come to the doctor's office barefoot!" Each player takes a turn telling a tall tale about any object within his field of vision. (At the end of each tale, I like to show respect for the storyteller by announcing, "I did NOT know that" with great fanfare.)

Friendship

Play is a natural way for children to develop strong social skills and fine-tune their emotional intelligence. Whether your child prefers one best friend or moves easily among many friends, friendship matters. If you ask a six-year-old boy or girl what he or she does with friends, you get variations of the same answer: "We play!"

Here's a quick look at some of the excellent ways your child can grow and learn while playing with friends:

- He learns that each friend has different wants, needs, feelings, and interests, distinctly different from his own.

- She learns to cooperate, take turns, and negotiate.

- He discovers that he can say or do something to help a friend. He can cheer him up, make him laugh, or lend a helping hand. His words and actions can make a difference to others.

- She realizes that there are times when she has to speak up for herself or for what she feels is right.

- He has a chance to practice managing emotions—anger, frustration, impatience.

- She learns that she *can* bounce back after experiencing teasing or rejection from another child.

- He understands the value of trust and loyalty.

- She learns to take responsibility for hurting someone's feelings and learns how to apologize.

559 What's That You're Eating?

This simplified version of charades is always good for a few laughs.

AGE: 6–10 YRS

CATEGORY: PARENT & CHILD/ INDOOR

NUMBER OF CHILDREN: ONE OR MORE

Play:

The first player thinks of a food and silently pretends to eat this particular food without props of any kind. The other players guess at what the food is. The wide range of possible pantomimes can make things very interesting. Think of peeling an orange, slicing an apple, picking up one shelled peanut at a time, dipping chicken fingers in honey-mustard sauce, or french fries in ketchup, or eating a hamburger. Everyone takes a turn acting out eating a particular food while the others do the guessing.

560 Rhyming Riddles

There's a rhythm to playing this game, and once your child gets it he'll create loads of quick mismatched sentences for you to figure out.

AGE: 6–10 YRS

CATEGORY: PARENT & CHILD/ INDOOR

NUMBER OF CHILDREN: ONE OR MORE

Play:

Think of a sentence with familiar words, like "I went to the park and played on the slide." Now say this sentence out loud, substituting rhyming words for one or more of the words in the sentence; you might say, "I went to the park and played on the *Clyde.*" Your child tries to guess the correct word or words in the original sentence. (Accent the mismatched word to let your child know which

word is out of sync.) After a few rounds of play, give your child a chance to create sentences while you take a turn guessing. (Provide pencil and paper so your child can write down the original sentence and experiment with rhyming words on paper before announcing his Rhyming Riddle.)

★CLASSIC★
561 Hangman

Who needs Wheel of Fortune*? This classic word game is fun for adults and kids and can be played whenever and wherever there's a pencil and paper.*

AGE: 6–10 YRS

CATEGORY: PARENT & CHILD/ INDOOR

NUMBER OF CHILDREN: ONE

Materials:
Paper
Pencil

Play:

One player will be the Hangman for the first round of play. The Hangman thinks of a word and marks a row of blank dashes on the paper, one dash for every letter of the mystery word. The other player tries to guess a letter in the mystery word. If she guesses incorrectly, the Hangman draws the first line of his "gallows"–the base. He also writes the incorrect guess on the paper as a reminder not to guess it again. If she guesses correctly, the Hangman fills in the appropriate blank, and she can choose to take a guess at the mystery word. If she guesses the mystery word, she beats the Hangman and becomes the new Hangman. If the Hangman completes his drawing before anyone guesses the word, he wins that round of play and takes a second turn at being Hangman.

Craft Activities

Some of the best children's crafts are made from inexpensive, everyday materials. A few scraps of yarn, a shoelace or two, a box of macaroni, or an ordinary shoe box may be all you need to get things started. Rummage through the house to round up your materials, place newspapers (or an old tablecloth) over the kitchen table to designate your craft corner, and you're heading in the right direction. Here are some ideas that allow your child to transform these ho-hum ingredients into something clever, creative, and original with a little help from Mom or Dad.

562 Drip-Drop Postcards

These postcards are colorful and truly unique works of art, though they are created quite simply. (What's more, you can make 45 postcards from one sheet of matte board, so they are quite inexpensive to make.)

AGE: 6–10 YRS

CATEGORY: PARENT & CHILD/ ARTS & CRAFTS

NUMBER OF CHILDREN: ONE OR MORE

Materials:

Yardstick

Pencil

Scissors

32" by 40" sheet of matte board

Washable paints

Disposable foil muffin tin

Plastic eyedroppers (1 for each print color)

Fine-tip marker

Setup:

Using the yard stick, pencil, and scissors, mark and cut up 4"-by-6" postcards from the large sheet of matte board. (You can make 45 postcards from one sheet of matte board!) Pour a small quantity of each color of paint in the compartments of the muffin tin. Lay out one eyedropper for each color of paint.

Create:

You and your child work with two postcards each; place the cards textured (matte) side up on the table. Dip the end of one of the eyedroppers in paint and squeeze the bulb until the dropper is full of paint. Carefully and quickly place this eyedropper over one of the postcards and squeeze to release small circles of color on the postcard. Select another color of paint and, using a clean eyedropper, repeat the same process on this first card. Continue adding additional colors of paint drops in random designs or controlled shapes or letters. (Overlap some of the drops to create different colors altogether.) Pick up the second, blank postcard and gently place it matte side down over the paint-drop card. Use your hand to apply some pressure to the card "sandwich." Gently pry the cards apart and place them faceup on the table to dry. Once they're thoroughly dry, turn them over and use a fine-tip marker to draw a vertical line down their center. Now you've got a postcard!

Tip: These postcards will be a bit heavier, so check that you have the right postage before mailing.

563 Rainbow Necklace

Take a pinch of blue, red, and yellow salt-dough, roll it around, and a beautiful rainbow design comes alive!

QUICK & EASY

AGE: 6–10 YRS

CATEGORY: **PARENT & CHILD/ ARTS & CRAFTS**

NUMBER OF CHILDREN: **ONE OR MORE**

Materials:

Homemade salt-dough (see recipe)

Paper plates

Scissors

Plastic drinking straws

Long, new shoelaces

Cookie sheets (1 for each child)

Setup:

Mix up a batch of homemade salt-dough (see recipe this page). Use scissors to cut about 10 drinking straws in half.

Create:

Pinch off small pieces of dough in each color and roll them together between the palms of both hands, into approximately ²/₃-inch-size balls. Place them on a paper plate. Push a straw through the center of each ball to create holes for stringing. Use a fresh straw piece for each bead, as the straws tend to get clogged with clay. Arrange beads on cookie sheets and bake them for 5 to 7 minutes (depending on the size) at 325°F, then remove them from the oven. (They'll pop in the oven if baked too long.) Allow the beads to cool before handling. The beads will be dry enough to handle (with care) for immediate stringing, but will continue to dry over the next 24 to 48 hours. Tie a large triple knot at one end of a shoelace. Now your child can begin threading her beads onto the string. When the shoelace is filled, untie the triple knot and tie the ends together in a double knot to make a long necklace that easily fits on and off your child's head.

564 Rainbow Noodle Necklace

Make the rainbow beads described above and allow them to dry thoroughly. Thread the beads along with (uncooked) rigatoni pasta pieces to create a necklace with its own unique personality.

*SAFETY ALERT: Keep beads away from infants and toddlers to avoid risk of choking.

Salt-Dough

1 cup salt

½ cup cornstarch

¾ cup water

Assorted food coloring

Mix the salt, cornstarch, and water together in a small saucepan. Place the pan on the stove over low heat and stir the mixture constantly so it does not stick to the bottom. Continue to cook and stir until the mixture thickens and clumps and becomes difficult to stir. (The mixture in the center of the pan will thicken first, so stir that to the side and keep heating and stirring until every bit of the liquid has turned to thick clumps.) Remove from the heat and place the lump of dough on the paper plate, letting it cool to room temperature. Knead the dough until the texture becomes smooth. Divide into smaller lumps and knead a different color of food coloring into each to create colored clay. (Use a little dish detergent and the scouring side of a kitchen sponge to easily remove the food coloring from your hands.)

★ CLASSIC ★

565 Papier-Mâché Bowl

There is something almost indescribable about the pleasure of getting your hands in slippery papier-mâché goop. It's messy, and the goop takes days to dry. And that's part of the appeal.

AGE: 6–10 YRS

CATEGORY: PARENT & CHILD/ ARTS & CRAFTS

NUMBER OF CHILDREN: ONE OR MORE

Materials:

Papier-mâché goop (see recipe right)

Newspaper or recycled vinyl tablecloth

Newsprint paper

Scissors

Medium balloon*

Felt-tipped marker

Large plastic margarine tub

Duct tape

Cookie sheet

Safety pin

Washable paint or nontoxic poster paint

Paintbrush

Setup:

Make the goop (see recipe, page 287) and let it cool. Cover your kitchen table with newspapers. Place a large bowl of goop on the table. Tear or cut newsprint pages into strips about 1" wide and 6" long. (It's best to tear a large quantity of these strips before proceeding to the messy part of this project.) Blow up the balloon and tie it off. Use the marker to draw a line all the way around the balloon, about halfway up from the bottom. (You'll be using the balloon as a mold for the bowl, and your child will be lining up newsprint strips along this marker.) Place the knotted end of the inflated balloon inside the margarine tub and secure the bottom of the balloon to the tub with strips of duct tape. Place the margarine tub (with balloon attached) on the cookie sheet to catch any drips while you work and while the project dries.

Create:

Dip a newsprint strip into the bowl of goop, making sure it is completely covered. Pull the strip out, holding it over the goop bowl, and smooth off any excess goop by sliding your index and middle fingers down the length of the paper strip. Place this strip around the balloon. Add more strips until you've completely covered the balloon up to the "stop line." Now begin to layer, applying four layers of strips. Use your hands to smooth out each strip so that it doesn't have huge bumps or lumps (but don't go crazy here—the finished bowl will have a handmade texture which adds to its beauty).

Allow the bowl three or four days to dry completely (drying time may vary depending on your climate and humidity level). Once the newspaper is dry, pop the balloon with the safety pin and decorate the bowl with paints.

NOTE: You may use newspaper instead of newsprint, but painting over the black ink can be a bit of a challenge.

*SAFETY ALERT: Supervise all balloon play to prevent children less than eight years old from choking on uninflated balloons or balloon pieces. This is a decorative bowl and is not intended for holding food of any kind.

Papier-Mâché Goop

2 cups cold water
½ cup flour
2 cups boiling water
4 tablespoons sugar

Stir the cold water and flour together in a bowl, blending well to dissolve all lumps. Pour 2 cups of water into a saucepan and bring to a boil. Add the cold water and flour mixture, stirring constantly, and bring to a boil. Remove from heat and stir in the sugar. Let this mixture cool.

566 Papier-Mâché Masks

This project is excellent for children with a little prior papier-mâché experience and a flair for creative details.

AGE: 6–10 YRS

CATEGORY: **PARENT & CHILD/ ARTS & CRAFTS**

NUMBER OF CHILDREN: **ONE OR MORE**

Materials:

Newspaper or recycled vinyl tablecloth
Papier-mâché goop (see recipe above)
Newsprint paper
Scissors
Large balloon* (to make 2 masks)
Large plastic margarine tub
Duct tape
Cookie sheet
Safety pin
Washable paint or nontoxic poster paint
Yarn, ribbon, feathers, fabric, etc.
Single-hole punch

Setup:

Cover your kitchen table with newspapers. Make the goop, let it cool, and place a large bowl of it on the table. Tear or cut newsprint into 1" by 6" strips. Tear a large quantity before proceeding to the messy part of this project. Blow up the balloon and tie it off. Place the knotted end of the inflated balloon inside the margarine tub and secure the bottom of the balloon to the tub with duct tape. Place the margarine tub and balloon on the cookie sheets.

Create:

Dip a newsprint strip into the bowl of goop, making sure it is completely covered. Pull the strip out, holding it over the goop bowl, and smooth off any excess goop by sliding your index and middle fingers down the length of the paper strip. Place this strip around the balloon. Repeat this process until the entire balloon is covered with about four layers of goopy paper strips. Allow three to four days for it to dry completely. (Drying times will vary depending on your climate and humidity.) Pop the balloon with a safety pin. Insert scissors at the bottom of the oval and cut the balloon-shaped paper creation in half lengthwise to create two masks. You can help your child cut out eyes and a mouth opening or simply draw eyes, nose, and lips with paints and markers. Decorate with paint, glitter, glue, yarn, feathers, etc. Punch holes on each side of your masks (by the ears) and tie ribbons through the holes, knotting them off on the inside of the masks. Tie the ribbons in a bow to hang this artwork on the wall or tie them to fit your child's head.

TIP: Clean up any spilled goop while it's still damp. (Once it dries, it is more difficult to remove from floors and other surfaces.)

*SAFETY ALERT: Supervise all balloon play to prevent children less than eight years old from choking on uninflated balloons or balloon pieces.

Grade School Play (age 6 to 10)

567 Eco Beads

A green parent's dream—recycling magazines destined for the dump and unleashing your child's creative spirit!

QUICK & EASY

AGE: 6–10 YRS

CATEGORY:
PARENT & CHILD/
ARTS & CRAFTS

NUMBER OF
CHILDREN: ONE
OR MORE

Materials:

Colored pages from magazines

Scissors

Pencil

Nontoxic white glue

String, yarn, dental floss, or rawhide laces

Create:

1. You and your child cut large and small triangles from colorful magazine photos.

2. Roll a paper triangle tightly around a pencil.

3. When you have nearly rolled the entire triangle, place a dab of glue on the point of the triangle still left sticking out, then roll it tightly in and hold in place a few seconds to let the glue begin to set.

4. Slide the bead off the pencil and allow the glue to continue to dry.

5. String these assorted beads on string or yarn, knotting the ends of the string together to create a long necklace that can be easily slipped on and off.

568 Jagged Eco Beads

Use thin sheets of colored paper or tissue paper to create the triangles. Roll as described above, but leave a half-inch of the paper point dangling. Glue the rolled paper at the last point of contact

and hold for a few seconds to let the glue dry. This creates a varied bead with ragged edges. After letting these beads dry completely, string them on the yarn to create a necklace.

569 Personalized Treasure Box

Children love to have a special place for treasured keepsakes; these boxes take on added value over time, so be sure to keep them somewhere safe.

AGE: 6–10 YRS

CATEGORY:
PARENT & CHILD/
ARTS & CRAFTS

NUMBER OF
CHILDREN: ONE
OR MORE

Materials:

Nontoxic white glue

Aluminum pie pan

Small shoe box or chocolate box with lid

Pasta in various shapes
(wheels, macaroni, ziti, shells, etc.)

Paintbrushes

Poster paint

Create:

Pour glue into the pie pan and add a little water to make it more spreadable. Spread a generous layer of glue on the shoe box lid and decorate with pasta pieces. (If you or your child are working slowly or creating an elaborate design, put glue on only one section of the lid at a time so it doesn't dry out before you've done the sticking.) Paint the sides of the box with poster paint, embellish with drawings and designs, and be sure to allow a bit of space for your child's name and age. If your child is willing to go the extra mile, decoratting the sides of the box with strips of fabric is also a nice finishing touch.

570 Button Treasure Box

Decorate the lid with assorted buttons to create a colorful design or spell out your child's name.

Outdoor Play

What can be better than heading outdoors on a warm sunny day to play with your child? You might join in because you know your child enjoys this outdoor playtime, but chances are that you too will reap many benefits and build memories of your own. (And don't be shy about taking a trip down memory lane to recall some of *your* favorite childhood games. Chances are, if it was a fun game for you many years ago, it will be a fun game to play with your child now. Perennial favorites like catch, Frisbee toss, and croquet absolutely never go out of style.) Here are some game suggestions that celebrate the joy of playing together in the great outdoors.

571 | Neighborhood Number Trail

Celebrate the simple pleasure of an afternoon walk—turned into a mathematical scavenger hunt where numbers lurk around every corner.

QUICK & EASY

AGE: 6–10 YRS

CATEGORY:
PARENT & CHILD/
OUTDOOR

NUMBER OF
CHILDREN: ONE

Materials:
Pencil
Paper

Setup:
Walk down your block or around your neighborhood without your child and create a list of clues about 10 things in your neighborhood that have a number attached to them—"The number of stones around Mrs. Johnson's mailbox," for example. Write these clues on lined paper, skipping lines for answers and leaving room at the bottom for the grand total.

Play:
Give your child the list of clues you made and set off on a walk together around the neighborhood. (Remember to bring a pencil and follow the same route that you traveled while making your list.) Your child reads each clue, figures out what number the clue refers to, and writes that number on the list. (Give additional tips and clues as needed along the way.) Once you're back inside, add up all the numbers to come up with a grand total, the Neighborhood Number of the day.

572 | The Magic Number Is . . .

This is a terrific game for family walks. Let your child pick a number from 10 to 20. As you walk, hunt through the neighborhood for the magic number. Look on mailboxes, license plates, phone numbers painted on trucks and vans, house numbers, and anywhere else you can think of. Carry a small notepad and pencil and keep track of how many magic numbers were found.

> **"**With television it's so easy to become a passive viewer of other people's ideas and other people's lives instead of becoming the creator of your own life and your own ideas.**"**
>
> **—T. A. Barron**
> author of *The Lost Years of Merlin* series

573 Horse

Children always love games that look like grown-up sports, and here's one that can easily be modified to fit your child's age and abilities.

AGE: 8–10 YRS

CATEGORY: PARENT & CHILD/ OUTDOOR

NUMBER OF CHILDREN: TWO OR MORE

Materials:
Adjustable basketball hoop
Playground ball or basketball

Setup:
Set the basketball goal (hoop and net) at the right height for the players. Toss a coin to see which player goes first.

Play:
The first player takes a shot from anywhere on the court or pavement and attempts to sink the ball in the basket. If she doesn't make a basket, she earns an *H* (the first letter of the word *horse*) as a penalty, and the second player takes a turn. If she does make the basket, the second player must stand in the exact same spot as she did for his shot. If the second player misses the shot, he earns the letter *H*. The game continues in this way, with the letters progressing through the word *horse*. The first player to collect all the letters in the word *horse* loses the game.

574 Beanbag Horseshoes

Here's a kid-friendly variation of the old favorite.

AGE: 6–10 YRS

CATEGORY: PARENT & CHILD/ OUTDOOR

NUMBER OF CHILDREN: TWO OR MORE

Materials:
Hula-Hoop
Beanbags
Roll of 2"-wide painter's tape

Setup:
Mark starting and finish lines, tailored to your child's age and tossing skills by placing a 6-foot-long strip of tape on the grass. (Roll out the tape, sticky side down, in 12-inch sections, pressing it down with your feet as you go.) Place the Hula-Hoop on the ground near the finish line.

TIP: If the lawn is wet, and your tape lines aren't sticking, see "Start and Finish" box, page 348.

Play:
Eacjh player stands behind the starting line and gets three turns tossing beanbags inside the hoop. Each bag that lands squarely inside scores two points. Each beanbag landing on the hoop scores one point. The first player to score 15 points wins.

Toys and Games for a Sunny Day

Badminton racket and birdie

Balsa-wood plane

Basketball

Bike (with helmet)

Bubble wand and bubbles

Croquet

Frisbee

Gloves and ball (for catch)

Hula-Hoop

In-line skates (with helmet, knee, and elbow pads)

Kickball

Kite

Nerf football (for catch)

Sidewalk chalk

Soccer ball and goal

Stopwatch

Styrofoam glider plane

Wagon

Wiffle ball and bat

Playing with Others

In the six- to ten-year-old range, friendships become increasingly important. The way children build friendships (and learn friendship skills) is by playing with others. The more diverse the assortment of games, the more likely they are to test different approaches to getting along with their peers. Some ideas work, while others need improvement. And so it goes in the world of learning as you play.

Set the Stage for Successful Playdates at Your Home

In this age range there's a fine line between *setting the stage* for successful playdates and *micromanaging*. Children can benefit from a bit of help behind the scenes to set things up or handle problems, but they also need the freedom to direct and manage their own play. Here are a few appropriate things you can do to encourage positive play with other kids at your home:

- Plan ahead. Have your child call a friend to set up a playdate several days in advance.

- Arrange playdates with a child who seems to share some interests with your own child.

- Prior to the playdate, ask your child which unplugged games would be most fun for the two children to play together. (Brainstorming in this way makes it less likely the children will automatically gravitate toward video games.)

- When children say "We're bored," be ready with a few suggestions to help rejuvenate their play.

- Try to keep siblings occupied with other activities so they don't interfere with the playdate. (This is a terrific time for some one-on-one attention from Mom or Dad.)

- Have healthy snacks on hand. When children run and play they get hungry and tired and need to recharge. Be aware of any food allergies your child's friend may have.

- Supervise to ensure the children's safety, and be aware of what they are doing and where they are at all times.

- Get to know the parents of your child's friends. (Write down their phone numbers too.)

Grade School Play (age 6 to 10)

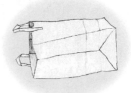

Indoor Play

Some of the games here are silly. Some are guessing games, card games, and storytelling games that result in incredible tall tales. There are also classic play ideas that have stood the test of time like putting on a play or creating a band. So let's celebrate friendship and fun with some of these wonderful games!

★ CLASSIC ★

575 Forts and Hideouts

Watch a pile of blankets magically turn into a spaceship, a dollhouse, or a tent on the edge of the Grand Canyon.

QUICK & EASY

AGE: 6–10 YRS

CATEGORY: PLAY WITH OTHERS/INDOOR

NUMBER OF CHILDREN: TWO

Materials for fort building:
Blankets

Flat or fitted bedsheets

Tablecloths

Large pillows

Tables, chairs, or other furniture

Heavy cushions or books

Materials to bring inside the fort:
Sleeping bag

Safe camping gear (compass, pots and pans, water bottles)

Maps and books

Action figures or dolls

Play:
The children drape the sheets and blankets over furniture to create a hideout or fort they can cozy up in. (Secure the sheets with heavy cushions or books. Use tape on the sheets if needed.) Once the fort is complete, the children enter—and from there, their imaginations take over.

576 Giant Cardboard Box Forts

Huge appliance boxes make some of the best indoor or outdoor forts for playtime with friends. Gather up one or two of these boxes before your child's playdate and you'll be amazed at how much time and imagination goes into turning this ho-hum box into something special. (See pages 152–153.)

577 Last Laugh

Warning: This game may cause excessive giggling in some children.

QUICK & EASY

AGE: 6–10 YRS

CATEGORY: PLAY WITH OTHERS/INDOOR

NUMBER OF CHILDREN: THREE OR FOUR

Setup:
One player volunteers to be the comic and moves to the middle of the room; the other players form a semicircle around him so that everyone can see the comic's face.

Play:
The comic begins making silly faces and comical movements in silence. The other players try their best to keep a straight face through all the comic actions. Every player who laughs must move to the center and team up with the comic to make the other players laugh. The person who maintains a straight face when all the other players have moved to the middle wins. Another comic is then selected for the next round.

578 Animal Style

For a noisier version of the game, allow the comic to add animal sounds to his antics. (This version moves rather quickly, as it's hard for the children not to laugh at the donkey noises of a clever comic.)

579 Unbelievable!

In this game of fill in the blanks, each tall tale should get more preposterous than the next.

AGE: 6–10 YRS

CATEGORY: PLAY WITH OTHERS/INDOOR

NUMBER OF CHILDREN: THREE OR MORE

Materials:
Magazines (with lots of photos/ advertisements)

Scissors

Large paper grocery bags

Markers

Newsprint paper or large writing tablet

Pencils

Setup:
Clip 10 interesting photos from magazines from each of the following categories:

1. Person (a grandmother, a baby, a farmer, a man with a red hat)

2. Machine (a car, a washing machine, a bicycle, a wagon, an airplane)

3. Place (a house, a restaurant, a garage, a park bench, a forest)

4. Food (a pumpkin, some pasta, a hamburger, a bowl of soup)

Write the numbers 1 through 4, each on its own grocery bag. Place the magazine clippings in the appropriate bags, keeping each category separate.

Copy the following four lines on one sheet of newsprint paper:

The _____
(describe the person from bag #1)

drove the _____
(describe the machine from bag #2)

over to the _____
(describe the place from bag #3)

and ate a very large _____.
(describe the food item from bag #4)

He didn't feel very well after eating the

_____.
(food item above)

So here's what happened next: _____

_____.
(make up a silly or serious ending to the story)

Play:
The children sit in a circle with the four grocery bags in the center. The first child draws one photo from each of the four bags and places them side by side. He reads (with your help if necessary) the first line of the story and fills in the blank by describing the appropriate photographs, embellishing with great detail.

Here's how a sample story might go: "The <u>man with big bushy eyebrows</u> drove the <u>washing machine</u> over to the <u>barn</u> where he ate <u>a 500-pound french fry</u>. He didn't feel very well after eating the <u>big, greasy french fry.</u> So, here's what happened next: <u>He went home to lie down, and in the morning, there were 500 potatoes in the bed with him!</u>"

At the end of the story, the other players shout, "Unbelievable!"

The second player draws photos from the four grocery bags and begins the next story in the same way. (Write down these embellishments in

Grade School Play (age 6 to 10)

UNPLUGGED PLAY

a notebook; that way you can revisit and revise these marvelous stories for more fun in the future.)

580 One Fine Day!

Clip photos from four categories:

1. Food

2. Household appliance, furniture, kitchen or bathroom item

3. Large object of any kind

4. Tool

Proceed as above, substituting this story line:

Mamma called the repairman today, because a

_____
(describe the food from bag #1)

had gotten stuck in the _____.
(describe the appliance from bag #2)

But when the repairman went in there he found more trouble!

A _____ was stuck in there too!
(describe the large object from bag #3)

So, he got a _____
(describe the tool or gadget from bag #4)

and was finally able to get the _____ out and saved the day.
(very large object above)

When the repairman left, Mamma sat down at the kitchen table and said (pause): "This has been one fine day!"
(All the players join in on "one fine day!")

Tip: For maximum fun, and to inspire a variety of outlandish stories, gather both popular magazines and professional magazines (with focus topics such as medicine, farming and gardening, culinary arts, etc.)

581 Haywire

Can you make the other players go "haywire" by saying one thing and doing another?

AGE: 6–10 YRS

CATEGORY: PLAY WITH OTHERS/INDOOR

NUMBER OF CHILDREN: THREE OR MORE

Setup:
One child moves to the middle of the room as the leader; the other players form a semicircle around her, so that everyone can see her face.

Play:
The leader turns to one player and touches one part of her own face or body while naming another part; if she touched her chin, she might say, "This is my eyebrow." The player must respond by doing the reverse (touching his eyebrow and saying, "This is my chin"). The leader tries to stump this player with five more mixed-up messages. Players get one point for each correct response; the leader doesn't play for points. Each player has the same number of turns and the one with the most points wins.

Deciding Who Goes *First*

Forget Shakespeare's "To be, or not to be?" . . . When children play, it's "Who goes first?"—now *that* is the question! Here are some easy, no-grumbling ways to decide:

• Toss a coin, with one player tossing and the other calling "heads" or "tails" prior to the toss.

• Roll a set of dice, agreeing ahead of time that the player with the highest number goes first.

• The youngest player goes first!

★ CLASSIC ★

582 Grand Canyon

This is a great memory game to play with a group of children who are just getting to know one another.

QUICK & EASY

AGE: 6–10 YRS

CATEGORY: **PLAY WITH OTHERS/INDOOR**

NUMBER OF CHILDREN: **TWO TO FOUR**

Setup:
All the children sit in a circle.

Play:
One player begins the game by announcing, "I'm going to the Grand Canyon and I'm going to take _____," filling in the blank with any word that begins with the same letter as the name of the player to his right. (If her name is Mary, for example, he might say, "I'm going to the Grand Canyon and I'm going to take *mustard*.") Then the player to his right takes a turn, and so on. When each player has taken a turn, the first player announces, "I'm going to the Grand Canyon and I'm going to take _____," filling in the blank with an item beginning with the *second* letter of Mary's name, *"almonds,"* for example. The game continues with all the letters of each child's first and last names.

583 Grand Canyon Names

In this more challenging version of the game, the first player lists one item for each letter of her own name in one single round of play ("I'm going to the Grand Canyon and I'm going to take *mustard, an apple, a radish, and yogurt*.") The next child in the circle must remember and recite everything mentioned by the previous player before going on to the items that correspond to all the letters in his first name.

584 Green-Groceries

This is a fast-action guessing game using alphabet cards that can be easy or very challenging.

QUICK & EASY

AGE: 6–10 YRS

CATEGORY: **PLAY WITH OTHERS/INDOOR**

NUMBER OF CHILDREN: **THREE OR FOUR**

Materials:
  23 blank index cards
  Marker
  A die

Setup:
Using the index cards, write one letter of the alphabet on each card, except for the letters *V, X, Y,* and *Z.* Shuffle the cards and place the deck facedown on the floor. The children sit in a circle with the die and alphabet cards in the center.

Play:
One player draws an alphabet card from the deck and rolls the die. The number he rolls determines the number of grocery store items, beginning with the letter on the alphabet card, he must think of. If, for example, he draws the letter *B* and rolls the number 4, he must quickly call out four items found in a grocery store starting with the letter *B*—beans, bananas, bread, and beets. This game is fun to play without keeping score, or you can give each player one point for every item called out. (Chance is a big part of this game, as the player who rolls the highest numbers has the best chance of winning.)

> ❝*Activities are the gel for the friendship!*❞
>
> **—Fred Frankel, Ph.D.**
> coauthor of *Good Friends Are Hard to Find*

Grade School Play (age 6 to 10)

585 Milk Shake Mix-Up

Here's a card game inspired by a milk shake maker who got an eggplant confused with blackberries.

AGE: **6–10 YRS**

CATEGORY:
PLAY WITH OTHERS/INDOOR

NUMBER OF CHILDREN:
THREE OR MORE

Materials:

Garden seed catalog

54 blank playing cards (or 3"-by-5" index cards)

Markers

Setup:

Using a seed catalog for ideas and spelling, the group creates 14 playing cards with the name of a different veggie on each card: eggplant, rutabaga, cabbage, and so on. Then the group does the same with fruit on 26 of the blank cards: peach, plum, date, strawberry, repeating fruits as needed to fill out the cards. On the remaining 14 cards, the group writes, "Enjoy a milk shake." Shuffle the deck of cards and place it facedown in the middle of the table.

Play:

A player may have no more than four cards at any time; fruit cards are worth one point and vegetable cards are worth zero. When a player gets a "Milk shake" card, she must show all her cards, receive her score, and turn her four cards facedown in the "discard" pile in the center of the table. Immediately after discarding her hand, this player takes four new cards from the dealer's deck to continue the game.

To begin, each player draws four cards from the deck without letting the other players see their cards. One player is chosen to start the game. If the first player has only fruit and veggie cards, she says "pass" and holds on to all four of her cards; then the player to her right proceeds in the same way, passing or showing his cards, depending on his hand.

Once everyone has either passed or shown their cards, each player must discard one card and select another from the dealer's deck in the center of the table (not to be confused with the discard pile); a player's best bet is to discard veggie cards. Once the deck of cards is depleted, shuffle the discard pile and continue playing. The first player to get 20 points wins the game. (Or you can set the kitchen timer; the player with the most points at the buzzer takes the game.)

A Little Help for the Bossy Child

Children notice when another child is bossy and always wants to run the show. If your child tends to boss her playmates around, a casual conversation behind the scenes can help her think of other ways to play. A good starting point for this conversation might be, "What would it feel like to you if Susan was always deciding what to play and bossing you around?" Then, brainstorm with your child about a plan that would allow each child to go "first" in a game or to decide what to play next, and practical ideas for sharing toys. When a playmate arrives, you might encourage the children to write a list of their three favorite things to play. Write each play idea on a little slip of paper, fold these papers in half, and drop them in a jar. The visiting playmate gets to pick a play idea from the jar first. Whenever they tire of a game, they can take turns drawing the next play idea from the jar.

586 Monkeyshines

Put a few heads together and see what kind of outlandish stories you can come up with.

AGE: 6–10 YRS

CATEGORY: **PLAY WITH OTHERS/INDOOR**

NUMBER OF CHILDREN: **THREE OR MORE**

Materials:
- Full-color magazines (1 for each child)
- Scissors
- Large basket or bowl
- Kitchen timer

Setup:

The group cuts one photo from a magazine of a person or animal who will become the "main character" in this progressive, collaborative story. This photo is placed faceup on the table for everyone to see. Next, each child cuts photos of 10 or more objects, such as a washing machine, car, door, shoe, baby bottle, and so on. Fold the photos in half and place them in the basket. Set the kitchen timer for 5 to 8 minutes, depending upon the number of players. Once the children get into the spirit and rhythm of quickly inventing these tall tales, you may choose to shorten or lengthen the playtime.

Play:

One player begins the story by giving the main character a name and three traits or details (his age, his job, where he lives, his best friend's name). Then the opening storyteller passes the photo to the next person, who draws two "object photos" from the basket. This player invents the next few lines of this outlandish story by looking at the two items in the photos. If, for example, the items are a shoe and microwave, he might weave a tale in which the character is late for school because his shoe explodes in the microwave. Each player draws two photos from the basket and uses these items to create a progressive story of mayhem and monkeyshines. This story goes round and round, with each player adding to the story, and when the buzzer finally sounds, the player next in line pulls two photos from the basket and creates an audacious ending to the story!

PARENT TIP

587 Winners and Losers

"We try to communicate the idea to our seven-year-old son that it's a fact of life; when you play a game, sometimes you win and sometimes you lose. And it's this way for everyone. He really likes professional baseball, so we read the scores in the paper together. He sees for himself that his favorite players have good days and bad days and their teams win sometimes and lose other times. We like to say to our son, 'The fun happens while you're playing the game, not at the end when you see who wins!'**"**

—Pete from Illinois

Theatrics and Music

The marvelous thing about six- to ten-year-olds inventing stories, puppet shows, and songs is that their emerging interests (favorite heroes, book characters, etc.) can easily be worked into the action. If, for example, your son is a big sports fan, he may try his hand at writing a skit called "The Night Before the Super Bowl" (see Center Stage, page 300), with his favorite quarterback becoming the main character in the plot. Or perhaps your child loved reading *Charlotte's Web*. The beloved animals in this classic can experience new adventures in your child's puppet show. If you encourage your child to follow his interests and stretch his imagination, all sorts of plots and theatrics will unfold. Here are some activities to launch your child into the magical world of at-home theatrics, storytelling, and music making.

588 Stick Puppets

Gather up a few supplies so your child can make clever stick puppets with his friends.

AGE: 6–10 YRS

CATEGORY:
PLAY WITH
OTHERS/THEATER
& MUSIC

NUMBER OF
CHILDREN:
TWO OR MORE

Materials:
Wooden paint stir-sticks
(available at building supply
or paint stores)

Markers

Yarn

Scraps of ribbon and fabric

Play:
The children wrap ribbon and fabric scraps around the stick to create clothes and costumes. They can then attach them to the stick with tape, rubber bands, or yarn. Make a braid or wrap yarn around the top of the stick to create hair, and finish the puppet off by using markers to draw eyes, nose, mouth, and a mustache.

589 Puppet Stage

A cardboard box makes quite a creative stage for a puppet show.

AGE: 6–10 YRS

CATEGORY:
PLAY WITH
OTHERS/THEATER
& MUSIC

NUMBER OF
CHILDREN:
TWO OR MORE

Materials:
Large or medium cardboard box

Scissors

Construction paper

Scotch tape

Markers

Assorted props

Play:
Remove all four flaps from the bottom. Tuck the four top flaps into the box for support. Turn the box on its side to create an open "window" or stage. The children use construction paper and tape to make a front curtain on the box that runs along the top and partway across each side. They can also decorate the inside walls and floor of the stage, and add props that go along with the story. Set this box on the kitchen table, and the puppeteers will crouch or kneel behind to put on the production. They will hold the puppets up in the air, just high enough to see the characters, without seeing the puppeteers' arms.

★CLASSIC★

590 Put on a Puppet Show

There's a lot of creativity going round and round when kids invent their own puppet show.

AGE: 6–10 YRS

CATEGORY:
PLAY WITH OTHERS/THEATER & MUSIC

NUMBER OF CHILDREN:
TWO OR MORE

Materials:

Large bedsheet or blanket

Book of favorite fairy tales

Paper and pencil

Small props for the stage (doll furniture and other small pieces)

Puppets and small stuffed animals

Roll of tickets (available at office supply or party supply stores)

Chairs

Setup:
Drape a large bedsheet over the kitchen table (or make your own puppet stage). The puppeteers will hide under the covered table, with the puppets performing in front of the curtain.

Play:
The children select a story, create the characters, write a short script, set up the stage, and rehearse the play. This process can stretch over several hours and finish off with a real audience of parents and siblings watching the puppet show at the end of the afternoon.

Jump-start:

- *Fairy Tale* Pick a classic fairy tale and have each child pick one or two characters to play. The children then write or plan out a short script with the basic action of the fairy tale reduced to several scenes. Each child can write his character's lines and read them (after rehearsing) or simply have the action in mind and ad-lib one or two lines for each scene.

- *After the Happy Ending* The children write an extension (or new ending) for a classic fairy tale.

- *Laying Down the Law* The children invent a magical city with an evil king or queen who has made a new law that everyone dislikes. (Perhaps all the dogs and cats must move away to another town!) The children work together to invent the main characters and assign them names and decide what the town's people (or animals) will do to stop the law from being passed. Once the basic story is decided, the children work together to write a few lines for each character in the play.

George, the Seven-Year-Old Playwright

My friend Kiki said to her son George one day, "When I was a kid, I had a friend who wrote his own play, got his friends to be the actors, and charged their parents $1.50 to come watch!" It's a funny thing how a little comment like this can launch a child into action. Indeed, George was smitten. He wrote his own story about favorite superheroes, turned it into a script, gathered friends and siblings to be the actors, assembled costumes from the dress-up box, and put props in the garage to create the set; the actors rehearsed their lines, they set up chairs for the audience, and he really, truly did charge all the parents $1.50 to watch the play. It was a memorable day for the writer and director, the actors and audience alike.

591 | Center Stage

Some kids will enjoy inventing a short story and ad-libbing a play on the spot, while others will string this activity over several days.

AGE: **6–10 YRS**

CATEGORY: **PLAY WITH OTHERS/THEATER & MUSIC**

NUMBER OF CHILDREN: **TWO OR MORE**

Materials:

Paper and pencil for script writing

Costumes and makeup for the actors

Furniture and props for the stage

Setup:

Two or more children work together to create the story for the play and turn it into a script. (One child will often take the lead, working favorite childhood stories or action heroes into the play.) Parents, siblings, grandparents, and neighbors can be invited to attend the performance; if that's the case, help the children by setting out chairs for the audience. (The children can make tickets themselves or use real tickets, available at office supply stores.)

Play:

This creative venture may occur spontaneously over the course of one afternoon or be planned and stretched out over several weekends. This is a wonderful collaborative play idea for children to undertake primarily on their own. Some plays will involve one scene and two friends acting, others may be more elaborate.

Let's Play Band

Sure, lots of children six to ten years old take formal music lessons, but they *still* get a charge out of playing around with musical instruments or singing with friends. In fact, if you have kid-friendly musical instruments around, children this age are notorious for creating their own impromptu "band" for the day. Here are some kid-friendly instruments that are excellent for spontaneous jam sessions:

Bongos

Boomwhackers (percussion tubes)

Calypso steel drum for children

Castanets

Child's dulcimer

Child's guitar

Claves

Conga (child's)

Cowbell with mallet

Drums

Glockenspiel

Glock-guitar

Handbells

Harmonica

Kazoo

Maracas

Melody lap harp

Piano or keyboard

Recorder

Slide whistle

Tambourine

Triangle

Ukulele

Xylophone

Guessing Games and Wordplay

There's a whole lot of thinking going on when children six to ten play the guessing games and wordplay games below. And each player brings his unique personality to the table—so be prepared for some silly antics and wild and crazy guesses. Sometimes it's a quick response that wins out, and other times mulling over the clues guarantees success. In either case, your child will discover the pleasure of using brain power, memory, and observation skills for play.

592 Alphabet Detective

What letters are missing from the alphabet? Is it the Q? Maybe the Z. Spot the missing letters quickly!

QUICK & EASY

AGE: 6–10 YRS

CATEGORY:
PLAY WITH
OTHERS/GUESSING
& WORDPLAY

NUMBER OF
CHILDREN:
TWO OR MORE

Materials:
Index cards
Pencils
Kitchen timer

Setup:
Write one letter of the alphabet on each index card (*A* to *Z*).

Play:
Shuffle the deck of cards and place the deck facedown on the ground. Player no. 1 takes three cards from the deck and, keeping them facedown, sets them aside. He sets the timer for two or three minutes and shouts "Go!" Player no. 2 begins laying the rest of the cards faceup in a horizontal line, trying to get them back into alphabetical order so he can figure out which three letters are missing before the timer sounds. One point is scored for each correct letter guessed, for a total of three possible points per round of play. On the next round, the players switch roles. When they come to a stopping point where they've had the same number of turns, the player with the most points wins.

> *" Friendship skills are learned. There's no gene for them. That means you can teach them. Each month look at your child a little closer. What's the one little friendship skill that my child needs this month to be a better human being? "*
>
> **—Michele Borba, Ed.D.**
> former classroom teacher and author of
> *Parents Do Make a Difference* and
> *12 Simple Secrets Real Moms Know*

593 Mystery Circle

This is an excellent game for mind readers (or very good friends)!

QUICK & EASY

AGE: 6–10 YRS

CATEGORY:
PLAY WITH
OTHERS/GUESSING
& WORDPLAY

NUMBER OF
CHILDREN:
TWO OR MORE

Materials:
Large sheets of newsprint paper
Pencils

Setup:
Place a sheet of paper and the pencils on the table. One child will be the Lead Artist and the other child will be the Supporting Artist.

Play:
The Lead Artist thinks of a specific object or animal that could be partially represented by

a circle (a bicycle, for instance). She writes the name of the object she plans to draw on a small piece of paper and, without the other artist seeing it, folds it and puts it in her pocket. The Lead Artist draws the circle on the paper and then adds two more marks, shapes, or lines to the drawing. The Supporting Artist looks at the partial drawing and silently tries to guess the object, and based upon his guess, the Supporting Artist finishes the drawing. (No speaking is allowed until the drawing is complete.) When the drawing is complete, he announces his guess aloud (in other words, he announces the finished object he has just completed). The Lead Artist takes the small, folded paper from her pocket and reads the name of the mystery object to determine if the Supporting Artist made the correct guess. This is a cooperative game, with both players working together and at times trying to stump each other.

Give Your Child a Vocabulary to Handle Emotions

Sometimes when children play together, emotions flare. Frustration or anger may wash over a child like a wave, with an angry outburst putting an end to the play. Children who learn to label their feelings of frustration, anger, crankiness, or sadness are often more able to control those feelings. The child who is familiar with what frustration feels like and can use the word to describe it might be more inclined to say, "Hey, you've been using that big shovel for a long time now. Let's trade and you use this little shovel for a while."

594 Nosy Parker

That pile of old magazines is full of colorful characters to use in this mystery-person guessing game.

AGE: 6–10 YRS

CATEGORY: PLAY WITH OTHERS/GUESSING & WORDPLAY

NUMBER OF CHILDREN: THREE OR MORE

Materials:
Full-color magazines
Scissors
Markers
Construction paper
Large paper grocery bag

Setup:
Tear out 36 photos, each featuring one person, from the magazines. (Select a wide variety of people of varying ages, looks, and clothing.) Trim around the photos so that you focus on one person or their face, with little or no background. Line these photos up on the floor, six rows across and six rows down, creating a square. Using a marker, write a number from 1 to 36 at the bottom right corner of each photo. Cut 36 small rectangles of construction paper and write a number from 1 to 36 on each piece, folding the pieces in half so the numbers are hidden. Put all these strips of paper in the grocery bag. Stir or shake the bag to mix up the numbers.

Play:
The first player draws a slip of paper from the bag and looks at the number without letting the other player see it. The photo with the matching number represents the "mystery person." The player to the first player's right tries to figure out the identity of the mystery person by asking questions. ("Is it a man?" "Does he have blond hair?" "Is he wearing a blue shirt?") Once the correct picture has been identified, it is removed from the floor and set aside; the second player takes a turn drawing a number from the bag, and the player to his right takes a

turn at guessing. (For more of a team approach to guessing, two children can alternate asking questions.) This is a fabulous game to play without keeping score, but if the children want to keep score, they might score one point for every question asked before the correct guess. The person with the *least* number of points wins the game.

Tip: Some children will prefer a guessing game that features only 12 or 24 mystery people, so tailor this game to your child's abilities and interests.

595 Quiz Master

How many foods can you come up with that start with the letter F?

AGE: 6–10 YRS

CATEGORY:
PLAY WITH
OTHERS/GUESSING
& WORDPLAY

NUMBER OF
CHILDREN:
THREE OR MORE
(with adult
assistance for the
youngest children)

Materials:
32 blank playing cards or
   index cards
Markers
Paper and pencils for each player
1-minute egg timer
   (or kitchen timer)

Setup:
Create a card for each letter of the alphabet, omitting the letters *Q, X, Y,* and *Z.* Create another set of cards of familiar "categories" like girls' names, boys' names, sports, creatures, places, foods, books, or book characters. Select one person to be the Quiz Master. Give each child a pencil and paper. Decide in advance how many rounds to play.

Play:
The Quiz Master announces the start of the game, draws one card from the category deck and one card from the letters deck, holding the cards up for everyone to see, and immediately starts the timer. The children quickly write down as many words as possible that start with the selected letter of the alphabet and fall within the selected category. When the time is up, the Quiz Master looks at each child's answers; the child with the most answers wins the round and is given the alphabet card. After the first round, another child becomes the Quiz Master, and the game continues. At the end of the game, the child with the most cards wins. To play without scoring, mix the alphabet cards right back in the deck of cards. In this version, new Quiz Master is selected after five cards have been played.

Good Things Can Happen Through Mixed-Age Play

In the old days, neighborhood kids, siblings, and cousins of various ages played together. The younger kids intently watched the older ones in action. The older kids sometimes paused to let the little ones take a turn. This scenario was not always picture-perfect, but there was a positive benefit to mixed-age play. For one thing, the older kids had a chance to play the role of mentor, showing patience and kindness to someone smaller and less experienced. And the younger kids had access to models who were more experienced than their own peers but more accessible than grown-ups. Today, your children may have fewer opportunities built-in, but on occasion you can set up mixed-age play when friends and family come to visit. If you have an older child at home and a younger child is coming to visit, ask your child to think of two or three things he can show the little one how to play.

Grade School Play (age 6 to 10)

Outdoor Play

Outdoor games provide tremendous opportunities for building friendships and physical fitness. Children experience the thrill of running, chasing, racing, throwing, and hopping—a welcome aternative to the sitting and thinking that goes on during the school day. They learn about being on a team, playing by the rules, and being a good sport. They learn to take turns, to make amends, to take a joke, and to dust themselves off after minor mishaps and misunderstandings. And they blow off steam in a way that just can't be replicated indoors. Here are some games that mix fun, fitness, and friends.

★ CLASSIC ★

596 Call-Ball

Quick reflexes are a plus in this game that involves more than a little scrambling.

AGE: 6–10 YRS

CATEGORY:
PLAY WITH OTHERS/ OUTDOOR

NUMBER OF CHILDREN:
THREE TO FOUR

Materials:

Playground ball or tennis ball

Safe, outdoor play area

Setup:
Players form a circle around one player. Each player in the circle is assigned a number between 1 and 10.

Play:
The player in the center throws the ball high into the air; the moment the ball is airborne, she calls out the number of one of the players. The player assigned that number runs to the center and tries to catch the ball. If she does catch the ball, she becomes the new tosser. If she does not catch the ball, she goes back to the circle and the original tosser continues to throw the ball and call numbers. (For mixed ages or abilities, let everyone take a set number of turns tossing the ball.) This game can also be played by assigning the players days of the week instead of numbers.

597 Obstacle Course Croquet

Designing your own obstacle course with lawn chairs and Hula-Hoops is half the fun.

AGE: 6–10 YRS

CATEGORY:
PLAY WITH OTHERS/ OUTDOOR

NUMBER OF CHILDREN:
TWO OR MORE

Materials:

Lawn chairs, basketballs, Hula-Hoops, or other safe objects to use as obstacles

Welcome mat or magazines

Child's (plastic) croquet set (use the mallets and balls)

Setup:
The children create an obstacle course on the lawn using lawn chairs, basketballs, Hula-Hoops, old shoes, and anything else they can find. Place the welcome mat at the starting point to create "home base," and designate the last obstacle in the course as the endpoint. They should also decide whether the croquet balls go under or around each item in the obstacle course.

Play:
The first player places his croquet ball on the ground just in front of home base and uses the

mallet to tap the ball toward the first item on the obstacle course. The next player places his ball at home base and takes a turn tapping a ball toward the first item. The game continues until each player has maneuvered the entire obstacle course with his croquet ball and mallet.

598 Croquet

The traditional version of croquet is played with mallets, hoops (wickets), stakes, and wooden balls on the lawn. The stakes and hoops are laid out on the lawn in a particular (double-diamond) pattern. The players take turns driving their balls through each of the hoops and scoring points along the way. For children six to ten, you may wish to set up a short course and adjust the rules to suit your child's age and skill level.

PARENT TIP

599 3-Minute Work-It-Out

❝*My sons were having a lot of trouble working out squabbles when they played together, so I instituted the 'three-minute work-it-out-on-your-own' rule. When I overhear them arguing while they play, I'll say, 'Hey, boys, it's time for a three-minute work-it-out alone.' This is basically a signal that they need to come up with a fair way to resolve the argument or I'll come in and settle things. They know that when I settle things, sometimes they have to go to their room or the toy is put away for a few days. So they are motivated to find a friendly solution to their problem.*❞

—Michael from Ohio

600 Beach Blanket Toss

Send the beach ball soaring, run in unison to catch it.

AGE: 6–10 YRS

CATEGORY: PLAY WITH OTHERS/ OUTDOOR

NUMBER OF CHILDREN: TWO

Materials:
   Beach towel or king-size pillowcase
   Inflatable beach ball

Setup:
Spread the beach towel out on the ground with one player standing at each end. Place the inflated beach ball in the center of the towel.

Play:
Each player grabs the two corners at her end of the beach towel or pillowcase. Players take a step or two backward so that the cloth is pulled tight. On the count of three, the players jerk the towel up and send the ball into the air. They catch the ball and work as a team, sending the ball into the air again, and running to catch it with the towel.

Grade School Play (age 6 to 10)

601 | Flyswatter Volleyball

"What could you do with a flyswatter besides swatting flies?" I asked two six-year-old boys in my neighborhood. What a wild assortment of ideas came tumbling out.

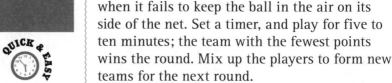

QUICK & EASY

AGE: **6–10 YRS**

CATEGORY: **PLAY WITH OTHERS/ OUTDOOR**

NUMBER OF CHILDREN: **TWO OR MORE**

Materials:

Roll of 2"-wide painter's tape (or masking tape)

Balloons* (or inflatable beach ball)

Unused plastic flyswatters

Kitchen timer or stopwatch

Setup:

In your backyard or the park, create an alternative volleyball net by stretching a 12- to 15-inch piece of painter's tape across the lawn in a straight line. (Roll out about 12 inches of tape at a time, sticky side down, on the lawn, and press it down with your feet, section by section, to hold it firmly in place on the grass.) Use painter's tape to create a boundary behind each side of the net as well.

Tip: If the lawn is wet, and your tape lines are not sticking, see "Start and Finish" box, page 348.

Play:

Create two teams with an equal number of players. Each team is positioned on one side of the net. One player tosses the beach ball in the air and swats it toward the opposite side of the net with his flyswatter. (Players can swat underhand or overhand.) The idea is to keep the ball moving from one side to the other without touching the ground. There is no limit to the number of times a player can swat the ball to keep it in play before sending it to the other side of the net. This game can be played without keeping score, or a simple scoring system can be devised by assigning one point to a team when it fails to keep the ball in the air on its side of the net. Set a timer, and play for five to ten minutes; the team with the fewest points wins the round. Mix up the players to form new teams for the next round.

Note: Balloons are lighter and easier to swat than beach balls.

602 | Chaos

For eight or more players, use two beach balls, which will be swatted from player to player simultaneously. Similar rules are in effect. The object is to keep both balls in the air simultaneously, moving from player to player and side to side. (When one ball touches the ground, the nearest player simply tosses it back into the air.) This version of the game is fast-moving and can be played without keeping score.

603 | Flip-Flop Volleyball

Use clean, adult-size flip-flops instead of flyswatters!

*Safety Alert: Supervise all balloon play to prevent children less than eight years old from choking on uninflated balloons or balloon pieces.

❝ *What a parent wants to do is to be a coach—'I like the way you handled that. You were so nice to that girl.' And you do positive coaching in the friendship arena. And the other thing is: You model it. Kids are great imitators of adults.* ❞

—Michael Thompson, Ph.D.
clinical psychologist and coauthor of
Best Friends, Worst Enemies: Understanding the Social Lives of Children

604 Scoop-Ball

Scooping isn't an Olympic sport, but maybe it should be.

QUICK & EASY

Materials:
Large plastic pet food scoops
  (1 for each child)
Tennis balls or small rubber balls

AGE: 6–10 YRS

CATEGORY:
PLAY WITH
OTHERS/
OUTDOOR

NUMBER OF
CHILDREN:
TWO OR MORE

Setup:
Position players on the lawn a short distance away from each other.

Play:
For two players, one player tosses the ball with his hand and the other player catches the ball with his scoop; or both players toss and catch the ball with the scoops (a bit more challenging). The players can increase the challenge by moving farther away from each other.

605 Scoop-Ball Relay

For four or more players, pair the players off in teams of two. Mark a "net line" in the middle of the lawn, and line the teams up with one player on each side of the line, directly opposite his teammate. Each player has a scoop in hand and each team gets one tennis ball. One player shouts "Scoop," and the ball is tossed from one player's scoop to his teammate's. (No hands are used in this version of the game.) Each time a team successfully tosses and catches the ball, they score one point. When the balls have all been caught, all players take one giant step backward. The designated shouter (player) shouts "Scoop" again as the signal for the next toss to begin. (Only one toss is made by each team, each time "Scoop" is called out.) The team with the most points at the end of each round wins.

★CLASSIC★

606 Monkey in the Middle

Jump up and down, wave your arms in the air, add a few sound effects, and you've got a lively round of play.

QUICK & EASY

AGE: 6–10 YRS

CATEGORY:
PLAY WITH
OTHERS/
OUTDOOR

NUMBER OF
CHILDREN:
THREE

Materials:
Playground ball
Safe, outdoor playing area

Setup:
One child is the "monkey" and stands in the middle of the lawn; the other two players line up on opposite ends of the lawn, about 8 to 10 feet away from the monkey.

Play:
The two ball tossers throw the ball back and forth across the lawn, over or around the monkey. The monkey tries to catch the ball in midair or on a bounce when a player has dropped it. The last player to touch the ball before the monkey catches it becomes the new "monkey" in the next round. (Set a time limit of 2 or 3 minutes for each monkey's turn so that nobody gets stuck out there for too long.)

> **"**In play, you learn how to fix the basketball hoop; you learn how to fix the bicycle chain; you learn how to do the math problem. **"**
>
> **—Edward Hallowell, M.D.**
> psychiatrist and author of
> *Delivered from Distraction* and *CrazyBusy*

Grade School Play (age 6 to 10)

UNPLUGGED PLAY

★ CLASSIC ★

607 Four Square

Four score and seven years ago, were children lucky enough to play this game? Let's hope so!

QUICK & EASY

AGE: 8–10 YRS

CATEGORY:
PLAY WITH
OTHERS/
OUTDOOR

NUMBER OF
CHILDREN:
FOUR OR MORE

Materials:

Chalk

Blacktop or concrete
   playing area

Playground ball

Setup:

Draw a large chalk square—16' by 16' or larger—on the concrete. Divide this square into four equal-size boxes. Label the box in the upper-left corner with the letter *A;* moving clockwise, label the other boxes *B, C,* and *D.* Select one player to start the game in square A. The goal in this game is to spend the most time possible in square A; the B square is second best, C is third, and D is the least desirable square.

Play:

Each of the four players stands in one of the lettered squares. (Any additional players stand in a waiting line several feet away from the box; they'll enter at the D square.) The player in the A square bounces the ball once on the ground and bats it underhand, using one or both hands. She tries to bounce the ball into any other player's square, and then that player bats the ball into another player's square. The ball keeps moving in this way, from square to square, until one of the players gets an "out." A ball is out when any of the following things happens:

- The ball bounces on a line rather than inside a square.

- The ball bounces out of bounds.

- A player hits the ball overhand, or with a closed fist, or doesn't use her hands to bounce the ball.

- A player fails to hit the ball out of her box when attempting to bounce it to another player.

When a player in squares A, B, or C makes an out, he moves into the D square, and each of the other players advances into a more favorable square to continue playing. If there are only four players playing and the player in the D square makes an out, she remains in the D square. If there are players in the waiting line, the player steps out of the square and moves to the end of the waiting line; the first player in the line moves to the D square. There is no particular scoring for this game, but the children try to stay in the A square as long as possible.

608 Playgroup Four Square

This version of Four Square is especially geared to six- and seven-year-olds who can't master the tap and serve routine of ordinary Four Square. This version allows the children one bounce before they catch the ball in their square, and rather than batting the ball they can catch and toss it.

609 Beanbag-Hat Race

Do you run like the wind or take it slow and steady? Give this game a try and discover the answer.

QUICK & EASY

AGE: 6–10 YRS

CATEGORY:
PLAY WITH
OTHERS/
OUTDOOR

NUMBER OF
CHILDREN: FOUR

Materials:

Roll of 2"-wide painter's tape

Beanbags

Kitchen timer

Setup:

Mark a starting and finish line by placing a 6-foot-long strip of tape on the grass. (Roll out the tape, sticky side down, in 12-inch sections, pressing it down with your feet as you go.)

TIP: If the lawn is wet, and your tape lines aren't sticking, see "Start and Finish" box, page 348.

Play:

Each player lines up behind the starting line with a beanbag on his head. Announce, "Ready, set, go!" and set the kitchen timer for 3 minutes. The players run the race with a beanbag on their heads. One point is scored every time a player completes one lap of the race (start to finish and back again). If a child drops his hat, he must go back to the closest start or finish line and resume racing. Keep track of the scores as the players cross the lines.

610 Beanbag-Hat Relay

Divide a larger group into two teams for a relay race. The first player runs one lap with the beanbag on his head; when he reaches the starting line, he hands his hat to the next player, who puts it on his own head and runs a lap. The relay continues in this manner, with the two teams running side by side.

> **❝** Physically challenged children sometimes have problems opening and closing their hands quickly enough to catch a ball. Try taking a child-size baseball glove and putting Velcro in the inside webbing. Then, put Velcro on the ball, use a batting tee, and you've got all the adaptations for throwing, catching, and striking during a five-, six-, or seven-year-old's tee ball game. **❞**
>
> **—Kristi Sayers Menear, Ph.D., CAPE**
> Assistant Professor of Human Studies at the
> University of Alabama at Birmingham

611 Waterlogged

A friendly game of catch using water balloons.

QUICK & EASY

AGE: 6–10 YRS

CATEGORY:
PLAY WITH
OTHERS/
OUTDOOR

NUMBER OF
CHILDREN:
TWO OR MORE

Materials:

Balloons*

Water

Bathing suits

Plastic laundry basket

Setup:

Fill balloons with water. Gently place them in the laundry basket. Position two players 3 feet apart, facing one another. With three or more players, they'll stand in a circle.

Play:

One child begins a game of toss. Each time the balloon is caught, the players each take a small step backward. Replace balloons as needed.

*SAFETY ALERT: Supervise all balloon play to prevent children less than eight years old from choking on uninflated balloons or balloon pieces.

612 Hopscotch

Toss, hop, and balance—a physical test of coordination and concentration.

AGE: 6–10 YRS

CATEGORY:
PLAY WITH OTHERS/ OUTDOOR

NUMBER OF CHILDREN:
TWO OR MORE

Materials:

Chalk

Sidewalk

Smooth, flat stone or bottle cap for each player

Setup:
Draw the hopscotch grid on the pavement using chalk.

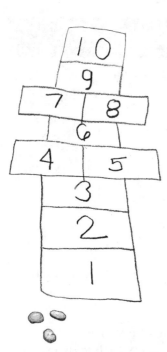

Play:
Select one player to go first. This player tosses his stone on the square marked 1. He then jumps over this square, hopping on one foot, taking care not to step on the lines or hop out of bounds. The player hops on one foot on any square that is positioned single file (the 1, 2, 3, 6, 9, and 10 squares) and may hop and land on two feet on the squares arranged side by side, such as the 4 and 5, and the 7 and 8 squares. On each play, when the player gets to the number 10 square, at the end of the grid, he must hop into that square using one foot, turn around (without his other foot touching the ground), and head back to the beginning square. When he gets back to the square that is in line immediately before the square with his stone, he pauses, stoops down, and retrieves the stone and the hops back to the starting line on each remaining square. If he has successfully hopped from one end to the other without stepping on a line, going out of bounds, or putting his other foot down when on a single file square, he takes another turn and tosses his stone on the number 2 square and continues. Once a player fouls out, the next player takes a turn. (When the fouled-out player's turn comes around again, he starts out all over again on the numbered square that he fouled out on during his previous turn.) The game continues in this way until one player completes the entire grid and wins the game.

613 Beanbag Hopscotch

Draw a starting line about 2 feet behind the first square. Using the same hopscotch grid, the children play the game by tossing a beanbag onto the numbered squares in sequence. If the first child makes his first toss into square number 1, he picks up the beanbag, returns to the starting line, and aims for square number 2. When his beanbag hits the line or goes out of bounds, the second child takes a turn. When it's time for a second turn, the children start wherever they left off, aiming for the square they fouled out on. The first child to move through all the squares and land on the 10 wins the game.

614 Inside

If it's raining outside, stay indoors and use tape to mark the grid on the floor or carpet.

615 | # Spaghetti and Meatballs

Tonight's special is flying meatballs with a side of giggling and tumbling.

QUICK & EASY

Materials:

Large colander with handles

Laundry basket

Ping-Pong balls or newspaper balls
(crumpled up pieces of newspaper)

AGE: 6–10 YRS

CATEGORY: **PLAY WITH OTHERS/ OUTDOOR**

NUMBER OF CHILDREN: TWO

Play:
Both children stand in the middle of the lawn with one child designated as the Meatball Tosser and the other as the Catcher. (The catcher is given the colander and the tosser has a laundry basket full of balls.) The tosser throws the meatballs one at a time way up into the air, and the catcher runs to catch each ball in her strainer. After all the balls have been thrown, the players swap positions and play another round.

The Importance of "I'm Sorry"

One of my parenting mottos is *Every child needs to learn to apologize.* I offer this in part because of the adults we have all encountered who step on the toes of others and can't bring themselves to apologize. Young children are just learning to get along with others, and they will make mistakes. The truth is, we all do from time to time, so it's important that making amends becomes an acceptable part of life. In fact, children like having something concrete they can do when they know they've been unkind. Let your kids know that they can say "I'm sorry" and that they can also *show* they are sorry with actions and kind deeds. Here are a few ways to help your child learn this important friendship skill:

• Be a good role model. Take responsibility when you have hurt someone's feelings or been short-tempered, and make appropriate apologies.

• Teach your child that if he realizes he's been unfair while playing, he can immediately say, "I'm sorry" and offer "You go first," or an extra or longer turn.

• Let children know it's okay to apologize later too. When your child comes home after making a mistake, let him know he can follow up with a call to the friend to say, "I was thinking about what I said (or did) and I'm sorry to have hurt your feelings (or been unfair). It won't happen again. I hope we can still be friends."

• Sometimes both friends have been unkind. In this case, your child can extend the olive branch by saying, "I'm sorry for my part of the argument we had today." Often, this prompts the other child to reciprocate and gives both a bridge back to friendship.

• Encourage your child to make amends if he has damaged or broken a friend's toy. He should use his own (allowance) money to buy a replacement toy and give it to his friend along with a short apology.

UNPLUGGED PLAY

616 Net-less Badminton

Sounds spiffy, easy to learn, and those little birdies are just so cute.

QUICK & EASY

AGE: **6–10 YRS**

CATEGORY:
PLAY WITH OTHERS/ OUTDOOR

NUMBER OF CHILDREN:
TWO OR MORE

Materials:
- Roll of 2"-wide painter's tape
- Badminton rackets
- Birdie (officially known as a shuttlecock)

Setup:
Mark off a large rectangular playing area on the lawn using tape for the boundaries. (Roll out about 12 inches of tape at a time, sticky side down, pressing it down with your feet as you go to hold it firmly in place on the grass.) Divide the court in half with another strip of tape, creating a "net."

TIP: If the lawn is wet, and your tape lines aren't sticking, see "Start and Finish" box, page 348.

Play:
Each player stands on one side of the net. One player serves the birdie; he can tap it as many times as he needs to get it over to his opponent's side. The opponent returns the birdie, using as many swats as necessary. They try to keep the birdie in the air as long as possible—no scoring necessary.

617 Classic Badminton

In the traditional game, a net is placed in the center of the lawn. A serving line is created about 3 inches behind each back boundary of the court, and the players take turns serving and volleying the birdie, trying to keep it

airborne when it's on their own side. The serving player only scores if he is serving and his opponent drops or misses the birdie. (The server continues to serve until he makes an error—either sending the birdie out of bounds or missing a returned birdie.) When the server makes an error, the other player becomes the new server. The first player to score 21 points wins.

Deciding Who Is "It"

Gather the players in a circle and have each child place both fists in the center. One child calls out the following rhyme, tapping each of the players (including herself) on one or both hands on the beat of the rhyme: "One, two, three, out goes he (or she)!" The person tapped on the last word is eliminated from the circle. The players continue with the rhyme until only one person is left in the circle. This person is "It."

Here are some other rhymes to try:

Eeny, meeny, miney, mo

Catch a tiger by the toe,

If he hollers, let him go,

Eeny, meeny, miney, mo.

One potato, two potato,

Three potato, four,

Five potato, six potato

Seven potato, more.

NOTE: See also "Deciding Who Goes *First*" box, page 294.

618 Skipping Rope

Introduce your child to your favorite jump rope rhymes of yesteryear!

Materials:
Jump rope (9' long)
Sidewalk or paved playing area

AGE: 6–10 YRS

CATEGORY:
PLAY WITH
OTHERS/
OUTDOOR

NUMBER OF
CHILDREN:
THREE OR MORE

Play:
Two children hold the rope while one child jumps to the rhythm of the rope. First-time holders will need a bit of practice synchronizing their rope twirling. See the following variations for classic rhymes to recite while jumping.

619 Red Hot Pepper

Mabel, Mabel, set the table,

Just as fast as you are able.

Salt, sugar, vinegar, mustard . . .

And don't forget the red-hot pepper!
(rope holders turn the rope at high speed)

620 One-Two

One, two, buckle your shoe.
(quickly bend down and touch shoe)

Three, four, shut the door.
(pretend to shut door)

Five, six, pick up sticks.
(quickly bend and pretend to pick up sticks)

Seven, eight, lock the gate.
(pretend to close gate)

Nine, ten, do it again!
(close gate again)

NOTE: With novice jumpers, the children can sing the song and skip the actions; more experienced jumpers can imitate the actions while they jump.

621 Silly-Billy

My boyfriend's name is Billy

He is so silly-silly.

He has forty-nine toes

And a pickle for a nose,

And that's the way the story goes.

622 Down in the Meadow

Down in the meadow where the green grass grows,

There sat Ann as pretty as a rose.

She sang, she sang, she sang so sweet,

Along came her boyfriend
and kissed her on the cheek.

How many kisses did she get that week?

One, two, three, four, five, six . . .

623 Alphabet Rhyme

My name is ___
and I have a dog named ___

We live in ___
and ___ likes to eat ___

One jumper starts with the letter A *and fills in the blanks: My name is Alice, and I have a dog named Andy, We live in Alabama and Andy likes to eat apples. The next jumper takes a turn and repeats the rhyme with words starting with B. This jumping rhyme continues through the letters of the alphabet and can be easily altered to create other silly alphabet rhymes.*

Grade School Play (age 6 to 10)

UNPLUGGED
PLAY

624 Teddy Bear, Teddy Bear

Teddy bear, teddy bear,

Turn around.
   (turn around while jumping)

Teddy bear, teddy bear,

Touch the ground.
   (touch the ground in between jumps)

Teddy bear, teddy bear,

Shine your shoes.
   (bend your leg to touch hand to shoe)

Teddy bear, teddy bear

Read the news.
   (perform action)

Teddy bear, teddy bear,

Go upstairs.
   (lift knees while jumping as if climbing stairs)

Teddy bear, teddy bear,

Say your prayers.
   (perform action)

Teddy bear, teddy bear,

Turn out the light.
   (perform action)

Teddy bear, teddy bear,

Say good night!

625 Dutch Girl

I'm a little Dutch girl

Dressed in blue.

Here are the things

I like to do:

Salute to the captain,
   (perform action)

Bow to the queen,
   (perform action)

Turn my back

On the submarine.
   (perform action)

I can do the tap dance,
   (perform action)

I can do the split,
   (perform action)

I can do the holka-polka

Just like this.
   (perform action)

626 I Love Coffee, I Love Tea

I love coffee, I love tea,

I want ___ to jump with me!

The jumper fills in the blank with the name of a friend he invites to jump with him. They try to jump simultaneously.

> " When a child makes a social mistake, instead of punishing the child for it, sit down with the child and do an autopsy on the situation. What went wrong? What could you have done? What options did you have? What will you do next time? And, through that kind of careful coaching, the social skills of kids can be greatly improved. It's a very, very significant job that parents have. "
>
> **—Richard Lavoie, M.Ed.**
> special education teacher and author of
> *It's So Much Work to Be Your Friend: Helping the Child with Learning Disabilities Find Social Success*

Grade School Play (age 6 to 10)

627 Hop, Stick, and a Jump

"Why don't grown-ups ever hop?" a five-year-old boy asked his grandpa.

AGE: 6–10 YRS

CATEGORY: PLAY WITH OTHERS/ OUTDOOR

NUMBER OF CHILDREN: TWO OR MORE

Materials:
  12 Popsicle sticks or craft sticks (available at teacher supply stores)

Setup:
Place six sticks in a line on the ground about 2 feet apart. Several feet away, create a second line of craft sticks parallel to the first line for a second player.

Play:
Each player stands behind her line of sticks. On one player's "Go," the players start hopping over each stick in their line on one foot. (If a player loses her balance or drops her other foot to the ground momentarily, she has to turn around and hop back over the last stick and then continue on her way.) When a player hops over the last stick in the line, she switches to the other hopping leg and hops back to the starting line, picking up the sticks as she hops. The player who gets back to the starting line first wins.

628 Relay Hop

Divide the players into two teams. You will need six extra sticks for each team. Designate one player on each team as the stick-layer who takes charge of these extra six sticks. As players hop back toward the finish line, picking up their sticks before handing off the relay to the next player, the stick-layer quickly lays down a fresh set of sticks parallel to the (vanishing) first set.

629 Peanut Picnic

Hunt for nuts like little squirrels on a rampage.

AGE: 6–10 YRS

CATEGORY: PLAY WITH OTHERS/ OUTDOOR

NUMBER OF CHILDREN: TWO OR MORE

Materials:
  Colored markers
  50 peanuts or walnuts in the shell
  Paper lunch bags
  Kitchen timer

Setup:
Use the markers to write the number 2 on ten of the peanuts. (These nuts will each be worth 2 points.) Hide all of the nuts outdoors, including the unmarked ones, without the children seeing. Give each player a paper bag.

Play:
Once all the children are outside, announce "Ready, set, go!" as a signal for the hunt to begin. Set the timer for 7 minutes. Each player scours the yard for peanuts. When the timer buzzes, players count the peanuts in their bags and add up the points. Unmarked peanuts are worth 1 point, marked peanuts are worth 2. The player with the most points wins.

630 Team Peanut Picnic

If four players are playing, divide them into two teams. The team with the most points at the end of the hunt wins.

SAFETY ALERT: Find out in advance if any child has a peanut allergy; if so, use wooden clothespins as a substitute.

Grade School Play (age 6 to 10)

631 Pirate's Map Treasure Hunt

Arrrrrr! There's nothing a little pirate likes better than a treasure hunt.

AGE: 6–10 YRS

CATEGORY:
PLAY WITH OTHERS/ OUTDOOR

NUMBER OF CHILDREN: **FOUR**

Materials:

2 shoe boxes or paper grocery bags (treasure chests)

4 apples (treasures)

Newsprint paper

Markers

Setup:

Hide two "treasure chests" indoors or outdoors before the children arrive or while they're otherwise occupied. Try hiding one upstairs and one downstairs, or one inside and one in the backyard, so that each pair of hunters is searching for their treasure in a separate area. Create two separate map-making stations with paper and markers.

Play:

Divide the four children into two pairs. Whisper one treasure location to each pair, so that each team can draw a different treasure map for the other team to follow. Give the mapmakers a few mapmaking hints to help them. It works well for the children to combine a few drawn objects, like trees, bushes, or the back door, with instructions like "Take 10 giant steps, turn right, and take 30 baby steps." Suggest that each pair try to have their pirate maps finished in 20 minutes, and let the treasure hunt begin.

632 Treasure for Two

In this version for two, the children hide the treasure and draw the map, and Mom or Dad searches for the hidden treasure box.

★ CLASSIC ★

633 Statues

The winner isn't just the person who can run the fastest, but also the person who can freeze the fastest.

AGE: 6–10 YRS

CATEGORY:
PLAY WITH OTHERS/ OUTDOOR

NUMBER OF CHILDREN: **THREE OR FOUR**

Materials:

Roll of 2"-wide painter's tape

Setup:

Mark a starting line and finish line on the lawn by placing a 6-foot-long strip of tape on the grass. (The easiest way to do this is to roll out the tape, sticky side down, in 12-inch sections, pressing down with your feet to secure it as you go.) Select one player to be "It."

Tip: If the lawn is wet, and your tape lines aren't sticking, see "Start and Finish" box, page 348.

Play:

All the players except "It" stand at the starting line. "It" stands at the finish line with his back to the other players. After calling out, "Ready, set, go!" he loudly counts to 10; he may vary his speed, counting very fast or very slowly and changing his pace suddenly. While he counts, all his opponents run toward him to try to tag him; as soon as he stops counting, all players must freeze in their tracks like statues. "It" does a quick about-face, and anyone he catches moving is "out" and must move back to the starting line and begin over again. Once "It" has been tagged, he chases all the players as they run back to the starting line; if he manages to tag a player before the starting line, that player becomes the new "It" and the game starts over. If "It" does not manage to tag anyone, he continues to be "It"). (For younger children and mixed-age play, set in place a rotation where every child takes one turn being "It" and chasing players.)

> ❝ Parents of children with disabilities should visit the websites for the Paralympics —www.paralympics.org—and for the Special Olympics—www.specialolympics.org—to see a wide range of individuals with a variety of disabilities participating in individual and team sports. It offers the opportunity to say, 'Oh my goodness, if this person can do this, perhaps my child can too,' because unfortunately, in the general media, we don't often see pictures or news clips of individuals with disabilities being physically active. ❞
>
> **—Kristi Sayers Menear, Ph.D., CAPE**
> Assistant Professor of Human Studies at the University of Alabama at Birmingham

634 Hide-and-Seek

What would summertime be without Hide-and-Seek—running, hiding, counting, and finding—with peepers peeping in the background, and a cool breeze stirring!

AGE: 6–10 YRS

CATEGORY: PLAY WITH OTHERS/ OUTDOOR

NUMBER OF CHILDREN: THREE OR MORE

Setup:
Select a safe grassy area of play. One child is chosen to be "It" to start the game.

Play:
"It" closes her eyes and counts to 100 while all the other players scatter about the playing area and find a place to hide. After she's done counting, "It" calls out "Ready or not, here I come!" and goes about finding people. When she sees someone, she calls out the person's name and describes his hiding place. ("I see Peter hiding behind the palm tree next to the swing set.") Once all the players have been found, a new player is selected to be "It" and another round of play begins.

635 With Home Base

Designate out-of-bounds areas and a home base, such as a tree, lamppost, or wall. No one is allowed to hide within 50 feet of home base, however, and "It" may not hang around home base while looking for players. When "It" spots a player, he announces, "One, two, three, I see *(the players name)*." Then "It" and the found player race for home base. If "It" gets there first, the hidden player is out for the rest of the game. If the hider gets there first, he calls out, "Home free!" and is safe. Hidden players can also sneak out of their hiding places when "It" is not looking and attempt to race to home base before being tagged or before "It" reaches home base. The game continues until everyone is caught or free. The first person who was found becomes the new "It." Or, for a less competitive version, everyone takes a turn being "It" (in alphabetical order based on first name).

> ❝ By not overscheduling your child, you allow her to make up her own activities and fill the time; there are opportunities for dreaming, for playing, for making up things. And, ultimately, to become the kind of creative person who really makes up their own life. That's what you're doing by making sure that there's a little bit of time in every day for a child to be a child. ❞
>
> **—T. A. Barron**
> author of *The Lost Years of Merlin* series

Grade School Play (age 6 to 10)

Beach Day

Six- to ten-year-olds are at the prime age for soaking up all that the beach has to offer. They enjoy frolicking in the water, and have the physical stamina to play all day on the shore (with sunscreen, of course), building sand castles, digging intricate tunnels, and probably making friends with the children on nearby beach blankets. Expect to spend more time in the sun than you ever thought possible, because kids in this age group will play from sunrise to sunset, and maybe beyond!

636 Seaside Habitat

Playtime at the beach turns into a building extravaganza, digging canals and ponds, making roads, bridges, and beachside dwellings of every kind!

QUICK & EASY

AGE: 6–10 YRS

CATEGORY: PLAY WITH OTHERS/ OUTDOOR (BEACH)

NUMBER OF CHILDREN: TWO OR MORE

Materials:
Plastic sand buckets and shovels

Giant spoons and scoops

Assorted plastic tubs (sherbet tubs, yogurt containers, loaf pans)

Wood scraps (to create bridges across the canals)

Small plastic boats

Play:
Create a giant (but shallow) lake in the sand by digging a hole with the shovels, or dig a narrow canal, by scooping a 4- to 5-inch-wide trench in the sand. Angle the banks of the river a bit so that the sides won't cave in when you add water. Fill buckets with ocean water and dump it in the hole or trench. Build homes, buildings, roads, and trees all along the edge of the lake or canal. Use wood scraps or twigs to make small bridges across the canal. Create trees along the landscape by using the Drip Castle technique (this page). Add some boats to the water for the finishing touch.

★CLASSIC★

637 Drip Castle

Try a neat alternative to traditional sand castle construction that requires patience, good muscle coordination, and some serious creativity.

AGE: 6–10 YRS

CATEGORY: PLAY WITH OTHERS/ OUTDOOR (BEACH)

NUMBER OF CHILDREN: TWO OR MORE

Materials:
Buckets

Shovels

Sand castle tools

Play:
Using buckets, shovels, or other sand castle tools, create sturdy sand bases for the castle walls. Then fill an empty bucket with water and add enough sand to make a wet, goopy mixture (the consistency of pancake batter). Cup your hand, dip it into the bucket, and collect a handful of watery sand. With your fingertips pointing downward, slowly let a stream of sand drip, drip, drip to form a tall, steeple-shaped turret (the pattern will resemble hot wax dripping down the side of a candle). Repeat this process to create more turrets along the top and base of the castle. You can make a whole drip castle kingdom!

638 Giant Creatures of the Sea

*Look what just crawled in—
a gian sandy sea turtle!*

QUICK & EASY

AGE: 8–10 YRS

CATEGORY: PLAY WITH OTHERS/ OUTDOOR (BEACH)

NUMBER OF CHILDREN: TWO OR MORE

Materials:

Scoops or shovels

Play:

Use scoops or shovels to create a large, round mound of sand. Turn this mound into a giant sea turtle by adding a head, legs, and tail, and drawing texture to form the shell plates. Or add more sandy mounds and shapes to create a whale, a dolphin, an octopus, a Loch Ness Monster, or other creatures of the deep.

*SAFETY ALERT: Supervise all beach play to ensure your child's safety.

★ CLASSIC ★

639 Back-to-Back Beach Run

Lock elbows with your buddy and run up and down the beach in this classic.

QUICK & EASY

AGE: 8–10 YRS

CATEGORY: PLAY WITH OTHERS/ OUTDOOR (BEACH)

NUMBER OF CHILDREN: TWO OR MORE

Materials:

Flat, sandy stretch of beach

Setup:

Use your foot (or a stick) to carve a starting line in the sand; make a "turning line" about 50 feet down the shore. Two players stand back-to-back at the start and lock elbows (so they are linked at each side by their bent arms). They position themselves so that one (the "forward runner") faces the turning line and the other (the "backward runner") faces backward and will be running backward down the beach while linked to the forward runner.

Play:

The forward runner says, "Ready, set, go!" and the two begin running down the beach, with one player running forward, and the other running backward. (They'll learn to pace themselves so that the backward runner can keep up with the forward runner without tripping.) Players will run from one line to the second, then turn and run back to the starting line once the play begins. When the runners cross over the turning line, the forward runner announces, "Circle round!" and then leads the way, shuffling in a semi-circular pattern, back across the turning line in order for the pair to run back to the starting line. Once back at the beginning, the players swap positions before running down the beach again.

TIP: If you have more than two players, set up the race relay-style.

> "I was just reading a piece of research that basically said that the worst thing the parent of a typical child can do is get too involved with the child's friendships. The flip side of that coin is, when it comes to a special-needs child, the parent needs to get involved, helping the child select friends, having a home where friends are comfortable coming by, and entertaining the friends when the friends are there. The parents have to play a very, very direct role in friendship for kids with special needs."
>
> **—Richard Lavoie, M.Ed.**
> author of *It's So Much Work to Be Your Friend: Helping the Child with Learning Disabilities Find Social Success*

Grade School Play (age 6 to 10)

Let It Snow!

If you live in a part of the world that experiences all four seasons, you know that outdoor play can take on a whole new meaning in the winter. A layer of snow creates a spectacular wonderland for all sorts of play. Pull on the snow pants, zip up the coat, and pull that hat on tight! Here are a couple of classics (that require few or no props) to keep your kids busy playing for hours.

640 Snow Angels

I imagine kids have been making snow angels since the first blanket of snow fell on the earth.

Play:
Find a fresh, untrampled layer of snow. Your child lies on his back on top of the snow, and begins moving his arms up and down and his legs together and apart (a horizontal jumping jack). When he stands up and steps out of the impression his body made in the snow, the resulting shape resembles an angel—the arm movements have become wings, and the legs, a gown. This can also be wonderful solo play (with a parent), but a group of friends can make a whole host of angels (see variation). Create a new challenge by trying to leap out of the impression while disturbing as little of the design as possible!

AGE: 6–10 YRS

CATEGORY: PLAY WITH OTHERS/ OUTDOOR (SNOW)

NUMBER OF CHILDREN: **FOUR**

641 Snow Angel Paper Doll Chain

When two or more kids get together to play in the snow, they can create a continuous line of snow angels that resembles a chain of cutout paper dolls strung together across a snowy lawn. The idea is for one child to create an angel in the snow and a second child to create an angel a few feet away so that the tips of the wings connect. The children continue to take turns adding more angels to create a long chain.

642 Snow Sculpture

Let your children experiment to transform the whole backyard into a snowy sculpture garden.

Materials:
Shovels
Buckets
Muffin pans
Plastic egg cartons
Plastic spray bottle filled with water
Twigs and sticks
Raisins, nuts, or small stones

AGE: 6–10 YRS

CATEGORY: PLAY WITH OTHERS/ OUTDOOR

NUMBER OF CHILDREN: **FOUR**

Play:
While younger kids may stick to the traditional snowman, the older ones may instead choose to fashion a turtle, a dragon, a duck, or an octopus! Or how about a snow wizard? Ski slopes for a doll's winter break vacation? Or try to recreate a summer sand castle. A masterpiece can be made out of packable wet snow using plastic shovels and buckets. Muffin pans and plastic egg cartons from the kitchen make great forms for mounds and decorative additions. Use the plastic spray bottle to add a little moisture to powdery snow so it's more moldable. Sticks and other underbrush can be gathered for accents (a shaggy mane, eyebrows, the pattern on a turtle's shell). Raisins and nuts make good eyes and noses.

643 Snow Forts

A more organized form of snow play, fort building is a great group activity for an outdoor winter birthday party. It opens the door to wonderful opportunities for creative construction play.

AGE: 6–10 YRS

CATEGORY: **PLAY WITH OTHERS/ OUTDOOR (SNOW)**

NUMBER OF CHILDREN: **FOUR**

Materials:
Shovels

Buckets

Plastic snow-block maker (optional)

Play:

Allow the children to make the fort "freestyle" by packing together walls or digging tunnels. Invite them to tell you about their fort. Is it a castle? A modern ice mansion? Are there any special secrets inside? Your child will enjoy pushing snow around while building walls and designing little alcoves. All snow play should, of course, be well-supervised, as things can get slippery!

"Let's Play Army!"

Children six to ten years old often pretend to capture or fight the enemy during their play; they seem fascinated with play scenarios pitting good versus evil, and enjoy pretending they are all-powerful and can outsmart or overpower their opponent. Some of these play themes are harmless and natural. On the other hand, sometimes war and fighting play can become truly aggressive and violent. So what's a parent to do? Here's my best advice:

- Talk in simple, age-appropriate ways with your child about the difference between real violence and weapons and pretend. Make your own personal values and beliefs known to your child and set clear rules to prevent play from escalating into violence.

- If you make the decision to not buy toy weapons of any kind, realize that your child might still turn ordinary sticks and LEGOs into pretend guns and knives from time to time to act out fantasy war play.

- Children are sometimes satisfied with chase, capture, and rescue games; each side has a safe zone where players can't be captured and a jail for captured opponents. Provide huge cardboard boxes and props for each home base and the children are likely to spend hours creating their base camps or hideouts.

- If your child is allowed to have a toy sword (with a non-blunt end) for fantasy play, set very clear rules: The sword may only hit another sword, not a playmate or any living thing. (Provide a costume box with tunics, belts, and fantasy gear for knights, kings, and queens.)

- If you decide to allow some types of toy weapons but not others, consider something low-tech like small water pistols that clearly look like toys (perhaps forbidding the realistic high-powered gear). Provide a couple of buckets of water for frequent "fill-ups" to keep the focus on running, movement, and fun rather than aggression.

Grade School Play (age 6 to 10)

Birthday Party and Large Group Games

What good things can happen when your six- to ten-year-old plays with a large group of children at a party? He discovers that the really quiet, new kid at school does the best yo-yo tricks. He learns that you have to be really patient to "wait your turn" when twelve kids are in front of you in the cake and ice cream line. He discovers that it's more fun to win, but everyone loses sometime. He makes new friends and learns new games. He learns you have to play fair and follow the rules. He discovers that he's really good at guessing riddles.

Team and Group Play

Children ages six to ten typically love a good challenge. But sometimes competition creates more friction than fun. With that in mind, I designed and tested many of the games in this *Birthday Party* section with two distinct ways to play. Team Play assumes there will be two opposing teams playing, while Group Play puts all the children on one large team, racing against the stopwatch or kitchen timer rather than against one another. Experiment to see which version of these games suits your style and is right for the mix of children at the party.

In each of these games, the stopwatch should be set for a specific amount of time that not only offers the group a bit of a challenge, but also allows a good chance of beating the clock. Because the number of players may vary and the

> *When kids see that they can actually go outside and play with other children and have fun, and that it's a reasonable alternative to spending all their time in front of the TV set, they might not be so resistant. I mean, if you give a kid a ball, and take him to a park to play, he might actually enjoy it.*
>
> **—Henry Joseph Legere, M.D.**
> pediatrician and author of *Raising Healthy Eaters: 100 Tips for Parents of Children of All Ages*

distance each child must run during the relay varies too, it's best to stage a test run with your child a day or two before the party to estimate how much time might be needed for each round of play.

Create a Party Plan

You can create an action-packed party for a group of boys and girls with a little advance planning. Select six to eight games (or more) to keep the party moving along quickly and smoothly. And remember to improvise, to repeat a second round of play for any game that is a big hit with the children. Here is a sample party schedule:

Sample Party Itinerary (2 hours)

1. Obstacle Course, page 337

2. Fish Out of Water, page 331

3. Memory, page 324 (during cake time)

4. Who Am I?, page 328 (during cake time)

5. Collage-Covered Journals, page 329

6. Elbows to Go, page 332

7. Treasure Hunt, page 344

8. Flip-Flop Wheelbarrow, page 334 (backup game)

9. Price Tag, page 325

10. Sneaker Scramble, page 346

Birthday Party Butterflies

Sometimes a low-key conversation with a dose of brainstorming or role-playing is all that's needed to help a child who has anxiety or shyness about an upcoming birthday party he's been invited to attend.

- Some children may be comforted by knowing where the party is, who will be there, and how long the party will last. Provide some basic information so he can begin to get a mental picture about what this party is all about.

- If your child is particularly shy, help him learn two simple social skills that send a positive signal to other children: Look others in the eye when you talk to them (rather than looking at the ground), and learn to smile when you meet someone new. (The smile is a warm welcome that says, "I'm happy to meet you" or "I'd like to play with you.")

- If talking to others in a group setting is a problem, role-play a few things that your child might actually say to one other child to break the ice. Children have their own variety of "small talk" that sends a signal of friendliness to others. Brainstorm with your child about what kids might talk about in a relaxed and friendly setting.

Grade School Play (age 6 to 10)

Indoor Party (Group) Games

Get your child's birthday party off to a good start by having some play activity in motion as soon as the children arrive. Have an assortment of felt-tip markers and stickers on the table so the children can personalize their own party-favor bags. The bottom line is that you need to have something nonelectronic and fun planned the moment they step inside the party arena.

★CLASSIC★

644 Memory

Cookie cutter, banana, keys, teddy bear, sock, spoon, stapler!

QUICK & EASY

Materials:
Assortment of 10 to 15 small
    familiar objects
Cookie sheet
Dish towel
Paper
Pencils
Stopwatch or kitchen timer
Kitchen table and chairs

AGE: **6–10 YRS**

CATEGORY:
**BIRTHDAY PARTY
(GROUP GAMES)/
INDOOR**

NUMBER OF
CHILDREN: **SIX
OR MORE**

Setup:
Before the party begins, place 10 to 15 objects on the cookie sheet and cover it with a dish towel to keep it hidden for the time being.

Team Play:
Divide the players into two teams and send each team to a different room in the house to keep them separate. (My experience has been that one team can distract the other team if they're in the same room.) Gather the children from the first team in a circle on the floor, place the cookie sheet in the middle of the circle, and remove the towel. Provide one player with a piece of paper and pencil and give him the task of writing down the list of objects. Give the group about 20 seconds to look at the objects on the cookie sheet. When the time is up, put the towel over the cookie sheet and set it aside. The group now has 2 minutes to collectively name as many objects from the tray as possible; the note taker keeps a list. At the end of the 2 minutes, uncover the tray and count up the number of correct answers on the team's list. Repeat this same game in another room with the second team, using the same tray of objects. The team that lists the most objects correctly wins. Keep each team occupied during the other team's round with a quick game of Alphabet Detective (page 301) or Smelly-Stuff (page 326). To up the challenge, you can create three separate trays of objects and have each team take three turns.

Group Play:
Prepare three trays of objects and cover with dish towels. Gather the children around the kitchen table. Uncover one tray and give the group 20 seconds to look at the objects. Cover the tray. Set the timer for 2 minutes and challenge the group to list every object on the tray. When the buzzer sounds, bring the tray back to see if the team has named each object correctly. Play two more rounds with the other trays. Adjust the time as needed to give the children enough time for guessing.

645 Price Tag

Give the children at your child's birthday party a chance to work on their appraisal skills.

QUICK & EASY

AGE: 6–10 YRS

CATEGORY:
BIRTHDAY PARTY
(GROUP GAMES)/
INDOOR

NUMBER OF
CHILDREN: SIX
OR MORE

Materials:
- *6 to 8 store-bought items (toy, camera, toothpaste, hammer, wig, can of corn, etc.)*
- *Index cards*
- *Pencil*

Setup:
Before the party begins, place each item on the counter or table in a long line. Fold index cards, one for every object, in half, and stand them up in front of each item to create "price tags." Assign a number to each item, and mark that number in the top corner of its price tag. Write three possible prices on each tag, one being the true purchase price (you can estimate). Use your imagination, varying the prices wildly. Create a list of the correct prices for each item, and put this list in your pocket.

Play:
The children form a long line, with the birthday child at the head of the line. Give each child a pencil and index card; have them write the numbers 1 through 8 along the left margin of their cards so they can write down their price guesses for each item. Once everyone has moved through the line of objects and written down their guesses, read out the correct price for the first item and announce, "Raise your hand if you had this price written down for this item." (Keep a list of winners for each item.) Go through this process with each of the items; the child with the most correct guesses wins.

646 Artistes

Assemble art supplies (brushes, paints, easel, erasers, paint rollers, bucket, drawing paper, picture frame, glitter, glue, scissors, etc.) and assign each item three prices, with one being the correct selling price for the item. The player with the most correct guesses wins.

★ CLASSIC ★

647 Orange Passing Relay

This game is older than your great, great, great, great grandmother, but many children today have never played it.

QUICK & EASY

AGE: 6–10 YRS

CATEGORY:
BIRTHDAY PARTY
(GROUP GAMES)/
INDOOR

NUMBER OF
CHILDREN: EIGHT
OR MORE

Materials:
- *Oranges (1 for each team)*

Team Play:
Divide the players into two teams and arrange each team in a line. Give the player at the end of each line an orange. She puts the orange under her chin, and from this point forward players aren't allowed to use their hands. On your "Go," the teams pass their oranges from player to player, using only their necks and chins. If a player drops the orange, she can either pick it up with her neck and chin and

pass it on *or* pick it up with her hands, in which case she must run it back to the start of the line. The first team to get the orange to the end of the line wins.

Group Play:

Line up all the players in one long line and have them play against the kitchen timer.

648 Touchy-Feely

I think it's the gross-out factor that makes this game such a hit with six- to ten-year-olds. It's gooey and messy, and they like it!

QUICK & EASY

AGE: 6–10 YRS

CATEGORY:
BIRTHDAY PARTY
(GROUP GAMES)/
INDOOR

NUMBER OF
CHILDREN: SIX
OR MORE

Materials:

Assortment of 5 objects
Small ziplock bags
   (1 for each object)
Paper lunch bags
Cookie sheets
Bandana (blindfold)
Paper and pencil

Setup:

Before the party, select five familiar, safe objects that you think could be identifiable by touch alone (cooked spaghetti, grapes, bread, Cheerios, an eraser, a golf ball, a pack of gum, a tube of toothpaste, a bar of soap, a hair clip, an empty saltshaker, a necktie). Place each item in a ziplock bag and seal it to avoid leakage. Then place each ziplock in a paper lunch bag. Folding the bags closed, and store them on cookie sheets until it's time to play the game.

Play:

Place the paper bags in a line on the kitchen table and bring one child in the room. Blindfold the child and open the first paper and ziplock bags. Place his hand inside the ziplock bag to let him

feel its contents. Allow him 10 or more seconds to make a guess. Repeat this touchy-feely routine with each lunch bag, and then bring in the rest of the children one at a time to take their turn. (If you want to make this a competitive game, keep track with pen and paper of how many correct guesses each child makes.)

649 Smelly-Stuff

In this version of the game, select safe, edible foods with a recognizable odor (an onion slice, a lemon, hard-boiled eggs, mustard, ketchup, cinnamon, apples, strawberries, cheese, bananas). Put each food inside several layers of plastic grocery bags to conceal the contents, and proceed as above.

Quick Games to Keep the Waiting Blues Away

If you have a large group of kids waiting to take their turn, they are likely to get antsy. Set up some quick waiting games to keep them busy, with a grown-up or helper in charge. Games might include:

• Three Nerf balls and a laundry basket—each child tries to get all three balls in the basket.

• A basket of beanbags—time for some juggling practice!

• Plastic golf club and three Wiffle golf balls—place a Hula-Hoop on the ground 10 feet away and let each child try to send the ball inside the hoop.

• Disposable camera—time to experiment with some silly poses (each child makes one silly face or pose).

650 Mixed-Up Message

This collaborative word puzzle will have everyone scrambling to figure out the mystery phrase before the time is up.

AGE: 6–10 YRS

CATEGORY: **BIRTHDAY PARTY (GROUP GAMES)/ INDOOR**

NUMBER OF CHILDREN: **EIGHT OR MORE**

Materials:

Markers

Construction paper

Paper bag

Stopwatch or kitchen timer

Setup:

Before the party, think of a phrase with two or three short words that would be familiar to the children ("What's Up?" "Hey Dude," "See Ya Later," "Happy Birthday, Billy," etc.). Write each letter of the phrase on a separate sheet of construction paper and mix the pieces up inside a paper bag.

Play:

One child dumps all the letters on the floor, and the group quickly (and spontaneously) places all the letters in a horizontal line (faceup) on the floor. One child is appointed to be the Letter Mover. Set the stopwatch for 1 to 3 minutes, depending upon the challenge involved. The team members stand back and work together to spell out the mystery phrase. As they guess possible words, the Letter Mover moves the letters around to form these words. Be prepared with several bags of "mystery letters" for extra rounds of play. If the children haven't unscrambled the message in the allotted time, you can start calling out hints.

651 Mixed-Up Colors

Play the game with letters that spell the names of one, two, or three colors. For example, you might include letters for the words *pink, white,*

and *blue* in a grocery bag. (For the youngest players, choose only one color.) The group of children must quickly create the words by arranging the individual letters on the floor, announcing one color at a time as that word is assembled. (Make it known that players may not simply guess random colors without lining up the letters on the floor!) Once all the colors have been identified for that bag, the players grab another bag, dump out the letters, and begin another quick round. In this variation, set the timer for 2 to 4 minutes, so that the children can try to guess as many of the colors before the buzzer sounds.

★ CLASSIC ★

652 San Diego, CA

This game is just like Pin the Tail on the Donkey, but it starts with a map of the United States.

AGE: 6–10 YRS

CATEGORY: **BIRTHDAY PARTY (GROUP GAMES)/ INDOOR**

NUMBER OF CHILDREN: **FOUR OR MORE**

Materials:

Invisible tape

Large map of the United States

Marker

Bandana (blindfold)

Sticky tabs (from office supply store)

Setup:

Use the invisible tape to hang the map at the children's eye level on a blank wall or door. Use the marker to draw a circle around San Diego, California, and point out this city to all the players before the game begins. Give each child a sticky tab.

Play:

Line up the players in front of the map. Blindfold and spin the first player three times, then point him in the direction of the map. With his hands outstretched he feels his way to the map and tries to tape his sticky tab on San Diego. Use the marker to write that child's name on the tab once it's on the map. Each child takes a turn, and the player whose sticky tab is closest to San Diego is the winner. Play additional rounds by selecting other cities on the map.

653 Pin the Tail on the Donkey

In this traditional version of the game, you draw a large donkey on a sheet of poster board, omitting the donkey's tail. Use the marker to draw an *X* where the tail should be located. Cut a donkey tail out of construction paper for each player, writing each player's name on his tail; attach a large piece of invisible tape to the top of the tails so that half of the tape is sticking out. One by one each child is blindfolded, spun around three times, and pointed in the direction of the donkey drawing. The child whose tail is taped closest to the *X* wins the game.

654 Odd Man Out

Size up each opponent and make your best guess for this fast-moving guessing game.

QUICK & EASY

AGE: 6–10 YRS

CATEGORY: BIRTHDAY PARTY (GROUP GAMES)/ INDOOR

NUMBER OF CHILDREN: SIX OR MORE

Materials:
  Dried beans (navy or kidney)
  Paper lunch bags (1 for each child)

Setup:
Put 20 beans inside each bag and distribute to all players except the birthday child, who gets an empty paper bag.

Play:
Line all the players up in a long line, with the birthday child at the head. With the exception of the birthday child, each player picks a small number of beans out of his paper bag, closing his fist around the beans to keep them hidden. The

birthday child stops at the first player, who asks him, "Even or odd?" The birthday child must guess whether the opponent has an even or odd number of beans in his hand; then the player opens his hand to reveal the truth. If the birthday child guessed correctly, he gets to keep the beans. He travels down the line, repeating this same routine, putting any beans he wins into his own paper bag. The next player in line then moves through the line in the same way. When every player has moved through the line, count the beans; the player with the most beans wins.

655 Who Am I?

Idle time makes for trouble when you have 12 rambunctious kids sitting around the table eating birthday cake. Here's a fast-paced guessing game for entertaining the troops for 10 minutes during cake and ice-cream time.

QUICK & EASY

AGE: 6–10 YRS

CATEGORY: BIRTHDAY PARTY (GROUP GAMES)/ INDOOR

NUMBER OF CHILDREN: SIX OR MORE

Setup:
Pick a person in the children's universe, such as a teacher, a classmate, a teammate, or someone's sibling. Write down clues about this mystery person that gives a small amount of information, such as, "I am a man with black hair" or "I am four years old." (It will be to your advantage to write these clues out in advance so you don't forget them once the party gets into high gear!)

Play:
Recite clues about the mystery person to the children. Continue with more specific clues until the correct person is named. You could also describe sports or music figures familiar to the group of children. Start with very broad clues and keep adding more descriptive clues until someone in the group gives the correct answer.

656 Telephone

This game has been around for a couple of generations now, and it never fails to elicit some laughs.

AGE: 6–10 YRS

CATEGORY: BIRTHDAY PARTY (GROUP GAMES)/ INDOOR

NUMBER OF CHILDREN: SIX OR MORE

Setup:
The children sit on the floor in a tight circle.

Play:
One child is selected to start the game. This child thinks of a serious or silly message of any kind and whispers the message clearly to the child on her left. The message might be: "I left a baloney sandwich in my lunch box at school today," or something nonsensical like "My teacher ate three watermelons and a shoe for lunch today." After the first child whispers the message to her neighbor, the message is repeated from child to child around the circle. Each whisperer may say the message only once, and if the neighbor does not fully understand the message she must still pass along whatever message she believes she heard. The last child in the circle receiving the message announces it to the entire group (and it's usually quite a garbled concoction!). Once the laughter has settled down, the first whisperer announces her original message for comparison.

657 Collage-Covered Journals

A journal becomes even more precious when children make it from scratch.

AGE: 6–10 YRS

CATEGORY: BIRTHDAY PARTY (GROUP GAMES)/ INDOOR

NUMBER OF CHILDREN: FOUR OR MORE

Materials:
Colored computer paper

Scissors

Ruler

Utility knife (for adult use only)

Colored foam board (poster board with foam backing)

Single-hole punch

Yarn or rawhide shoelaces

Markers

Magazine photos and captions

Nontoxic white glue

Glitter

Setup:
Before the party begins, cut the paper in half so that each piece is 5½" by 8½". Use the utility knife to cut two pieces of foam board, approximately 6" by 9". Along the left side of each piece of foam board, cut one hole (using the hole punch) 2½ inches from the bottom edge and another hole 2½ inches from the top edge. These will serve as your front and back covers. Now punch holes in your paper that line up with those in the journal covers. (The journal covers will be about ½ inch larger than the paper on every side.)

Create:
Each child takes a front and back journal cover and a slim stack of paper. The children assemble the journal by threading yarn or rawhide laces through the paper and covers and tying a knot or bow in each lace. They can decorate the front and back covers using markers, magazine photos and captions, and glitter.

658 Collage-Covered Notebooks

Make a simpler version of this journal by purchasing a small spiral notebook for each child. Provide precut poster board to glue onto the front and back covers of the notebook to create a colorful background for each cover collage.

659 Photo-Op Journal

Take a Polaroid of each child at the party so they can glue their photo onto the journal covers and work them into a collage.

660 Personalized Party Shirts

Who says you need to spend an arm and a leg to send the gang home with special keepsake T-shirts?

AGE: 6–10 YRS

CATEGORY: BIRTHDAY PARTY (GROUP GAMES)/ INDOOR

NUMBER OF CHILDREN: FOUR OR MORE

Materials:

Recycled tablecloth or newspapers

Fabric markers or squeezable fabric paints

Poster board or cardboard

Plain white paper

Plain white T-shirts

Assorted colored pencils

Setup:

Create a work station at the kitchen table by putting an old tablecloth or newspapers down. Have fabric markers or paints and precut blotters available in the center of the table.

Create:

Each child pulls his T-shirt over a large cardboard blotter so the paint doesn't bleed through. Give each artist a plain sheet of paper and colored pencils so she can sketch her design—this way she can work out the size, color, thickness of lines, and placement of her design on paper prior to putting paint on her one-of-a-kind T-shirt. Once she's satisfied with her design, she uses this sample to help lay out and create a painted masterpiece on her T-shirt. Let the paints dry, with the cardboard blotter still in place. Remove the blotter when the T-shirt is completely dry and allow each artist to model her fashion statement.

661 Personalized Nightshirts

Use large or extra-large T-shirts to make Personalized Nightshirts for a sleepover party.

> " A birthday is a celebration of the life of your child. It's a day to set aside to think about where she was last year or five years ago and to reflect on her growth. "
>
> **—Shelley Butler**
> coauthor of *The Field Guide to Parenting*

Outdoor Party Games

When the weather is warm and dry, move the birthday crowd outside to play. Let them run, toss, and flip and flop around the backyard, or stage the party at a nearby park. These high-energy, active games are perfect for burning off a little excitement, and the party cleanup is a breeze. Here are some of my favorite relays and group games for outdoor birthday party play. There are games in this section that require strategy and patience and others where fast thinking or physical speed win out. And always bring your sense of humor to the party—some of the props and play gear are very wacky to wear and even wackier to play with.

662 Fish Out of Water

Last summer, I was sitting out on our dock at high tide when a big fish jumped up on the dock beside me and scared me silly. I was inspired to write this game for the neighborhood children as a way to tell the story of my visit from Mr. Mullet.

QUICK & EASY

AGE: 6–10 YRS

CATEGORY:
BIRTHDAY
PARTY (GROUP
GAMES)/OUTDOOR

NUMBER OF
CHILDREN: FOUR
OR MORE

Materials:
Permanent marker
2 Ping-Pong balls
2 small plastic pitchers of equal size
Card table or picnic table
2 medium to large buckets
2 one-cup plastic measuring cups with handle
   (or large plastic margarine tubs)
Kitchen timer or stopwatch

Setup:
Draw a simple fish (or write the word *fish*) on each of the Ping-Pong balls. Place one ball in each of the empty pitchers. Place these pitchers side by side on top of the picnic table or card table outside. Mark a "starting line" by placing two buckets (one for each team) filled with water about 20 to 30 feet away from the picnic table. Place one plastic measuring cup on the ground next to each water bucket.

Team Play:
Create two teams of players and position all the players behind their team's bucket of water. Call out "Ready, set, go!" and the first player on each team fills the measuring cup with water, hustles down to the picnic table, and dumps the water into his team's pitcher. (The players must be fast, but they must also try not to lose water along the way.) The player runs back to the starting line and gives the measuring cup to his teammate, who repeats the same routine. The players continue this relay until a cup of water causes the fish to spill out onto the ground. (Not as easy as it seems; when the pitcher is filled to the brim, the ball continues to teeter on the top.) The players on the winning team shout, "Fish Out of Water!"

Group Play:
Position all the players behind the bucket of water. (Only one ball, one measuring cup, one bucket, and one pitcher are needed in this version.) Call out "Ready, set, go!" and set the kitchen timer for about 4 to 8 minutes, depending on the size of the water pitcher and the distance each player must travel with the cup of water. (Do a trial run with your child before the party and adjust the time according to the abilities of the players, allowing enough time so the group has a good chance of

filling the pitcher with water before the buzzer sounds.) The game continues as above. Most kids love to play a second round to try to improve their racing time and "beat the clock."

Mix Up the Teams for Fun and Fairness

For games that require teams, I like to continually mix up the teams after each round of play. This gives all the children an opportunity to cooperate with every member of the larger group. A simple way to make this work is to say "Rotate" after every round. This signals the first player in the line of each team to switch to the opposing team and move to the back of the line. This way no one ever feels they're unfairly stuck on a team.

663 Elbows to Go

The grandpa at the next booth said to the waitress, "Miss, could you put my elbows in a to-go cup?" (referring to the macaroni salad on his plate). That night, driving back to our cabin, I invented this game.

AGE: 6–10 YRS

CATEGORY:
BIRTHDAY PARTY
(GROUP GAMES)/
OUTDOOR

NUMBER OF
CHILDREN: SIX
OR MORE

Materials:
Roll of 2"-wide painter's tape

2 cookie sheets

Baseball caps (1 for each child) or plastic margarine tubs (more challenging)

Box of macaroni

Stopwatch or kitchen timer

Setup:
Mark a starting line and finish line by placing a 6-foot-long strip of tape on the ground. (The easiest way to do this is to roll out the tape, sticky side down, in 12-inch sections, pressing it down with your feet as you go to secure it.) Place the cookie sheets on the ground at the finish line with at least 3 feet of space between them.

Tip: If the lawn is wet, and your tape lines aren't sticking, see "Start and Finish" box, page 348.

Team Play:
Divide the players into two teams, and have both teams line up behind the starting line. Give each child a small plastic margarine tub or baseball cap filled with six macaroni elbows. The first player on each team puts the tub or upside-down baseball cap on his head. On your "Go," the two players run to the finish line, dump their elbows into their team's cookie sheet, and run back to the starting line. If a player drops his tub or cap during the race, he must stop to pick up the elbows and put them back in his tub or cap before continuing. The next player in line repeats this routine. When all the players have crossed the finish line, the team with the most elbows in the team's cookie sheet wins.

Group Play:
Use only one cookie sheet and tub or cap for this variation. Set the kitchen timer for about 4 to 8 minutes. Challenge the team to get all the players back and forth across the finish line before the buzzer sounds. Vary the time according to the number of children playing and the distance they must travel to reach the team cookie sheet. (Do a trial run with your child before the party begins to get an approximate idea of how much time is needed for each player to run the course, then allow a bit of extra time for gathering up lost macaroni!)

Theme Parties

Invite the kids to wear costumes and adapt the games to fit the theme. Be sure to add other favorites to the party game lineup so that you create a good mix of physically active, high-energy games with creative activities, and guessing and thinking games too!

Mindbenders:

• **Costumes** Ask the children to dress like their favorite "genius" (from real life or fiction—Einstein or Hermione, anyone?) Once all the guests have arrived, kick off the party by letting the group guess the identity of each genius present. As an alternative, provide each child with a plain T-shirt and bright fabric markers on arrival so that each child can design his own "brainy" design on the shirt—perhaps a favorite genius from a story or movie, or a picture of the human brain at work!

• **Games** Memory (page 324), Price Tag (page 325), Mixed-Up Message (page 327), Pirate's Map Treasure Hunt (page 316)

Arts and Crafts:
• **Costumes** Invite the kids to come as their favorite color (and expect color-coordinated costumes from head to toe!).

• **Games** Mixed-Up Message (page 327), Price Tag Artistes (page 325), Personalized Party Shirts (page 330), Drip-Drop Postcards (page 284), Rainbow Necklace (page 285), Eco Beads (page 288), Personalized Treasure Box (page 288), Collage-Covered Journals (page 329).

Beach Party:
• **Costumes** Invite the children to come in bathing suits and T-shirts (or cover-ups). Or, put a silly (and creative) spin on this beach party—ask the children to wear a bathing suit that might have been worn 100 years ago and see what they come up with. (Expect to see adult-size bathing suits over leggings and T-shirts and long underwear!)

• **Games** Bucket-Head Water Brigade (page 343), Water Balloon Toss (page 349), Water Balloon Basketball or Water Balloon Baseball (page 350).

Sports Party:
• **Costumes** Each child comes dressed in their favorite sports gear: soccer, baseball, football, hockey, and basketball jerseys and uniforms.

• **Games** Obstacle Course (page 337), Heave-Ho (page 335), Sneaker Relay (page 346), Water Balloon Baseball (page 350), or make Personalized Party Shirts (turned into sports jerseys), (page 330).

664 Flip-Flop Wheelbarrow

Here's a funny twist on the classic wheelbarrow relay race.

QUICK & EASY

AGE: **6–10 YRS**

CATEGORY: **BIRTHDAY PARTY (GROUP GAMES)/ OUTDOOR**

NUMBER OF CHILDREN: **SIX OR MORE**

Materials:
- *Roll of 2"-wide painter's tape*
- *2 pairs of flip-flops*
- *Stopwatch or kitchen timer*

Setup:
Mark a starting line and finish line by placing a 6-foot-long strip of tape on the grass. (The easiest way to do this is to roll out the tape, sticky side down, in 12-inch sections, pressing down with your feet to secure it as you go.)

Tip: If the lawn is wet, and your tape lines aren't sticking, see "Start and Finish" box, page 348.

Team Play:
Divide the players into two teams, and line up all the players behind the starting line. One player on each team puts flip-flops on his hands by sliding the thong between the index and middle finger of each hand. This player and the next player in line assume the "wheelbarrow" position: The child with the flip-flops bends over and places her weight on her hands while her teammate holds both her legs up in the air behind her. On your "Go," both teams take off clomping down the lawn to the finish line and back. They pass the flip-flops to the next two players in line, who perform the same routine. The team whose last players finish the lap first wins.

Group Play:
Use only one pair of flip-flops and set up the players in one line. Set the kitchen timer for about 4 to 8 minutes. (The time varies according to the number of players and distance they must travel. Do a trial run with your child before the party begins to gauge the time needed to beat the clock.) The group tries to beat the clock, and on the second round, to beat their first time.

Note: For a simpler game, play without the flip-flops. To prevent cuts on the hands, make sure you've checked the lawn for any sharp rocks or other objects!

PARENT TIP

665 Used Toys for Sale

❝*About once a month on a Saturday morning, my kids and I go to yard sales in search of toys they might want to buy with their allowance money. This has turned out to be a lot of fun for the three of us, but they have also become really savvy about looking for toys and managing their money. I chuckle each time one of my sons says, 'Look at this toy, it costs ten times as much at the toy store!' They have actually become much more appreciative of what they already have and less likely to whine for something expensive they've seen on TV. In fact, one time I heard my ten-year-old tell his young brother, 'That's a lot of money to spend on a truck. If I were you I'd wait and see if you can get it at a yard sale.'*❞

—Debra from Nebraska

666 Heave-Ho

Here's a game that allows for a little bravado!

Materials:
- Rope
- Hula-Hoop
- Nerf football
- Stopwatch or kitchen timer

AGE: 6–10 YRS

CATEGORY:
BIRTHDAY PARTY
(GROUP GAMES)/
OUTDOOR

NUMBER OF
CHILDREN: FOUR
OR MORE

Setup:
Tie one end of the rope to the Hula-Hoop and tie the other end of the rope around a sturdy branch of a tree (this is definitely an adult task– and take care while you're up there). Position the hoop at a good tossing level for the players.

Team Play:
Divide the players into two teams and position them behind the starting line. The first player on one team takes a turn tossing the football through the hoop. If he is successful, he takes two giant steps backward and has another try. (His teammates keep track of how many balls go through the hoop.) Once the player misses, the first player on the other team takes a turn, following these same rules. The game alternates back and forth, with players from each team stepping up to take a turn. Once every player has had a turn the game is over. The team with the most scores wins this round of play.

Group Play:
Create two tossing lines, one a little farther from the hoop, for varying degrees of difficulty. Challenge the team to get a certain number of scores (successful tosses) in 10 minutes, and set the kitchen timer. (Set a manageable number of scores during the first round of play so that the team has a realistic chance of achieving their goal with players of mixed tossing abilities.) Each player gets two tries at tossing the football,

one at each of the two tossing lines, and then the ball is quickly handed to the next player in line, who takes his two turns. The players continue to take quick tosses, with each player getting repeated turns in the 10-minute time limit. If the team is successful, increase the number of expected scores on the next round.

667 Water Balloon Heave-Ho

Play the same game as described above, but jazz things up a bit by tossing water balloons instead of a football. This game gets a lot of "oohs" and "ahs" as the water balloons break after sailing through the hoop.

*SAFETY ALERT: Supervise all balloon play to prevent children less than eight years old from choking on uninflated balloons or balloon pieces.

668 Windbag

One clever little boy taught me that it's nearly impossible to blow three bubbles in a row if you are laughing hysterically at a silly imitation of a baboon!

AGE: 6–10 YRS

CATEGORY:
BIRTHDAY PARTY
(GROUP GAMES)/
OUTDOOR

NUMBER OF
CHILDREN: TEN
OR MORE

Materials:
- Roll of 2"-wide painter's tape
- 2 folding chairs
- 2 plastic bowls
- Bubble solution
- 2 plastic bubble wands
- Plastic whistle
- Stopwatch or kitchen timer

Setup:
Mark a starting line and finish line by placing a 6-foot-long strip of tape on the grass. (The easiest way to do this is to roll out the tape,

sticky side down, in 12-inch sections, pressing it down with your foot to secure it as you go.) Open the folding chairs and place them just across the finish line, facing backward, about 3 feet away from each other. Fill the bowls with bubble solution and place on the chairs, laying a bubble wand on each chair.

Tip: If the lawn is wet, and your tape lines aren't sticking, see "Start and Finish" box, page 348.

Team Play:

Create two teams and line everybody up behind the starting line. The scorekeeper blows a whistle to start the game. The first player on each team races to the finish line, stands behind the chair (facing her teammates), and blows three consecutive bubbles, calling out "1, 2, 3" once she has been successful. (She can only run back to the starting line after she has done so.) She races back to the starting line with the bubble wand and hands it to the next player in line, who repeats the same actions. The team to get all its players back to the starting line after successfully blowing and announcing the bubbles wins that round of play. (Be prepared with lots of extra bubble solution, and refill the bowl quickly if a spill occurs.)

Group Play:

You only need one bowl, chair, and wand for this version. Line up all the children behind the starting line. The scorekeeper blows a whistle to start the game and starts the kitchen timer. (Allow enough time for the children to have a chance to win but at the same time feel challenged enough to beat the clock.)

669 Double-time

For a wackier version of this game, increase the number of bubbles required for each player to 10 or 20; counting is required for each set of bubbles blown in one breath. If a player blows only three bubbles in one breath, she must say, "1, 2, 3," and then resume blowing, counting, "4, 5, 6," and so on after each group of bubbles blown. When a player forgets to call out the numbers, her teammates can remind her to announce the numbers before running back to the team.

670 Flapping Flops

Somebody's mom is bound to be calling out, "Hey, your shoes are on the wrong feet!" when this game is under way.

QUICK & EASY

AGE: 6–10 YRS

CATEGORY: BIRTHDAY PARTY (GROUP GAMES)/ OUTDOOR

NUMBER OF CHILDREN: SIX OR MORE

Materials:

Safe outdoor playing area

Roll of 2"-wide painter's tape

2 pairs of medium to large flip-flops

Stopwatch or kitchen timer

Setup:

On a flat, grassy lawn (without bumble bees or fire ants), mark a starting line and finish line by placing a 6-foot-long strip of tape on the grass. (The easiest way to do this is to roll out the tape, sticky side down, in 12-inch sections, pressing down with your feet to secure it as you go.) Create one or two teams to play.

Tip: If the lawn is wet, and your tape lines aren't sticking, see "Start and Finish" box, page 348.

Team Play:

The first player on each team puts the flip-flops on the *wrong* feet. On the command "Ready, set, go!" the players dash down to the finish line, take off the flip-flops, and run barefooted back to the starting line, handing the flip-flops to the next teammate, who repeats this routine. The team whose last player crosses the finish line first wins.

Group Play:

You only need one pair of flip-flops in this version. Set the kitchen timer for 4 to 8 minutes, depending on the number of children, and give the command "Ready, set, go!" The game proceeds as above, with one player at a time running from start to finish, and everyone finishing the relay before the buzzer sounds.

★ CLASSIC ★
671 | Obstacle Course

It's always a camp favorite, so it's such a treat for children to be able to have their very own obstacle course.

QUICK & EASY

AGE: 6–10 YRS

CATEGORY:
BIRTHDAY PARTY
(GROUP GAMES)/
OUTDOOR

NUMBER OF
CHILDREN: SIX
OR MORE

Materials:
Junior football or Nerf football, twine, Hula-Hoop

Wiffle golf ball, plastic golf club, flowerpot

Loops of rope or Hula-Hoops

Wooden board

3 beanbags and a bucket

Backyard slide or swings

Small soccer ball and goal

Safety cones and beach ball

Index cards and markers

Whistle

Stopwatch

Setup:
Before the party begins, set up six to ten stations using the props above. Use index cards and markers to number each of these stations (you might have to be creative about where on the station to stick the card). Here are some obstacles you might try, along with general directions for the players:

1. Football, twine, and Hula-Hoop: Hang the hoop from a branch on the tree, sail the ball through the hoop.

2. Wiffle golf ball, plastic club, and flowerpot turned on its side: Stand back and tap the ball in the pot.

3. Loops of rope, placed in parallel lines on the lawn: Hop from loop to loop, alternating feet.

4. Board on the ground: Walk the plank quickly from one end to the other.

5. Three beanbags and a bucket: Stand back at the line and keep tossing until one beanbag goes in the bucket.

6. Slide or swings: Player must slide down the slide or swing back and forth three times before moving on to the next obstacle.

7. Small soccer ball and goal: Shoot the ball into the net one time.

8. Safety cones and beach ball: Arrange the cones in a line, with about 4 feet between cones. Players must use their feet to dribble the ball (soccer style) around each of the cones before moving on to the next obstacle.

Play:
Line the players up, with the birthday child at the head of the line. Blow the whistle and start the stopwatch. The first player begins to run through each obstacle. When he has finished the entire course, you blow the whistle to signal that it's time for the second player to take a turn. All the children complete the course as quickly as possible in an effort to beat the clock. (You might challenge them to beat last year's total team time, or "Mom's or Dad's best time" multiplied by the number of players on the team.)

Grade School Play (age 6 to 10)

672 Spillin' the Beans

The bobbing helmets add a marvelous sense of silliness, but there's a good dose of challenge to this game as well.

AGE: 6–10 YRS

CATEGORY: BIRTHDAY PARTY (GROUP GAMES)/ OUTDOOR

NUMBER OF CHILDREN: SIX OR MORE

Materials:

Scissors

Velcro with sticky-back adhesive (sold at discount or hardware stores)

Heavy-duty paper bowls (1 for each child)

Plastic headbands (1 for each child)

2 large plastic tubs

Dried navy beans or kidney beans

Stopwatch or kitchen timer

Setup:

Cut four sets of Velcro pieces into 1-inch-long long pieces. Turn each paper bowl upside down. Peel the tape off one of the fuzzy pieces, center it on the bottom of the bowl, and press firmly. Now peel the tape off one of the scratchy strips of Velcro, center it at the top of the headband, and press firmly. Allow the sticky tape to set for 5 minutes. Next, attach the headband to the bottom of the bowl by using the interlocking Velcro.

Create a starting line and finish line on the lawn. Put two plastic tubs at the finish line. All players put on their Spillin' the Beans headgear. An adult is designated as Official Bean Counter (O.B.C.); the O.B.C. counts out 10 beans for each player and places them in the players' bowls.

Team Play:

The O.B.C. shouts, "Ready, set, go!" and sets the kitchen timer for 3 to 5 minutes or more. The first player on each team begins running toward the finish line (trying to spill as few beans as possible), positions his head directly over his team's tub, and carefully tips his head to spill all the beans into the tub. (Players may learn that it's best to kneel before dumping the beans.) He runs back to the starting line and tags the next player, who repeats the action. The O.B.C. refills the bowls of players in the rear of the line as needed, since players may take a second or third turn before the timer goes off. When it sounds, the O.B.C. counts the beans in each team's pan. The team with the most beans wins that round.

Group Play:

Decide ahead of time on the number of beans needed to win the game. The O.B.C. puts 10 beans in each player's bowl and lines players up behind the starting line; he shouts, "Ready, set, go!" and starts the kitchen timer. The players proceed as above. When the timer sounds, the O.B.C. counts the beans in the tub to determine if the team did beat the clock *and* get the desired number of beans into the tub.

673 Bean Grabber

To spice things up, any player heading toward the goal can choose to stoop down and pick up spilled beans on the way—a tricky business that may prove to be more trouble than it's worth. This option may appeal to the older, more confident players in the crowd and creates an unpredictable element to the play!

Play-Rehearsal

Play a few new games with your child before a playmate arrives so he becomes comfortable with the rules and confident about playing. Then, when friends arrive, your child will have a whole repertoire of new games to play without needing you to step in with instructions.

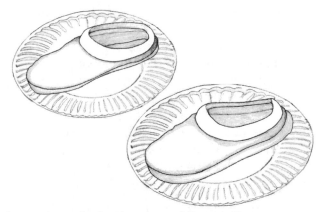

674 | Platypus Maximus

My neighbors are still wondering what in the world we were doing with "snowshoes" on our feet last summer and why a grown man was rolling on the ground laughing.

AGE: 6–10 YRS

CATEGORY: BIRTHDAY PARTY (GROUP GAMES)/ OUTDOOR

NUMBER OF CHILDREN: FOUR OR MORE

Materials:

4 dinner-size, extra-sturdy paper plates (do not use plastic plates)

Scissors

5" roll of Velcro with sticky-back adhesive (sold at discount stores)

2 pairs of inexpensive children's slippers

Roll of 2"-wide painter's tape

2 large plastic tubs or roasting pans (1 for each team)

Dried kidney beans

4 plastic cups

Stopwatch or kitchen timer

Setup:

First, make the "Platypus Plates" (snowshoes): Put two paper plates on the ground. Cut four pieces of fuzzy Velcro strips slightly shorter than the length of the slippers. Peel off the paper backing and stick that Velcro to the bottom of each slipper, right down the center. Now cut four strips of the scratchy Velcro to the same length, peel off the paper, and stick these strips to the center of each of the paper plates. Next, stick each slipper to a paper plate.

Shortly before the party, create a starting line and finish line in the grass by placing a 6-foot-long strip on the grass. (The easiest way to do this is to roll out the tape, sticky side down, in 12-inch sections, pressing down with your feet to secure it as you go.) Place two large plastic tubs or roasting pans at the finish line a few feet apart. Place 10 beans in each plastic cup, and line up the cups on a table or other level surface nearby.

Tip: If the lawn is wet, and your tape isn't sticking, see "Start and Finish" box, page 348.

Team Play:

Create two teams. Line up all the players and give the first child in each line a pair of the Platypus Plates. Select one adult as the Official Bean Counter (O.B.C.). The O.B.C. places 10 kidney beans around the players' feet on their Platypus Plates. On your "Go," the first players begin to walk or shuffle down to the finish line without spilling their beans. (Players should be encouraged to figure out what works best; sometimes a slower pace spills fewer beans!) When the players reach the finish line, they lift one foot at a time and gently spill the beans into their team's tub. They then quickly shuffle back to the starting line, take the Platypus Plates off their feet, and hand them off to the next player; the O.B.C. dumps 10 beans on the next players' plates. The relay continues until all the players have taken a turn, at which point the O.B.C. counts the total number of beans in each team tub. The team with the most beans wins.

Group Play:

Decide ahead of time on the number of beans (100 beans, for example!) the team has to get into the team's tub before the buzzer sounds.

To get things started, the O.B.C. puts 10 beans on the first player's plate and shouts, "Ready, set, go!" Set the kitchen timer for 5 to 10 minutes, depending on the number of players. Proceed as above. When the timer sounds, the O.B.C. counts the beans in the pan to see if the team has met or exceeded the total number of beans needed to beat the clock. If not, alter the required number of beans or time and challenge the children to a second try, and with a bit of luck, the repeat performance will be a winner.

NOTE: This game requires coordination and strategy, so it's wise to give each child a practice run before the competition begins.

675 Ping-Pong Platypus Maximus

For a simpler version of this game, create the Platypus Plates (snowshoes) described above, and put two to four Ping-Pong balls (or plastic Wiffle golf balls) on the Platypus Plates as each child shuffles down to the finish line (and dumps the balls into the team tub). The team with the most balls in the team tub at the end of the game wins. Or, create a Group Game where all the children are on one team and they each take a turn shuffling down the lawn with Ping-Pong balls on their Platypus Plates, working together to get 20 Ping-Pong balls into the tub before the timer sounds.

676 Platypus Toss-Amus

Create the Platypus Plates (snowshoes) described above, and mark a starting line on the lawn with a finish line approximately 6 feet away (adjust the distance to suit the tossing abilities of your players). Place a plastic laundry basket at the finish and six Ping-Pong balls or plastic Wiffle golf balls on the lawn at the starting line. Each player takes a turn wearing one of the Platypus Plates (left foot or right foot), standing at the starting line, and launching one ball at a

time toward the laundry basket. Score one point for each ball that is pitched inside the laundry basket, and the team with the most points at the end of the game wins. Or, create a Group Play version of Platypus Toss-Amus where all the children are on one team and they work together to get 20 balls into the basket before the timer sounds.

*SAFETY ALERT: Use only paper plates for this game, not slippery disposable plastic plates. These Platypus Plates are only to be worn on grassy areas of the lawn; do not allow the children to wear them anywhere else.

677 Wacky Waiter

Don't dillydally, your customers are waiting! Tonight we are serving a special dish: essence of Ping-Pong ball.

AGE: 6–10 YRS

CATEGORY: BIRTHDAY PARTY (GROUP GAMES)/ OUTDOOR

NUMBER OF CHILDREN: SIX OR MORE

Materials:
  1 or 2 plastic dinner plates
  1 or 2 Ping-Pong balls
  Stopwatch or kitchen timer

Setup:
Designate two starting points and two finish points.

Team Play:
Divide the players into two teams, and line up each team at a starting point. The first player on each team is given a large plastic dinner plate and a Ping-Pong ball. The players place the ball on their plates and, putting one or both hands under the plate, carry it waiter style to their respective finish points, running if they can, and trying not to drop the ball. (If a player does drop the ball, he simply stops, picks it up, and resumes the race.) He heads back to his starting

point and hands the platter to the next teammate in line. Each player runs the race, balancing the ball on the platter. The first team to have its last player return to its starting point carrying the ball on the platter wins that round of play.

Group Play:

Line up the team behind a single starting point and start the kitchen timer. Proceed as above. The object is for all the players to run the race, carrying the platter and ball before the buzzer sounds.

678 Zigzag Wacky Waiter

For older players, create a slightly more challenging game. Create two teams. Each team forms a single-file line, with the players spaced about 3 feet apart. The player at the back of each line grabs the platter and ball and after your "Go," takes off toward the other end of the line and back again, weaving around each teammate. When he gets back to his original starting place, he hands the platter and ball to the second teammate in line, then quickly dashes to the other end of the line to take his place. The second player begins weaving around the line of players, carrying the platter, going from one end of the line and back again. The game continues in this way until all the players have had a turn repeating this routine. The team whose last player gets back to his starting place first wins the game.

679 Bucket-Head How-To

All of the Bucket Head games require Bucket-Head gear, of course, and once you give a quick demo, children really enjoy making these on their own.

AGE: 6–10 YRS

CATEGORY: BIRTHDAY PARTY (GROUP GAMES)/ OUTDOOR

NUMBER OF CHILDREN: SIX OR MORE

Materials:

Scissors

5" roll of Velcro with sticky-back adhesive

Plastic whipped-topping containers or margarine tubs (8-ounce size, 1 for each child)

Inexpensive plastic headbands (1 for each child)

Marker

Create:

Cut four sets of 2-inch-long Velcro pieces. Turn one container upside down. Peel the tape off one of the fuzzy strips of Velcro and center it on the bottom of the container; press firmly. Now peel the tape off one of the scratchy strips of Velcro, center it on the top of the headband, and press firmly. Allow the sticky tape to set for 5 minutes. Next, attach the margarine tub to the headband. Repeat this process with the other margarine tubs so that you end up with six Bucket-Head hats. Write each child's name or initials on the tub part of the hat. The children are now ready to play Bucket-Head games.

Choosing Sides

Cut a small piece of paper for each child. Write the number 1 on half of the slips and the number 2 on the others. Fold these papers in half twice, toss them in a bowl, and mix them up. Have each child pull out one piece of paper. Their number determines their team: ones on this team, twos on that team.

Grade School Play (age 6 to 10)

680 Ping-Pong Bucket Brigade

"What's a bucket brigade?" my son asked years ago, when I began to weave a tale about a magical group of animals and the bucket brigade they created to douse a campfire. Here is a game that involves fast-action teamwork and wobbly buckets on each player's head.

AGE: 6–10 YRS

CATEGORY: BIRTHDAY PARTY (GROUP GAMES)/ OUTDOOR

NUMBER OF CHILDREN: SIX OR MORE

Materials:

Bucket-Head hats
 (1 for each child, see directions page 341)
2 large plastic buckets
24 Ping-Pong balls
Stopwatch or kitchen timer

Setup:

Divide the players into two teams. Position a Bucket-Head hat on each child's head so that it sits at a somewhat level position. Set two large plastic buckets on the ground to create a finish line. Mark a starting line about 30 feet from the buckets and position one player from each team at this starting line, sitting on the ground. Have the second players from each team sit about 20 feet from the buckets, and the third players about 10 feet from the buckets. (Add additional lines farther away from the buckets for every two players.)

Team Play:

Dump a Ping-Pong ball in the hats of the two players sitting at the starting line. On your "Go," the starting-line players jump up, run to the second players, and each carefully bends over to dump the Ping-Pong ball into their teammate's Bucket-Head hat. (If the ball is dropped, the child standing simply picks it up, puts it back inside his own hat and tries again.) When the ball has been successfully transferred, the first players say, "Bucket-Head!" When the second players hear this signal, they jump up and run to the third players to repeat the action. (Meanwhile, the first players return to their spots, and one of the adults puts another ball in the first players' hats—one adult is assigned to each team.) The last players run over to the bucket, where they dump their balls, shouting "Bucket-Head Brigade!" as a signal to the first players to get going. The game continues in this way. The first team to get ten balls into their big bucket wins that round of play.

Group Play:

Use only one bucket for this version. After setting up the bucket, position all the players in their own spot on the lawn in incremental distances from the bucket. Dump one Ping-

Pong ball in the hat of the player sitting at the starting line (the player farthest away from the bucket). Set the timer for 3 to 5 minutes (depending on the number of players) and say, "Ready, set, go!" The game proceeds as above, with the players trying to dump 10 balls into the team bucket before the kitchen buzzer sounds.

NOTE: Let the players know that they may use their hands to hold the headbands in place while playing all of these Bucket-Head games. This makes it manageable and fun for even the youngest players.

681 Bucket-Head Water Brigade

This game is perfect for a hot summer day and beach-themed birthday party.

AGE: 6–10 YRS

CATEGORY: **BIRTHDAY PARTY (GROUP GAMES)/ OUTDOOR**

NUMBER OF CHILDREN: **FOUR OR MORE** (plus two adults)

Materials:
Large-size plastic bucket or tub full of water

2 large, clear plastic pitchers

2 Ping-Pong balls

Bucket-Head hats (1 for each child, see directions on page 341)

2 plastic cups

Setup:
Form two teams with equal numbers of players. Place a large bucket of water to designate a starting point and a picnic table or card table as the finishing point. Place two clear plastic pitchers on the table, one for each team. Drop a Ping-Pong ball into each empty pitcher. Back at the start, have the giant bucket of water ready (for filling the Bucket-Head hats throughout the game).

Play:
Put the Bucket-Head hats on all the children in the group and line them up at the starting point. Use the cups to fill each Bucket-Head about halfway full with water. (Before the race begins, test the stability of the hats to see how much water they can hold without tipping off each child's head. Remember that it's fine for the children to use their hands to steady their buckets as they run.) One at a time, players scurry down to the table where they dump their water into their team's pitcher. This routine continues until one team fills its pitcher so high with water that the Ping-Pong ball spills out on the table. The team shouts "Water Brigade!" and wins that round of play. (Two adults should be on hand to constantly refill the players' hats with water.)

682 Water Brigade Group Relay

Use only one team pitcher and one Ping-Pong ball, and set up the children in one line. Proceed as above, setting the kitchen timer for 10 minutes before giving the group of children your "Go."

★ CLASSIC ★

683 Treasure Hunt

Transform your house or yard into a wonderland filled with treasure and mystery.

AGE: 6–10 YRS

CATEGORY: BIRTHDAY PARTY (GROUP GAMES)/ OUTDOOR

NUMBER OF CHILDREN: FOUR OR MORE

Materials:

Treasure box with prizes

Pencils

Paper

Tape

Setup:

Before the party, hide a treasure box filled with trinkets, treasures, or treats in a good hiding spot indoors or outdoors. Next, write a series of 10 to 12 progressive clues on individual pieces of paper (one clue should lead to the hiding place of the next clue). Hide each of these clues, except for the first clue, around the playing area. Consider hiding places like inside a cupboard, under the corner of an area rug, in a plastic container in the refrigerator, in a red shoe in the closet, inside an empty pitcher on the kitchen counter, or inside the pages of a favorite book on the shelf. A clue to a hiding place in the freezer might read, "Go to the coldest spot in the house." Be sure to keep a copy of all the clues in sequence on a "master clue list" that only you can review, and give hints to the children if needed.

Group Play:

Gather the group of treasure hunters together and present them with the first clue. Stick with the children throughout the treasure hunt to offer minor clues and make sure they are safe and not creating unnecessary messes. The final clue will send the group to the treasure box filled with treats. (At certain clues along the way, you can also include a very small treat for the players, like sticks of sugarless gum.)

Team Play:

Create two teams and give each team its own list of treasure clues to follow, with each clue leading to a separate bag of treats or treasures. In this variation, it's best to fill both treasure boxes with exactly the same treats to keep everyone satisfied.

684 Many Clues, Many Treasures

Create a list of clues, with each clue leading directly to a small hidden treasure. Give each child at the party a paper bag marked with her name containing three or four individual treasure clues on small pieces of paper. Tailor the prizes to the age, gender, and interests of each child. As the child finds a prize and puts it inside her bag, she calls out "Treasure!" before moving on to her next clue.

★ CLASSIC ★

685 Egg-on-a-Spoon Relay

Have a few extra hard-boiled eggs on hand—someone is sure to smash one!

AGE: 6–10 YRS

CATEGORY: BIRTHDAY PARTY (GROUP GAMES)/ OUTDOOR

NUMBER OF CHILDREN: FOUR OR MORE

Materials:

Roll of 2"-wide painter's tape

Large gift bow (made from ribbon)

Tablespoons (1 for each team)

Several hard-boiled eggs in their shells (or use Ping-Pong balls for easy cleanup!)

Stopwatch or kitchen timer

Setup:

Mark a starting line and finish line by placing a 6-foot-long strip of tape on the ground. (The easiest way to do this is to roll out the tape in 12-inch sections, pressing down with your feet to secure it as you go.) Place the large gift bow on the ground at the finish line.

Tip: If the ground is wet, and your tape lines don't stick, see "Start and Finish" box, page 348.

Team Play:

Create two teams with an equal number of players. Line up the teams behind the starting line. The first player on each team is given a spoon and a hard-boiled egg. On your "Go," the first players run to the finish line and back, balancing the egg on their spoon. (If a player drops his egg, he picks it up and goes back to the starting line to begin again.) When a player touches the finish line and returns to the starting line, he hands the egg and spoon to the next teammate, who repeats this same routine. The first team to have all its players successfully return to the starting line wins the game.

Group Play:

All the players form one team and are given this challenge: Everyone on the team must run the egg on the spoon to the finish line and back (relay style) before the buzzer sounds.

★ CLASSIC ★

686 Three-Legged Race

If your child's ever wondered what life would be like as a three-legged animal, here's his chance to find out.

QUICK & EASY

AGE: 6–10 YRS

CATEGORY:
BIRTHDAY PARTY
(GROUP GAMES)/
OUTDOOR

NUMBER OF
CHILDREN: FOUR
OR MORE

Materials:
Roll of 2"-wide painter's tape
Large bandanas (or cloth scarves)
Stopwatch or kitchen timer

Setup:

Mark a starting line and finish line on a safe, grassy area by placing a 6-foot-long strip of tape on the ground. (the easiest way to do this is to roll out the tape, sticky side down, in 12-inch sections, pressing down with your feet to secure it as you go.) Match up two similar-size partners; each pair of partners stands side by side with their legs touching and one arm around each other's shoulders. Loosely tie a cloth scarf around the partners' ankles, binding their adjoining legs together with just enough pressure so that the scarf stays in place.

Tip: If the ground is wet, and your tape lines aren't sticking, see "Start and Finish" box, page 348.

Play:

On your "Go," all the partners begin running toward the finish line, cross over the line, turn and run back to the starting line. The first pair to return to the starting line wins. You can also play this game as a relay race, either by dividing the children up into two teams or by playing against the clock as a group.

*SAFETY ALERT: Children may trip and fall, so provide a safe playing area.

687 Sneaker Relay

Velcro and brightly colored sneakers provide an undeniable advantage in this game.

Materials:
- Roll of 2"- wide painter's tape
- 2 large cardboard boxes
- Sneakers
- Stopwatch or kitchen timer

AGE: 6–10 YRS

CATEGORY: BIRTHDAY PARTY (GROUP GAMES)/ OUTDOOR

NUMBER OF CHILDREN: EIGHT OR MORE

Setup:
Find a safe, grassy area suitable for barefoot play. Mark a starting line and finish line by placing a 6-foot-long strip of tape on the grass. (Roll out the tape, sticky side down, in 12-inch sections, pressing it down with your feet to secure it as you go.) Place two cardboard boxes across the finish line.

Tip: If the ground is wet, and your tape lines aren't sticking, see "Start and Finish" box, page 348.

Team Play:
Divide the players into two teams, and line up the teams at the starting line. On your "Go," the first players run to the finish line, take off their shoes, deposit them in the team box, and race back (barefooted) to tag the next teammate in line. The games continues in this way. When everyone has had a turn, players continue the relay race in reverse, running to the finish line to search for their shoes, putting them back on, and racing back to tag the next teammate in line. All the players continue in this way, putting their shoes back on. The first team to finish the race wins.

Group Play:
Play as above, using only one cardboard box and having the group race against the clock. Set the kitchen timer or stopwatch for 3 to 4 minutes (depending on the number of players and distance they run).

★ CLASSIC ★

688 Sneaker Scramble

Get those sneakers on and then run like the wind!

Materials:
- Roll of 2"- wide painter's tape
- Sneakers
- Laundry basket
- Stopwatch or kitchen timer

AGE: 6–10 YRS

CATEGORY: BIRTHDAY PARTY (GROUP GAMES)/ OUTDOOR

NUMBER OF CHILDREN: EIGHT OR MORE

Setup:
Mark a starting line and finish line on a safe, grassy area using a 6-foot-long strip of tape. (Roll out the tape, sticky side down, in 12-inch sections, pressing down with your feet to secure it as you go.) Have all the players take off their shoes and deposit them in the laundry basket. Stir the shoes around so they are thoroughly mixed up. Place the basket at the finish line.

Tip: If the ground is wet, and your tape lines aren't sticking, see "Start and Finish" box, page 348.

Team Play:
Line up both teams behind the starting line. On your "Go," the first player on each team runs to the pile of shoes, scrambles around to find his shoes, puts them on, ties the laces, and races back to tag the next player in line. Each player continues in the same way. The first team to have all its players cross the finish line wearing their own shoes wins the game.

Group Play:
Line all the kids up behind the starting line. Announce, "Ready, set, go!" and set the kitchen timer. All the players proceed as above. The goal is for all the players to finish the race before the buzzer sounds.

★CLASSIC★

689 Sack Race

Is that a ghost, a jumping bean, or a kangaroo?

AGE: 6–10 YRS

CATEGORY:
BIRTHDAY PARTY
(GROUP GAMES)/
OUTDOOR

NUMBER OF
CHILDREN: FOUR
OR MORE

Materials:

Roll of 2"-wide painter's tape

Old pillowcases or burlap sacks
    (1 for each child)

Setup:

Mark a starting line and finish line on the lawn by placing a 6-foot-long strip of tape on the ground. Give each child a sack and line them up behind the starting line. Help each child step inside his sack, showing him how to grab the top corners of the pillowcase with both hands.

Play:

On your "Go," the players begin hopping toward the finish line. Once they reach the line, each child crosses over it, turns, and hops back to the starting line inside his sack. If a player falls, he must get back up, get back in the sack, and continue hopping. The first player back to the starting line wins. This game can also be played as a relay, either as a group or in teams.

★CLASSIC★

690 Pack-It-Up Relay

If your child oversleeps, there's a good chance she has had to get dressed really quickly. That skill will come in handy in this game!

AGE: 6–10 YRS

CATEGORY:
BIRTHDAY PARTY
(GROUP GAMES)/
OUTDOOR

NUMBER OF
CHILDREN: SIX
OR MORE

Materials:

10 articles of assorted clothing

2 small suitcases or tote bags

Roll of 2"-wide painter's tape

Stopwatch or kitchen timer

Setup:

Pack five varied articles of clothing in each suitcase and shut the suitcase. Mark a starting line and finish line by placing a 6-foot-long strip of tape on the ground. (Roll out the tape in 12-inch sections, pressing down with your feet to secure it as you go.)

Tip: If the ground is wet, and your tape lines aren't sticking, see "Start and Finish" box, page 348.

Team Play:

Divide the players into two teams. Line up the teams behind the starting line and give the

> "There is a reason why children all over the world, in every generation, forever, have tended to play the same sorts of games in the same sorts of ways with the same sorts of objects. There are always balls, there are always hoops, there are always things that look like dolls. There are always chasing and tagging and running and climbing and rolling games. The reason? The human brain has a need for it."
>
> **—Jane M. Healy, Ph.D.**
> educational psychologist and author of *Your Child's Growing Mind*
> and *Failure to Connect: How Computers Affect Our Children's Minds*

Grade School Play (age 6 to 10)

first player on each team a suitcase. On your "Go," the players pick up the suitcases and run to the finish line. At the finish line, they open the suitcases and put on every single item over their clothes. They must put on the items as they were intended to be worn. They then close the suitcases and dash back to the starting line. Once there they open the suitcase, take off all the clothes and pack them back up, closing the suitcase and handing it to the next teammate. This routine continues with each player. For the second round, the teams swap suitcases.

Group Play:

Play as above, using only one suitcase and having the children compete against the timer. Set the timer for 4 to 8 minutes, depending on

the number of players and distance they must travel during the relay. (Do a trial run with your child the day before the party, to estimate how much time is needed per child and share a few laughs as you test the game together.)

691 Cardboard Box Relay

To simplify and speed up this game, start out with each outfit in a cardboard box at the starting line. The first player puts the entire outfit on, runs to the finish line and back again, takes off the outfit, and puts each item back in the box; when the last item of clothing has been dropped in the box, the second player in line repeats the same routine. The first team to complete the entire relay wins the game.

Start and Finish

Many games played on the lawn need a starting line, finish line, center line, or pitching (free throw) line. Here are two easy and effective ways to create official-looking lines on any lawn whether it's dry or wet:

1. With Tape Use a 2-inch-wide roll of painter's tape (masking tape) placed sticky side down on the lawn. (Yes, it sticks to the grass, and stays in place, so long as the grass is dry!) The easiest way to place a long strip of tape on the lawn is to roll out about 12 inches of tape at a time, pressing it sticky side down, with your feet to secure it on the grass.

2. With Flour Remove the screw-on lid from an empty 36-ounce ketchup bottle, wash it out, and dry it thoroughly. (Speed up the drying process by inserting a paper towel into the bottle and using a butter knife to move it around to absorb any drops of water.) Once the bottle is dry, use a funnel to fill it with flour. Screw the plastic lid back onto the bottle. Go outside, open the cap, tip the bottle upside down a few inches above the grass, and squeeze the bottle to draw a line on the lawn with the flour. (Make the line thick enough so that a few feet trampling over it do not "erase" it.) For large group play (and lots of feet running back and forth across the finish line), have extra flour on standby to repair any sections of erased finish line. Once the games are over, use the garden hose to thoroughly flush the flour from the lawn so it doesn't damage the grass.

Water Play Party Games

Setting up a sprinkler or hose in the backyard makes for some great freestyle splishing and splashing, slipping and sliding, but I've given the games in this section a little more structure to make way for the occasional surprise drenching—like when a water balloon bursts on the ground right at your feet. Or when a player hits a soggy home run in Water Balloon Baseball. Expect lots of squeals and giggles, but also keep in mind that some children love group water play and others are reluctant to get wet. One thing for sure is that many of these games are good for a real soaking, so bathing suits or a change of clothes are a must. Let the water games begin!

★ CLASSIC ★

692 Water Balloon Toss

Great refreshing fun on a hot-hot-hot summer day!

QUICK & EASY

AGE: 6–10 YRS

CATEGORY:
BIRTHDAY PARTY
(GROUP GAMES)/
WATER PLAY

NUMBER OF
CHILDREN: SIX
OR MORE

Materials:
Balloons*
Water
Plastic laundry basket
Bathing suits

Setup:
Fill a dozen or more balloons with water. Gently place them in the laundry basket.

Play:
Pair off the children. Create a line down the center of a safe, grassy lawn; line up the children on the line. Each set of partners should face each other, standing about 3 feet apart, with the line in between them. Give a water-filled balloon to each player on the right side of the line. On your "Go," each player gently tosses the balloon to her partner. (It takes finesse to toss and catch these balloons without breaking them.) If a player's balloon breaks, she and her partner are out of the game during the rest of the round of play. After each successful catch, the player who caught the balloon takes one giant step backward. Call out "Ready, set, go!" when all the players are ready for the next throw, so that all the balloon-throwing happens simultaneously. The game continues in this way until only one duo is left.

*SAFETY ALERT: Supervise all balloon play to prevent children less than eight years old from choking on uninflated balloons or balloon pieces.

> ❝As kids get out on the playground, it gives them an opportunity to negotiate and to cooperate. When each child just sits in front of a computer or video game, we are depriving them of the opportunity to develop those social skills.❞
>
> **—Dr. Marilyn Benoit, M.D.**
> Clinical Associate Professor of Psychiatry at Georgetown University Medical Center; past president, American Academy of Child & Adolescent Psychiatry

Grade School Play (age 6 to 10)

693 Soggy-Susan

A wet beach towel flappin' and slippin' and drippin' while you run is silly fun for a summer day.

AGE: **6–10 YRS**

CATEGORY: **BIRTHDAY PARTY (GROUP GAMES)/ OUTDOOR**

NUMBER OF CHILDREN: **EIGHT OR MORE** (plus two adults)

Materials:

Roll of 2"-wide painter's tape

2 large buckets

2 heavy-duty beach towels

Bathing suits

Stopwatch or kitchen timer

Setup:

Play on a safe, grassy lawn. Mark a starting line and finish line by placing a 6-foot-long strip of tape on the ground. (The easiest way to do this is to roll out the tape, sticky side down, in 12-inch sections, pressing down with your feet to secure it as you go.) Fill both buckets with water and place them at the finish line. Thoroughly dunk each of the beach towels in a bucket so that they are soaked to the max. You'll need two adults to continuously refill the buckets during the game.

Tip: If the ground is wet, and your tape lines won't stick, see "Start and Finish" box, page 348.

Team Play:

Hand the first player on each team a thoroughly drenched beach towel. The players wrap the towels around their waists or chests (toga style) and tuck the ends of the towel firmly in place. On your "Go," the players race to the finish line, take off the beach towels, and dunk them in the buckets of water. They then race back to the finish and hand their teammates the sopping-wet towels. This routine continues until the last member of the team crosses the finish line. Anytime a player loses the beach towel while running, he must stop, pick it up, place it back around his waist, and resume running.

Group Play:

Play as before, using only one towel and bucket and having the group racing against the clock.

694 Water Balloon Baseball

This is an equal-opportunity activity. Everybody gets soaked!

AGE: **6–10 YRS**

CATEGORY: **BIRTHDAY PARTY (GROUP GAMES)/ OUTDOOR**

NUMBER OF CHILDREN: **SIX OR MORE**

Materials:

Balloons*

Water

Plastic laundry basket

Foam bats

Setup:

While the children put on their bathing suits, fill up the water balloons and gently place them in the laundry basket.

Play:

This is a free-form game where one player pitches the balloons while the other players try to hit a home run by popping the water balloons with the bat. (Even a "foul ball" or "strike" makes a splash.) There are no winners or losers in this game, just lots of fun, laughs, and cooling off.

695 Water Balloon Basketball

Players take turns holding a small plastic colander while their teammates toss water balloons into the basket. The basket holder can move about to assist in "catching" the balloon.

*SAFETY ALERT: Supervise all balloon play to prevent children less than eight years old from choking on uninflated balloons or balloon pieces.

696 ★CLASSIC★ Bobbing for Apples

Make like a horse and use only your teeth to grab the shiny red apples.

AGE: 6–10 YRS

CATEGORY:
BIRTHDAY PARTY
(GROUP GAMES)/
OUTDOOR

NUMBER OF
CHILDREN: FOUR
OR MORE

Materials:

Newspapers

Large washtub or dishpan

Apples

Large towels

Safety pins

Setup:
Put several layers of newspapers on the floor. Place the washtub on top of the papers and fill with clean, drinkable water. Float several apples in the tub.

Play:
Select one player who'll begin the game: The other players stand several feet away and may not touch or taunt this player in any way. Create a makeshift bib for this player, using a towel and safety pin. The player kneels on the floor near the washtub, holds both hands behind her back, and attempts to grab one of the apples, using only her teeth. If she is successful at biting an apple, she carefully lifts the apple out of the tub and onto the floor.

SAFETY ALERT: Provide continuous adult supervision for this game. Set clear rules forbidding any player from pushing another player's head into the water.

Learning to Play Fair

Childhood is full of real-life opportunities to teach your child about playing fair. When your seven-year-old daughter comes home from school and mentions that she saw someone cheating, you have a perfect opportunity to have a chat about why cheating is wrong. When your six-year-old son sees another boy on the playground pushing the younger kids out of the way and jumping ahead on the slide, another conversation unfolds. Fairness can be explained quite simply to children: no cheating or hurting other players, giving everyone an equal turn to play, treating other players respectfully, and following the rules. Of course, parents' words and expectations about fairness are important, but children need to see their parents playing fair too.

Grade School Play (age 6 to 10)

Large Group Games

Getting together to play with a large group of friends offers great excitement for children six to ten. Large group games give them the chance to play many roles—each child can take a turn at chasing or fleeing, kicking or catching, leading or following. Sometimes the rules must be followed to a T; other times the children ad-lib new rules and alternate ways of playing. Here are some crowd-pleasing games that can be played competitively or just for fun.

Sunday Afternoon Play Club

Children today have busy lives, with friends often spread across town rather than right down the block. These two facts often make it difficult to organize a good game of kickball or hide-and-seek in the neighborhood. How about starting a play club or playgroup that meets once a month, perhaps on a Sunday afternoon? Test the waters for this idea by contacting a group of families with children of similar ages and interests. (Each family would commit to hosting a monthly party at their home or nearby park.) These playgroups are a great way for parents and kids to play kickball or other large group games together. (Other favorites might include: Wiffle baseball, water balloon toss, wheelbarrow relays, and so many others.) You might agree in advance that each family hosting will end playtime with a simple dinner of sandwiches or pizza to make this a real party.

> **❝**I like to work with kids on how they can prevent conflict, rather than just dealing with conflict resolution. In my book, I talk about two brothers whose younger cousins are coming over to play for the day. One brother has good social skills; the other has poor social skills. The brother with good social skills takes all of his delicate toys and puts them away so the younger cousins can't break them. The child with poor social skills meets the young cousins at the door and says, 'If you go into my room and you touch one of my models, you are never coming back again,' not understanding that he could prevent that conflict by taking some preventive action.**❞**
>
> **—Richard Lavoie, M.Ed.**
> author of *It's So Much Work to Be Your Friend:*
> *Helping the Child with Learning Disabilities Find Social Success*

697 Bandana Base

What's your team color?

Materials:

4 objects to use as bases

Bucket

An even number of red and blue bandanas (1 bandana for each child)

Stopwatch or kitchen timer

AGE: 6–10 YRS

CATEGORY:
**BIRTHDAY PARTY
(GROUP GAMES)/
LARGE GROUP**

NUMBER OF
CHILDREN: SIX
OR MORE

Setup:

Set up one home plate and three bases on the lawn, in baseball-diamond formation, with each base about 20 feet from the next. Place the bucket near home plate.

Team Play:

Form two teams. One team is given the red bandanas, and the other the blue; all the players tuck their bandanas into their side pockets or the side of their waistbands, with the edge sticking out about 3 inches. Designate one team as team 1 and the other as team 2. Set the kitchen timer for 5 minutes; on your "Go," the first player on team 1 takes off running around the bases. When he reaches home plate, he drops his bandana in the bucket and the second player begins running the bases. When this second player reaches home plate, he drops his bandana in the bucket and the third player takes off around the bases. (If the game is played with a small number of players on each team, each player must be given two or three bandanas and take two or three turns running around the bases.) The players continue running the bases and dropping bandanas in the team bucket when they return to home plate. When the buzzer sounds, count the bandanas inside the bucket to find the team's score. The timer is set for 5 minutes again, with team 2 taking a turn in exactly the same way. After each team has had

their turn, the one with the most bandanas in their bucket wins.

Group Play:

Play as above, using a single color of bandana, or mix them up randomly; have the group race against the clock.

698 Backward Bandana Relay

Mark a starting line and a finish line and create two teams. Place two empty buckets at the starting line and give each child two or three bandanas. Set your kitchen timer for 3 to 5 minutes (depending on the number of players and distance each must run). The first player runs or quickly walks backward to the finish line and then runs normally to the starting line; when he drops his bandana in the bucket, the next player on his team starts his backward jaunt. Use a timer set for a specific amount of time. When the buzzer sounds, the team with the most bandanas in their team bucket wins.

> "The two easiest skills to teach, which we know are the two most highly correlated traits of well-liked kids—they smile and they use eye contact. And you can reinforce both of those. 'Oh, I love that smile!' 'Oh, you were looking at your friend. He looked like he was interested in what you were saying, and you were looking like you were interested in what your friend was saying.'"
>
> **—Michele Borba, Ed.D.**
> former classroom teacher, author of
> *Parents Do Make a Difference* and
> *12 Simple Secrets Real Moms Know*

Grade School Play (age 6 to 10)

699 Chain Chase

This game eventually melds the children into one long tagging machine.

QUICK & EASY

AGE: 6–10 YRS

CATEGORY: BIRTHDAY PARTY (GROUP GAMES)/ LARGE GROUP

NUMBER OF CHILDREN: SIX OR MORE

Materials:

Roll of 2"-wide painter's tape

Setup:

Create a starting line by placing a 6-foot-long strip of tape on the ground. (Roll out the tape, sticky side down, in 12-inch sections, pressing down with your feet to secure it as you go.) Create a finish line 50 feet away in the same manner. Mark off sidelines to designate the out-of-bounds areas, and to keep play restricted to one area of the lawn. One player is selected to be the tagger and stands between the starting line and finish line. All the other players line up behind the starting line.

Tip: If the lawn is wet, and your tape lines aren't sticking, see "Start and Finish" box, page 348.

Play:

The tagger calls out, "Ready, set, run!" and all the players try to run to the finish line without being touched by the tagger. When a player is tagged, she instantly joins hands or locks elbows with the original tagger and helps tag runners on the next round of play. When all players who haven't been tagged have reached the finish line, the tagger calls out, "Ready, set, run!" again, and the players run back to the other side. Once the chain has three or more players, only the players on the end of the chain are allowed to do the tagging. The game continues until every player has been tagged. On the next round, the first person who was tagged becomes the starting tagger.

700 Roaming Hoops

The power of simple toys like a ball and a hoop goes way, way back in time.

QUICK & EASY

AGE: 6–10 YRS

CATEGORY: BIRTHDAY PARTY (GROUP GAMES)/ LARGE GROUP

NUMBER OF CHILDREN: SIX OR MORE

Materials:

Roll of 2"-wide painter's tape

Hula-Hoops

Inflatable beach balls

Stopwatch or kitchen timer

Setup:

Create a free-throw line and a backboard line about 20 feet away by placing a 4- to 6-foot strip of tape on the lawn sticky side down. Have the children do a test run tossing the ball into the hoops before the game begins, to decide the best distance between the free-throw line and the backboard line. The lines should be positioned far enough apart to create a bit of a challenge, but close enough for a good shot at success.

Team Play:

Form two teams and select two players from each team to be the hoops. These players stand at the backboard line, holding a large

Hula-Hoop for the beach balls to pass through. The other players on the team take turns shooting the beach ball from behind the free-throw line. Though the hoops start at the backboard line, they are allowed to move toward the ball in order to help get it through the hoop. Each team gets 20 shots, and the team that sinks the most baskets wins.

Group Play:

Play as above, using a single hoop and having the group race against the clock.

★ CLASSIC ★

701 Kickball

This old-time favorite is tailor-made for kids, but grown-ups seem to like it too!

AGE: 8–10 YRS

CATEGORY: BIRTHDAY PARTY (GROUP GAMES)/ LARGE GROUP

NUMBER OF CHILDREN: ELEVEN TO TWENTY

Materials:

Squares of carpet or bath mats

Playground ball

Setup:

Create a baseball diamond in the lawn, with home plate, a pitcher's mound, and first, second, and third bases. For older kids, place the bases 30 feet apart; half that distance for younger kids. Divide the children into two teams.

Play:

Toss a coin to see which team goes first. The team in the field disperses players at each base and in the outfield. The team "at bat" lines its players up to establish a kicking order. (Every player gets a turn before anyone can kick a second time.)

The team in the field chooses from the following four positions: the *pitcher* stands at the pitcher's mound and rolls the ball to the

kicker; the *catcher* stands behind the kicker at home plate, trying to catch the ball and get the player out; the *base players* are positioned at each of the three bases to try to catch the balls, kicking them to whichever base the kicker is approaching to get him out; the *outfielders* stand farther out and perform the same role as the base players.

Once everyone is in place, the pitcher rolls the ball to the first kicker. When he kicks the ball into the field, he runs the bases. The batting team scores a point for every player who runs home. Additional rules follow:

Strikes:

If the kicker attempts to kick the ball but misses it, this is a strike. If the ball is kicked outside the "foul line" (the line that runs from home plate to first base and home plate to third base), the kicker receives a strike. Three strikes (of any kind) and the kicker is out.

Balls:

If the pitcher rolls the ball high or way off course, his pitch counts as a ball. Four balls means the kicker gets to walk to first base, and any player on first moves to second base, and so on.

Outs:

If a player on the field catches a ball before it hits the ground or tags a base before the kicker gets there and while the kicker is still between bases, the kicker is out.

If the kicker gets tagged (touched lightly) by the ball while running to a base, he is out. Any other player running between bases can also be tagged by the ball.

After three outs, the inning is over, and the teams switch places and roles.

Steals:

Players on any base may attempt to run to the next base as soon as the pitcher rolls the ball to the kicker, but before he actually kicks it. However, if this stealer is tagged by the ball in the process, he is out.

Runs:

One point is scored for every player who runs to home base on any play.

Innings:

Traditionally there are nine innings in the game, but shorten the game to only a few innings and mix up the teams if you like to keep younger children interested.

NOTE: Since this is a game with fairly complex rules, be flexible and improvise as you see how children respond.

★ CLASSIC ★

702 Dragon's Tail

This dragon doesn't breathe fire, but it sure doesn't like it when you pull its tail!

QUICK & EASY

Materials:
2 bandanas or small scarves
Stopwatch or kitchen timer
Paper
Pencil

AGE: **5–8 YRS**

CATEGORY:
**BIRTHDAY PARTY
(GROUP GAMES)/
LARGE GROUP**

NUMBER OF
CHILDREN: **EIGHT
OR MORE**

Setup:

Form two teams; each team creates a dragon by lining up, facing the same direction, with each player holding on to the waist of the player in front of him. The player at the end of each dragon tucks a bandana in his back pocket or into the back of his waistband, leaving the end dangling so that the tail is hanging out. Players then decide upon the in-bounds and out-of-bounds areas for this chasing game.

Play:

Begin with each team at opposite ends of the yard. Set the kitchen timer for 8 to 10 minutes, and as one player calls out, "Dragon's Tail," both teams run toward the center. Now the dragons try to steal each other's tails! The first player in line is the only player allowed to try to do this. Each time a team successfully yanks the other's tail it scores a point. Keep track of the points so the players can concentrate on the task at hand.

★ CLASSIC ★

703 Red Rover

This game gives the players a chance to see how strong they can be when they combine muscle power with strategy.

QUICK & EASY

AGE: **6–10 YRS**

CATEGORY:
**BIRTHDAY PARTY
(GROUP GAMES)/
LARGE GROUP**

NUMBER OF
CHILDREN: **EIGHT
OR MORE**

Materials:
Kitchen timer

Setup:

Create two teams and have them each select a team captain. One team lines up at one end of the lawn, with all team members holding hands tightly, the other team lines up facing the first team at the other end of the lawn. Allow some extra room behind each team line for space to run. Set the timer for 10 to 15 minutes.

Play:

The captain of the first team picks one member of the second team and extends him this invitation: "Red Rover, Red Rover, let ____ come over" *(insert the player's name).* The selected player runs toward the line of opposing players and attempts to break through their hands. If he is successful, he picks one opponent from the line (other than the captain) to join his own team at the other end of the field. However, if the charging player is *not* successful at breaking through the line, then he becomes a member of the team that caught him. Then it's the second team's turn to call Red Rover, and each team continues taking turns. When the buzzer sounds, the team with the most players takes the round.

★ CLASSIC ★

704 Capture the Flag

With its multiple choices and fast-moving action, Capture the Flag is both tactical and athletic.

AGE: **8–10 YRS**

CATEGORY: **BIRTHDAY PARTY (GROUP GAMES)/ LARGE GROUP**

NUMBER OF CHILDREN: **EIGHT OR MORE**

Materials:
Roll of 2"-wide painter's tape
Bandanas in 2 different colors (1 for each child)

Setup:
Divide the children into two teams and assign each team a bandana color. Create a square playing area and mark a line down the center by placing a length of tape on the lawn, sticky side down. Assign each team to a half. All players place their bandanas on the ground along their back boundary, and stand slightly in front of them.

Tip: If the lawn is wet, and your tape line isn't sticking, see "Start and Finish" box, page 348.

Play:
On your "Go," each team rushes toward the other team's end of the field, trying to capture their opponent's "flag" (bandana) and carry it to their own end of the field. If a player is tagged on the opposing team's field before he has successfully captured a flag, he is considered captured. Once captured, he must stand behind his opponents' flags until one of his own teammates manages to cross over and tag him, setting him free. (So tagging is an action with two uses in this game: You can tag a captured member of your own team to set him free, or you can tag an opponent to imprison him.) If a player is successful in grabbing an opponent's flag, he runs back to his own side of the field and cannot be tagged along the way. (But players can only capture one flag at a time, and can't capture a flag and free a teammate in the same run.) The team that captures all its opponents' flags wins the game; or set a kitchen timer for 10 minutes, and the team with the most flags at the sound of the buzzer wins the round.

> ❝As an adult at a party, when you want to be involved in a conversation, you just don't go up and say, 'What are you talking about? Can I talk?' You listen to the conversation, you figure out what people are talking about, and you say something that's relevant. Young kids have to learn this same sort of thing. To a certain extent you have to adapt to the group rather than the group adapting to you. If we give children the opportunity to learn these kinds of entry skills and learn how to share, they'll be much more successful than if we do the intervention for them.❞
>
> —**William Corsaro, Ph.D.**
> professor of sociology and author of *We're Friends, Right? Inside Kids' Culture*

Grade School Play (age 6 to 10)

What to Do When Your Child Loses

Elementary-age children have a natural tendency to compete with others. They are at a stage where they are trying to figure out who they are and what they're good at. Up to a point, this tendency is okay. But sometimes children get carried away and feel they must win at all times and at all costs in order to feel worthwhile; or they may feel so disappointed when they lose that they burst into tears. So what's a parent to do?

• Take notice of your child's many strengths and talents and be careful not to put a huge emphasis on one thing (such as his baseball abilities).

• Help your child develop an attitude of fair play and learn what it means to be a good sport.

• Encourage your child to do his personal best, to go for practice and improvement rather than being better than everyone else.

• Listen attentively when your child expresses disappointment about losing, and let him know that everyone loses sometimes.

10-Minute Cleanup Rule

Whether they're playing bandana relays, building forts, or putting on puppet shows, all that fabulous fun usually leaves a mess in its wake. Let your kids (and their playmates) know in advance that they need to allow for 10 minutes of cleanup time at the end of playtime. You might even want to talk to the other parents in your child's group of friends and try to get everyone to set this house rule in place. When everyone is on the same page about this rule, children come to expect and respect this cleanup responsibility.

Appendix I:
Family Game Night

One first-rate way to vote *yes* for family playtime is to create a Family Game Night that both parents and children can count on. Put it on your calendar, once a month or once a week, and make a commitment to this family tradition. (Yes, even during the teen years.) Of course, what you do together will change as the children move through each stage of their development, but the main ingredients remain the same—fun, play, and time together!

What Goes on at Family Game Night?

Here are a few words of wisdom to make your Family Game Night successful and exciting. Start with some easy foods like pizza or sandwiches eaten picnic style on a blanket on the floor, or decide to have breakfast for dinner. Set aside two hours for the event, and select a variety of games. (Nearly everyone will get bored with ninety minutes of playing one board game.) You may find it best to play two short, silly games that require a bit of moving around, followed by a guessing game or two. Then move on to twenty minutes of a truly engaging board game. (I've listed my favorites on the following pages.) Create your personalized Family Game Night to suit your family's style, interests, ages, and individual personalities. Here's one last bit of advice before you get started: Toddlers love to be included in the fun and excitement of family games. You'll see some activities and games listed that are toddler-friendly. (Babies will be fascinated watching and listening to all the sounds and action too.) So, without further ado, here are the best games in this book for family playtime.

Games that Require Moving About Indoors

To get everyone engaged and their energy up, a few active games are just the thing. Pick a few to try, taking into consideration the age range of the children playing, and then move on to a game around the kitchen table.

Animal Charades (ages 3–10), page 362

Beanbag Horseshoes (ages 3–10), page 290

Camelback Crawl (ages 3–10), page 183

Color Dot Hide-and-Seek (ages 1–2), page 45

Elbows to Go (ages 6–10), page 332

Hidden Stars (ages 1–2), page 80

Last Laugh (ages 3–10), page 292

Musical Cake Pan (ages 1–2), page 70

Orange Passing Relay (ages 6–10), page 325

Sock Toss (ages 1–2), page 89

Stop and Go Dancing (ages 1–2), page 88

Toddler Basketball (ages 1–2), page 54

Toddler Style Follow the Leader (ages 1–3), page 55

Games Played at the Kitchen Table

The kitchen table is a bustling center of family activity, and why should it stop after the last dish is cleared after dinner? Save the dishes for later—it's time to play! Pick your favorite word or guessing game, tabletop craft, or classic board game and go.

Alphabet Garden (ages 6–10), page 246

Blind Sketching (ages 6–10), page 246

Concentration (ages 3–10), page 279

Desert Island (ages 3–10), page 281

Dictionary Detective (ages 6–10), page 275

Did You Know? (ages 3–10), page 282

Dog Diaries (ages 3–10), page 247

Draw Me a Story (ages 6–10), page 249

Family Favorites (ages 3–10), page 281

Going on a Picnic (ages 6–10), page 278

Grand Canyon (ages 6–10), page 295

I Spy (ages 3–10), page 279

I'm Thinking of a Food (ages 3–10), page 275

Memory (ages 6–10), page 324

Odd Man Out (ages 6–10), page 328

One Fine Day! (ages 3–10 with adult help), page 294

Opposites (ages 5–10), page 141

Paint Dabber (ages 1–2), page 50

Quiz Master (ages 6–10), page 303

Rhyming Riddles (ages 5–10), page 283

Ringer-Ball (ages 1–2), page 54

Roller-Painting (ages 1–2), page 51

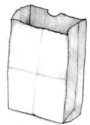

Scribble Lunch Bags (ages 1–2), page 47

Scribble Bookmarks (ages 1–2), page 47

Story Basket (ages 3–10), page 108

Story Detective (ages 3–10), page 135

Classic Board Games for Family Game Night

Games for Outdoors

When the weather outside is warm (and far from frightful), here are a few suggestions for outside play that the whole family can get in on. From the classic pastimes of kite flying, Frisbee-throwing, and horseshoes to Bubble-Clapper, Flyswatter Volleyball, and Paint Party—enjoy an afternoon in the fresh air.

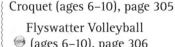

Family Game Night Favorites

It's often said that traditions are the glue that hold families together. Likewise, a few well-placed game traditions can be the glue that holds Family Game Night together through all the ages and stages of childhood. Many families have one family favorite that is *always* included on game night—one that both children and parents come to expect to play come rain or shine. It's a bit like comfort food when it comes to play routines. Though you'll certainly find your own favorites, here are four of mine: Family Trivia, Animal Charades, Celebrity, and Twenty Questions. I hope one of these games is the glue of just the right consistency to make game night a tradition that sticks with your family.

★ CLASSIC ★

705 Family Trivia

Ask "Trivia" questions about the people and events in your own family.

AGE: 3–10 YRS

CATEGORY: FAMILY

NUMBER OF CHILDREN: THREE OR MORE

Object:
Answering small questions about your unique family.

Play:
Ask a question about some current or past detail related to your family members, home, pets, etc. Pose a different question for each player at the table. For a three-year-old player you might ask, "What did Grandpa drink last summer that he said was the worst thing he ever tasted in his life?" (Answer, "tomato juice") You are likely to hear more details like, "Grandpa didn't have his glasses on and thought he was drinking orange juice.") For older children, familiar with family history, you might ask, "What was our next-door neighbor's name who lived in the pink house when we lived in Summerville?" Let the children take a turn posing questions to Mom or Dad too.

★ CLASSIC ★

706 Animal Charades

This variation of the classic is great fun for kids of all ages to play with parents. The animal antics can get pretty silly and sound effects can be added to help the youngest children in the group.

AGE: 3+

CATEGORY: FAMILY

NUMBER OF CHILDREN: THREE OR MORE

Materials:
Paper
Markers
Scissors
Bowl

Setup:
Brainstorm with your children a list of 20 familiar animals. (Include zoo animals, farm animals, pets, and every sort of animal in between.) Write the name of each animal on a small slip of paper and fold it over two times. Place these papers in the bowl.

Play:
One player is selected to draw a slip of paper from the bowl, silently read the animal name,

and act out the actions of that animal without saying a word. All the other players make guesses. (Younger animal actors may also add animal sounds as needed to help with the guessing.) Each player takes a turn as the animal actor. Play this game without keeping score just for fun, or give one point to the person who guesses the correct animal first.

Tip: For young children who can't yet read, one adult becomes the reader, and whispers the name of the selected animal to the animal actor. Or for a picture version of the game, copy photos of familiar animals (or tear photos from magazines), fold these papers in half and fold them again. Place all the photos in the bowl and each player acts out the actions and sounds of the animal selected.

707 Traditional Charades

If you're playing with an older crowd (ages seven and up), try a more traditional game of charades, with a mix of different categories. Instead of animals, write book or movie titles, famous people (fictional characters, musicians, actors, politicians), song titles, or quotations on the slips of paper. Indicate the categories by pantomiming opening a book (book title), cranking an old-fashioned movie camera (movie title), putting hands on your hips (person), making air quotes with your fingers (quotation), and so on. As clues, you may hold up a number of fingers to indicate the number of words in the particular title; hold up a number of fingers again to indicate which word you're acting out; lay a number of fingers on your forearm to indicate the number of syllables in a particular word; tug on your earlobe to indicate that the word "sounds like" another word or action; and touch a finger to the tip of your nose if one of the players has guessed correctly. Rules often vary from family to family, so make sure everyone is on the same page before starting the

first round. For older children and adults, time each acting session for about 3 minutes. For large groups, split the group into two competing teams.

★ CLASSIC ★

708 Celebrity

This family classic is a game that goes by many different names including Who?, Who Am I?, Hollywood Minute, and, one of my favorites, Mies van der Rohe.

AGE: 6+

CATEGORY: FAMILY

NUMBER OF CHILDREN: THREE OR MORE

Materials:

Paper

Scissors

Markers

Bowl

Timer

Setup:

Start by cutting or tearing many small slips of paper. Have everyone in the group write as many names of famous people on the slips of paper (one name per piece of paper), fold the pieces of paper in half, and drop them into the bowl. The people's names you might write down may include cartoon characters, TV personalities, politicians, actors, musicians, inventors, sports figures, or family friends that everyone knows—even family pets are fair game!

Play:

The group is split into two teams. The team that goes first chooses one person to be the "celebrity." The celebrity draws names from the bowl one at a time and gives clues in the first person as to her new identity. The celebrity's goal is to get her teammates to correctly guess as many identities as possible in one minute. For example, if the first slip of paper she draws is George Washington, she might say, "I was the first president of the United States" or "I chopped down a cherry tree." If she draws Winnie the Pooh, she might say, "I live in the Hundred-Acre Wood." Someone might guess Piglet, to which she might reply, "My favorite food is honey." After one of her teammates guesses Pooh, she sets the slip of paper aside and draws another one: "I'm an amphibian in love with a pig." Someone guesses "Kermit the Frog!" After one minute, her team counts up all the correct guesses—one point is awarded for each correct guess. One point is subtracted from the score for each slip of paper the celebrity "passes" on. Then play goes to the other team. Play continues between the two teams until each person has had the role of "celebrity" an equal number of times.

★ CLASSIC ★

709 Twenty Questions

Invent an easy (or silly) version of play for preschoolers or step it up for older kids, who love a good challenge.

QUICK & EASY

AGE: **3+**

CATEGORY: **FAMILY**

NUMBER OF CHILDREN: **THREE OR MORE**

Object:
Guessing the mystery word by asking a series of twenty questions.

Play:
Select one player to think of a person, place, or thing that will become the mystery word for the first round of play. The other players take turns asking questions that might reveal the mystery word. Let's say the player is thinking of a hamburger. With young children playing, he might start out by mentioning the category of his mystery word. For example, he might say, "I'm thinking of something to eat." The first player on the right then asks any question that can be answered by yes or no, such as, "Do you eat it with a spoon?" After each answer is given, the person who asked the question is allowed to take a guess. (If all the players are six and up, no need to mention the category; instead the players will take turns asking "Is it a person?" or "Is it a thing?" or "Is it a place?" in order to get more information to reveal the mystery word.) No need to keep score in this group version of the game.

710 Team Twenty Questions

If you prefer to keep score, form two teams, with one team playing against the other. Score one point for every question your team had to ask in an effort to guess the correct mystery word. (So if you asked six questions before you guessed the right answer, your team has six points for that round.) At the end of four or five rounds of play, the team with the *fewest* points wins.

> ❝We're not saying no to TV time, we're saying yes to 'come and let's play a family board game, let's play together, let's have family time.' Saying no doesn't have to be negative, it can be the most positive thing you say in a day because it allows you to do what is important—it allows you to have the family life you want to have.❞
>
> **—William Ury, Ph.D.**
> Director of the Global Negotiation Project at Harvard University and author of
> *The Power of a Positive No* and coauthor of *Getting to Yes*

Appendix II:
The Well-Stocked Toy Cupboards

The Well-Stocked Toddler Toy Cupboard

For Freestyle Play

Balls (playground balls, Wiffle balls, tennis balls, Ping-Pong balls)

Barn and farm set (includes animals)

Beanbags

Blocks (wooden, plastic, giant cardboard)

Books for read-aloud (see page 41 for a list of favorite toddler books)

Bowls (unbreakable)

Bubbles (adult supervision)

Cars and trucks

Doll stroller

Dolls and doll accessories (baby bottle, crib, blankets)

Dress-up hats, purses, wallets, backpacks

Giant bead-maze (the type found in many doctors' office waiting rooms)

Giant LEGOs

Giant (plastic) popping beads

Hula-Hoops

Jack-in-the-box

Kitchen set and plastic foods

Miniature wagon

Nesting cubes and blocks

Noah's ark (wooden set with boat and animals)

Peg-board with giant pegs

Plastic animals

Plastic lawn mower

Plastic slide

Plastic spinning top

Plastic or wooden tool set (toddler-safe)

Play dough and tools

Play grocery cart and groceries (empty yogurt containers, pudding boxes, rice boxes, etc.)

Playing cards

Pop-up activity boxes

Pots and pans, and cooking toys

Pounding bench with plastic or wooden hammer

Pretend money

Pretend picnic set (plastic or wooden)

Pull-toys

Puppets

Push toys

Puzzles (lift-out style)

Ride-on toys (without pedals, propelled by scooting feet)

Sandbox and clean sand

Sandbox toys

Shape-sorting cube

Sprinkling can

Stacking rings

Stacking wooden clown

Stuffed animals

Swings (toddler-safe type)

Tea set (unbreakable)

Toddler-size cleanup toys: little broom, dustpan

Toddler tool set (chunky plastic hammer, saw)

Toddler/Freestyle Play, contd.

Toy camera

Toy phone

Tub toys

Wading pool (adult supervision)

Waterwheel (plastic tub toy)

Wooden or plastic people and animals

Wooden or plastic toy train

Wooden train

Household Items

Bedsheets and tablecloths

Cardboard boxes, shoe boxes, and hat boxes

Cardboard tubes

Cloth napkins

Cookie sheets

Dress-up clothes

Egg cartons (cardboard)

Envelopes (new or junk mail)

Fishnet (tiny, used for fish tanks)

Funnel

Laundry basket (plastic)

Measuring cups and spoons

Metal roasting pan

Muffin tins

Notepad

Office supplies, toddler-safe

Paint rollers and sponges

Paper and/or cloth grocery bags

Phonebook

Pillowcases

Plastic and/or cardboard containers (margarine tubs, Tupperware, spice jars, tennis ball tubes, cups, yogurt cartons, milk jugs, bottles, diaper wipe boxes, etc.)

Plastic colander or kitchen strainer (no small parts)

Plastic cookie cutters

Plastic disposable plates

Plastic ice-cream scoop

Plastic lids

Plastic wastebasket

Pots, pans, safe kitchen utensils, measuring cups, bowls

Salt and pepper shakers (unbreakable and empty)

Scarves

Shovels (plastic and toddler-safe)

Socks

Towels (bath, hand, dish, beach, washcloth)

T-shirts (adult-size)

Water bottles and squirt bottles

Whistle

Wooden clothespins

For Arts and Crafts

Cardboard or foam board

Cardboard scalloped-edge border (pre-cut)

Chalkboard and chalk*

Child-size rolling pin

Colored gift bags

Crayons*

Flour and/or cornmeal

Flour tortillas

Food coloring (adult use)

Glue (sticks, liquid, glitter), all nontoxic

Library pockets

Nontoxic finger paint*

Nontoxic markers*

Paintbrushes with short handles*

Paper (butcher, notebook, copy, construction, newsprint)

Plastic nonspill paint pots*

Plastic pencil pouch

Poster board

Ruler

Safety scissors*

Scraps of ribbon and fabric

Streamers

Three-ring binder

Tissue paper or wrapping paper

Washable paints (nontoxic)

Waxed paper*

Wooden board (no nails or jagged edges)

Wooden paint sticks or giant craft sticks*

NOTE: An asterisk indicates that the toy is suitable only for older toddlers, typically ages two and a half to three, who have stopped putting everything in their mouths.

For Music

Cong-Itas*	Rattles	
Hand drums	Rhythm sticks*	
Jingle bells*	Sand blocks*	
Maracas (toddler style)	Shakers	
Pots and pans with safe spoons for tapping	Tambourine*	
	Triangle*	
	Wooden clackers	
	Wooden train whistle	

Musical Play Props

The only electronic gear mentioned in this book, these props provide music for many classic movement games.

Music (CDs, electronic files, records, tapes)

Music player (CD, mp3, record)

NOTE: An asterisk indicates that the toy is suitable only for older toddlers, typically ages two and a half to three, who have stopped putting everything in their mouths.

Is It a Good Toddler Toy?

There are loads of colorful and attractive toddler toys on the market. You've probably discovered that some of these toys have true staying power and others are more ho-hum. Of course you'll need to select toys that seem to captivate your child's individual likes and toddler passions, but here are some general guidelines to keep in the back of your mind. A toddler toy should be:

1. Safe Does it meet the following guidelines:
- Made from durable, nontoxic materials.
- No small parts that can come loose (and create a choking hazard) including balloons.
- No sharp edges or corners.
- No long, loose strings or cords that could cause a strangulation hazard.

2. Age Appropriate Toys should cater to your child's physical and mental capabilities. Keep in mind that the toy manufacturer's *recommended age for play* is just a suggestion and might not tell the whole story concerning your child's matchup with this toy. Also, toddlers do become frustrated rather easily, so be sure to avoid toys that are far too difficult to manipulate or handle. (A toy that is a *little challenging* is good, but too much challenge can be overwhelming for your child.)

3. Interesting or Fascinating Toddlers love to make things happen—action is the name of the game. Particularly look for toys that your child can use or manipulate in multiple ways. A medium-size ball, for example: Your child can roll it and chase it across the floor, push it off the couch and watch it bounce from place to place, put it in a basket and dump it out, swat at it, and discover many other spontaneous ways to play.

The Well-Stocked Preschool Toy Cupboard

For Freestyle Play

Balls (playground ball, soccer ball, tennis ball, beach ball, plastic Wiffle golf balls)

Beanbags

Blocks (wooden, cardboard, or large interlocking plastic blocks)

Boats and plastic tub toys

Dollhouse

Dolls and accessories (doll stroller, highchair)

Dress-up clothes (hats, jewelry, briefcases, purses, boots, crowns, uniforms)

Masks

Miniature basketball hoop and ball

Noah's ark (wooden or plastic animals, boat)

Plastic grocery cart

Play furniture (doll table and chairs, fences, ladders)

Play picnic set

Play vehicles (cars, trucks, planes, road signs)

Pots and pans and toy utensils

Pretend doctor's set (stethoscope, rubber hammer, lab coat)

Pretend play kitchen set (stove, fridge, counter, and pretend food)

Puppets

Puzzles

Stuffed animals

Tea set

Tool set and tool box for preschoolers

Toy cash register and money

Toy telephone

Wooden train set

Zoo or farm animals (plastic or wooden)

> 66 *When looking at toys, go for the ones that offer the most flexibility in play. Blocks, obviously, are always a huge success with young children. Also cars and trains and things like that, because they're very familiar to children. Any kind of activity that can relate to in their everyday lives is very valuable. They can make connections with their real world.* 99
>
> **—Sheridan Turner**
> early childhood educator,
> President of Kohl Children's Museum of Greater Chicago

For Building, Inventing, and Creating

Cardboard boxes of all sizes (from small gift boxes and shoe boxes to huge appliance boxes)

Plastic, wooden, or cardboard blocks

Preschool (large size) LEGOs,

Classic Junior Building Set (no small parts), Lincoln Logs, and Tinkertoys

For Outdoor Play

Bubbles and bubble wands

Bucket

Camp accessories (sleeping bags, flashlights, canteen)

Frisbee

Garden tools and watering can

Hula-Hoops

Jump rope

Large paintbrushes

Outdoor sprinkler

Pebbles

Playhouse

Tennis racket
(for adult use only)

Sandbox

Sandbox toys (shovel, bucket,
sieve, molds)

Sidewalk chalk

Swing set with slide

Toy lawn mower

Tricycles and riding toys

Wading pool and water toys

Wagon

Watering can

Wheelbarrow

Household Items

Aprons

Bedsheets, blankets,
and tablecloths

Bicycle pump

Binoculars

Birthday candles

Blank index cards
or flash cards

Briefcase, backpack,
or suitcase

Button box filled with buttons

Cake decorating set (empty)

Calculator

Calendar

Catalogs, magazines, maps, tour
books, coupons, fliers

Cleaning utensils (mop, bucket,
broom, dustpan)

Clipboard

Clocks (alarm, wall, wristwatch)

Coffee filters

Coins and coin sorter

Colander or kitchen strainer

Color dot stickers

Communication accessories
(headphones, walkie-talkies,
pretend microphones)

Cookie sheets
and/or pizza pans

Credit cards and
checkbooks (expired)

Dice

Dowel rods

First-aid supplies
(Band-Aids, cotton swabs,
cloth bandages)

Fishing tackle (no hooks,
plastic only)

Flyswatter (new)

Food coloring

Funnel

Helmet

Hinged hair clip

Ice-cube tray

Juice glasses (plastic)

Jumbo drinking straws

Life jackets

Lunch boxes

Magnets

Mesh shower poufs

Metal roasting pan

Muffin tins

Occupation tools and supplies
(builder's level, babysitter's
storybooks, photographer's
backdrop, astronaut's "space
food")

Office supplies (paper, envelopes,
ruler, stapler, single-hole punch,
safety scissors, pencils, file
holders, pens, desk calendars,
notebooks)

Paper chef's hat

Paper plates, towels, napkins,
coffee cups, cupcake holders

Pasta of every shape

Photos of family and friends

Pillows

Ping-Pong balls

Place mats

Plastic cake or pie plate

Plastic and cardboard containers
(buckets, margarine tubs, milk
cartons, oatmeal canisters, film
containers)

Plastic flowers

Plastic headbands

Plastic laundry basket

UNPLUGGED PLAY

Prescholl/Household Items, contd.

Plastic pet-food scoops (with rounded edges)

Plastic spice jars (filled with old spices or empty)

Poker chips

Pots, pans, safe kitchen utensils, measuring cups, bowls

Radio (pretend)

Rags

Scales (kitchen or bathroom)

Seashells

Serving utensils (spoons, spatulas, pie servers, pizza cutters), all plastic

Shoe horn

Shoelaces

Small work bench

Socks

Soup cans and/or other canned goods

Standard playing cards

String

Tape (duct, invisible, masking, painter's)

Tape measure

Thread spools

Timers (kitchen and/or egg timers)

Tins (cookie, candy, coffee)

Towels (dish, beach, bath, washcloth)

Uncooked grains and legumes (rice, beans, lentils)

Utility knife (for adult use only)

Wastebasket or wire basket

Water bottles and pitchers

Waxed paper bags

Whistle

Wire coat hanger

Wooden clothespins

Wooden planks

Yardstick

Ziplock bags

For Arts and Crafts

Artist's easel

Bottle caps

Buttons

Child-size rolling pin

Colored pencils

Confetti

Crayons

Crepe paper or streamers

Felt rectangles

Foam board

Glue, glitter glue (nontoxic)

Index cards

Invisible tape, clear packaging tape

Magazines with color photos

Markers, fabric markers (nontoxic)

Paintbrushes

Painter's smock

Paint roller and pan

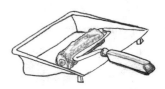

Paints (washable, nontoxic)

Paper (construction paper, newsprint, butcher paper, copy)

Paper lunch bags

In Search of Wooden Toys

Are you nostalgic for the wooden toys you remember playing with as a child? Would you like your child to enjoy similar toys? Good news. You may find these toys hidden away right in your own community. If you're lucky, you might find a small selection of wooden toys at the major toy (chain) stores in your area. But for a truly wide variety of wooden puzzles, tool kits, trains, trucks, cars, kitchen sets, blocks, nesting cubes, and more, you'll need to visit a toy store specializing in creative (or educational) toys or a local teacher supply store.

Pencils

Pipe cleaners

Play dough and tools for working clay

Popsicle sticks

Poster board

Scissors (for adult use only)

Scraps of ribbon and fabric

Sequins

Sponges

Tissue paper

Tracing paper

Velcro

Watercolor paints

Waxed paper

Yarn

Zigzag trim

For Music

Bells

Castanets

Drum (see make-your-own drum instructions, page 175)

Harmonica

Kazoo

Maracas

Musical shakers (see make-your-own musical shakers instructions, page 174)

Piano

Recorder (flutelike wind instrument)

Slide whistle

Tambourine

Ukulele

Xylophone

Musical Play Props

The only electronic gear mentioned in this book, these props provide music for many classic movement games.

Music (CDs, electronic files, records, tapes)

Music player (CD, mp3, record player)

Store-Bought Games

Barrel of Monkeys*

Berries, Bugs & Bullfrogs

Boggle Jr.

Candy Land

Chutes and Ladders

Cootie

Dominoes (make up preschool rules of play)*

Don't Wake Daddy

Dr. Seuss's ABC Game

Go Fish

Goodnight Moon Game

Hi Ho! Cherry-0*

Honey Bee Tree*

Hungry Hungry Hippos

I Spy Preschool Game

Lady Bug Game

Memory*

Memory Game

Mr. Mouth*

Operation*

Preschool Bingo*

Preschool Lotto*

Puzzle Card Opposites

Puzzles*

Tickle Bee*

Trouble*

Uncle Wiggily

*Noted games lend themselves well to independent preschool play.

NOTE: Remember to include books in your well-stocked preschool play cupboard too! See page 130 for some excellent read-aloud books to enjoy together.

Two great sources for classic and cooperative games are Back to Basics Toys (www .backtobasicstoys.com) and Family Pastimes Inc. (www.familypastimes.com).

The Well-Stocked Grade School Toy Cupboard

For Freestyle Play

Action figures
Balloons*
Beanbags

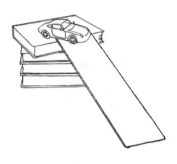

Blocks (wooden, cardboard, plastic)
Dolls, dollhouse, and accessories
Dress-up clothes
Gyroscope
Jacks
LEGOs and construction toys
Miniature cars and ramps
Models (planes, spaceships, boats, cars)
Pick-up sticks
Playing cards

Puppets
Puzzles
Safe hand tools, tool belt, and toolbox
Stuffed animals
Yo-yo

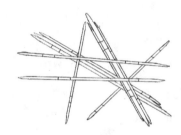

For Outdoor Play

Backyard swing set and/or slide
Badminton racket and birdie
Balsa wood plane
Baseball glove and ball
Basketball and hoop (adjustable)
Bicycle (and helmet)
Child-size (or toy) golf clubs and tees
Croquet
Frisbee
Giant bubble wand and bubbles
Giant Styrofoam glider (plane)
Hula-Hoop
Inflatable beach ball

In-line skates (with helmet, knee, and elbow pads)
Jump rope
Kickball croquet
Kites
Nerf (soft) baseball and bat
Nerf football
Ping-Pong balls
Plastic snow-block mold
Playground ball
Rubber balls
Sand and beach toys

Sidewalk chalk
Soccer ball and goal

Sports cones
Swings and climbing gym
Tennis balls
Tetherball
Volleyball
Wagon
Water and squirt toys
Water balloons*
Wiffle ball and bat

*SAFETY ALERT: Supervise all balloon play to prevent children less than eight years old from choking on uninflated balloons or balloon pieces.

Household Items

Bandanas and scarves

Bath mats or carpet squares

Bedding (blankets, bedsheets, sleeping bags, pillowcases, and pillows)

Books (cookbooks, travel books, baby name books)

Bowls (unbreakable)

Buckets (plastic and/or metal galvanized)

Buttons

Camping supplies (compass, canteen, etc.)

Cardboard boxes and shoe boxes

Colander, large

Cooler, small

Dice

Dry grains and legumes (beans, rice, lentils)

Envelopes

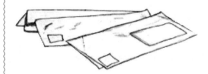

Flip-flops

Flower pots, empty

Flyswatter, new

Food stuffs (apples, oranges, peanuts in the shell, hard-boiled eggs, dry pasta)

Funnel

Grocery bags (plastic, paper, cloth)

Jumbo drinking straws

Kitchen utensils (pots, pans, muffin tins, cookie sheets, pie pans, pitchers, measuring cups and spoons)

Laundry basket (plastic)

Office supplies (notepads, pens, sticky notes, paper clips)

Paper cups, bowls, towels, plates

Photos of family and friends

Beat the Boredom Blues

Create a Challenge Jar by filling a jar with small slips of paper with creative play challenges. When your child says "I'm bored," open the jar, have your child pull out a play challenge, and let the fun begin. Fill the jar with interesting ideas that test your child's thinking skills or memory, imagination, or physical stamina. Create challenges that will appeal to your child's interests and abilities. Here are a few ideas to get your creative juices flowing. (You may increase interest in these games if you set the kitchen timer for a specific amount of time allowed to complete each challenge.)

• Write down the names of all the professional athletes you can think of.

• Think of as many places, names, and foods as possible that begin with the letter ___. (Throw some Scrabble letters into the jar.)

• Build three LEGO buildings before the timer goes off.

• Complete three puzzles in twenty minutes.

Grade School/Household Items, contd.

Plastic containers (margarine tubs, yogurt cartons, Tupperware)

Plastic headbands

Plastic kitchenware (utensils, cups, plates)

Plastic pet-food scoops

Roll of tickets

Rope or twine

Sheets and tablecloths

Shoelaces, new

Shovels, large scoops, and spoons (plastic and child-friendly)

Spray bottles

Suitcases

Tape (duct, invisible, packing, masking, and painter's)

Timers (egg timer, kitchen timer, stopwatch)

Towels (dish, beach, bath, washcloth)

Utility knife (for adult use only)

Whistle

Wooden boards or planks

Yardstick and/or ruler

For Arts and Crafts

Artist's easel

Artist's portfolio

Artist's smock

Blank journal and/or sketchbook

Cardboard boxes

Colored pencils

Construction paper

Crayons

Crepe paper or streamers

Eyedroppers

Fabric

Fine-tipped markers, washable markers, fabric markers

Foam board, cardboard, matte board, poster board

Glitter

Glue (nontoxic)

Index cards

Kneaded eraser

Lunch bags

Magazines with color photos (catalogs, fliers, pamphlets)

Modeling clay

Unplugged Toys at Your Local Teacher Supply Store

Your local teacher supply (school supply) store is a fabulous source for toys, games, and art supplies. These stores sell to teachers, nursery schools, and child care centers, but they are a fabulous resource for parents as well. At a well-stocked teacher supply retailer, you'll find all sorts of amazing gadgets, gizmos, toys, and arts and crafts supplies too, to delight your six- to ten-year-old child. (You'll also find some first-rate birthday presents that won't break the bank.) To find a teacher supply store in your area, do a quick search on the National School Supply Equipment Association website, www.teacherstores.com.

Needle and thread

Paintbrushes, assorted

Paint roller and pan

Paints (nontoxic, washable)

Paper (sketch, newsprint, butcher, printer, drawing)

Pastel chalk

Pencils

Play dough

Safety pins

Scissors

Shoe boxes

Single-hole punch

Sponges and/or Sponge Ums

String, yarn, rawhide laces, dental floss, and ribbon

Tempera paints and fabric paints

T-shirts (adult- and child-size)

Velcro

For Music

Bells

Bongos

Boomwhackers (percussion tubes)

Calypso steel drum, child-size

Castanets

Claves

Conga, child-size

Cowbell with mallet

Drums

Dulcimer, child-size

Glockenspiel

Glock-guitar (string instrument)

Guitar, child-size

Handbells

Harmonica

Kazoos

Maracas

Melody lap harp

Musical shakers

Piano or keyboard

Recorder (wind instrument)

Slide whistle

Tambourine

Ukulele

Xylophone

Two of my favorite sources for musical instruments for young children who want to experiment with music are Hearthsong (www.hearthsong.com) and Groth Music (www.grothmusic.com).

Musical Play Props
The only electronic gear mentioned in this book, these props provide music for many classic movement games.

Music (CDs, electronic files, records, tapes)

Music player (CD, mp3, record)

Board and Card Games

Backgammon

Bingo

Checkers

Chess

Chinese Checkers

Chutes and Ladders

Clue, Clue Jr.

Connect Four

Crazy Eights

Dominoes

Great States Game*

Guess Who?

Ker Plunk

Mancala

Marbles

Grade School/Board Games, contd.

Monopoly,
   Monopoly Junior

Mouse Trap

Mr. Mouth

Ogres and Elves**

Parcheesi

Pick-up Sticks

Pitt

Rush Hour, Rush Hour Junior

Scrabble,
   Scrabble Junior

Sorry!

Spill and Spell

> **"** When kids play a board game like Monopoly or Chutes and Ladders, they're watching the other players. They're learning social skills and strategies that can't be learned in computer games. **"**
>
> **—David Elkind, Ph.D.**
> Professor of Child Development at Tufts University
> and author of *The Hurried Child* and *The Power of Play*

Topple Game

Twister

Uno

Yahtzee

*Great States Game and other classic games are available from Back to Basics Toys, www.backtobasicstoys.com.

**Ogres and Elves is a cooperative game; the players work together to win. For this and other cooperative board games, check out Family Pastimes Inc. at www.familypastimes.com.

Parent Planner

Birthday Party Itineraries

Event: _____

Date: _____

Number of Guests: _____

Games and Activities:

_____ *Page:* _____

_____ *Page:* _____

_____ *Page:* _____

_____ *Page:* _____

_____ *Page:* _____

_____ *Page:* _____

Other notes: _____

Event: _____

Date: _____

Number of Guests: _____

Games and Activities:

_____ *Page:* _____

_____ *Page:* _____

_____ *Page:* _____

_____ *Page:* _____

_____ *Page:* _____

_____ *Page:* _____

Other notes: _____

Event: _____

Date: _____

Number of Guests: _____

Games and Activities:

_____ *Page:* _____

_____ *Page:* _____

_____ *Page:* _____

_____ *Page:* _____

_____ *Page:* _____

_____ *Page:* _____

Other notes: _____

Playdate Contact Information

Child: _____

Parent(s): _____

Address: _____

Phone number(s): _____

Allergies: _____

Favorite games:

_____ *Page:* _____

_____ *Page:* _____

_____ *Page:* _____

_____ *Page:* _____

_____ *Page:* _____

Child: _____

Parent(s): _____

Address: _____

Phone number(s): _____

Allergies: _____

Favorite games:

_____ *Page:* _____

_____ *Page:* _____

_____ *Page:* _____

_____ *Page:* _____

_____ *Page:* _____

Child: _____

Parent(s): _____

Address: _____

Phone number(s): _____

Allergies: _____

Favorite games:

_____ *Page:* _____

_____ *Page:* _____

_____ *Page:* _____

_____ *Page:* _____

_____ *Page:* _____

Our Family Favorites

Game: _____ *Page:* _____
Game: _____ *Page:* _____
Game: _____ *Page:* _____
Game: _____ *Page:* _____
Game: _____ *Page:* _____
Game: _____ *Page:* _____
Game: _____ *Page:* _____
Game: _____ *Page:* _____

Games We Invented

Game: _____
Materials: _____
Play: _____
_____
_____
_____

Variations: _____
_____

Game: _____
Materials: _____
Play: _____
_____
_____
_____

Variations: _____
_____

Game: _____
Materials: _____
Play: _____
_____
_____

Variations: _____
_____

Unforgettable Moments in Play

Child: _____ *Date:* _____
Game: _____
What happened: _____
_____
_____
_____
_____
_____

Child: _____ *Date:* _____
Game: _____
What happened: _____
_____
_____
_____
_____
_____

Child: _____ *Date:* _____
Game: _____
What happened: _____
_____
_____
_____
_____
_____

Child: _____ *Date:* _____
Game: _____
What happened: _____
_____
_____

Index

About the Author

Bobbi Conner is the creator and host of the award-winning syndicated radio program *The Parent's Journal,* broadcast weekly nationwide since 1986 on public radio stations. Known for her in-depth interviews about child-development topics, Conner's program, books, and articles have been featured in *The Washington Post, Redbook, Parade, USA Today, Parents, Woman's Day,* and *Child.* Conner is also the author of *Everyday Opportunities for Extraordinary Parenting* and the mother of three children. She lives in Mount Pleasant, South Carolina.

For more information, access to hundreds of audio interviews with child-development experts, and a chance to share your play tips and activities with other moms and dads, visit www.unpluggedplay.com.